THE GIVE AND TAKE OF SUSTAINABILITY

Sustainability strives to meet the needs of the present without compromising the future, but increasingly recognizes the tradeoffs among these many needs. Who benefits? Who bears the burden? How are these difficult decisions made? Are people aware of these hard choices? This timely volume brings the perspectives of ethnography and archaeology to bear on these questions by examining case studies from around the world.

Written especially for this volume, the essays by an international team of scholars offer archaeological and ethnographic examples from the southwestern United States, the Maya region of Mexico, Africa, India, and the North Atlantic, among other regions. Collectively, they explore the benefits and consequences of growth and development, the social costs of ecological sustainability, and tensions between food and military security.

MICHELLE HEGMON has dedicated her career to expanding the reach of archaeology, drawing insights from her own research in the Mimbres region of the US Southwest. She has contributed to archaeological theory, the study of style and ceramics, gender research, and social perspectives on ecology. Currently, she is developing a new paradigm, the Archaeology of the Human Experience (AHE), concerned with understanding what it was actually like to live in the past that archaeologists study. The study of tradeoffs, the hard choices people have to make, is part of that AHE perspective.

NEW DIRECTIONS IN SUSTAINABILITY AND SOCIETY

Published in conjunction with the School of Sustainability at Arizona State University and The Amerind Museum and Research Center in Dragoon, Arizona, New Directions in Sustainability and Society features a program of books that focus on designing a resilient and sustainable future through a rich understanding of past and present social and ecological dynamics. Collectively, they demonstrate that sustainability research requires engagement with a range of fields spanning the social and natural sciences, humanities, and applied sciences. Books in the series show that a successful transition to a sustainable future will depend on the ability to apply lessons from past societies and link local action to global processes.

For more information about the series, please visit http://newdirections.asu.edu/.

Title in the Series:
SUSTAINABILITY IN THE GLOBAL CITY Edited by Cindy Isenhour, Gary McDonogh, Melissa Checker.

The Give and Take of Sustainability

Archaeological and Anthropological Perspectives on Tradeoffs

Edited by
MICHELLE HEGMON
Arizona State University

CAMBRIDGE
UNIVERSITY PRESS

One Liberty Plaza, New York, NY 10006, USA

Cambridge University Press is part of the University of Cambridge.

It furthers the University's mission by disseminating knowledge in the pursuit of education, learning, and research at the highest international levels of excellence.

www.cambridge.org
Information on this title: www.cambridge.org/9781107078338
DOI: 10.1017/9781139939720

First published 2017

Printed in the United States of America by Sheridan Books, Inc.

A catalogue record for this publication is available from the British Library.

ISBN 978-1-107-07833-8 Hardback

Contents

Figures

Tables

Contributors

Rimjhim M. Aggarwal
School of Sustainability, Arizona State University.

John M. Anderies
School of Human Evolution and Social Change and
School of Sustainability, Arizona State University.

Bill Angelbeck
Department of Anthropology and Sociology, Douglas College,
British Columbia.

Jette Arneborg
Department for Middle Ages, Renaissance and Numismatics,
National Museum of Denmark, Denmark.

Randall B. Boone
Department of Ecosystem Science and Sustainability,
Colorado State University.

Seth D. Brewington
Department of Anthropology, Hunter College,
City University of New York.

Todd J. Brinkman
Institute of Arctic Biology, University of Alaska Fairbanks.

Shauna BurnSilver
School of Human Evolution and Social Change, Arizona State University.

Jacob Freeman
Department of Sociology, Social Work and Anthropology, Utah State
University.

Colin Grier
Department of Anthropology, Washington State University.

Scott Heckbert
InnoTech Alberta, Edmonton, Alberta, Canada.

Michelle Hegmon
School of Human Evolution and Social Change,
Arizona State University.

Alf Hornborg
Human Ecology Division, Lund University, Sweden.

Scott E. Ingram
Department of Anthropology, Colorado College, Colorado Springs.

Christian Isendahl
Department of Historical Studies, University of Gothenburg,
Gothenburg, Sweden.

Ann P. Kinzig
School of Life Sciences and Julie Ann Wrigley Global Institute of
Sustainability, Arizona State University.

Gary P. Kofinas
School of Natural Resources and Extension and
The Institute of Arctic Biology, University of Alaska Fairbanks.

Amanda L. Logan
Department of Anthropology, Northwestern University.

Ben A. Nelson
School of Human Evolution and Social Change,
Arizona State University.

Margaret C. Nelson
School of Human Evolution and Social Change and Barrett Honors
College, Arizona State University.

Paul Roscoe
Department of Anthropology, University of Maine.

Katherine A. Spielmann
School of Human Evolution and Social Change,
Arizona State University.

Richard Streeter
Department of Geography and Sustainable Development, University of
St Andrews, UK.

Andrea Torvinen
School of Human Evolution and Social Change, Arizona State University.

Preface

Tradeoffs are in the news almost daily, and most people experience many tradeoffs in their daily lives. As anthropologists (archaeologists who study the past and ethnographers who study living people) my colleagues and I see many tradeoffs in the situations we study. In some cases we can see people making difficult choices between two important goals; in other cases our long-term perspective allows us to see tradeoffs that develop over time, so that the benefits and losses cross generations. The goal of this volume is to share our insights about tradeoffs with a broader audience so that they may contribute to policy and decision making that affects today's world.

One of the joys of this work, the conference at the Amerind Foundation and the many, many conversations that followed, was the collaboration. So many of the ideas throughout this volume came out of that collaboration. This is especially the case for the introductory Chapter 1; although it was authored by me, it is truly a product of all of our collaborative work. All of the conference participants (including John Ware, then director of the Amerind Foundation, and Frances Hayashida, who attended but was unable to contribute a chapter) should share the credit. Alf Hornborg graciously contributed a post-conference concluding chapter that helped to round out this work, asking us to think about tradeoffs inherent in the very concept of tradeoffs.

This volume is part of the New Directions in Sustainability and Society series, organized and supported by the Global Institute of Sustainability at Arizona State University and the Amerind Foundation, under the guidance of Christopher Boone (Dean, School of Sustainability) and Norman Yoffee (Board of the Amerind Foundation). I am grateful for their guidance and input every step of the way, from the formulation and revision of the proposal to the final manuscript. A number of anonymous reviewers also provided valuable input on the initial proposal and the final manuscript. And, on behalf of all of the participants, I offer many thanks to the staff at the Amerind Foundation, especially Deb Mechigian, for making us so comfortable and allowing us to focus on our work.

1

Introduction

Multiple Perspectives on Tradeoffs

MICHELLE HEGMON

> Sustainable development "meets the needs of the present without compromising the ability of future generations to meet their own needs"
>> (World Commission on Environment and Development [aka Brundtland Commission] 1987:8)

> Sustainability is defined "by the joint objectives of meeting human needs while preserving life support systems and reducing hunger and poverty" and sustainable development involves "the reconciliation of society's development goals with its environmental limits over the long term"
>> (National Research Council 1999:21, 22).

> The three grand challenges of the 21st century are "freedom from want, freedom from fear, and the freedom of future generations to sustain their lives on this planet"
>> (United Nations Secretary-General Kofi Annan in his Millennium Report to the UN General Assembly 2000).

Implicit in these eloquent words is a sense of tension among the goals: Some of the needs of the present are met most efficiently with non-renewable resources such as fossil fuels that will not be available for future generations and that are contributing to what may be irreversible climate change. Living within environmental limits may be good for the long term, but it prevents some people from meeting their needs today. Subsequent work recognized these tensions and tried to untangle these multiple goals, recognizing that they involve different scales, actors, institutions, and targets (e.g., Martens 2006; Parris and Kates 2003). Even more recently, it is recognized that hard choices and tradeoffs are often necessary, because it is not always possible to alleviate poverty and preserve the environment simultaneously (e.g., Campbell et al. 2010; McShane et al. 2011; Turner et al. 2003). As a result, there is a growing concern with understanding tradeoffs, conceptually and in practice. This volume is designed to address that need.

A brief story illustrates: At a recent conference in Taiwan, Margaret Nelson (the lead author of Chapter 8) presented a paper entitled "Sustainability, Resilience and Policy" based on her archaeological research about vulnerability tradeoffs (see Nelson et al. 2010, 2013). In the ensuing discussion, one of the national research directors, who was developing national policy regarding sustainability for Taiwan, told her that he thought he had solutions (such as recycling) to various problems, but her talk helped him to realize that his "solutions" also had consequences and he needed to reevaluate parts of his strategy. The point is not that recycling is bad – it is usually better than dumping trash in a landfill – but rather that it also has costs. Recycling is often energy intensive, may involve poor labor conditions, and can encourage wasteful behavior such as the continued use of small plastic bottles of water. The director was able to make more carefully considered plans because Nelson's talk led him to consider the tradeoffs of his sustainability solutions.

We hope that this volume will inspire people like that open-minded director to become more cognizant of tradeoffs and think broadly about their implications. Some tradeoffs have clear or immediate losses and benefits that are identified by vocal opposing stakeholders. In other cases, the tradeoffs may not be obvious, either because losses are incurred in the future, or because they are borne by the dispossessed. A major goal of this volume is to bring awareness to these less obvious tradeoffs.

To this end, in April of 2014, a group of anthropologists (both ethnographers who work with living peoples and archaeologists who study the past) came together at the Amerind Foundation in Dragoon, Arizona, to talk about the tradeoffs we observed in our research, a conference supported by the Global Institute of Sustainability at Arizona State University. We were joined by Ann Kinzig, an ecologist and sustainability expert, who is a co-author of a key article that argues for the importance of recognizing tradeoffs (McShane et al. 2011). As that article shows, there is an intense discussion of tradeoffs in the growing field of sustainability science. In contrast, although the concept of tradeoffs is found throughout anthropology, the word itself is rarely used. It seemed clear that the fields could inform one another. Anthropology could provide more perspective and awareness to sustainability's concern with tradeoffs, and the concept of tradeoffs could sharpen anthropological analyses and provide new perspectives.

The overarching goal of this work is to create a broad awareness of tradeoffs. Together, we worked toward two sets of more specific goals. (1) In our considerations of tradeoffs, we sought to maintain focus on the human costs and human experience, in part linking this work to ongoing efforts to develop an approach known as the Archaeology of the Human Experience (Hegmon 2016a). In particular, it is important to understand who experiences the advantages and disadvantages of a particular policy or action. If the losses are borne disproportionately by some – often those already disadvantaged – that should be viewed as a serious tradeoff. For example, in Chapter 10, Brewington shows how long-term ecological resilience on the Faroe Islands was achieved by disenfranchising a large proportion of the population, and in Chapter 9 Grier and Angelbeck illustrate how unequal resource ownership contributed to the sustainability of those resources among the Coast Salish. (2) Individually and especially in combination, the chapters are organized to provide a broad multi-scalar perspective on tradeoffs. The deep time perspective of archaeology, the detailed understanding of particular situations provided by both eth-nography and computer modeling, and the comparative tradition in anthropology as a whole all allow us to understand how tradeoffs some-times cross time and space and social group. For example, Spielmann and Aggarwal (Chapter 11) use insights from the archaeology of small-scale societies to gain insights into issues facing farmers in India today. Specific-ally, archaeological examples demonstrate the effectiveness of household-level storage, which in turn allows them to explore the tradeoffs incurred by national-level storage. Logan (Chapter 5) also links past and present with a long-term archaeological and historical study of foodways in Ghana. She explores the short- and long-term tradeoffs involved in the adoption of new and potentially highly productive crops, a perspective that helps her explain both the relatively slow rate of adoption and the difficulties farmers face in today's market-based economy.

Definition

Tradeoffs involve "a giving up of one thing in return for another" (Merriam-Webster Dictionary 1984:1250). At one level, tradeoffs are omni-present simply because resources are finite and multi-tasking is literally impossible; doing one thing precludes doing another. This broad definition is given focus in statements that emphasize costs or sacrifices vs. benefits or desirable objectives (italics mine):

> *Hard choices* ... are faced when there are trade-offs ... between different interests and priorities ... between long-term and short-term time horizons ... and between *benefits* at one spatial scale and *costs* at another (McShane et al. 2011:968).

> In trade-off situations it is impossible to achieve two or more *desirable objectives* simultaneously (Hahn et al. 2010:219).

> Tradeoffs involve "compromise situations when a *sacrifice* is made in one area to obtain *benefits* in another" (Byggeth and Hochschorner 2006:1420 cited by Hahn et al. 2010:220).

The concept of tradeoffs is a central concern of what has come to be called the "Robustness-Vulnerability Framework" (Anderies 2006; Anderies et al. 2004; Anderies et al. 2007; Carpenter et al. 2001; Janssen et al. 2007; Nelson et al. 2010). This view, which is linked to resilience thinking and derived from engineering, emphasizes that a strategy or construction can be robust only to certain kinds of shocks, and that robustness in one realm incurs vulnerabilities in others. The goal is to understand how these trade-offs work in order to minimize vulnerabilities that are likely to be realized and those that have particularly severe consequences. Some of the chapters in this volume (Chapter 2 by Freeman et al., Chapter 3 by BurnSilver et al., and Chapter 8 by Nelson et al.) explicitly draw on this framework. And all of the chapters are concerned with understanding tradeoffs that are truly difficult. These also include those in which different actors have different needs that cannot be met simultaneously. Often gains and losses are separated across time or space or social groups, and those who experience losses (whether a disadvantaged group today or people of the future) have minimal or no representation.

In contrast, in a win-win situation two or more objectives can be gained simultaneously. In sustainability, there is a great deal of debate (reviewed in the next section) about whether and how win-wins can be achieved. In general, as is shown in the analyses in Chapter 2 by Freeman and colleagues, win-wins are possible in some cases, depending on (1) the empirical setting and (2) the scope of what is considered. The first point is perhaps obvious: there is no need to make hard choices about resources in abundant settings. The latter point is key to our awareness of tradeoffs. If the scope is narrowly defined to include only two or very few objectives, then it might be possible to satisfy all simultaneously and achieve a win-win. But if the scope is broadened, it reveals that there are always costs or tradeoffs in some realm – time spent, things not done, or resources utilized. A narrow scope that focuses on a few neatly specified objectives is easier to analyze, but the broader view, which recognizes that there are always tradeoffs somewhere, expands understandings and might point to import-ant tradeoffs that would otherwise be missed. Throughout the volume authors draw on both the narrower and broader perspectives, as appropri-ate. Two examples illustrate:

Chapter 2, by Freeman and colleagues, explains the essence of tradeoffs with a mathematical model of corn and agave farmers that is the basis of two experiments; each utilizes the narrower view of tradeoffs, considering two neatly specified objectives in a particular empirical setting. For example, their Experiment 1 shows that when rainfall is very abundant it is possible to both maintain balanced reciprocity and minimize the farmers' exposure to famine; thus there is a win-win with respect to these two variables. However, they call this scenario a "qualified win-win" because in order to achieve these two objectives not all farmers can have their preferred level of maize consumption. Thus, the broader view reveals a tradeoff, and the question becomes whether the tradeoff is difficult at some level. The answer depends in part on one's perspective, an issue considered in the penultimate section.

The second example should be generally familiar to anyone who has seen the 1974 film *Chinatown*. In the early twentieth century, Los Angeles engineered an aqueduct that diverted water from the Owens Valley to a reservoir that supplies the city. The Owens Valley was transformed from a productive agricultural area to an unhealthy dustbowl and many people lost their livelihoods. Los Angeles kept some water in Owens Lake in an attempt to reduce the dust, and recently the city agreed to control the dust through other means. As described by Little (2015:7, emphasis mine), the city is using "enormous bulldozers to dig deep furrows that capture and retain loose dust. The agreement promises clean air for Owens Valley and allows Los Angeles to save 3 billion gallons of water annually—*a classic win-win.*" It is a win for California's water and a win for residents of Owens Valley who want less dust. However, a broader view recognizes that there are tradeoffs at other levels, such as the energy cost for the bulldozers and the implication that difficult situations can be resolved with technofixes. A broader historical view also considers how this difficult situation came to be, including the tremendous losses suffered by Owens Valley residents and landscapes when the water was originally diverted. The point is that whether a situation is considered a tradeoff or a win-win (or something else) depends on what is included and who is defining the outcomes. This case in particular shows that both narrow and broad perspectives contribute insights: Like recycling, the bulldozers provide a solution at some levels, but there is always something more to consider.

The Importance (and Difficulty) of Recognizing Tradeoffs

Both the difficulty and the importance of recognizing tradeoffs is illustrated by a brief history of what came to be called integrated conservation and development programs (ICDPs; Brandon and Wells 1992), which emerged primarily in the last decades of the twentieth century. At their core was the belief that alleviating poverty and protecting the environment (mostly in the developing world) should go hand-in-hand, a perspective underlying the quotes that open this chapter. A brief history of this approach is provided by Adams et al. (2004). The union of these two goals was an important part of the 1992 Earth Summit at Rio de Janeiro and of the Millennium Development Goals of 2000. Among the many resulting development programs were the commercial gathering of non-timber products in forests and ecotourism around parks. Both kinds of initiatives involved local people deriving income from natural resources in ways that would inspire those people to protect their environment. Thus, the dual goals of conservation and poverty reduction were tightly linked (Christensen 2004:34).

This paradigm is strongly win-win, and it led to a very optimistic view of what good programs could achieve. For example, Gibson (2006) argues that sustainability should find solutions that involve "multiple reinforcing gains." He also dismissed solutions that involve compromises as undesirable and says "trade-offs are acceptable only as a last resort when all the other options have been found to be worse" (2006:172). This view assumes that well-designed programs will be able to alleviate poverty and preserve the environment simultaneously (with the implication that if a program cannot do both, the failure lies with the program).

The difficulty, of course, is that this paradigm created unreasonable – though appealing and easily marketable – expectations. A "deadly combination of wishful thinking, quickly contrived policy poultices, and ... poor information ... induced policy professionals to declare that in tropical settings biodiversity conservation is de facto compatible with sustainable economic development" (Redford and Sanderson 1992:38). It also led to what is described as a "vicious cycle of optimism and disenchantment"

(McShane et al. 2011:967), in which planners who refused to acknowledge or report failures could not understand why the expectations were so often unmet. As these quotes suggest, much was at stake and the argument was often heated. The work of Kent Redford is one of many examples (described by Christensen 2004). Redford had studied the commercial gathering of forest products in Amazonia, and reported his findings in an essay entitled "The Ecologically Noble Savage" (1991), which questioned the ICDP win-win paradigm. He argued that indigenous people using modern hunting technologies have a strong negative impact on forest ecology. The people have been terribly wronged, their rights to land should be recognized, but they should not be "faulted for failing to live up to Western expectations of the noble savage." Redford was vilified as a result, even to the point of receiving hate-mail.

Eventually, the same points were made with data from many case studies and less controversy. W. M. Adams had been an early skeptic of "sustainable development" (2008 [1st edition in 1990]), and in 2004 he led a paper that concluded "success with integrated strategies is elusive" (Adams et al. 2004:1146). That paper also developed a typology aimed at better understanding the relationship between poverty alleviation and conservation. A special feature of *Ecology and Society* was devoted to assessing the numerous ICDPs in the Malinau District of Indonesia, where a majority of people live in poverty (Campbell et al. 2010). Authors recognized some cases where conservation was improved and poverty alleviated, but they also noted many failures. Importantly, they argued that one reason for the failures was refusal to acknowledge tradeoffs: "Fundamental to success is the recognition of the significant trade-offs that occur between conservation and development goals." (2010:1). Ferraro and Hanauer showed that even the protected areas in Costa Rica, often seen as successful integrated programs with win-wins results, saw tradeoffs between deforestation and poverty alleviation (2011). Drawing on a comparative study of many projects, McShane and colleagues (2011) argued for the importance of acknowledging conservation-development tradeoffs and developed a set of principles for analyzing them.

The win-win paradigm that promised to alleviate poverty and promote conservation was full of heady optimism. But, as the people who were involved describe, it initially created unrealistic expectations and a myopia that could not see failures, with the result that the failures could not be addressed or understood. The tradeoffs approach may appear less optimistic, at least rhetorically, but its realism offers promise. In essence, what it says is that even the best programs with the best intentions often result in tradeoffs. We need to be aware of those tradeoffs to understand and manage them, and work to minimize their impact; and a great deal of current ecological research is working to do just that (e.g., Adams et al. 2014; Kareiva et al. 2007). For example, a study of mangrove forests found that there are strategies that both increase peoples' income through shrimping and protect the forests (McNally et al. 2011). This work was strengthened by the authors' explicit consideration of tradeoffs and their long-term view on how they can be alleviated. Win-win outcomes are sometimes possible, but they are more likely if potential difficulties are acknowledged and dealt with rather than ignored.

These kinds of ideas have also become part of sustainability thinking more generally, including the very concept of sustainability. The issues are articulated in the four key questions raised by Allen et al. (2003:36) and articulated by Tainter (2014):

(1) Sustain what?
(2) Sustain it for whom?
(3) Sustain it for how long?
(4) Sustain it at what cost?

These questions, and contemplation of their answers, implicate tradeoffs. Do we want to sustain our way of life? Make changes such as reducing poverty and inequality? Help endangered species recover? All of these benefits incur costs – there are always tradeoffs.

Most of the authors in this volume came to the conference at the Amerind with this realist perspective: There are often, or perhaps always, tradeoffs. Our collective goal is to advance research to create awareness of potential tradeoffs so they can be understood and thus better managed or possibly mitigated. We leave the debate about whether and how ICDPs should be changed to the many experts in that field, and instead work to create a broader multi-dimensional perspective on tradeoffs.

The Power of Words

Words matter. According to *The Concise Oxford Dictionary of Literary Terms*, the word "discourse" denotes "any coherent body of statements that produces a self-confirming account of reality by defining an object of attention and generating concepts with which to analyze it" (Baldick 1990:59). Or, as Brosius (1999:278) says in a review of anthropology and environmentalism, "environmental discourses are manifestly constitutive of reality (or, rather, of a multiplicity of realities)." Adams (2008) makes similar points regarding the idea of "sustainable development" (see also Crush 1995). Hornborg even suggests that serious problems and looming disaster are being ideologically disarmed by "the rhetoric on 'sustainability' and 'resilience'" (2009:239). And in his concluding Chapter 12, Hornborg questions the discourse implied by the economic calculus of "costs" and "benefits" and of the very concept of tradeoffs, which he suggests provides functionalist justification for injustice and inequality. Discourse has long been a key issue in political ecology (e.g., Escobar 1996), an approach that focuses on issues of power and control over resources as a means of understanding relations between nature and society. Talk about tradeoffs can be a powerful discourse, and those who control that discourse – whether policy makers or academics – focus our attention on some things and exclude others. There are at least three interrelated issues.

First, tradeoffs are often seen from analysts' omniscient perspective that assumes society is an integrated whole. There are losses, yes, but there are also gains, so the term connotes a sense of balance. But from the perspective of those involved in the tradeoff, on one side of the balance, there may be nothing but loss. The people removed from a newly created park don't see a tradeoff; they see their homes destroyed. Anthropology's recent concern with the ethnographer's "gaze" and how that differs from indigenous perspectives (see Clifford and Marcus 1986) may be helpful in navigating between perspectives.

Second, while a focused view on tradeoffs among a small number of realms is useful analytically, it necessarily excludes other realms. Much of the work regarding ICDPs discussed in the previous section concerns the conflicting goals of well-defined stakeholders, who are sometimes defined as "anyone affected by a particular World Bank project" (Brosius and Russell 2003:40). A broader perspective considers other less vocal classes of people, including those more distant in time or space.

Finally, the focus on a tradeoff "situation" provides a useful analytical focus but may exclude the structural forces that created the situation. An understanding of multiple scales – a basic tenet of political ecology and one emphasized here – shows how larger historical or global economic forces create or contribute to what is seen as a particular or local tradeoff situation.

These difficulties do not lead us to reject the concept of tradeoffs, but rather to use it carefully. The broad definition of tradeoffs brings awareness to tradeoffs beyond the interests of vocal stakeholders, and beyond the immediate time and place. This is the multi-dimensional perspective advocated by many researchers (e.g., Schoon et al. 2011) and explored in the next two sections that focus on tradeoffs over time, and then on those that cross space and social group. These in turn lead to consideration of how what we call tradeoffs are actually experienced and perceived, and thus how an understanding of tradeoffs might help us to make better decisions.

The Temporal Dimension

> I'm spending my children's inheritance!

This RV bumper sticker gets across a concept also known as "discounting the future." Possible losses (to be experienced in the future) are traded off for value experienced in the present. This is one characteristic of a poverty trap – the present value of a dollar always outweighs its future value because food or medicine or clothing are needed immediately, and saving for the future is an impossible luxury; this issue in agricultural decision making is explored in Bartlett (2013). For example, the Indian farmers described by Spielmann and Aggarwal (Chapter 11) are forced by circumstances to sell food at low prices (in order to get much-needed cash for other expenses) and then to buy food later at higher prices. In other situations, the future is simply not valued as much as the present, as may be the case when people are rewarded only for short-term profits. Sustainability is essentially the opposite; it is about *counting* the future. Sustainability recognizes that the way we currently meet the needs of (some people in) the present may compromise the ability of future generations to meet their own needs. The goal is to reduce this all-encompassing tradeoff, to figure out ways of meeting both present and future needs. However, as the earlier section on recognizing tradeoffs made clear, many of the strategies designed to meet that goal themselves lead to tradeoffs. And that's just the part we see. Even good plans and strategies have unanticipated consequences, cascading effects, and downstream consequences.

Perspectives on tradeoffs developed in the field of evolutionary biology, which has a long history of studying tradeoffs (Garland 2014), provide some insights into temporal processes. There is no question that evolution involves tradeoffs; the focus is on how the tradeoffs can be understood, including implications for both ecosystems and human health. Two examples introduce issues of concern in this volume.

The first involves immune systems and their effects, at two temporal scales. Over the course of evolution, and in many areas of the world today, humans faced many risks from parasites and infectious diseases. Studies of vertebrates (including humans) show that immunological defenses including inflammation are necessary for survival, but they adversely affect other processes including growth, reproduction, and thermo-regulation (Lochmiller and Deerenberg 2000). This tradeoff is experienced over individual life histories, with costs accumulating as organisms age. A longer temporal scale reveals further complications that partly involve what is known as the "selection shadow" (the idea that evolutionary selection has relatively little effect on aging processes that affect us in post-reproductive years). Research is finding that inflammation may contribute to chronic diseases of aging, which of course are more prevalent as lifespans increase in today's world (Gurven et al. 2008). Thus the tradeoff is becoming more difficult over the course of evolutionary time.

Another example derives from recent work regarding chilies, specifically the tradeoffs involved with hotness or pungency, which is produced by capsicum (Haak et al. 2011). Capsicum provides protection from fungi, but it is also genetically linked to traits that reduce drought tolerance. As a result of this tradeoff, capsicum is beneficial in wetter environments, where there is also a greater risk of fungus. This example points to the importance of understanding how tradeoffs involve different sorts of processes that may or may not be important in a particular time or place. The chapters by BurnSilver and colleagues (Chapter 3) and Nelson and colleagues (Chapter 8) consider analogous processes in their discussions of vulnerabilities and tradeoffs.

Path dependence, which connotes becoming increasingly stuck in a particular trajectory, is an important temporal component of tradeoffs (Hegmon 2016b reviews ideas of path dependence from the perspective of archaeology). Path dependence often comes about as a result of "critical junctures," times or actions that move a historical trajectory in a particular direction, and sometimes "lock-in" a path that is increasingly difficult to exit. Very often, the critical junctures involve actions or strategies that are initially beneficial but that become problematic in the long term.

There are at least two interrelated issues brought to the fore by a temporal perspective on tradeoffs, both involving path dependence. First, tradeoffs may play out over time, in that the gains are realized at one time and the losses felt at another. Isendahl and Heckbert (Chapter 6) and Hegmon (Chapter 7) both use a model developed by Tainter (1988; Tainter and Taylor 2014), in which the development of complexity is viewed as a means of solving problems, but complexity is expensive and over time it has diminishing returns. Thus both chapters discuss tradeoffs between advantages at one time and disadvantages at another. In the Mimbres case considered by Hegmon, there is a sort of feedback process as growth in a relatively rich area increases the attractiveness of the area. Thus in-migration occurs, which adds to the difficulties; one result, and a major focus of her chapter, is inter-generational tradeoffs. The same sort of sequence, though with a different starting point, is seen in the Maya region. Isendahl and Heckbert find that complex technological and organizational infrastructure develops in subregions that need considerable investment to capture and manage water. The complexity helps solve the water problem initially, but tradeoffs develop over time as long-term infrastructure costs coupled with decreasing returns on energy invested lead to economic decline.

Other chapters reach similar conclusions, drawing on different bodies of theory. Nelson and colleagues' Chapter 8 is based on research that assesses vulnerability to climatic challenges in a number of cultural sequences in the US Southwest and the North Atlantic. Some strategies are helpful in the short term but exacerbate vulnerabilities over the longer term. For example, in Greenland people coped with increased cold and storminess around 1310 CE (Greenland 2 in their analysis) by increasing their exploit-ation of marine mammals, thereby increasing their productivity but decreasing the diversity of their subsistence strategies. They thus were unable to cope with another severe shock at around 1421, which marks the end of Norse settlements on Greenland.

This kind of tradeoff – "kicking the can down the road" – is also described by Logan (Chapter 5). Maize, a New World crop, is highly productive but also less drought resistant than local and native crops in Banda, Ghana. If farmers make decisions that focus on the short term, the adoption of this high-yield crop seems like a good strategy; the tradeoffs are seen only with a different and longer-term perspective. Maize was initially adopted quite slowly, but once it became a dominant staple – "locked in" in the terminology of path dependence – it contributed to the potential for both high productivity and drought-induced failures.

Second, what appears to be a tradeoff situation in a particular time and context is often best understood as the result of historical and often path-dependent processes. For example, whether or not one agrees that using bulldozers to lessen dust in the bed of what was Owens Lake is a win-win or a tradeoff, it is best understood in a historical context that explores how Los Angeles was able to appropriate the water from this rural community.

Another stark and oft-discussed example involves the Miskito people on Mosquito Coast of Honduras and Nicaragua (Nietschmann 1979). They traditionally hunted or captured many marine animals – including lobsters and green sea turtles – as part of their subsistence regime, and they were much-admired for their skills. However, there was a demand for these animals on the world market, so the Miskito intensified their capture, aided by modern technologies. The situation today is a classic tradeoff between the income needs of the Miskito and the conservation of these species; the green sea turtles in particular are now listed as endangered by the International Union for Conservation of Nature. An understanding of how this difficult situation came to be provides perspective and may point to solutions beyond the immediate situation: that is, the problem isn't just the Miskito's hunting; it is the larger socio-political situation and lack of alternative sources of income, as Nietschmann shows (1979).

A final example from this volume is Spielmann and Aggarwal's (Chapter 11) exploration of tradeoffs between national and local food security in India. They show how the former has been emphasized at the expense of the latter and argue for a return to more local and household-level storage. Importantly, although they reveal the flaws in the current centralized system, they also acknowledge the path-dependent processes that created a difficult-to-change situation that is locking in policy makers and small-scale farmers alike. By acknowledging the historical processes involved, they recognize that alleviating the situation will involve systemically complex decisions.

Social and Spatial Scales

> One person's degradation is another's accumulation
> (Blaikie and Brookfield 1987:14).

This now classic quote from *Land Degradation and Society* makes clear how tradeoffs involve social and environmental justice. Working toward a future in which there is freedom from want is, *ultimately*, good for everyone. However, to get to that future, some are asked to make more sacrifices than others. The difficult issue of coal mining illustrates this, with a series of complex and compounding tradeoffs. Moving away from coal as a source of energy will reduce carbon emissions and thus help slow climate change, but closing coal mines devastates already marginal mining communities. Some countries like the United States are able to decommission the most polluting coal-burning power plants and the heavy industry they support, thus reducing pollution and emissions (as well as manufacturing jobs) at home. But the tradeoff crosses national boundaries and oceans, because we in turn import goods from China, which produces those goods with power from coal-burning power plants. To add one more unhappy twist to this spiral, some of the Chinese power plants are the exceptionally dirty ones that were decommissioned in the United States and subsequently exported to China. In other words, the tradeoffs cross space and society: Some of us get to breathe relatively clean air and buy inexpensive imported consumer electronics, and others lose their jobs or live in heavily polluted areas. This complex spiral of tradeoffs distributes gains and losses unevenly across scales and between places or social groups.

These and related processes are explored in a number of critical perspectives. World Systems Theory (Wallerstein 1974) studies the uneven distribution of wealth and movement of goods that produce the First World (which reaps the benefits) and Third World (which experiences the losses). Marx's concept of "spatial fixes" (developed by Harvey 1982) concerns how immediate problems at home – such as over-accumulation resulting in declining returns – are relieved by moving capital or finding new and cheaper sources of labor elsewhere. Also, the concept of "environmental load displacement" (e.g., Hornborg 2009) concerns, among other things, the uneven and inequitable distribution of pollution and waste on a global scale and is a concern in recent approaches to World Systems Theory.

New work in the resilience perspective also emphasizes the importance of recognizing tradeoffs. Resilience scholars often analyze what they call "social-ecological systems" (SES), a perspective that sometimes assumes a degree of homogeneity among the people in a given system. However, a recent critique by Fabinyi et al. (2014) (published in the journal of the Resilience Alliance) emphasizes social differences and the experience of tradeoffs. They note that strategies beneficial for the system as a whole often disadvantage some, particularly marginal, individuals and argue that "focus on the societal winners and losers of resilient ... SESs could provide a much more politically sensitive approach to resilience science."

These general and global concepts serve to frame many of the chapters in this volume, although the chapters focus primarily on smaller spatial and social scales. BurnSilver and colleagues (Chapter 3) describe the process of sharing among people in Alaskan native communities as they engage in both subsistence hunting and wage labor. There are complex tradeoffs between households and the wider community that work out in different ways. At the simplest level, when households share food, the number of households receiving food increases as does intra-community equity. However, in these situations the amount of food available to individual households is lower – a classic tradeoff between the household and community scales. However, the effectiveness of sharing relationships depends on other conditions, including employment and resource scarcity, illustrating another aspect of tradeoffs: they change over time as conditions fluctuate.

Tradeoffs between scales are also the subject of Spielmann and Aggarwal's Chapter 11, which describes massive centralized food storage organized by the central government of India. In some ways, this policy has protected the nation from large-scale famines, but it has not ended – and may actually have worsened – food insecurity at the household level, because government agents buy so much food from households for storage in national repositories. The tradeoffs in this case are between benefits at the national scale and losses at local scale, and between food security in the context of periodic famines and intra-annual food security. This case in particular points to the important practical and policy implications of seeing and understanding tradeoffs. Specifically, by viewing these processes from a tradeoffs perspective, the authors (who are also informed by resilience thinking) suggest that the tradeoff could be mitigated by reviving long-term (ancient and historic) practices of household storage.

Tradeoffs are a key component of inequality. In *Inequality Reexamined* (1992), Amartya Sen argues that humans are intrinsically unequal in some respects, thus any attempt to reduce inequality in some realm incurs inequalities in other realms. For example, because people differ in health and physical mobility, the provision of equal access requires that more resources be used to help those with disabilities. Although he rarely uses the term, the concept of tradeoffs is central to Sen's perspective: It is not possible to simply eliminate all inequalities; rather, there are tradeoffs among inequalities in different realms, and it is important to understand those tradeoffs in order to choose wisely. This argument is not unlike recent perspectives on sustainability: It is not possible (or desirable) to simply sustain everything; rather, we must ask questions about what is to be sustained. Sen ultimately argues that it is most important to work for equality in what he calls capability, people's ability to function in and contribute to society, a perspective utilized by Brewington in Chapter 10.

Brewington's is one of two chapters that consider inequality in tradeoffs in which gains are broadly felt but the losses are concentrated on some disadvantaged people. The medieval Faroese contributed to the long-term conservation of rangeland by managing the use of wild resources and preventing over-grazing. The long-term gains were at the level of the society (and ecosystem) as a whole, but the losses were borne primarily by the poorest members of society. Similarly, in Chapter 7 Hegmon describes how the Mimbres land-tenure system regulated access to land in ways that were perhaps good for society overall; however, some people, those with ancestral rights to the best land, would have benefited at the expense of other later-comers. Hornborg (Chapter 12) asks if the concept of tradeoffs provides undue justification to the unequal distribution of benefits and losses.

Finally, several chapters specifically consider inequality as part of a tradeoff (Freeman and colleagues' Chapter 2, BurnSilver and colleagues' Chapter 3, Hegmon's Chapter 7, and Grier and Angelbeck's Chapter 9). The authors consider inequality to be a negative for society overall, a perspective supported by recent social and economic analyses that show, for example, that inequality erodes trust (e.g., Stiglitz 2012). The authors of some of these chapters report that the people in the societies they are studying share these views and value equality. For example, within Coast Salish territory, the values of equality are materialized in "transformer stones" that represent greedy individuals who were turned to stone. Similarly, as described by BurnSilver and colleagues (Chapter 3), in Alaskan native communities, successful hunting households share widely rather than accumulate food for themselves, a pathway that personifies what it means to be a member of the community. These chapters also explore tradeoffs between inequality and efficiency or sustainable land use practices. In addition, of course, inequality itself also involves a tradeoff between the haves and have-nots, especially since the wealth of some countries or some sectors of society is directly linked to the poverty of others. Grier and Angelbeck (Chapter 9) show how initially small inequalities translate into more major structural inequalities over time, and how these constructs are challenged, resulting in tensions and sometimes conflict. The role of values – that is, viewing inequality as negative – in considerations of tradeoffs is discussed in the penultimate section.

Analysis: Making Tradeoffs Less Difficult

Our goal in this volume is to contribute to an awareness and understanding of tradeoffs that will contribute to good decision making. Returning to the definitions in this chapter, there is always some kind of tradeoff, but some involve bigger losses or harsher sacrifices than others. By classifying, comparing, and considering the dimensions of tradeoffs, we can move toward understanding why some are more difficult and possibly what can be done about them.

Roscoe (Chapter 4) develops this point specifically in his discussion of feedback loops. Loose feedback loops involve a weak link between actions and their consequences, whereas tight loops have a much stronger link. In tradeoff terms, when feedback loops are loose, gains and losses are separated, whereas when loops are tight there is less separation such that those who experience gains also incur losses. In the latter situation, the tradeoff is better understood by those involved and there is more incentive to minimize its difficulty.

These principles are borne out in comparisons among a number of the cases presented in this volume. The endemic warfare in pre-contact New Guinea described by Roscoe (Chapter 4) is one end of the spectrum, exhibiting a very tight feedback loop. In this sad situation people must protect themselves from attack but at the same time must go out into the landscape to produce and gather food; there is a tradeoff between defensive and food security. The needs are immediate and experienced by the same people, and the result is that these two needs are balanced in the best ways possible, which vary across New Guinea depending on the exact nature of resources and population density. The experiments developed by Freeman and colleagues (Chapter 2) also have tight feedback loops, in this case a result of the mathematics that underlie the model.

In the other cases described in this volume the feedback is looser. The historical accounts show how short-term benefits involve longer-term losses. Complex institutions and infrastructure in the Maya (Isendahl and Heckbert, Chapter 6) and Mimbres cases (Hegmon, Chapter 7) or the adoption of highly productive crops such as maize (Logan, Chapter 5) are advantageous, to at least some people, in the short run, but result in difficulties for future generations. A similar challenge is reflected in situations where the setting – and thus tradeoffs or their intensity – change over time (BurnSilver and colleagues' Chapter 3). This, of course, is a key issue of sustainability. Even if decision makers strive to minimize long-term losses, the absence of tight feedback makes it difficult for them to know what those losses might be. Long-term studies such as those in this volume can contribute insights into future tradeoffs and thus improve decision making.

The uneven distribution of benefits and losses is a component of social inequality. In the case of the Coast Salish (Grier and Angelbeck, Chapter 9) and the Faroes (Brewington, Chapter 10) the benefits included long-term environmental and food security, but the losses were borne unevenly, including (in the Faroes) by lower classes who could not own land and in some cases were not allowed to marry. An unfortunate example in today's world is environmental load displacement (see Hornborg 2009), sometimes instantiated in the not-in-my-backyard phenomenon (NIMBY). Most people do not want to live near polluting or dangerous facilities such as coal-burning power plants or toxic waste sites. However, wealthy and powerful people are best able to oppose or move away from such facilities, with the result that they are sometimes built in other countries with looser environmental laws. People who "successfully" fight the facility receive the benefits – power for their electric cars or cheaply made goods – without incurring the costs of the pollution.

Finally, the situation in India described by Spielmann and Aggarwal (Chapter 11) demonstrates the difficulties resulting from a lack of feedback, even when decision making is intended to benefit all. In this case, decision makers created a massive system of centralized food storage intended to reduce hunger and starvation. This strategy did improve food security at the national level and seems to have prevented large-scale famines such as those seen in earlier times. However, it also has costs that are mostly borne at the household and local scales since people are forced to sell crops immediately after harvest and then buy more expensive food later. Lack of feedback between centralized decision making and local consequences seems to have contributed to these problems. As Spielmann and Aggarwal note, the decision makers as well as the farmers are caught up in a historical situation that is not easily changed.

Perspective and Values

Many of the examples discussed so far make clear that whether a situation is seen to involve difficult tradeoffs depends on perspective, on what is considered a benefit or a loss and by whom. Most of the introduction thus far has moved between narrow and broad perspectives on tradeoffs – the broader one's view, the more likely one will perceive a tradeoff somewhere. Here I focus more specifically on how values influence that perspective, with two examples.

First, as was discussed earlier in the chapter, the authors of several chapters saw a tradeoff when increased productivity was linked to increased inequality. A different perspective, one that considers classes or castes or other forms of inequality to be a normal part of society, might see the same situation as a win-win. This is much more than academic speculation. It is very likely that many of the peoples discussed in the chapters – such as the Norse colonists of the Faroes and Greenland – did not share contemporary liberal social scientists' opinion about inequality. This does not mean that we cannot consider and learn from tradeoffs that we see analytically, as long as we are aware of the values and assumptions involved.

A second example also considers values and (literally) tastes. As was discussed previously, one of the experiments in Chapter 2 by Freeman and colleagues resulted in what the authors called a "qualified win-win" because in order to meet the dual goals some agents had to accept a less-preferred diet. The question, especially relevant in the real world, is whether that tradeoff is difficult. As modelers and analysts, we can ignore the preferences of voiceless virtual subjects, but in the world today this is a very difficult choice. Myriad evidence shows that plant-based diets are both healthier and more ecologically sustainable than diets heavy in animal products (Pan et al. 2012; Tilman and Clark 2014; UNEP 2010). Thus following Michael Pollan's seven words of advice "Eat food, not too much, mostly plants" (2008:1) would seem to be a win-win: good for you and good for the planet. That's easy for me, a long-time vegetarian, to say or preach. But for people who like meat, who think it gives them strength or energy, or who derive prestige from being able to afford it, switching to a plant-based diet is a real sacrifice. Policy (or friendly advice) about plant-based diets is far more likely to be successful if perceived tradeoffs are taken into account.

Conclusions: Moving on to the Volume

As a group, the chapters that follow consider all of these issues, and more, moving across and among dimensions and temporal and spatial scales. Three chapters that focus on tight and clearly defined tradeoffs begin the volume. These are followed by others that that consider tradeoffs over time and across multiple dimensions or scales. The various chapters also illustrate the importance of perspective in understanding tradeoffs.

In Chapter 2, Freeman and colleagues use mathematical models to consider two clearly defined tradeoffs, asking whether and in what situations win-win scenarios are possible. The models focus on issues of food production, sharing, and inequality. In Chapter 3, BurnSilver and colleagues synthesize mathematical models and ethnographic work to consider tradeoffs in an Alaskan community that still relies on traditional subsistence hunting. They explore the iterative tradeoffs of combining subsistence and wage economies and dealing with resource scarcity, and the role of social relationships in mitigating these tradeoffs at household and community scales. They also report that these trade-offs are much on people's minds and a common topic of discussion. Roscoe's Chapter 4 provides another view of immediate tradeoffs between the need for military defense and the need to go out into the bush to gather and grow food in New Guinea societies. He emphasizes the tight feedback in this tradeoff, in that the gains and losses are felt by the same group of people.

The next four chapters focus on looser tradeoffs over time, in which gains and losses cross generations. In Chapter 5, Logan considers food security in Africa, particularly the tradeoffs involved with the introduc-tion of new kinds of productive but drought-susceptible crops. The benefits of these crops, particularly their increased productivity, were realized at one time but the costs – tradeoffs – were felt generations later at times of increased aridity. In Chapter 6, Isendahl and Heckbert focus on water management in the Maya region to show how technologies that confer advantages at one time introduce complexities and conse-quences in later times. Hegmon uses a similar approach in Chapter 7, examining the tradeoffs – some inter-generational – involved with growth and complexity in the Classic Mimbres sequence in the US Southwest. She also considers tradeoffs involved with inequality, a theme that is explored in more detail in some of the later chapters. In Chapter 8, Nelson and colleagues examine two cases, Mimbres (also the focus of Chapter 7) and Greenland, the latter concerning tradeoffs over time. At a time of climatic challenge the Norse (Viking) Greenlanders shifted their resource base to focus more on marine animals, a strategy that provided more food in the short run but increased their long-term vulnerability to changing marine conditions experienced a few gener-ations later.

The next set of issues involves tradeoffs across scales and across different components or dimensions of society, a perspective developed in one of the examples considered in Chapter 8. Specifically, in their work with the Mimbres case, Nelson and colleagues consider the human securities (identified by the United Nations Development Pro-gramme) and find tradeoffs between food and community security. This demonstrates the importance of a broad and multi-dimensional view of tradeoffs, a point especially important to the following Chapters 9 and 10. Grier and Angelbeck (Chapter 9) examine two sets of tradeoffs among the Coastal Salish. On the one hand, there are tradeoffs involved with resource stewardship, in that a degree of inequality involved with ownership of certain resources contributes to ecological management of those resources. On the other hand, there is also a tradeoff between organizational inefficiency and social equality, and the authors argue that the Salish were consciously willing to tolerate the inefficiency inherent in an anarchic organization in order to preserve social equality. In contrast, inequality was an inherent part of ancient Norse society, including those who colonized the Faroe Islands, the subject of Chapter 10 by Brewington. There is a complex interplay between tradeoffs over time, inequality, and human well-being in the Faroes, and Brewington uses a multidimensional perspective on well-being to show that while everyone had reasonable material well-being, the poor, who were not allowed to own land or marry, had less social well-being. He uses his conclusions to make policy recommendations for the management of common resources, emphasizing local management and flexibility.

Chapter 11, by Spielmann and Aggarwal combines a consideration of household practices documented archaeologically and historically with an analysis of a case study in the contemporary world and tradeoffs across social scales. They consider food storage practices in the past and current food storage in India, and the tradeoffs incurred by a system of massive centralized storage. While the system does improve food security at the national level, and it seems to have made severe famines less likely, it makes things much more difficult for small farmers who are caught in a cycle of selling their crops and then needing to buy more expensive food later in the season. The authors develop specific policy recommendations, arguing for the viability of local and household storage, in part by drawing examples from the archaeological record.

The volume concludes with Hornborg's (Chapter 12) consideration of the tradeoffs brought on by the tradeoffs perspective. There are gains – including the insights discussed in this chapter – but also losses. He is particularly concerned with two issues: Many of the chapters use the economic terminology of "costs" and "benefits," which has the benefit of enabling analysis but at the cost of "loss of awareness of complexities and contexts." Second, Hornborg maintains focus on the uneven distribution of the advantages and disadvantages of tradeoffs. Although the issue is addressed in many chapters, he notes that, especially when a society or system is considered to be an integrated whole, inequality is somehow justified because of the purported benefits it provides to "the system." Hornborg's chapter provides a cautious starting point for further work: Thinking about tradeoffs can help us understand and analyze many difficult situations and think about the future, but we must also be aware of how it directs our perspective.

References

Adams, W. M. 2008 *Green Development: Environment and Sustainability in the Third World.* Third edition, Routledge, London.

Adams, William. M., Ros Aveling, Dan Brockington, Barney Dickson, Jo Elliott, Jon Hutton, Dilys Roe, Bhaskar Vira, and William Wolmer 2004 Biodiversity Conservation and the Eradication of Poverty. *Science* 306:1146–1149.

Adams, V. M., R. L. Pressey, and N. Stoeckl 2014 Navigating Trade-offs in Land-use Planning: Integrating Human Well-being into Objective Setting. *Ecology and Society* 19(4):53.

Allen, Timothy F. H., Joseph A. Tainter, and Thomas W. Hoekstra 2003 *Supply-Side Sustainability. Complexity in Ecological Systems Series.* Columbia University Press, New York.

Anderies, John M. 2006 Robustness, Institutions, and Large-scale Change in Social-ecological Systems: The Hohokam of the Phoenix Basin. *Journal of Institutional Economics,* 2(2):133–155.

Anderies, John M., Marco A. Janssen, and Elinor Ostrom 2004 A Framework to Analyze the Robustness of Social-ecological Systems from an Institutional Perspective. *Ecology and Society* 9(1):18.

Anderies, John M., A. A. Rodriguez, Marco. A. Janssen, and O. Cifdaloz 2007 Panaceas, Uncertainty, and the Robust Control Framework in Sustainability Science. *Proceedings of the National Academy of Sciences of the United States of America,* 104(39):15194–15199.

Annan, Kofi 2000 *We the People: The Role of United Nations in the 21st Century.* Millennium Report of the Secretary General of the United Nations.

Baldick, Chris 1990 *The Concise Oxford Dictionary of Literary Terms.* Oxford University Press, Oxford, UK.

Blaikie, Piers, and Harold Brookfield, editors 1987 *Land Degradation and Society.* Methuen, London & New York.

Brandon, Katrina Eadie, and Michael Wells 1992 Planning for People and Parks: Design Dilemmas. *World Development* 20(4):557–570.

Brosius, J. Peter 1999 Analyses and Interventions: Anthropological Engagements with Environmentalism. *Current Anthropology* 40(3):277–310.

Brosius, J. Peter, and Diane Russell 2003 Conservation from Above: An Anthropological Perspective on Transboundary Protected Areas and Ecoregional Planning. *Journal of Sustainable Forestry* 17(1):39–66.

Campbell, Bruce M., Jeffrey A. Sayer, and Brian Walker 2010 Navigating Trade-offs: Working for Conservation and Development Outcomes. *Ecology and Society* 15(2):16.

Carpenter, Scott, Brian Walker, John M. Anderies, and N. Abel 2001 From Metaphor to Measurement: Resilience of What to What? *Ecosystems* 4(8):765–781.

Christensen, Jon 2004 Win-win Illusions. *Parks: The International Journal for Protected Area Managers.* 14(2):32–41.

Clifford, James, and George E. Marcus, editors 1986 *Writing Culture: The Poetics and Politics of Ethnography*. University of California Press.

Escobar, Arturo 1996 Construction Nature: Elements for a Post-Structuralist Political Ecology. *Futures* 28(4):325–343.

Fabinyi, Michael, Louisa Evans, and Simon. J. Foale 2014 Social-ecological Systems, Social Diversity, and Power: Insights from Anthropology and Political Ecology. *Ecology and Society* 19(4):28.

Ferraro, Paul J., and Merlin M. Hanauer 2011 Protecting Ecosystems and Alleviating Poverty with Parks and Reserves: "Win-Win" or Tradeoffs? *Environmental and Resource Economics* 48(2):269–286.

Garland, Theodore 2014 Trade-offs. *Current Biology* 24(2):R60–61.

Gibson, Robert B. 2006 Sustainability Assessment: Basic Components of a Practical Approach. *Impact Assessment and Project Appraisal* 24:170–182.

Gurven, Michael, Hillard Kaplan, Jeffrey Winking, Caleb Finch, and Eileen M. Crimmins 2008 Aging and Inflammation in Two Epidemiological Worlds. *Journals of Gerontology Series A: Biological Sciences and Medical Sciences* 63(2) (February):196.

Haak, David C., Leslie A. McGinnis, Douglas J. Levey, and Joshua J. Tewksbury 2011 Why Are Not All Chilies Hot? A Trade-off Limits Pungency. *Proceedings of the Royal Society B* 279:2012–2017.

Hahn, T., F. Figge, J. Pinkse, and L. Preuss 2010 Trade-offs in Corporate Sustainability: You Can't Have Your Cake and Eat It. *Business Strategy and the Environment*. 19:217–229.

Harvey, David 1982 *The Limits to Capital*. University of Chicago Press, Chicago.

Hegmon, Michelle (editor) 2016a *The Archaeology of the Human Experience*. Archaeological Papers of the American Anthropological Association, Volume 27.

— 2016b Path Dependence: Approaches in and for Southwest Archaeology. In *The Oxford Handbook of the Archaeology of the American Southwest*, edited by B. J. Mills and S. Fowles. Oxford University Press. Forthcoming.

Hornborg, Alf 2009 Zero-Sum World: Challenges in Conceptualizing Environmental Load Displacement and Ecologically unequal Exchange in the World System. *International Journal of Comparative Sociology* 50(3–4):237–262.

Janssen, Marco A., John M. Anderies, and Elinor Ostrom 2007 Robustness of Social-Ecological Systems to Spatial and Temporal Variability. *Society and Natural Resources* 20(4):307–322.

Kareiva, Peter, Sean Watts, Robert McDonald, and Tim Boucher 2007 Domesticated Nature: Shaping Landscapes and Ecosystems for Human Welfare. *Science*, 316(5833):1866–1869.

Little, Jane Braxton 2015 Ted Schade: Dust Devil: A Civil Engineer Tackles a Massive Cleanup. *High Country News* 47(4):6–7.

Lochmiller, Robert L., and Charlotte Deerenberg 2000 Trade-offs in Evolutionary Immunology: Just What Is the Cost of Immunity? *Oikos* 88(1) (January): 87–98.

Martens, Pim 2006 Sustainability: Science or Fiction. *Sustainability: Science, Practice, & Policy* 2:36–41.

McNally, Catherine G. Emi Uchida, and Arthur J. Gold 2011 The Effect of a Protected Area on the Tradeoffs between Short-Run and Long-Run Benefits from Mangrove Ecosystems. *Proceedings of the National Academy of Science* 108(34):13945–13950.

McShane, Thomas O., Paul D. Hirsch, Tran Chi Trung, Alexander N. Songorwad, Ann Kinzig, Bruno Monteferri, David Mutekanga, Hoang Van Thang, Juan Luis Dammert, Manuel Pulgar-Vidal, Meredith Welch-Devine, J. Peter Brosius, Peter Coppolillo, and Sheila O'Connor 2011 Hard Choices: Making Trade-offs between Biodiversity Conservation and Human Well-being. *Biological Conservation* 144:966–972.

Merriam-Webster Inc. 1984 *Webster's Ninth New Collegiate Dictionary*. Merriam Webster, Springfield, Massachusetts.

National Research Council, Board on Sustainable Development. 1999 *Our Common Journey: A Transition Toward Sustainability*. National Academy Press, Washington, D.C.

Nelson, Margaret C., Keith W. Kintigh, David R. Abbott, and John M. Anderies 2010 The Cross-scale Interplay between Social and Biophysical Context and the Vulnerability of Irrigation-Dependent Societies: Archaeology's Long-term Perspective. *Ecology and Society* 15(3):31.

Nelson, Margaret C., Michelle Hegmon, Keith W. Kintigh, Ann P. Kinzig, Ben A. Nelson, John Marty Anderies, David A. Abbott, Katherine A. Spielmann, Scott E. Ingram, Matthew A. Peeples, Stephanie Kulow, Colleen A. Strawhacker, and Cathryn Meegan 2013 Long-Term Vulnerability and Resilience: Three Examples from Archaeological Study in the Southwestern United States and Northern Mexico. In *Archaeology and Sustainability*, edited by Scarlett Chiu and Cheng-hwa Tsang, pp. 104–128. Center for Archaeological Studies, Academia Sinica, Taipei, Taiwan.

Nietschmann, Bernard 1979 Ecological Change, Inflation, and Migration in the Far Western Caribbean. *Geographical Review* 69(1):1–24.

Pan, An, Qi Sun, Adam M. Bernstein, Matthias B. Schulze, JoAnn E. Manson, Meir J. Stampfer, Walter C. Willett, and Frank B. Hu, 2012 Red Meat Consumption and Mortality: Results from Two Prospective Cohort Studies. *Archives of Internal Medicine* 172(7):555–563.

Parris, Thomas M., and Robert W. Kates 2003 Characterizing a Sustainability Transition: Goals, Targets, Trends, and Driving Forces. *Proceedings of the National Academy of Science* 100(14):8068–8073.

Pollan, Michael 2008 *In Defense of Food: An Eater's Manifesto*. Penguin, New York.

Redford, Kent H. 1991 The Ecologically Noble Savage. *Cultural Survival Quarterly* 15(1):46–48.

Redford, Kent H., and S. E. Sanderson 1992 The Brief, Barren Marriage of Biodiversity and Sustainability. *Bulletin of the Ecological Society of America* 73(1):36–39.

Sen, Amartya 1992 *Inequality Reexamined*. Harvard University Press, Cambridge.

Schoon, Michael, Christo Fabricius, John M. Anderies, and Margaret Nelson 2011 Synthesis: Vulnerability, Traps, and Transformations—Long-term Perspectives from Archaeology. *Ecology and Society* 16(2):24.

Stiglitz, Joseph E. 2012 *The Price of Inequality: How Today's Divided Society Endangers Our Future*. WW Norton & Company, New York.

Tainter, Joseph A. 1988 *The Collapse of Complex Societies*. Cambridge University Press, Cambridge.

2014 Keynote Address to the Workshop "Social Transformations to Sustainability," organized by the International Social Science Council and the Potsdam Institute for Advanced Sustainability Science, Potsdam, Germany, 17–19 November 2014.

Tainter, Joseph A., and Temis G. Taylor 2014 Complexity, Problem-Solving, Sustainability and Resilience. *Building Research and Information* 42(2):168–181.

Tilman, David, and Michael Clark 2014 Global Diets Link Environmental Sustainability and Human Health. *Nature* 515(7528):518–522.

Turner, Billie Lee, Pamela A. Matson, James J. McCarthy, Robert W. Corell, Lindsey Christensen, Noelle Eckley, and Grete K. Hovelsrud-Broda 2003 Illustrating the Coupled Human–environment System for Vulnerability Analysis: Three Case Studies. *Proceedings of the National Academy of Sciences* 100(14):8080–8085.

United Nations Environment Programme 2010 *Assessing the Environmental Impacts of Consumption and Production: Priority Products and Materials*. A Report of the Working Group on the Environmental Impacts of Products and Materials to the International Panel for Sustainable Resource Management.

Wallerstein, Immanuel 1974 *The Modern World-System I: Capitalist Agriculture and the Origins of the European World-Economy in the Sixteenth Century*. Academic Press, New York.

World Commission on Environmental Development 1987 *Our Common Future*. Oxford University Press, New York.

2

Diversity, Reciprocity, and the Emergence of Equity-Inequity Tradeoffs

JACOB FREEMAN, ANDREA TORVINEN, BEN A. NELSON, AND JOHN M. ANDERIES

The mutual exchange of gifts, or what anthropologists call reciprocity, is a core social institution that binds diverse individuals into cohesive groups capable of collective action. In this chapter, we use a model of specialization and reciprocal exchange to study how social actors with diverse capabilities, *but the same goals*, might collectively achieve win-wins. By win-win we mean situations in which the goals of multiple stakeholders are simultaneously achieved. Our study is an outgrowth of previous work that seeks to understand the role of social and ecological diversity in the rapid development and decline of the Mesoamerican northern frontier (Figure 2.1) (Anderies et al. 2008; Freeman et al. 2014). In the context of this case study, we investigate how the interaction of reciprocity, social diversity, and the productivity of resources generate tradeoffs. Our study of tradeoffs contributes to understanding how diversity affects the ability of actors in social-ecological systems (SES) to cooperate and meet the challenges of sustainable development.

A challenge of sustainable development is to craft policies, at appropriate levels of governance, "that protect human well-being and ecosystems simultaneously in ways that are socially inclusive and equitable" (Bokova 2013:4). This statement embodies the laudable win-win paradigm (Gibson 2006). The realization of win-wins, however, is not only difficult, but, perhaps, unlikely because the dynamics of SES generate tradeoffs (Anderies et al. 2013; Janssen et al. 2007; McShane et al. 2011; Sen 1992). As Hahn et al. (2010) chide us, "we cannot have our cake and eat it too." But it is one thing to recognize that tradeoffs make win-wins

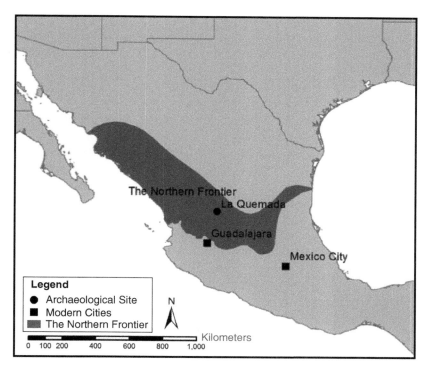

FIGURE 2.1. The northern frontier of Mesoamerica

difficult to achieve and quite another to understand the interaction of factors in SES that generate tradeoffs and the *kinds* of tradeoffs that may preclude win-wins.

Previous work tells us that two factors in SES contribute to tradeoffs that make the development of win-win situations difficult. First, SES are composed of individuals with diverse goals. The potentially negative effect of diverse goals is straightforward to imagine. The now infamous golf outings of Speaker of the House John Boehner and President Barack Obama produced little in the way of agreement on taxes or budget priorities, largely because both individuals represented competing interest groups with different goals for the allocation of capital. Diverse goals contribute to tradeoffs in sustainability contexts, for example, where the goal of environmental advocates is to protect a forest and the goal of forest inhabitants is to secure their livelihood. These different goals can contribute to a tradeoff; protect the forest at the expense of livelihoods, or better livelihoods at the expense of the forest (Chhatre and Agrawal 2009). Not exactly a win-win.

Second, feedback processes in SES make the negative outcomes of a policy difficult to anticipate. This is intuitively captured by the concept of "blow-back" in political science; policies designed in today's political milieu to aid today's freedom fighters can also foster tomorrow's well-armed terrorists as the political milieu changes. In the context of sustainability, many researchers draw on the concept of a robustness–vulnerability tradeoff to describe how strategies for managing resources often create negative outcomes in other realms. Robustness is the ability of an entity to consistently achieve a goal despite uncertainty, such as that generated by environmental change (Anderies et al. 2004:1; Csete and Doyle 2002:1664; Jen 2003; Page 2011:148–166). Vulnerability is "the state of susceptibility to harm from exposure to stresses associated with environmental and social change and from the absence of capacity to adapt" (Adger 2006:268). For instance, in order to achieve a consistent yield of crops, farmers in arid environments often invest in irrigation and, thus, gain robustness to inter-annual changes in yield caused by drought. However, this strategy makes every farmer in an irrigation system vulnerable to extreme, infrequent floods that destroy large sections of the system (Anderies 2006; Nelson et al. 2010). This example illustrates robustness to drought, but vulnerability to flood – solve one problem, create another (Anderies et al. 2007).

More difficult to intuit, and the topic of our chapter, is that a third factor in SES – diverse capabilities – may contribute to tradeoffs that make win-wins difficult to realize. Capabilities are simply how individuals function to achieve a goal, and diverse capabilities should be a good thing. Simple models and empirical studies indicate that diverse capabilities lead to creativity and foster effective collective action in small groups that have a common goal over a short period of time (Page 2008:328; Watson et al. 1998). Over longer periods of time, however, self-organizing groups with diverse capabilities may experience equity-inequity tradeoffs. As Amartya Sen (1992:20) states, "One of the consequences of 'human diversity' is that equality in one space tends to go, in fact, with inequality in another space." In short, diversity creates equity-inequity tradeoffs. Equity-inequity tradeoffs can constrain win-wins because they generate conflicts of interest, which make collective action difficult. Thus, it is important to understand whether and how diverse capabilities lead to equity-inequity tradeoffs and associated conflicts of interest in self-organized SES. In particular, we explore the role of reciprocity, over time, in mitigating or amplifying equity-inequity tradeoffs in a SES composed of actors with diverse capabilities.

The agroecology of the northern frontier of Mesoamerica grounds our model of diverse capabilities, how they may engender tradeoffs in SES, and how those tradeoffs might make win-win scenarios difficult to achieve. In particular, we ask: (1) Are there social-ecological contexts in which equal exchange (what we call balanced reciprocity) makes it possible for individual farmers with different capabilities to minimize, simultaneously, their exposure to famine? (2) Are there reciprocity arrangements that can distribute the experience of famine equally among individuals and, simultaneously, minimize the experience of famine at the group level? In our model, a simple diversity of capabilities (even among actors with the same goals) produces equity-inequity tradeoffs. Equity-inequity tradeoffs underlie potential conflicts of interest in our model, and may favor "winner take all" scenarios, as opposed to win-wins. However, all is not lost. If resources are abundant enough, we observe the potential for qualified win-wins.

Background: The Northern Frontier and Tradeoffs

From the perspective of sustainable development, the northern frontier of Mesoamerica provides an interesting situation. Around 200–450 CE, the semi-arid regions of the modern day states of Zacatecas and Durango, Mexico, were inhabited by small-scale farming societies (Kelley 1985). The production of food was mainly carried out by the household, and the distribution of food occurred in a network of kin and friendship sharing obligations. However, around 500 CE, this region transformed rapidly, as evidenced by the development of Mesoamerican-style artifacts and architecture, and, presumably, socioeconomic relationships characteristic of more urbanized societies in the Central Mexican Highlands, where these life-ways had long existed. This rapid transformation is epitomized by large archaeological sites, such as La Quemada (Nelson 1997). Such population centers dominated the landscape for about 400 years, but experienced a precipitous depopulation around 900–1050 CE.

This chapter is part of a long-term effort to understand how social and ecological diversity interact in ways that affect the sustainability of human societies (Anderies et al. 2008; Freeman et al. 2014; Hegmon et al. 2008; Nelson et al. 2011; Torvinen et al. 2015). We are particularly interested in the sustainability of Mesoamerican farmers along the northern frontier, and the rapid development and decline of Mesoamerican life-ways in the region (Anderies et al. 2008; Freeman et al. 2014). Our strategy has been to build a simple model that describes the agroecology of a Mesoamerican cultivation system that included maize (an annual seed crop from the grass family) and agave (a perennial succulent plant with a large starchy "heart" that is generally drought resistant). In our framework, maize and agave are assets in a portfolio of crops that a farmer might adopt. Maize is analogous to stocks, which are high yield, high risk assets; while agave is analogous to bonds, which are lower yield but also lower risk assets. Our work has progressed in three steps. First, we built a simple model of a generalist farmer who can either choose to grow maize or both maize and agave (Anderies et al. 2008). Next, we used our understanding of the generalist model to develop a more complex model of specialization and exchange (Freeman et al. 2014). Our current work is the third link in this chain of research.

Our initial study evaluated the hypothesis that the integrated cultivation of maize and agave was necessary for the expansion of Mesoamerican socioeconomic systems into the semi-arid zones of Zacatecas and Durango (Parsons and Parsons 1990; Sauer 1963). In particular, we investigated the potential tradeoffs of adding agave to an agroecological system focused on the production of maize for reducing the risk of famine (Anderies et al. 2008). Our analysis indicated that generalists (i.e., farmers who grow both crops simultaneously), could, in fact, reduce their risk of famine by integrating the cultivation of maize and agave under some ecological conditions. However, simply increasing diversity by adding agave to the agroecological system engendered a tradeoff for a farmer. While agave increased the reliability of the food supply, it also required the farmer to work harder (Anderies et al. 2008: 419). We call this a *functional tradeoff*. An individual must choose how to achieve a goal and accept the gains and losses that come with such a choice; in the example in this section, a farmer reduces the risk of famine by growing agave, but must also work harder to do so.

Given the increase in labor that is required in order for a generalist farmer to reduce the risk of famine by adding ecological diversity to a system, we decided to ask a follow-up question. Farmers could also add ecological diversity to their economy by specializing in different crops and exchanging these crops. There is evidence of both specialist production and exchange in Mesoamerica as a whole (Hirth 2009; Schortman and Urban 2004). Groups in the northern frontier had specialized potters (Strazicich 1995); and they, at the least, interacted with specialists who produced mirrors (Lelgemann 2000), obsidian blades (Darling 1998), shell ornaments (Jiménez 1992, 1995), and copper bells (Hosler 1994). Thus, we asked: Under what social-ecological conditions might a specialist or generalist agroecological system best reduce the risk of famine for individual farmers? Our analysis revealed two tradeoffs (Freeman et al. 2014: 306).

First, in many environments, the production and exchange of agave by specialists made the food supply of all of the farmers more consistent (i.e., robust to minor droughts), but the agave specialists were vulnerable to severe droughts. When, for instance, hit by a major drought, the agave specialist would experience famine for 10–15 years at a time. This result occurs because agave is a perennial plant; its annual yield is affected by the crop's age structure, and cohorts of agave age-mates are vulnerable to the same conditions. For instance, when a drought hits, the juvenile age cohort (plants less than three years old) is wiped out. Thus, one very bad year followed by a good year and then another very bad year will create a continuous five-year gap in production. Conversely, droughts only affect the immediate maize crop and thus have less of a long-term impact on maize specialists. A bad-good-bad annual sequence of rainfall would still produce one good yield. We call this a *robustness–vulnerability tradeoff*. Everyone becomes robust to minor droughts, but the agave farmers become more vulnerable to severe droughts.

Second, in benign environments, the robustness–vulnerability tradeoff described in this section is likely worth tolerating because really bad droughts are so rare that the vulnerability of agave farmers to prolonged famine is never realized. However, even in the most productive and reliable environments, strategies that reduce famine still require some actors to accept something less than their preferred outcome. For example, in benign environments, our modeled agave specialist reduces her exposure to famine by consuming only 20 percent of their carbohydrate diet from maize (Freeman et al. 2014:table 3), as opposed to a preference of 70 percent, which is an ethnographically documented estimate for Mesoamerican societies (Parsons and Parsons, 1990). In this example, the different capabilities of the specialists to grow crops led to different endowments of surplus crops over time. As we discuss in this chapter, it is important to note that the only difference between farmers in our model is what crop they grow or what we call their capability to grow crops. Even though the goals of the modeled farmers are identical, an *equity-inequity tradeoff* emerges. One farmer must give up her preferred level of maize (an inequality) in order for everyone to experience virtually no famine (an equity).

However, the equity-inequity tradeoff noted in this section emerged in a model in which *reciprocity was held constant*. In a real system, individuals are likely to adjust their reciprocity arrangements in response to the emergence of such equity-inequity tradeoffs. Furthermore, our previous results illustrate tradeoffs between individuals but do not consider the group-level effects of reductions in famine. A group might become more robust to drought overall at the expense of some individuals, which might justify some level of inequality.

In sum, our previous work demonstrates three types of tradeoffs that occur in SES: functional, robustness–vulnerability, and equity-inequity tradeoffs. All three may occur simultaneously, although we parse them here for analytical convenience. The questions that we address in this chapter are designed to help us understand how diverse capabilities might lead to equity-inequity tradeoffs. We are particularly interested in equity-inequity tradeoffs that might lead to conflicts of interest, which are costly to resolve and may hamper the development of win-wins. If equity-inequity tradeoffs are a consequence of a diversity of capabilities in particular social-ecological settings, then we need to understand how such tradeoffs are produced and the kinds of conflicts of interest that they might generate. Our analysis, grounded by a particular archaeological case study, contributes to understanding the relationship between diverse capabilities and tradeoffs in the context of crop specialization and reciprocal exchange.

A Model of Specialization and Exchange

Our model is inspired by the agroecology of the northern frontier of pre-hispanic Mesoamerica, but it does not seek to simulate what might have happened in this region in the past. Rather, the goal of the model is to capture essential features of the agroecology and the potential exchange dynamics that occur in a system in which actors are bound together by reciprocity. Our modeled agroecological system is composed of two crops, maize and agave, and two actors who specialize in the production of these crops. Each farmer has the goal to obtain a sufficient level of carbohydrates, and each farmer uses a combination of two strategies – growing their own crops and exchange – to reach that goal. These strategies determine how farmers interface with their resource base (arable land). The resource base is subject to rainfall, which generates variation in the yield that farmers reap over time. Based on their yield signal, farmers compare their yield with their preferred amount of food and decide how much to exchange. In this way, our model describes feedbacks between the yield of the respective specialists and their exchange behavior. The details of our model are described in Anderies et al. (2008) and Freeman et al. (2014:appendix). We provide a summary in this section.

The Agricultural Component

Maize and agave were two staples of Mesoamerican societies. Maize is an annual seed crop that can be eaten as either a vegetable (sweet corn) or stored as a grain, though the latter is our focus here. Agave is a perennial plant with a large above-ground storage organ, the heart, which contains large quantities of carbohydrates and water. Here we are concerned with the production of agave hearts, though other parts of the agave plant are useful for products such as textiles (Freeman et al. 2014; Parsons and Parsons 1990).

Maize and agave have different responses to the availability of moisture. Farmers in our model plant maize and agave each year in an attempt to meet their total carbohydrate production goal, U_t. Specifically, they attempt to meet their carbohydrate needs with a mix of 70 percent maize and 30 percent agave and plant in accordance with these percentages. Farmers aim to produce a surplus as a hedge against future variation in their supply of food, thus U_t is greater than that required to meet the total carbohydrate desire of the farmers, U_d, in time period t.

In our model, the yield of maize per unit area is a function designed to capture the basic relationship between the productivity of maize and the availability of water, and it conforms reasonably well to experimental results (e.g., Calviño et al. 2003; Glover 1957). Below a minimum level of annual rainfall, maize yield is zero. Above this threshold, maize yield increases linearly with rainfall up to a maximum level, beyond which additional rainfall has no impact on yield (see Figure 2.2a). Note that mean annual rainfall is scaled such that 100 units is the point at which maize reaches its maximum productivity (r''_m on Figure 2.2a) and 50 units is the limit below which maize yield is zero (r'_m). This means that if mean annual rainfall is 80 units, then the yield of maize is 60 percent of the maximum potential yield for a given year. We scale the parameters in the model as described because the dynamics of the model are independent of the choice of units (i.e., whether yield is measured in tons per hectare or ounces per square foot).

Agave exists in age-structured populations. Age structure affects the population dynamics of agave because individual plants at different stages of development respond to the availability of moisture in different ways. We assume that young agave plants from one to three years old are less tolerant of periods of extremely low moisture availability and are more likely to fail, whereas well-established agave plants of four years or older can better tolerate dry periods. The moisture-dependent effects of age structure are represented by splitting the survival of agave populations into two functions. For juveniles aged one to three, survival is a function of rainfall and has the shape shown in Figure 2.2b. For adults, the survival function has the shape shown in Figure 2.2c. The function described in Figure 2.2b is an if-then statement. If rainfall is greater than or equal to r'_j, then juvenile agave plants survive, otherwise juveniles perish. The function described in Figure 2.2c says that the survival of adult agave increases in proportion to rainfall until the upper limit of r'_a, after which an increase in rainfall no longer increases the rate of survival.

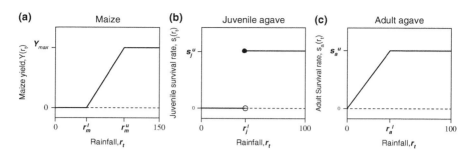

FIGURE 2.2. (a) Depiction of the relationship between maize yield and annual rainfall. Agave survival rates as a function of annual rainfall for (b) juveniles and (c) adults.

We represent the growth of agave with a discrete time, density dependent growth model, $g(x) = exp[a(1\text{-}x)]$ (Ricker 1954), where x is biomass. This function describes the conversion of resources into biomass by individuals (the intrinsic growth rate a) and competition for scarce resources (the (1-x) term). As x approaches the carrying capacity of 1, the population stabilizes due to intra-specific competition. We assume that agave matures in 15 years. Thus, a dry period that kills juvenile plants will cause a shortfall in agave production 12 years later, and the shortfall will last for three years. Relative to maize, however, agave is better able to tolerate a water deficit. Thus, the point at which young agave fail (r^J_j) is less than the rainfall level at which maize fails (r^J_m). We emphasize that this difference in tolerances is the fundamental assumption of our model that drives differences in the productive capacities of farmers. In real farming systems, individuals will engage in strategies such as mounding sediment around maize to conserve moisture during critical points in the plant's life cycle. Similarly, farmers will pot-irrigate juvenile agave in an attempt to mitigate the negative effects of moisture deficits (Trombold and Israde-Alcántara 2005:350). We don't deny such strategies; we simply assume that they are only partly effective. One can think of these strategies as "baked into" our different tolerance values for maize and juvenile agave, respectively. Finally, we assume that maize is stored for up to seven years and that agave has a storage life of less than one year (Anderies et al. 2008).

The Social Component

In our model, exchange is motivated by the desire to conform to social expectations that are based on reciprocal gifts (Gluckman 1941; Monaghan 1996; Richards 1961; Sahlins 1972). Gift exchange occurs in a social market

(Fiske 1992) as opposed to a monetized market (Heyman and Ariely 2004). The logic of exchange in social markets is based on reciprocity rather than maximizing profit (Henrich et al. 2004; Mauss 2002[1954]; Sahlins 1972). Monaghan (1996) provides a concrete example of the logic that motivates exchange in our model. He describes an exchange system in which reciprocal gifting obligations serve as a means of financing fiestas within the Mixtec community of Santiago Nuyoo of southern highland Mexico. Fiesta contributions are integral components of a social contract. Each participant's gift is repaid and renewed on a cyclical basis, enabling community members to finance personal or communal fiestas. Thus, in our model, exchange between our specialists is motivated by a social contract that defines reciprocity obligations; the amount of food that a specialist gifts and receives in any year, however, depends on circumstance.

We consider how specialists make gift decisions in three different circumstances: 1) maize and agave are both in excess; 2) maize and agave are both scarce; and 3) one crop is scarce and the other in excess. The decision to gift in each scenario is determined by how much of each respective crop is available in a given year due to the availability of moisture and the level of inter-group trust within the system (K_{ji}). We define inter-group trust as belief that a gift will be reciprocated. The subscript j is the specialist j's belief that specialist i will reciprocate. When inter-group trust is one, each respective specialist trusts that one unit of agave will merit a reciprocal and equal (in caloric equivalents) gift of maize. Although our scenario is idealized, our gifting logic approximates that observed in some human societies (as noted previously) and thus serves as a fruitful point of departure. Additional research could compare the success of different rules for organizing exchange in the same environment (Hegmon 1996).

Methods of Analysis

We analyze our model numerically in XPPAUT (Ermentrout 2006). The parameters for the rainfall distribution, $\hat{r}$ and σ_r, are close approximations of the mean and standard deviation of rainfall. To simplify our presentation, we call these parameters mean rainfall and the standard deviation (see Freeman et al. 2014:308–309). We measure the robustness of farmers to negative variation in rainfall, which we quantify as the expected number of famine events that farmers experience in a given environment during a 100-year period. We assume that as a farmer experiences more famine events, she is more likely to abandon an agroecological system and the system is more likely to break down.

We use two summary statistics to evaluate the robustness of the food supply of each farmer and of the group to variation in rainfall. We calculate (1) the number of discrete famine events and (2) the number of total famine years experienced by each farmer over 100 years. We calculate the number of discrete famines by conducting 400 model runs for a given set of model parameters using Monte Carlo simulation. A single model run consists of a 100-year interval. A famine event of length i is simply the number of consecutive years when the minimum level of food required by a farmer is not achieved. The total number of famine years experienced by a farmer, on average, is the sum of the number of famines of length i experienced by a farmer. For example, if the maize specialist experiences two 1-year famines, one 2-year famine, and one 3-year famine in an average 100-year period, then the maize specialist experiences, on average, 7 total years of famine in a 100-year period.

Due to the fact that our model is composed of two representative farmers, the question arises: If one farmer experiences a famine and the other does not, does the group experience a famine or is the experience of the famine weighted? Here we use a weighted sum to estimate robustness to negative variations in rainfall at the level of the group. We weight each famine of duration i by γ, the size of the group of maize specialists relative to the agave specialists. Group level famine events are calculated as follows: $(\gamma)(\sum x_{1,m} + x_{2,m} + x_{i,m}) + (1-\gamma)(\sum x_{1,a} + x_{2,a} + x_{i,a})$. Where $x_{i,m}$ is the mean of a famine with the length i for the maize specialist. Although we weight the measure of robustness at the group level, we recognize that one starving actor might make life miserable for another through incessant begging or robbery, or a satisfied actor may be moved to share more by a starving actor's misery.

Our Experiments

We conduct two experiments. First, we ask if farmers can use balanced reciprocity (equal exchange) to simultaneously minimize their risk of famine. Second, we ask if there are reciprocity arrangements that can equally distribute the experience of famine between individuals and, simultaneously, minimize the experience of famine at the level of the group. In our experiments we hold the standard deviation of rainfall constant at 0.20 because the net benefits of specialization and exchange likely outweigh the net benefits of a generalist strategy (Freeman et al. 2014:fig. 2).

Experiment 1: Balanced Reciprocity

Experiment 1 is designed to help us understand if win-win situations are possible when we privilege balanced reciprocity in a system in which farmers have different capabilities. In Sen's (1992) terminology, we answer the question "equality of what?" because we choose to privilege an equality of reciprocity. We investigate the consequences of balanced reciprocity at three levels of inter-group trust. (1) Farmers are generous and give 50 percent more than the other specialist desires ($K_{ji} = 1.5$), if they have the surplus to afford it. (2) Farmers trust that one unit of maize will merit a one unit reciprocal gift of agave and *vice versa* ($K_{ji} = 1$). (3) Farmers are selfish and give 50 percent less than the other specialist desires ($K_{ji} = 0.5$).

Experiment 1 illustrates two results. First, it is possible for farmers with diverse capabilities to achieve what we call a qualified win-win scenario. As long as resources are abundant, (i.e., rainfall is above 90), then balanced reciprocity results in an equal distribution of famine, and farmers experience very few famines. So, as long as rainfall is high and not very uncertain, things look pretty good. However, we call this a qualified win-win because, although everyone has enough food, not everyone has the preferred 70 percent maize and 30 percent agave. Specifically, the agave farmer has a smaller proportion of maize than the maize farmer, (see Background section), or *vice versa*, if there is a high degree of inter-group trust (i.e., farmers are generous).

Second, when resources are moderately productive (rainfall between 90 and 70), then balanced reciprocity results in winners and losers in terms of the distribution of famine. This is significant because when mean rainfall is moderate, Freeman et al. (2014) found that the net benefits of specialization and exchange might outweigh the net benefits of a generalist strategy. In this range of rainfall, too much generosity or too much selfishness erodes the robustness of the group as a whole to negative deviations in rainfall. At the same time, in this range it pays for the maize specialist to promote generosity and it pays for the agave specialist to remain more selfish. This conflict of interest is a result of the different capabilities of the maize and agave farmers. The implication is that win-wins (such as that achieved with rainfall above 90) may be fragile. Small declines in the productivity of resources interact with diverse capabilities to create an equity-inequity tradeoff and associated conflict of interest.

Figure 2.3 helps illustrate our two primary results. Figures 2.3a and b show that for the agave farmers, the best level of inter-group trust (i.e., the level that most reduces famine) is 1 or 0.5, while for the maize farmers, the best level of inter-group trust is 1.5. For the maize specialists, whenever mean rainfall is less than about 92 units, they experience much less famine if everyone is generous. The opposite is true of the agave specialists.

The result described in Figure 2.3 stems from the productivity of agave when mean rainfall is between 90 and 70 units. Between 90 and 70 units, the ability of farmers to avoid famine depends on their ability to eat excess agave. There is typically an excess of agave (i.e., more than the two farmers desire annually) in this setting because droughts that kill juvenile agaves are extremely rare. When inter-group trust is one or less, the agave specialist simply eats the excess agave and stores the maize that he receives for the very rare dry period in which agave actually fails. Thus, for the agave specialist, the agave becomes his stock and maize his bond. The maize specialist cannot engage in this strategy unless the agave specialist is generous. When generous, the agave specialist gives away the excess agave in the system. The result is that the agave specialist eats more maize on an annual basis, and the maize specialist can eat the excess agave, as well as put any surplus maize in storage as a hedge against future dry periods. In sum, the different capabilities of our modeled farmers result in different endowments of food over time, and exchange based on balanced reciprocity is not sufficient to mitigate the unequal distribution of famine whenever productivity is moderately high. Whether maize or agave specialists experience the most famine depends on the level of balanced inter-group trust.

Further, in the rainfall range of 90 to 70, at the level of the group (Figure 2.3c), the occurrence of famine is best reduced when inter-group trust is equal to 1. Thus, the agave farmer and the group (i.e., both farmers) are most robust to drought when inter-group trust is 1, but the maize farmer is most robust to drought when inter-group trust is 1.5. These results illustrate that as balanced inter-group trust declines, the agave farmer and the group gain robustness at the expense of the maize farmer. As long as mean rainfall is below approximately 90 units and balanced inter-group trust increases, all gains in robustness are made by the maize farmer and come at the expense of the agave farmer and, potentially, the group as a whole. This raises the possibility that even though maize farmers might gain more food security by pushing for more generosity, their gains at an individual level might be negated by losses at the level of the group.

Experiment 2: Unbalanced Reciprocity

Experiment 2 is designed to help us understand how unbalanced reciprocity effects the distribution of famine. Can unbalanced reciprocity

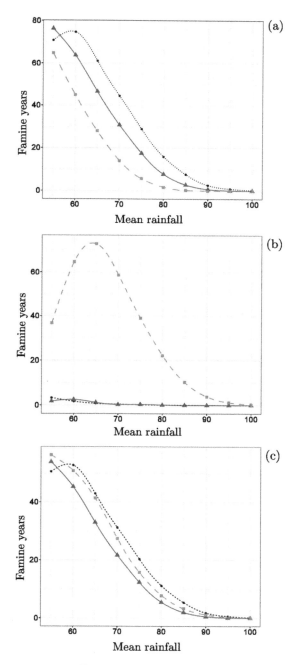

FIGURE 2.3. Famine years per 100-year period versus mean rainfall: (a) the maize specialists, (b) the agave specialists, and (c) the group level. In all three graphs: long dashed lines-$K_{sm} = K_{sa} = 1.5$; dotted lines-$K_{sm} = K_{sa} = 0.5$; and solid lines-$K_{sm} = K_{sa} = 1.0$.

result in the equal distribution of famine between individuals and, simultaneously, minimize the experience of famine for the group as a whole? Here, we privilege equality of famine, and we are willing to accept unbalanced reciprocity. Of course, equality does not necessarily mean that both farmers are well off. Both may experience 50 famines in a 100-year period. This would be an equal outcome, but one much worse than a distribution of 5 famines and 25 famines between our two specialists. A win-win requires a correspondence between our focal equality variable (the distribution of famines) and the ability of each specialist to minimize their experience of famine.

Experiment 2 demonstrates two points. First, for all levels of mean rainfall above 80 units, there is a level of unbalanced inter-group trust that minimizes famine at the group level and distributes famine events equally between the two specialists. By the very nature of unbalanced inter-group trust, one exchange partner gives more food than they receive. It is the agave farmer who must give more than she receives to equalize the distribution of famines in the system. The act of giving more agave than maize received results in an increase in the number of famine events that the agave farmer experiences. However, when mean annual rainfall is greater than approximately 80 units, the marginal loss of robustness for the agave farmer is potentially counterbalanced by gains in robustness at the level of the group.

Second, when mean annual rainfall is below approximately 80 units, an important conflict of interest arises between group level robustness and individual level equality (compare Figures 2.4 and 2.5). The maize and agave farmers cannot simultaneously minimize famine at the level of the group and equally distribute famine. In this environment, the robustness of the group is always highest when one farmer experiences far fewer famines and the other actor shoulders most of the hunger in the system.

In Figure 2.4, mean rainfall is held constant at 85 units and the ratio of inter-group trust is varied along the x-axis. A value of 1 indicates balanced reciprocity. For values greater than 1, the agave farmer gives more agave than she receives in maize equivalents. Values less than 1 indicate the opposite. In Figure 2.4, when the ratio of K_{sa}-to-K_{sm} is approximately equal to 1.15, the number of famines measured at the level of the system is minimized (marked by the red circle). At the same time, famine events are distributed equally (i.e., specialists experience the same number of famines where the dotted and dashed-dot curves intersect). In this rainfall setting, in fact, all settings above approximately 80 units of rainfall, there is a level of unbalanced inter-group trust that simultaneously minimizes the frequency of famine for the group and equitably distributes famine between the two specialists. This is, again, a qualified win-win scenario; individuals equally experience famine and the group gains robustness overall. The burning question is whether individuals are willing to accept unbalanced reciprocity.

In contrast, the curves in Figure 2.5 illustrate a rainfall setting in which the ratio of inter-group trust that produces the minimum number of famines at the system level does not correspond well with the ratio that produces the most equal distribution of famines between the two specialists. When K_{sa}-to-K_{sm} is equal to 1 and 1.5, there are approximately 14 famine events at the group level. But when K_{sa}-to-K_{sm} = 1, the maize farmers experience more of the famines, and when K_{sa}-to-K_{sm} = 1.5, the agave farmers experience the majority of famines. When K_{sa}-to-K_{sm} = 1.2, the maize and the agave farmers both experience 16 famine events. In terms of the distribution of famines, this is an equitable outcome, but nowhere near as good as a maize farmer could do if K_{sa}-to-K_{sm} = 1.5 or an agave farmer could do if K_{sa}-to-K_{sm} = 1. In sum, the interaction between the farmers' different capabilities and the

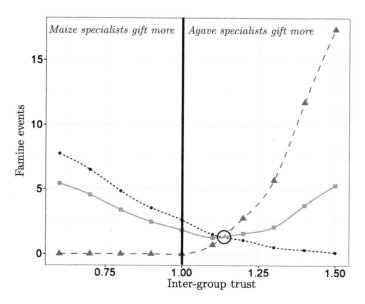

FIGURE 2.4. The relationship between inter-group trust and the number of famines experienced by the maize specialists (short dashed), agave specialists (long dashed), and at the system level (solid line). Mean rainfall = 85.

relative scarcity of rainfall reveals conflicts of interest that might make qualified "win-win" scenarios costly to achieve.

Discussion and Conclusion

We have addressed two different types of potentially desirable win-win situations: in one, two social actors simultaneously do well, in the other individuals and the group as a whole both win. Using a modeled agroecological system characteristic of the northern frontier of Mesoamerica, we conducted two experiments to answer two questions. (1) Are there social-ecological contexts in which balanced reciprocity exists and individual farmers with different capabilities simultaneously minimize their exposure to famine? (2) Are there reciprocity arrangements that can equally distribute the experience of famine between individuals and, simultaneously, minimize famine at the level of the group?

The answer to question one is, yes. Experiment 1 reveals that when rainfall is very abundant, individuals who engage in balanced reciprocity can simultaneously value balanced reciprocity arrangements and minimize the exposure of each specialist to famine. However, we call this a qualified win-win at the level of the individual because both farmers cannot achieve their preferred level of maize consumption. This is because it is excess agave that allows the farmers to reduce famine. This discrepant consumption may or may not be important. Certainly, preferences for certain foods can change, and, more generally, norms of social justice are negotiated beliefs. Nonetheless, someone has to accept less maize consumption on an annual basis in order for everyone to benefit, even in a rich environment.

Experiment 1 also reveals a subtle interaction between the different capabilities of farmers to grow crops and the productivity of a crop. Small declines in productivity lead to a more pronounced equity-inequity tradeoff between the distribution of famine and balanced reciprocity. In the rainfall range of moderate productivity (90 to 70 rainfall), generosity means that the agave specialist experiences more famine than the maize specialist, and selfishness means the opposite (Figure 2.3). This is a conflict of interest that may be quite costly to resolve. Thus, the qualified win-win is quite sensitive to small declines in the productivity of crops.

The answer to question two is, yes. If the productivity of the agricultural base is high enough, then individuals can equalize the number of famines that they experience, minimize the number of famines each individual experiences, and, *at the same time*, minimize the number of famines at the group level (Figure 2.4). This is a nice confluence. The only kicker is that

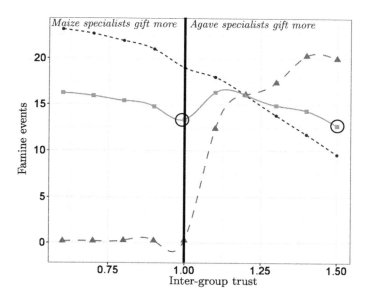

FIGURE 2.5. The relationship between inter-group trust and the number of famines experienced by the maize specialists (short dashed), agave specialists (long dashed), and at the system level (solid line). Red circles highlight the points where the group is most robust. Mean rainfall = 70.

individuals must accept unbalanced reciprocity that slightly favors the maize specialist (i.e., maize is worth more than agave). This might make sense over the long term in moderate-to-high mean rainfall environments (with only small deviations from the mean). This is because agave is more consistently productive (due to its drought tolerance) than maize, but maize has a much greater storage value. In other words, maize is worth more because of its storage value and the excess agave typically produced will go to waste if it is not consumed. In any case, individuals and the group win as long as mean rainfall is high enough in our experiment *and* individuals accept a norm of unbalanced reciprocity. This is an equity-inequity tradeoff, but may not result in conflicts of interest that constrain collective action.

Again, however, if mean rainfall decreases past an inflection of about 80 for our default parameters, the individual-group win-win is not possible. Figure 2.5 illustrates how the minimum experience of famine at the group level does not correspond to the minimization of famine for both specialists. One specialist wins and the other loses in terms of famine. If the farmers attempt to equalize the experience of famine, both end up in bad shape and sacrifice robustness at the level of the group. These are equity-inequity tradeoffs that result in a potentially stark conflict of interest and may reduce the incentives for individuals to cooperate in maintaining the system of reciprocal exchange and specialization.

So What?

The central challenge of sustainable development is to craft policies that are win-win, in the sense that they protect the biophysical environment over the long term and are socially just. This challenge requires sustained collective action on the part of social groups at multiple scales of govern-ance, a complex and difficult prospect. It also requires a normative agree-ment on what social justice entails, which is also difficult.

As researchers, we hope to contribute to the public good of knowledge that informs sustainable development. Thus our challenge is to simplify the complex systems of human–environment interaction in order to under-stand how they may foster or constrain win-win situations. SES are complex systems made-up of actors with diverse goals and capabilities, and are characterized by feedback processes that can generate uncertainty. Previ-ous studies show how diverse goals can lead to conflicts of interest that make collective action difficult and constrain the implementation of win-win policies. Previous work has also shown us how feedbacks create uncertainty in the functioning of SES and engender robustness–vulnerability tradeoffs. Such feedbacks can also constrain win-wins. The potential effects of diverse capabilities on tradeoff dynamics in SES have not been critically analyzed. In fact, it is generally argued that, *ceteris paribus*, diverse capabilities promote collective action. By extension, diverse capabilities among members of social groups who have the same goals should actually bolster the achievement of policies crafted to develop win-wins.

Our analysis illustrates that when individuals have diverse capabilities through which they interact with the environment, the result is different endowments of resources between actors over time. This necessitates exchange to distribute the flow of resources, which raises the possibility of conflicts of interest. Our model suggests that diverse capabilities, thus, may constrain pure win-win situations. The difficulty of achieving collect-ive action should increase as the productivity of the resource base declines because equity-inequity tradeoffs become more and more pronounced as the productivity of resources declines. In short, in small groups that have a common goal over a short period of time, diverse capabilities are beneficial (Page 2008). Diverse capabilities in such contexts lead to creativity and foster effective collective action. Over longer periods of time in self-organizing groups, however, diverse capabilities can lead to equity-inequity tradeoffs. That is, in order for a social group to achieve its goals, such as minimizing famine for everyone, someone in the group may have to accept an inequality. The questions are: What inequality is acceptable and who will be unequal (Sen 1992)?

Zooming Out: Types of Tradeoffs

We argue that three types of tradeoffs occur in SES: functional, robustness–vulnerability, and equity-inequity. We summarize the key processes that may generate each of the tradeoffs described in this section. These three tradeoffs interact, and we suggest that the evaluation of policies should focus on measuring all three tradeoffs over time rather than a singular performance measure of a given policy per se.

(1) *Functional tradeoffs.* These are tradeoffs that individuals must accept to satisfy conflicting but necessary goals. Roscoe (this volume, Chapter 4) provides a very clear example of a functional tradeoff. In New Guinea, the size of a settlement that best provides for the military security of individuals is larger than the size of a settlement that would allow individuals to most efficiently obtain food. A key feature of the New Guinea social environment is the persistent threat of war, raids, and ambushes. In this situation, members of communities either cooperate in defense as large groups or their capacity to defend against raids and ambushes is diminished. Thus, individuals sacrifice some efficiency in the food quest in order to obtain more personal security from the threat of raids. Individuals must trade off how they function to achieve these different goals. We argue that a diversity of necessary goals in a SES leads to functional tradeoffs. Clearly, functional tradeoffs can constrain win-wins. In the best of all worlds, individuals in the cases discussed by Roscoe could simultaneously maximize their personal security and food security. But these different goals require different ways of using time and organizing on a landscape that make such a win-win difficult.

(2) *Robustness–vulnerability tradeoffs.* These are tradeoffs between the ability of an actor to consistently achieve a goal and the vulnerability of an actor to environmental change. Isendahl and Heckbert (this volume, Chapter 6) provide an example (see also Nelson et al. and Brewington, this volume, Chapter 10). The Maya political

system on the Peten Karst Plateau and in Puuc-Nohkabab collapsed due to what we can characterize as a robustness–
vulnerability tradeoff, in which the vulnerability was realized. Political control in the Maya system was enmeshed in a tight feedback
loop centered on the royal courts, a situation that inclined nobles to
displace the costs of water management onto commoners at the
expense of the system's vulnerability to economic slowdowns.
Nobles controlled water management to increase production for
their own benefit. The more they increased production, the more
they benefited by increasing their status and control. However, this
strategy of basing authority and status on ever increasing production
through water management meant that the political contract was
vulnerable to an economic slowdown. The drive to increase production led to an exhaustion of soil nutrients and top soil erosion.
Eventually, the production system experienced a slowdown due to
declines in soil fertility and topsoil loss and the power base of the
elites evaporated. In this example, we see the importance of feedback loops that generate robustness–vulnerability tradeoffs in SES
(Anderies et al., 2007).

(3) *Equity-inequity tradeoffs.* The main thrust of our chapter, equity-
inequity tradeoffs occur when creating equality along one dimension of a SES leads to inequality in another dimension. We agree
with Sen's assertion that such tradeoffs are pervasive in human
societies. For example, even among hunter-gatherers, men using
the exact same technology, drawing on the same cultural traditions,
and hunting the same animals still often experience unequal outcomes in terms of hunting performance (Kaplan et al. 2000). The
reason is that some men have better eyesight, some are more experienced hunters, and/or some, by chance, hunt in more productive
areas. In this case, a diversity of individual capabilities leads to an
unequal production of meat *over time.* The inequality exists as a
latent feature of a SES composed of individuals with diverse capabilities. Where diverse capabilities mean different ways of interacting
with an environment, the result is equity-inequity tradeoffs. Such
tradeoffs may create conflicts of interest that make win-wins difficult.

Full Circle

What does any of this have to do with the northern frontier of Mesoamerica? The northward expansion of the frontier represents a

temporarily successful use of more arid areas. Armillas (1964) postulated that this expansion was associated with climatic change that temporarily made Mesoamerican agricultural systems possible. However, geomorphic and botanical study of the La Quemada landscape did not find evidence of such change, suggesting that the mechanisms of expansion and collapse may be social or biosocial (Elliott et al. 2010). Centers like La Quemada are examples of social, economic, and political elaboration, and exemplify complex farming societies pushing back against the limitations of aridity. This was "development," but it was not sustainable in the sense described in our introduction. First, social inequality was a feature of Mesoamerican sociopolitical organization that was as pervasive as ball courts, temples, and human sacrifice. Evidence of inequality at La Quemada includes extensive deposits of modified human bone, many comprising skeletal displays rather than burials (Nelson et al., 1992), as well as residences differing in size, construction materials, and centrality within the settlement (Nelson 2008). Importantly, some of the significant manifestations of inequality in the settlement are in the production, preparation, presentation, and consumption of food (Turkon 2004). It is hard to imagine that social justice, as defined in a sustainability context today, was achieved on the northern frontier. Second, Mesoamerican life-ways on the northern frontier collapsed rapidly (in Tainter's (2003) terms). This is not indicative of stable and sustainable social and political relationships, though the situation may have been beneficial for some segments of society.

Ultimately, the northern frontier of Mesoamerica is a case that does not meet the twin goals of sustainability. A useful strategy for informing sustainability research is to understand why. It is in this context that we have constructed a simple model of specialization and exchange that describes the core features of a Mesoamerican agroecological system in a semiarid environment. Our model illustrates that individual actors in this system with diverse capabilities to grow crops, but the same underlying goals, experience equity-inequity tradeoffs. The kinds of conflicts of interest generated by such tradeoffs are weakest in super-productive environments, but become starker as the productivity of the crop base declines. The northern frontier of Mesoamerica is not typically considered to be an environment with abundant arable land, especially when population is large. The ostentatiousness of La Quemada and the extreme coerciveness suggested by massive displays of human skeletons most likely represent recurrent interethnic violence in a context of scarce patches of highly productive agricultural land. They might also represent civil violence generated by stark equity-inequity tradeoffs in agricultural systems based more on specialization and exchange. La Quemada, along with many examples from the past, help us think critically about the goals of sustainable development in addition to our intrinsic curiosity about what happened in these places. Formal models help us flesh-out the logic of our thinking and begin to generalize our results, in this case, to understand the effects of diverse capabilities on tradeoffs in SES.

Acknowledgments

We would like to thank the participants of the Sustainability and Society seminar for thoughtful comments on earlier drafts of this work, especially Jim Roscoe and Seth Brewington. We would also like to thank the LTVTP group at ASU for their comments and input. We also gratefully acknowledge the National Science Foundation grants that supported excavation of La Quemada and study of its landscape, (BCS-0211109 and BECNH-0508001), as well as support provided by the NSF Dynamic Coupled Natural and Human Systems Program (#CNH-1113991).

References

Adger, W. Neal 2006 Vulnerability. *Global Environmental Change* 16(3):268–281.
Anderies, John M. 2006 Robustness, institutions, and Large-scale Change in Social-ecological Systems: The Hohokam of the Phoenix Basin. *Journal of Institutional Economics* 2(2):133–155.
Anderies, John, M. Janssen, and Elinor Ostrom 2004 A Framework to Analyze the Robustness of Social-ecological Systems from an Institutional Perspective. *Ecology and Society* 9(1):18.
Anderies, John M., Ben A. Nelson, and Ann P. Kinzig 2008 Analyzing the Impact of Agave Cultivation on Famine Risk in Pre-Hispanic, Arid Northern Mexico. *Human Ecology* 36:409–422.
Anderies, John M., Carl Folke, Brian Walker, and Elinor Ostrom 2013 Aligning Key Concepts for Global Change Policy: Robustness, Resilience, and Sustainability. *Ecology and Society* 18(2):8.
Anderies, John M., A. A. Rodriguez, M. A. Janssen, and O. Cifdaloz 2007 Panaceas, Uncertainty, and the Robust Control Framework in Sustainability Science. *Proceedings of the National Academy of Sciences* 104(39):15194–15199.
Armillas, P. 1964 Condiciones Ambientales y Movimientos de Pueblos en la Frontera Septentrional de Mesoamerica. In *Publicaciones del Seminario de Antropologìa Americana*, edited by Homenaje a Fernando Marquez-Miranda, pp. 62–82. Universidades de Madrid y Sevilla, Madrid.
Bokova, Irina, 2013 Preface. In *World Social Science report 2013: Changing Global Environments*, edited by Heide Hackmann, Françoise Caillods, Susanne

Moser, Frans Berkhout, Louise Daniel, Diana Feliciano, Orla Martin, and Eduardo Marques, pp. 3–5. UNESCO, Paris. DOI: 10.1787/9789264203419-en

Calviño, P. A., F. H. Andrade, and V. O. Sadras 2003 Maize Yield as Affected by Water Availability, Soil Depth, and Crop Management. *Agronomy Journal* 95(2):275–281.

Chhatre, A., and A. Agrawal 2009 Trade-Offs and Synergies between Carbon Storage and Livelihood Benefits from Forest Commons. *Proceedings of the National Academy of Sciences* 106(42):17667–17670.

Csete, M. E., and J. C. Doyle 2002 Reverse Engineering of Biological Complexity. *Science* 295(5560):1664–1669.

Darling, J. A. 1998 *Obsidian Distribution and Exchange in the North-Central Frontier of Mesoamerica.* PhD dissertation, Department of Anthropology, University of Michigan, Ann Arbor.

Elliott, M., C.T. Fisher, B.A. Nelson, R.S. Molina Garza, S. K. Collins, and D. M. Pearsall 2010 Climate, Agriculture, and Cycles of Human Occupation Over the Last 4000 yr in Southern Zacatecas, Mexico. *Quaternary Research* 74:26–35.

Ermentrout, B. 2006 XPPAUT 5.96.

Fiske, A. 1992 The 4 Elementary Forms of Sociality: Framework for a Unified Theory of Social-relations. *Psychological Review* 99(4):689–723.

Freeman, Jacob, John M. Anderies, Andera Torvinen, and Ben A. Nelson 2014 Crop Specialization, Exchange and Robustness in a Semi-arid Environment. *Human Ecology* 42(2):297–310.

Gibson, R. B. 2006 Sustainability Assessment: Basic Components of a Practical Approach. *Impact Assessment and Project Appraisal* 24(3):170–182.

Glover, J. 1957 The Relationship between Total Seasonal Rainfall and Yield of Maize in the Kenya Highlands. *Journal of Agricultural Science* 49(3):285–290.

Gluckman, Max 1941 *Economy of the Central Bartose Plain.* Rhodes-Livingston Institute, Livingston.

Hahn, T., F. Figge, J. Pinkse, and L. Preuss 2010 Trade-offs in Corporate Sustainability: You Can't Have Your Cake and Eat It. *Business Strategy and the Environment* 19(4):217–229.

Hegmon, Michelle 1996 Variability in Food Production, Strategies of Storage and Sharing, and The Pithouse-to-Pueblo Transition in the Northern Southwest. In *Evolving Complexity and Environmental Risk in the Prehistoric Southwest*, edited by J. A. Tainter and B. B. Tainter. Santa Fe Institute Studies in the Sciences of Complexity, Santa Fe.

Hegmon, Michelle, Matthew A. Peeples, Ann P. Kinzig, S. Kulow, C. M. Meegan, and Margaret C. Nelson 2008 Social Transformation and its Human Costs in the Prehispanic US Southwest. *American Anthropologist* 110(3):313–324.

Henrich, Joseph., Rob Boyd, S. Bowles, C. Camerer, E. Fehr, and H. Gintis 2004 Introduction. In *Foundations of Human Sociality: Economic Experiments and Ethnographic Evidence from Fifteen Small-Scale Societies*, edited by J. Henrich, R. Boyd, S. Bowles, C. Camerer, E. Fehr, and H. Gintis, pp. 1–7. Oxford University Press, Oxford.

Heyman, J. and Dan. Ariely 2004 Effort for Payment: A Tale of Two Markets. *Psychological Science* 15:787–793.

Hirth, Kenneth G. 2009 Craft Production, Household Diversification, and Domestic Economy in Prehispanic Mesoamerica. In *Housework: Craft Production and Domestic Economy in Ancient Mesoamerica*, edited by K. G. Hirth, pp. 13–32. Archeological Papers of the American Anthropological Association 19.

Hosler, D. 1994 *The Sounds and Colors of Power: The Sacred Metallurgical Technology of Ancient West Mexico.* MIT Press, Cambridge, MA.

Janssen, Marco, John M. Anderies, and Elinor Ostrom 2007 Robustness of Social-ecological Systems to Spatial and Temporal Variability. *Society and Natural Resources* 20(4):307–322.

Jen, E. 2003 Stable or Robust? What's the Difference? *Complexity* 8(3):12–18.

Jiménez Betts, P. 1992 Una Red de Interacción del Noroeste de Mesoamérica: Una Interpretación. In *Orígen y Desarollo en el Occidente de México*, edited by B. Boehm de Lameiras and P. C. Weigand, pp. 177–204. Colegio de Michoacán, Zamora.

    1995 Algunas Observaciones Sobre la Dinámica Cultural de la Arqueología de Zacatecas. In *Arqueología del Norte y del Occidente de México*, edited by B. Dahlgren and M. d. l. D. Soto de Arechavaleta, pp. 35–66. Universidad Nacional Autónoma de México, Mexico, D.F.

Kaplan, H., Kim Hill, Jane Lancaster, and A. M. Hurtado 2000 A Theory of Human Life History Evolution: Diet, Intelligence, and Longevity. *Evolutionary Anthropology Issues News and Reviews* 9(4):156–185.

Kelley, J. Charles 1985 The Chronology of the Chalchihuites Culture. In *The Archaeology of West and Northwest Mesoamerica*, edited by M. S. Foster and P. C. Weigand, pp. 269–288. Westview Press, Boulder, Colorado.

Lelgemann, A. 2000 *Proyecto Ciudadela de La Quemada, Zacatecas. Informe final al Consejo de Arqueología*, Instituto Nacional de Antropología e Historia, Bonn, Germany.

Mauss, Marcel 2002 [1954] *The Gift: The Form and Reason for Exchange in Archaic Societies.* Routledge, London.

McShane, Thomas O., Paul D. Hirsch, Tran Chi Trung, Alexander N. Songorwa, Ann Kinzig, Bruno Monteferri, David Mutekanga, Hoang Van Thang, Juan Luis Dammert, Manuel Pulgar-Vidal, , J. Peter Brosius, Peter Coppolillo, and Sheila O'Connor. 2011 Hard Choices: Making Trade-offs between Biodiversity Conservation and Human Well-being. *Biological Conservation* 144(3):966–972.

Monaghan, John 1996 Fiesta Finance in Mesoamerica and the Origins of a Gift Exchange System. *Journal of the Royal Anthropological Institute* 2(3):499–516.

Nelson, Ben A. 1997 Chronology and Stratigraphy at La Quemada, Zacatecas, Mexico. *Journal of Field Archaeology* 24(1):85–109.

    2008 Urbanism beyond the City: La Quemada, Zacatecas. In *El Urbanismo en Mesoamérica/Urbanism in Mesoamerica*, edited by A. G. Mastache, R. H. Cobean, Á. García Cook, and K. G. Hirth, pp. 501–538. Instituto Nacional de Antropología e Historia and Pennsylvania State University, México, D.F., and University Park, Pennsylvania.

Nelson, Ben A., J. Andrew Darling, and D. A. Kice 1992 Mortuary Practices and Social Order at La Quemada, Zacatecas, Mexico. *Latin American Antiquity* 3:298–315.

Nelson, Margaret C., Keith W. Kintigh, David R. Abbott, and John M. Anderies
2010 The Cross-Scale Interplay between Social and Biophysical Context and the Vulnerability of Irrigation-Dependent Societies: Archaeology's Long-term Perspective. *Ecology and Society* 15(3):31.

Nelson, Margaret C., Michelle Hegmon, Stephanie R. Kulow, Matthew A. Peeples, Keith W. Kintigh, and Ann P. Kinzig 2011 Resisting Diversity: A Long-Term Archaeological Study. *Ecology and Society* 16(1):25.

Page, Scott E. 2008 *The Difference: How the Power of Diversity Creates Better Groups, Firms, Schools, and Societies.* Princeton University Press, Princeton.
2011 *Diversity and Complexity.* Princeton University Press, Princeton.

Parsons, Jeffrey R., and Mary H. Parsons 1990 *Maguey Utilization in Highland Mexico: An Archaeological Ethnography.* Anthropological Papers of the Museum of Anthropology No 82, University of Michigan.

Richards, A. I. 1961 *Land, Labour and Diet in Northern Rhodesia: A Economic Study of the Bemba Tribe,* 2nd edition. Published for the International African Institute by the Oxford University Press, London.

Ricker, W. E. 1954 Stock and Recruitment. *Journal of the Fisheries Board of Canada* 11(5):559–623.

Sahlins, Marshall D. 1972 *Stone Age Economics.* Aldine-Atherton, Chicago.

Sauer, Carl O. 1963 *Land and Life: A Selection from the Writing of C. O. Sauer.* University of California Press, Berkeley.

Schortman, Edward M., and Patricia A. Urban 2004 Modeling the Roles of Craft Production in Ancient Economies. *Journal of Archaeological Research* 12(2):185–226.

Sen, Amartya 1992 *Inequality Reexamined.* Russell Sage Foundation, New York.

Strazicich, Nicola 1995 *Prehispanic Pottery Production in the Chalchihuites and La Quemada Regions of Zacatecas, Mexico.* PhD dissertation, Department of Anthropology, State University of New York at Buffalo.

Tainter, Joseph A. 2003 *The Collapse of Complex Societies.* Cambridge University Press, New York.

Torvinen, Andrea, Michelle Hegmon, Ann P. Kinzig, Margaret C. Nelson, Matthew A. Peeples, Karen G. Schollmeyer, Colleen Strawhacker, and Laura Swantek 2015 Transformation without Collapse: Two Cases from the U.S. Southwest. In *Beyond Collapse: Archaeological Perspectives on Resilience, Revitalization, and Transformation in Complex Societies,* edited by R. K. Faulseit, pp. 262–286. Southern Illinois University Press, Carbondale.

Trombold, Charles D., and Isabel Israde-Alcántara 2005 Paleoenvironment and Plant Cultivation on Terraces at La Quemada, Zacatecs, Mexico: The Pollen, Phytolith and Diatom Evidence. *Journal of Archaeological Science* 32:341–353.

Turkon, Paula 2004 Food and Status in the Prehispanic Malpaso Valley, Zacatecas, Mexico. *Journal of Anthropological Archaeology* 23(2):225–251.

Watson, Warren E., Lynn Johnson, Kamalesh Kumar, and Joe Critelli 1998 Process Gain and Process Loss: Comparing Interpersonal Processes and Performance of Culturally Diverse and Non-Diverse Teams Across Time. *International Journal of Intercultural Relations* 22:409–430.

3

Modeling Tradeoffs in a Rural Alaska Mixed Economy

Hunting, Working, and Sharing in the Face of Economic and Ecological Change

SHAUNA B. BURNSILVER, RANDALL B. BOONE, GARY P. KOFINAS, AND TODD J. BRINKMAN

In the Circumpolar North, mixed subsistence-cash economies are a livelihood form that is geographically widespread and culturally important for indigenous peoples (Nymand Larson et al. 2014; Poppel and Kruse 2010). Despite many ecological, subsistence, and political-economic differences, these economies have three components in common. People a) engage in market-based activities (e.g., employment for cash), b) carry out some form of subsistence production (harvesting, contributing, and processing), and c) share and cooperate, so that harvested foods, money, and other critical resources flow among households and interlink cash and subsistence activities (Natcher 2009; Nymand Larson et al. 2014).

Social relationships of sharing and cooperation both anchor cultural identities and contribute to food security and broader well-being (Poppel and Kruse 2010; Schweitzer et al. 2014). While research shows mixed livelihoods have persisted through time (BurnSilver et al. 2016; Forbes et al. 2009; Harder and Wenzel 2012; Kruse 1991; Langdon 1991; Wheeler and Thornton 2005) policy discussions around how future changes will occur in northern economies often assume opposing outcomes. Either mixed livelihoods will inexorably give way to market dynamics, or they are persistent, flexible, and robust under conditions of change. The subtext of these conversations is often sustainability. That is, are arctic mixed livelihoods sustainable? Are they able to persist while maintaining material, cultural, and ecological resources for present and future generations, or are they in decline (McCarthy et al. 2005)?

The processes and dynamics of adjustment associated with either market transformation or persistence outcomes are poorly understood, and the polemical arguments on both sides obscure important decisions and trade-offs for people that could characterize mixed northern livelihoods in the future. Decision making at individual, household, and community scales within the context of political-economic structures all contribute to import-ant outcomes for people and arctic landscapes. The emerging literature on tradeoffs emphasizes that there are costs and benefits associated with the strategies and preferred outcomes of different actors associated with any given human-resource-governance scenario (Brown et al. 2001; Campbell et al. 2010). But in the context of mixed economies, these costs and benefits are often framed in economic terms, and focus on maximizing economic utility rather than collective decisions that act to support the common good (Bates 1994; Plattner 1989). For example, common economic currencies for evaluating benefits (i.e., economic growth) are per capita income or village-level unemployment rates (Nymand Larsen and Huskey 2010). This approach essentially ignores the importance of cultural norms that emphasize other goals, such as equity, cooperation, or social cohesion. In this chapter we consider how the concept of tradeoffs represents a more useful rubric for understanding the iterative effects of decisions at house-hold and community scales in arctic mixed economies.

Our mechanism to explore tradeoffs is to simulate plausible scenarios of social, economic, and ecological changes currently facing northern house-holds and communities using an agent-based model called RASEM (Rural Alaska Social-Ecological Model). The linked concepts of vulnerability and robustness frame our thinking about tradeoffs within this modeled social-ecological environment. Vulnerability is a framework commonly used to analyze the effects of changes on households and communities (Eakin and Luers 2006; Smit and Wandel 2006). Adger (2006:269) describes vulner-ability as "the susceptibility to harm from the combination of exposures to ecological or social changes and the absence of capacity to adapt." Communities or households experience changes based on a range of pre-existing capabilities and assets (Adger 2003, 2006; Sen 1982). But vulnerability outcomes are usually framed as inherently negative (i.e., people have a predisposition to be harmed given x exposure and sensitivity combination, and y_1 to y_n capabilities). The focus is largely on the costs of changes for people or groups. The addition of the concept of robustness, however, makes conceptualization of potential outcomes of change more nuanced. Robustness emphasizes human behaviors and norms that shape how people respond to multiple perturbations. While people or a social-ecological system (SES) can be robust to a known set of perturbations, particularly those with which they have prior experience, they may be vulnerable to a new set of conditions. In this view change produces tradeoffs – both benefits and costs – for households and groups (Janssen and Anderies 2007; Janssen et al. 2007). Tradeoffs, or vulnerability-robustness combinations, appear as system components adjust to new or emergent circumstances (Janssen and Anderies 2007). For example, Alaska Iñupiat hunters prior to the 1950s traveled slowly across landscapes by dogsled and canoe, at a pace that was amenable to people developing nuanced understandings of weather patterns. Today, hunters use snowmachines and powerboats to travel more quickly (a benefit), but Elders describe how the knowledge of weather held by younger people is potentially less nuanced (a cost). This describes a robustness-vulnerability tradeoff, which may be further exacerbated under conditions of climate change that add an additional layer of uncertainty to weather knowledge (Berkes 2012; Ford et al. 2006). New vulnerabilities emerge as conditions change, thereby making existing knowledge-plus-technology-plus-climate tradeoffs more complex.

This example foreshadows the design of model scenarios in this chapter. The vulnerability and hazard literatures illustrate that drivers of change frequently act iteratively and cumulatively on households (Reynolds et al. 2014; Turner et al. 2003; Walker et al. 1987), and in the northern communities we have studied, changes do not act in isolation. Much more common are situations in which households and communities must respond to multiple and changing conditions concurrently or sequentially. A household may be able to ride out a job loss, but couple job loss with rising food and fuel prices, and existing tradeoffs may intensify or new vulnerabilities emerge.

How people in northern mixed economies experience these changes or perturbations depends very much on their communities and social relationships. Because many northern households do not act alone, but cooperate and share with others, sharing should increase equity and mitigate the effects of perturbations at the larger scale of the community. But these cross-scale dynamics have, so far, received little attention in the literature on tradeoffs (Carr 2008; Ericksen 2008). Instead, studies of vulnerability and robustness have focused primarily on a single scale, for example on households (Eakin and Borjorquez-Tapia 2008; O'Brien 2009), communities (Ford et al. 2006) or social-ecological systems (Nelson and colleagues, Chapter 8, this volume). Processes by which ecological and economic conditions accumulate, and subsequently mold emergent tradeoffs for households embedded within communities in the circumpolar north are unclear. Synthesizing these considerations through modeling is a goal of this chapter.

We parameterize RASEM to focus on three types of changes commonly addressed in the Alaska literature on mixed economies; changes in sharing norms, the effects of employment on subsistence, and changing ecological conditions that act to decrease the abundance of critical subsistence species. Relevant contexts for each of these manipulations are described in the following section, but our approach is similar to that of Reynolds and colleagues (2003), who simulated the differential effects of basic rules for sharing and exchange across a range of ecological conditions in the archaeological past (i.e., the Central Mesa Verde region). We pose the following questions in this chapter: (1) How do different sharing norms affect the distribution of wild food at household and community scales under conditions of change, and (2) As employment and ecological perturbations accumulate, how do identified tradeoffs change? Are they mitigated or intensified? Given the cultural importance of sharing and reciprocity in northern regions we intuitively expect that sharing results in more equity. However, whether changing economic and environmental conditions alter this fundamental relationship within mixed economies is an interesting question. The model's structure reflects a "baseline" community in Northern Interior Alaska, and is parameterized with a combination of biophysical base layers, ethnographic and empirical data on household socio-demographic attributes, and social networks (Figure 3.1). Model outcome variables of interest include the number of households with wild food, the amount of wild food stored by households, and the standard deviation of food stored. Standard deviation of available food is a way to examine equity of food distribution outcomes across scenarios.

We explore four scenarios in this chapter in which social, economic, and ecological perturbations accumulate (Table 3.1). The first scenario (*Exploratory*) applies the basic household model without biophysical layers in order to consider the effects of two types of sharing norms on outcome variables in isolation. In Scenario 2 (*Baseline*) household consumption is activated so households more realistically consume what they hunt and receive through redistribution. This run serves as a baseline against which subsequent scenarios are compared. Scenario 3 adds a distance limitation to subsistence travel as a proxy for employment (*Employment-Distance*). A fourth scenario subsequently overlays a 50 percent decline in resource densities onto distance constraints (*Employment -Scarcity*).

TABLE 3.1. *Cumulative design of model scenarios*

Scenario no.	Scenario name	Basic model	Sharing conditions	Household consumption	Geospatial model	Employment-distance conditions	Scarcity conditions
1	*Exploratory*	X	X				
2	*Baseline*	X	X	X	X		
3	*Employment-Distance*	X	X	X	X	X	
4	*Employment-Scarcity*	X	X	X	X	X	X

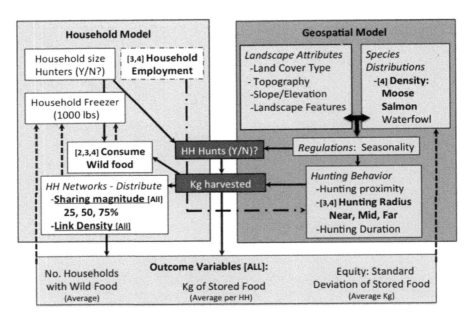

FIGURE 3.1. Conceptual diagram of RASEM showing two linked submodels, parameters and outcome variables. Bolded text represents parameters that are manipulated in modeling and numbers in brackets denote parameters that accumulate through scenarios [2, 3, 4]. Sharing conditions are applied across [All] scenarios. Processes within the model are represented as solid lines and feedbacks are dotted lines. The tradeoff between HH employment and Hunting Distance is mechanistically represented (hatched line).

Background to Mixed Economies

RASEM characterizes interactions between ecological, cultural, and economic changes within a mixed economy for a village of eighty-four households (the "agents" in the model). The model is parameterized using

FIGURE 3.2. Log home in Venetie, Alaska. Photo by Gary P. Kofinas.

ethnographic data from Venetie, a Gwitch'in Athabascan community in Interior Alaska (Figure 3.2). Thus, household agent decisions to hunt, work and share reflect both social values and economic goals that underlie real livelihood choices in a mixed economy. Key social and economic norms and ecological dynamics are described next.

Sharing Norms

Sharing and cooperation between households are integral to northern worldviews and take multiple forms (Damas 1972; Nelson 1982). Successful hunting households commonly provide food to kin or other households in need (e.g., elders or single women with children), and others may give or lend supplies to hunters in return for shares of a successful hunt. Social relationships could therefore compensate for inter-household shortfalls in time, skills, equipment, and money (Harder and Wenzel 2012). Subsistence production in Alaska Native communities historically follows a skewed distribution whereby 30 percent of households harvest 70 percent of wild foods (Magdanz et al. 2002; Wolfe and Walker 1987) and social relationships structure the distribution of food from key producers to other households. We use this 30:70 rule to specify the number of active hunters in model scenarios and parameterize redistribution of food. BurnSilver et al. (2016) found that almost 75 percent of total hunted/fished food in three northern Alaska communities circulated between village households based on a diverse set of social relationships (cooperative hunting, sharing/gifting, shares for helping others to harvest, and feasting), illustrating their importance as a component of mixed economies. We focus on one social relationship in the RASEM model – sharing. From a structural perspective, sharing relationships can be represented based on both the size of a household's network (each household connected to n others) and the magnitude of food given and received. The decision to share food with others is culturally valued, but it is, after all, a choice. Engagement in the cash economy could change social norms to the extent that individual accumulation of food becomes more important than sharing and cooperation, and households could decide to either share less or share with fewer others (Chabot 2003). Anecdotal evidence also suggests other factors, such as the 1970s advent of social services in villages, have already altered sharing norms. One Gwich'in Elder describes how, "...Before food stamps, returning hunters went door to door giving out food. Once food stamps came though, people still gave, but the door to door rounds stopped and people gave to fewer people" (personal communication, S. BurnSilver). In model scenarios we test the relative effects of changing sharing norms in two ways: first by varying the density of sharing networks (*connectedness*), and second by manipulating the proportion of a household harvest shared (*sharing magnitude*). Model outcomes are reported across all levels of these two sharing conditions (Table 3.1). In differentiating between sharing rules, we are able to compare the relative effects of network density versus sharing magnitude on food distribution, storage, and equity.

Household Employment

In Alaska native villages, the cash sector of mixed economies is typically constrained by limited employment opportunities, with unemployment ranging between 15 and 25 percent (Alaska Department of Commerce, Community and Economic Development 2015). Prices for basic necessities of food, fuel, and equipment in rural Alaskan communities are well above those in the mainland USA so access to some form of cash is important (Brinkman et al. 2014; Cochran et al. 2013; Loring and Gerlach 2009). In Venetie, a carton of twelve eggs, for example, costs $3.39, while an average T-bone steak runs at $14.99/lb (Alaska Food Cost Survey, 2010).

Household cash incomes may be supplemented by transfer payments in the form of village, regional, and state dividends or government assistance (Wheeler and Thornton 2005). Employment provides needed funds for fuel and equipment, while subsistence activities provide fresh, nutritious, and culturally important wild foods, without recourse to expensive local stores. However, employed but active harvesters must balance work time and subsistence activities, leading some to suggest that there is a core tradeoff in mixed economies between subsistence efforts and employment (Kruse et al. 1992; Wheeler and Thornton 2005). There is potentially some flexibility in employment forms as individuals may choose to work part-time, seasonally, or take "subsistence leave" if available. We model this potential work-time tradeoff in a simple way by constraining travel distance as a proxy for work time. In this initial effort we assume that hunting households are employed full-time and this equally constrains the travel distances of hunters in Scenarios 3 (*Employment-Distance*) and 4 (*Employment-Scarcity*) (Table 3.1).

Ecological Change

Climate change occurring in Alaska means that mixed livelihoods currently face multiple ecological changes (Chapin et al. 2008; Hinzman et al. 2005; Peterson et al. 2014; Trainor et al. 2009). Predictions suggest that the broader arctic region will warm an average of 2 degrees Celsius by 2100, with associated declines in summer sea ice extent, increasingly unpredictable storm patterns, increased frequency of forest fire, and thawing permafrost (Soja et al. 2007). Households may experience these changes in complex ways, through safety concerns (e.g., living with thin ice), less navigable landscapes due to timber deadfalls from fire or shallower rivers, increasingly uncertain weather patterns, or altered animal movements. These changes influence the ability of hunters to get out on the land and engage in subsistence (Berman et al. 2004; Brinkman et al. 2014; McCarthy 2001). We model ecological changes in RASEM in Scenario 4 by decreasing the densities of moose and salmon, two key Interior Alaska subsistence species (Stevens et al. 2012) (Table 3.1). Chinook (King) salmon have experienced steep declines in recent years across Alaska's Interior (JTC 2013). Significant restrictions on subsistence fishing have been put in place recently, and we mimic these restrictions by closing salmon harvests in Scenario 4 for five of ten years. Moose (Figure 3.3) densities in some regions of Interior Alaska are relatively high, while in other regions (e.g., Yukon Flats, Interior Alaska) moose densities are some of the lowest

FIGURE 3.3. Moose are a key subsistence species in Interior Alaska. Photo by Eduardo Wilner.

in the world (Lake et al. 2013). Moose numbers are thought to be primarily limited by predators (bear and wolf), but hunting pressure may also influence densities near communities. We model this condition by decreasing moose density in RASEM.

Methods: The Rural Alaska Social-Ecological Model (RASEM)

The agent-based representation of households for a generic Interior community in northeastern Alaska reflects basic household economic activities, key animals they harvest, and the resources that flow between households based on hunting and sharing. RASEM uses the NetLogo platform (Northwestern University, Evanston, IL). Two submodels have been developed, a geo-spatial and household model, which are linked (Figure 3.1). The coupled model reflects the interdisciplinary nature of the modeling team – two wildlife biologists, an environmental anthropologist, a resource economist, and a natural resource policy scientist. Data used to parameterize the model were collected in 2009–2010.

Geospatial Model

The current version (ver. 60) uses a daily time-step to represent the passage of time. The spatial arena represents an area 25 km × 25 km, with landscape cells each 50 m × 50 m. The landscape contains river and boreal forest habitats and represents moose, waterfowl, and salmon species. Spatial data layers, including land cover type and large rivers, are read into the model and their interactions affect animal distributions and mobility. Moose use different land cover types according to assigned rules and are hunted in two official seasons, two weeks in September and one additional week in December. Baseline moose densities are set at .66 km^2 (Taras and McCarthy 2011). Salmon are represented as a variable density in landscape cells classified as river and are fished in June in the current model. Waterfowl occur in water and wetlands and are hunted May–June as they migrate northward.

The behavior of hunters is controlled by tendencies, such as the desire to hunt near home, hunting radius, and maximum travel time away, plus seasonality constraints, hunting or fishing limits, and animal densities. Hunters select fishing or hunting sites randomly and move to that location. Success is determined by a probability (adjustable) plus published daily limits.

Household Network Model

The household network model reads in household attributes based on empirical data (BurnSilver et al. 2016; Kofinas et al. 2015). Households reflect heterogeneous agents based on a range of household sizes and levels of hunting activity. The eighty-four initialized households range in size from one to eight persons (mean of 2.89). A percentage of households is designated randomly as hunting or non-hunting and food flows into hunting households from hunting/fishing alone and hunting with others. Hunting and non-hunting households may then receive food through gifts. Households are assumed to accumulate food, which is stored conceptually in a "freezer" with a capacity up to 1,000 kg. Consumption is set at the rate of number of persons × .15 kg per day.

Sharing norms are manipulated across scenarios by varying two conditions: link density and proportion of food shared. We use the metric of link density to create a village network through which food moves between agents. The measure reflects the number of connections in a network divided by the total number of possible connections. To build

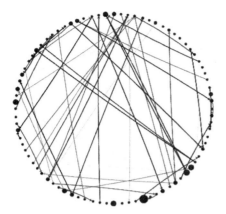

FIGURE 3.4. Screen shot of household network model for *Exploratory* Scenario. Sharing of twenty moose at Keep 50% condition. Nodes are households, sized by amount of meat received. Darker lines signify greater amounts of meat flowing between households.

a network, a house is selected randomly from which food will flow, and a household is selected to receive food (see example network, Figure 3.4). A directed link is made between these two houses, and a randomly generated weight from zero to one is assigned to the link, reflecting the strength of the relationship. In this sense, households within the network are faithful to their sharing partners, as they continue to pass specified proportions of what they receive until shared amounts of food decline to .1 kg, when sharing stops. That process is repeated across link densities from zero to .040, at .001 increments until a specified network link density is reached.

Households also share varying proportions of food. Interviews with Venetie hunters suggest that as a rule of thumb, hunters keep around 50 percent of what they harvest and redistribute the balance. Potential changes to community sharing norms are reflected by varying the percentage of wild food that households keep around this value: 25, 50, or 75 percent. Households then share (give) the balance of food remaining to other households (Figure 3.4).

Across scenarios, a factorial design is used, simulating the combination of each percentage value of food kept (25, 50, and 75 percent) and for each case, link density varies from 0 to 0.040. Each of these combinations (link density by sharing proportion) is simulated thirty times to account for the stochastic nature of the agent-based model.

Scenario 1: Exploratory

In this scenario, we focus specifically on the relative role of two sharing norms – magnitude and connectedness – on household to community scale tradeoffs in food distribution, provisioning, and equity. Without household consumption or geospatial interactions enabled, we assume meat from a single species (twenty moose) is shared between households given variable sharing rules and link densities. Twenty-five percent of households are designated as hunting in this scenario based on empirical results (25 percent of eighty-four households (n = 21) hunted for moose in Venetie).

Exploratory *Results*

This *Exploratory* scenario highlights an intuitive and basic tradeoff within mixed economies; under more generous and connected conditions, more households receive food (a benefit), but average kg received per household is lower (a cost) (Figure 3.5). This cost initially occurs at the scale of successful hunting households, and relative costs for individuals change as food is redistributed up to the community scale through networks. Equity in food holdings increases when households share more and are connected with many others (a community-level benefit). We term this a household to community scale distribution tradeoff.

Without consumption incorporated, both magnitude and connected-ness affect the shape of the basic distribution tradeoff, but in different ways (Figure 3.5). Varying connectedness structures the shape of the distribution – the number of households with food increases with higher link density, while average kilogram per household stored decreases. Varying the basic rules of sharing magnitude (25, 50 compared to 75 percent of food kept) significantly alters the intensity – i.e., the relative slope of the lines for each sharing condition – of the tradeoff at household and community scales. So for example, available food is highest in absolute terms for successful hunters under the most selfish condition (keep 75 percent of food). The difference in stored food from low to high connectedness is also greatest under this condition as average stored food steeply declines from 207 to 70 kg (Figure 3.5, hatched black line). To put this in perspective, for a family of four persons, each consuming approximately half of their daily 2,000 calories as wild food, 207 kg represents 1,597 kcal, or 399 days of available wild food. Seventy kg represents 540 kcal, or 134 days of consumption, so there is a significant decrease in stored food based on being connected to others. As well,

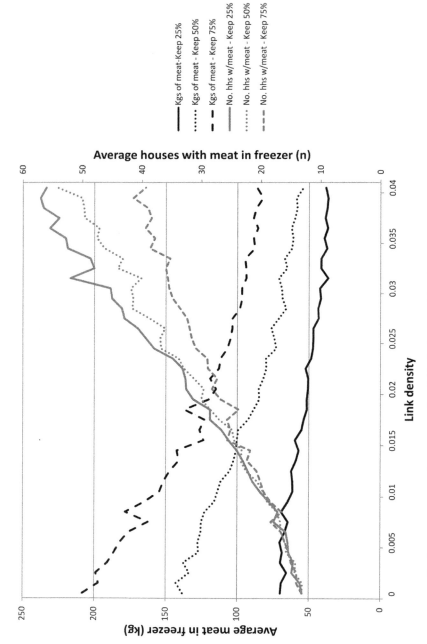

FIGURE 3.5. *Exploratory* scenario – Comparison of available food (y axis - black lines) and households with stored food (z axis - grey lines) for three magnitudes of sharing across link densities (x-axis, low to high).

equity in household food holdings is lowest under more selfish sharing conditions. At the 25 percent sharing level, the standard deviation in freezer holdings is 34.1 kg, while at 50 percent it rises to 60.5 kg, and at 75 percent of meat kept, the deviation is 86.0 kg.

Scenarios 2–4

In these scenarios we allow employment and scarcity perturbations to accumulate and examine how conditions modify the basic tradeoff identified in Scenario 1. These modeling scenarios more closely reflect "reality" as the household and geospatial models are linked and households consume what they hunt and receive. Thirty percent of households, in line with the 30:70 rule described earlier, are chosen randomly as hunters in simulations. Household sharing conditions are varied as previously. In the *Baseline* simulation hunters can travel any distance to hunt, but in subsequent scenarios hunters are constrained by employment characteristics that limit mobility from the village according to three conditions (i.e. Near, within 5 km – fully employed; Up to middle distance of 12.5 km – moderate employment; No distance limitation – little employment). In Scenario 4, distance conditions remain in place and additional scarcity conditions are added. The density of moose is halved to .33 km² and in years two, three, five, and six of the ten-year simulations, the salmon run fails. In all scenarios, ten repetitions of a given set of parameters are calculated to yield mean responses and a measure of deviation. We run each simulation for ten years, or 3650 days.

Scenarios 2, 3, 4 *Results*

We highlight general patterns across Scenarios 2, 3, and 4 first, then describe scenario-specific results in the following sections. The basic directionality of responses observed across all scenarios remains similar to those observed in the *Exploratory* scenario. The structure of the basic household to community scale distribution tradeoff is maintained, although the intensity and shape of the tradeoff changes significantly with employment and scarcity perturbations.

Across scenarios 2–4, a core pattern repeats: As link densities increase, the average number of households with meat increases (Figures 3.6a) and mean kg in household freezers decreases (Figures 3.6b). We report results only for sharing proportions of 25 and 75 percent, as observed patterns are largely redundant for the 50 percent sharing condition. Standard deviation

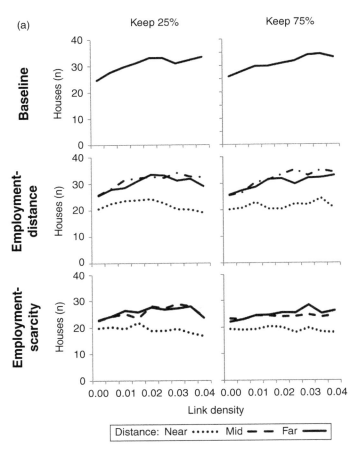

FIGURE 3.6. Households with wild food and stored food for scenarios 2–4. Results picture two sharing conditions (Keep 25 and 75 percent of hunted or received food) and link density increasing from .00 to .04. (a) Average number of households with stored wild food. The basic tradeoff (*Baseline*) suggests that the number of households with stored food increases at higher connectedness, but sharing more does not have significant effects on this outcome. The distribution of households with food shifts downward as hunting distance declines (*Employment-Distance Scenario*) and as scarcity occurs (*Employment-Scarcity Scenario*). (b) The amount of stored wild food for households with food. The basic tradeoff (*Baseline*) suggests that stored food per household declines at higher connectedness. At high connectedness keeping more food results in more stored food relative to other sharing conditions. The distributions of stored food shift downward as hunting distance declines (*Employment-Distance Scenario*) and as scarcity occurs (*Employment-Scarcity Scenario*).

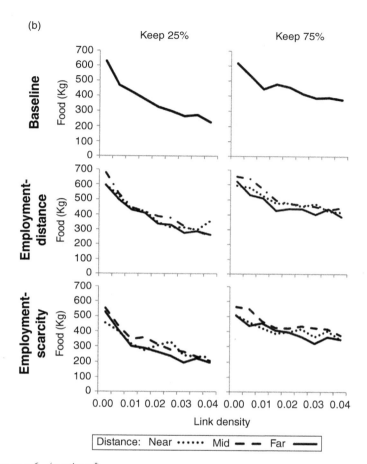

FIGURE 3.6. (*continued*)

of meat (kg) in freezers is lower at high link densities, although the size of the decrease varies (Figure 3.7). Thus, as observed in the *Exploratory* scenario, equity of available food among households is greater at higher connectedness.

Turning on household consumption modifies the basic tradeoff pattern in two ways. First, the number of households with food ranges between a low of seventeen and a maximum of thirty-six households. Thus, many households in these three scenarios (the majority of eighty-four households) may have received food from others, consumed it, and in the end have no stored food. Second, there are now few observed differences in patterns across sharing conditions by scenario

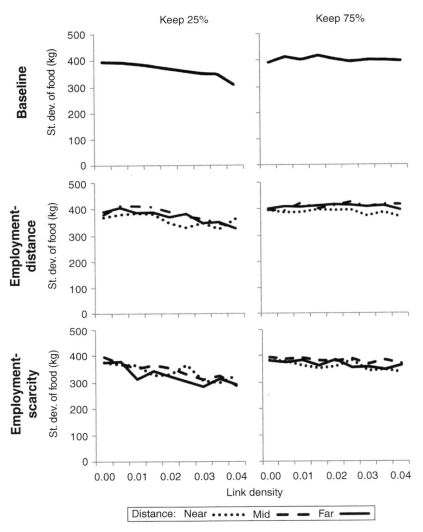

FIGURE 3.7. Standard deviation of stored food for scenarios 2–4. Results picture two sharing conditions (Keep 25 and 75 percent of hunted or received food) and link density increasing from .00 to .04. Equity increases as connectedness increases and households share more with others and keep less for themselves.

(Figure 3.6a). Consumption weakens the positive effects of generosity (keeping only 25 percent) on the number of households receiving food. The observed slopes of outcome variables across sharing norms are now very similar. Incorporating household consumption makes the model more realistic, but the striking accumulation and distribution differences seen in the *Exploratory* scenario based on sharing magnitude is muted. Based on the logic of household consumption in RASEM, hunting and receiving households receive food and then share the designated proportion. As they now consume what is in their "freezer" at daily time steps instead of storing it, less food accumulates on average to be stored over the ten-year period. In answer to our initial research question, connectedness emerges as most important in structuring the household to community distribution tradeoff.

However, two patterns linked to sharing conditions remained. Across all scenarios at high link densities, average food stored in freezers is highest when households keep proportionally more of their hunted and received food (Figure 3.6b, keep 75 percent condition). Under this sharing condition, the slope of the stored food line left to right – from low to high link density – flattens. There is less of a decline in food stored when households keep a higher proportion of food even when highly connected. When keeping only 25 percent, households (whether hunters or receivers) are not keeping enough food to sustain consumption over time even if they are well-connected and continue to receive food. Keeping more food under the 75 percent condition translates into more stored food stored at high link densities. The strategy to share less seems to pay off for the households who still have meat in their freezers. A second pattern involves equity. The general pattern remains that equity in stored food increases with link density, but the standard deviation of stored food is highest when households keep 75 percent of what they receive (Figure 3.7). When households share less generously, equity across households with food is lower.

Scenario 2: Baseline

In this *Baseline* scenario no limitations on distance or scarcity conditions are in place. The basic household to community distribution tradeoff and equity relationships are observed in this scenario. An average of between twenty-four and thirty-six households received food and have food stored at the end of the model run (Figure 3.6a). Sharing conditions seem to exert little effect, but the number of households receiving food rises across conditions when households are more connected. Distributions of food stored are similar across sharing conditions but increase with link density. As described previously, keeping 75 percent of hunted and received food at high link densities results in more stored food on average per household (Figure 3.6b, 375 kg compared to 293 kg, moving from 25 to 75 percent kept). At high link density, standard deviation in average food stored is lowest (and equity highest) under the most generous sharing condition (307 compared to 375 kg, moving from 25 to 75 percent kept, respectively).

Scenario 3: Employment-Distance

In this scenario, employment places increasing constraints on travel distance. Focusing first on number of households who have stored food (Figure 3.6a), there is no observed effect of diminished travel distance on average number of households with food in their freezer under middle distance constraints when compared to the baseline model. However, the average number of households with food declines when hunting area is most constricted (Near condition – dotted line). If high levels of employment act to constrict hunting distance within 5 km of the village, at most twenty-four households have meat in their freezers, compared to between twenty-five and thirty-six households with food when hunters can hunt at middle to far distances. As well, the slope of household distributions across link density flattens or becomes negative. Even greater connectedness between households cannot mitigate strongly constrained travel distance. This effect is true across sharing norms. There is, however, little observed effect of constrained hunting distance on average food kg stored in freezers (Figure 3.6b). When hunters only hunt close to the village, average stored food for households with meat is similar or higher than middle hunting distance conditions. When households are most connected, stored food is highest at the Keep 75 percent sharing condition.

Results here suggest an additional tradeoff between level of employment and subsistence distance. Additionally, while the shape of the core household to community distribution tradeoff holds, it is modified when hunting distance is most constrained. Many fewer households receive food on average; however, there is not a change in the amount of food households with food are able to store. Stored food (kg) declines in step as link density increases, regardless of distance or sharing norm. The shape of the basic household to community distribution tradeoff observed previously is weakened. The positive distribution side of the tradeoff – from few to many households provisioned – is mitigated as the movement of hunting households is constrained.

Scenario 4: Employment-Scarcity

Declines in moose and salmon species are layered onto employment-distance constraints in this scenario. The cumulative effect of scarcity and distance constraints again changes the strength of the baseline household to community distribution tradeoff. Compared to the *Baseline* and previous *Employment-Distance* scenarios, the average number of households with food declines across all successive distance conditions as resources become more scarce. The slope of distributions for households receiving food becomes increasingly flat as distance limitations intensify (from Far to Near). This effect occurs irrespective of amount shared and even at higher levels of connectedness. Only between seventeen and twenty-eight households receive food when households travel within 5 km distance from the village (Figure 3.6a, dotted line, *Employment-Scarcity Scenario*). Under the Near only condition, the slope of the distribution for households with meat becomes negative. The distributions of food stored shift downward under combined scarcity and distance conditions and these patterns intensify as households travel less. The range of stored food across sharing conditions declines to between 554 kg and 197 kg, never achieving 600 kg observed in previous scenarios. Consistent with other scenarios, however, keeping more food (75 percent) increases average kg of food stored at high connectedness (Figure 3.6b). Equity still increases at high link density, particularly if households share more, but this applies only to the very few households with food (Figure 3.7).

Under these cumulative perturbations, there is an iterative effect of both scarcity and distance, and the baseline distribution tradeoff is further weakened. Fewer households overall receive food, and stored food also declines on average. Even increased connectedness cannot mitigate these outcomes.

Tradeoffs in Mixed Economies

We applied RASEM to explore the structure of household to community distribution tradeoffs, and how these tradeoffs could change given potential social, economic, and ecological change perturbations. Simulations across the four scenarios integrated more realistic household dynamics (i.e., consumption) and cumulative exposures (employment constraints on travel and resource scarcity). Results highlight a core distribution tradeoff characteristic of mixed livelihoods, but illustrate that tradeoffs are sensitive to perturbations. These tradeoffs are not indicative of clear trajectories of change within mixed economies (i.e., either transformation or persistence), in part because what is gained from employment is not part of the current model. We find that employment can act as a drag on the subsistence system due to travel constraints, but the benefits (for example, cash available to purchase food and fuel) are not yet represented. However, modeled outcomes do reflect potential vulnerability-robustness tradeoffs within communities. Perturbations characterize some key ecological and livelihood dynamics under conditions of change, and as such, reflect conditions with which northerners themselves are grappling in real terms.

The *Exploratory* scenario highlights a conceptual – and intuitive – tradeoff at the foundation of mixed economies. As sharing occurs through networks, initial household-scale benefits from hunting transform into individual costs but broader community-scale benefits. As connectedness between households increases, food is redistributed more broadly. Equity of food stored increases but average kg of food stored at the household-scale declines. There is a cost (in stored food) associated with this basic tradeoff. It is borne particularly by initially successful hunters, but household decisions to share aggregate upward to benefit the community as redistribution continues through networks. This basic tradeoff is a structural outcome of the 30:70 production rule for subsistence systems when the choice to redistribute from high to low producers is maintained (Wolfe and Walker 1987). We first posed the question of how different sharing norms affect the distribution of wild food at household and community scales under conditions of change. At the purely conceptual level (i.e., without consumption included) the answer to this question is that both sharing magnitude and connectedness strongly affect distribution patterns. Varying connectedness structures the basic shape of the distribution tradeoff, and varying the basic rules of sharing magnitude significantly changes the intensity of the tradeoff at household and community scales.

In scenarios 2–4, increasing connectedness still improves the number of households with food and equity across households. But, the effects of sharing magnitude largely disappear. These scenarios incorporate household consumption and successive layers of employment constraints on distance and animal scarcity conditions. Results overall suggest *any* level of sharing and redistribution from hunters and between non-hunting households acts to distribute food initially beyond hunting households. But from the community perspective, giving more is not always better than giving less. Increasing the magnitude of food shared (keeping less) did not systematically improve the number of households receiving food, and food accumulation in average kg across link densities only marginally improves when households share more. In these more realistic scenarios, connectedness between households emerged as much more important than sharing magnitude in maintaining the basic household to community redistribution tradeoff.

Our second research question asked if and how cumulative changes would modify the core household to community distribution tradeoff. Results indicate that layered employment-distance and scarcity perturbations alter the *strength* of the tradeoff, and under highly perturbed conditions the *shape* of the tradeoff changes as well. We mechanistically represented an effect of employment on travel distance, such that at close distances moose are hunted intensively and abundance declines. Hunting success decreases, with subsequent negative effects on redistribution and number of households receiving food. Salmon and waterfowl abundance in RASEM are based on density rather than individual animals, such that many areas are available for harvesting, so decreased travel distance exerts little effect on their off take. The dynamic approximates overhunting that could arise if household employment limited hunting time – or, alternatively, if fuel prices rose such that long hunting trips were curtailed.

Layering on *Scarcity* conditions mirrors outcomes in the *Employment-Distance* scenario, but the distributions of households with food and average kg of food in freezers shifts downward starting even at the intermediate travel distance. The positive relationship between link density and number of provisioned households then disappears at the 5 km distance, suggesting that there may be a threshold, past which the benefits of household networking cease. Connectedness cannot compensate for lack of hunting success and the structure of the basic tradeoff is not maintained under these conditions. Results illustrate how cumulative changes could alter critical structures and dynamics characterizing subsistence-oriented communities.

The conceptual lens of vulnerability-robustness is useful in framing these findings on cumulative effects. The household to community distribution tradeoff is robust to distance constraints above 5 km, but below this point increasing link density is unable to compensate for lower hunting success and increase the number of households with food. The tradeoff is even less robust to cumulative effects of distance *and* scarcity. Turner and colleagues (2003) emphasize that multiple exposures within social-ecological systems usually act in concert to affect vulnerability outcomes, and this iterative characteristic of change is reflected in RASEM model outcomes. The distribution tradeoff basic to the mixed economy (as parameterized) is robust to a set of conditions, including changes in sharing magnitude and middle travel distance constraints. But it is less robust to declines in connectedness and combined distance and scarcity conditions. Under these conditions more households are potentially vulnerable to food insecurity. These iterative results echo those found by Nelson and colleagues (Chapter 8, this volume). Norse Greenlandic settlements were robust to a first climate shift, but, given emergent vulnerabilities, they were not robust to a second set of perturbations. Logan (Chapter 5, this volume) also provides an agricultural example of how crop transformation tradeoffs are mutable through time as conditions change.

Sharing and Cooperation

Sharing is a key feature of northern worldviews and remains integral to northern cultural identities. Manipulation of connectedness in RASEM clearly changes the strength of the distribution tradeoff and provisioning outcomes for households and communities. The historical narrative of sharing in the Circumpolar North is both material and moral. Decisions to share materialize as hunting success because animals only *give themselves* to hunters who share widely (Berkes 2012; Brewster 2004; Feit 1995; Slobodin 1981). Hunted and fished animals are morally deserving of respect, the expression of which mandates forms of generosity and respect between humans. Similarly, reciprocal relationships based on sharing and cooperation can mitigate expected periods of scarcity, although ethnographic evidence suggests that sharing networks may shrink under adverse environmental conditions (Burch 1980). Bodenhorn (2000) and Nelson (1982) highlight the significant prestige associated with possessing a reputation for generosity. Thus people make decisions to redistribute food for non-economic reasons that extend beyond simple individual scale cost/benefit calculations. Our modeling efforts do not capture the interplay between cultural and individual cost/benefit decision points. For example, exactly how much wild food is *enough* for households is unknown and will depend on many factors, but a household of four able to store ~189 kg of food would have access to 50 percent of daily calories from wild food sources for one year. Venetie hunters state that decisions on how much and how widely to share depend on the timing within a season (early vs. late) and perceptions of hunting success (excellent vs. poor) (BurnSilver, personal communication). A hunter may widely distribute 75 percent of a caribou in the early season when both community need and the potential to catch more is high, but hold onto 75 percent of an animal caught late in the season in order to store enough meat through to the next year. Decision making is fluid and may take into account both own need and the collective good of others through time.

The corn and agave reciprocity scenarios explored by Freeman and colleagues (Chapter 2, this volume) highlight similar individual cost vs. group level benefits, but they frame this tradeoff from a resource-maximizing perspective. In the Arctic context, ethnographic data for northern peoples highlight that while there may be a tradeoff from productive hunters to the wider community, this redistribution reflects a highly valued cultural choice to consider collective as well as individual benefits. In this sense, northern hunters themselves may not articulate this choice as a tradeoff at all. Instead of a *win-lose*, it may be a *win-win* even as hunter households have less food stored in their freezers.

Changing Context within Mixed Economies

Today, northern households have many more livelihood options than in the past. While multiple studies illustrate that mixed economies persist, the combined strength of mixed livelihoods (subsistence + employment + sharing/cooperation) is built on a series of individual and household decisions. An additional aspect of expanded livelihood choice is that households within communities are less and less homogeneous (Kruse 1991) as no longer are most households entirely dependent on subsistence. Employment levels vary, and households increasingly have a range of capabilities and financial, physical, or human assets that subsequently translate into heterogeneous capacities to adapt (Usher et al. 2003). As exposures act on communities, unique tradeoffs emerge for households based on their adaptive capacities and sensitivities to change (Adger 2003; Adger 2006; Turner et al. 2003). Freeman and colleagues (Chapter 2, this volume) examine the effects of heterogeneous capabilities on decisions to share resources. This household-level heterogeneity is not yet fully represented in RASEM, but this will be an important future question to explore.

The basic household to community tradeoff at the heart of mixed economies highlighted in this chapter is predicated on culturally mediated household decisions to share and redistribute even as economic contexts change. Over and above the simplistic rules explored here, households decide how often to engage in subsistence, who to hunt with, how much to work, how far to travel, and whether to share equipment and other supplies, thereby helping others to get out hunting. As households and communities face climatic, economic, and other challenges, mixed economies and outcomes for households could change if the cultural norms and values governing these decisions transform. Some households could become more focused on employment, act more individualistically (i.e., selfishly) and change sharing and cooperation patterns. Alternatively, non-economic values could maintain core social relationships and strengthen commitments to subsistence into the future. Results here show that there are potential community-scale costs in food security and community cohesion associated with decisions *not* to share and redistribute. Likewise, there are situations in which even sharing widely made little difference to distribution outcomes. These potential gaps are important to consider given that development pressures and climatic changes are only predicted to intensify in the Arctic going forward.

What do our results indicate regarding the strength of particular levers to affect basic tradeoffs under conditions of iterative change? We modeled sharing norms in two ways in RASEM; the magnitude of food given to others and the level of connectedness between households. Findings suggest that absolute sharing magnitude is irrelevant under some circumstances and level of connectedness is more critical to maintaining the shape of the basic redistribution and equity tradeoff. Sharing widely emerges as a more powerful form of social capital that may be more critical to maintaining an ability to cope with change by redistributing resources and food. Sharing widely also contributes to a sense of social cohesion within communities, such that even if the amount shared is small, it implies a connection between people that could be called on in periods of scarcity or stress.

It is important to recognize that in spite of the positive role of connectedness observed in model outcomes, many households under scenarios 2–4 end the model runs with no stored food. Sharing at higher link densities raises the number of provisioned households, but the proportion never goes above 42 percent (thirty-six households) in any scenario. Even at high link densities, we observe strong differences in stored wild food between households that accumulate food and those who do not. Within communities, options to increase available food include purchasing food, hunting more, or asking for help from others, and in recent times, applying for public assistance. We did not consider the effect of income on the ability to purchase food here, but either income inequality or lack of sharing could translate into disparate well-being outcomes, such as high and low food security within a community (Lambden et al. 2006; Loring and Gerlach 2009). This is a dimension of well-being that is not addressed in a straightforward consideration of household to community distribution tradeoffs.

Future Modeling

Models are always simplified representations of reality. RASEM mimicked basic dynamics characteristic of mixed economies and demonstrated utility to explore other scenarios and interactions. We only mechanistically represented the assumption that full-time employment would translate into diminished capacity to travel for subsistence. Future efforts will incorporate more complex household economic dynamics to explore how money or equipment factor into sharing relationships, and if flexible work schedules (i.e., full or part-time) or higher household income could offset the time/distance tradeoff modeled here. For example, households could purchase faster equipment to travel greater distances in shorter time periods. This is a realistic household coping strategy that Kruse (1991) and others documented (Chabot 2003; Wheeler and Thornton 2005) and modeled (Kruse et al. 2004). Integration of these key dynamics will allow more thorough consideration of additional economic and subsistence tradeoffs within mixed economies.

Perspective Taking

Alaska Natives, academics from multiple disciplines, and policy makers have long evaluated the mix of choices and outcomes represented by mixed economies (Langdon 1991; Wheeler and Thornton 2005). Alaska Natives themselves actively debate what it means to be someone who is active in subsistence, and who shares, works, and takes care of family under current conditions of social, economic, political, and environmental change. But implicit in the framing of these choices and their respective tradeoffs is perspective. Coulthard (2012), for example, poses the question, "Can households be both resilient and well?" Within our modeling framework, we might define "well" as the greatest number of households with enough stored food, employed but able to travel for subsistence, and high equity in food stored across households within the community. In contrast, a development economist might focus on employment opportunities and leave hunting and social relationships aside. There are an unlimited number of possible perspectives on what constitutes "well," "resilient," or "sustainable." Echoing the third theme of tradeoffs in Hegmon's introduction (Chapter 1) to this volume, each of these perspectives implies judgments about which tradeoffs are valuable to consider. Equity, *or the lack thereof*, has emerged as an important driver of change in case studies included in this volume. We explicitly parameterized RASEM based on

combined cultural and economic norms characterizing northern livelihoods, a perspective that prioritizes equity. Freeman and colleagues, as
well as Hegmon (Chapter 7) and Grier and Angelbeck (Chapter 9, this
volume), also focus on equity as a key component of sustainability tradeoffs.
However, their perspective on equity is externally informed. While achieving equity may not have been an explicit cultural goal in Mimbres,
Frontier Mesoamerica, Coastal Salish, or Greenlandic societies, their work
identifies that inequality was a potential factor in many of the tradeoffs and
transformations identified by these authors.

Coulthard (2012) and Armitage et al. (2012) highlight that positive
outcomes associated with a livelihood choice in one domain do not
necessarily imply equally positive outcomes in another domain. Brown
and Westaway (2011) similarly suggest that carefully differentiating
important outcomes across well-being and adaptive capacity domains is
key to representing tradeoffs associated with livelihood change. We agree
with these perspectives, and add that the process of choosing both
domains of interest and outcomes defines the tradeoffs to be considered
and the way benefits and costs are ultimately weighted. Northern cultural
groups, the Gwitch'in, the Inuit, and many others are increasingly full
collaborators and partners in discussions around critical outcomes and
tradeoffs associated with change. The process of framing a range of
choices, perspectives, and values across livelihood, policy, and academic
divides is critical to identification of important tradeoffs. Exploring *what if*
scenarios through conversations and modeling can be a key feature of
these conversations. We suggest further that application of modeling
frameworks to explore plausible scenarios and dynamics of change is
another method to transform consideration of tradeoffs away from polem-
ics and from implicit to explicit.

Acknowledgments

Research for this chapter was supported primarily by the project
"Modeling Harvesting Behavior to Understand Adaptation, Mitigation,
and Transformation in Northern Subsistence Systems," funded by the
Arctic Social Science Division of the National Science Foundation
(award # 0909570). Dr. Branka Valcic, who served as the original study
PI, developed initial modeling ideas. Partial support was received
through the Alaska EPSCoR program funded by National Science
Foundation (award #OIA 1208927), the State of Alaska, and the "IPY:
Impacts of High-Latitude Climate Change on Ecosystem Services and

Society" project (award # 0732758). Support for background research was provided by "The Sharing Project" of the Northwest Cooperative Ecosystems Studies Unit through US Department of the Interior Bureau of Ocean Energy Management Cooperative Agreement M07AC12496. The views expressed here are those of the authors and not the funders. A special acknowledgement is made to the many Venetie respondents who participated in interviews, to the Venetie Traditional Village Council for its guidance in making the project successful, and to Eddie and Sarah Frank for their hospitality and unwavering support of our work. An additional thank you goes to the Natural Resource Management Department of the Council of Athabascan Tribal Governments, based in Fort Yukon, for its work with Brinkman on the resource component of the model.

References

Adger, W. Neil 2003 Social Capital, Collective Action and Adaptation to Climate Change. *Economic Geography* 79:387–404.
    2006 Vulnerability. *Global Environmental Change* 16:268–281.
Alaska Department of Commerce, Community and Economic Development 2015 Electronic Database. www.commerce.alaska.gov/dcra/DCRAExternal/community, accessed May 15, 2015.
Alaska Food Cost Survey 2010 *Venetie, Alaska*. University of Alaska Fairbanks, Cooperative Extension Service. Accessed Online.
Armitage, Derek, Chris Béné, Anthony Charles, Derek Johnson, and Edward Allison 2012 The Interplay of Well-being and Resilience in Applying a Social-ecological Perspective. *Ecology and Society* 17(4):15.
Bates, Robert 1994 Social Dilemmas and Rational Individuals. In *Anthropology and Institutional Economics*, edited by James Acheson, pp. 43–66. University Press of America, Lanham.
Berkes, Fikret 2012 *Sacred Ecology: Traditional Ecological Knowledge and Resource Management* 3rd edn. Taylor and Francis, Philadelphia.
Berman, Matthew, Craig Nicolson, Gary Kofinas, Joe Tetlichi, and Stephanie Martin 2004 Adaptation and Sustainability in a Small Arctic Community: Results of an Agent-Based Simulation Model. *Arctic* 57(4):401–414.
Bodenhorn, Barbara 2000 "It's Good to Know Who Your Relatives Are but We Were Taught to Share with Everybody": Shares and Sharing among Iñupiaq Households. *Senri Ethnological Studies* 53:27–60.
Brewster, Karen (editor) 2004 *The Whales, They Give Themselves: Conversations with Harry Brower, Sr.* Oral Biography Series. University of Alaska Press, Fairbanks.
Brinkman, Todd, B. Maracle Karonhiakta'tie, James Kelly, Michelle Vandyke, Andrew Firmin, and Anna Springsteen 2014 Impact of Fuel Costs on High-Latitude Subsistence Activities. *Ecology and Society* 19(4):18.

Brown, Katrina, W. Neil Adger, Emma Tompkins, Peter Bacon, David Shim, and
    Kathy Young 2001 Trade-off Analysis for Marine Protected Area Management.
    Ecological Economics 37(3):417–434.
Brown, Katrina, and Elizabeth Westaway 2011 Agency, Capacity and Resilience to
    Environmental Change: Lessons from Human Development, Wellbeing, and
    Disasters. *Annual Review of Environment and Resources* 36:321–342.
Burch, Ernest 1980 Traditional Eskimo Societies in Northwest Alaska. *Senri Ethno-
    logical Studies* 4:253–304.
BurnSilver, Shauna, Jim Magdanz, Rhian Stotts, and Gary Kofinas 2015 Are Mixed
    Economies Persistent or Transitional? Evidence Using Social Networks from
    Arctic Alaska. *American Anthropologist*, 2016.
Campbell, Bruce, Jeffrey Sayer, and Brian Walker 2010 Navigating Trade-offs: Working
    for Conservation and Development Outcomes. *Ecology and Society* 15(2):16.
Carr, Edward 2008 Between Structure and Agency: Livelihoods and Adaptation in
    Ghana's Central Region. *Global Environmental Change* 18:689–699.
Chabot, Marcelle 2003 Economic Changes, Household Strategies, and Social
    Relations of Contemporary Nunavik Iñuit. *Polar Record* 39:19–34.
Chapin, F. Stuart, Sarah Trainor, Orville Huntington, Amy Lovecraft, Erika Zava-
    leta, David Natcher, David McGuire, Joanna Nelson, Lily Ray, Monika Calef,
    Nancy Fresco, Henry Huntington, T. Scott Rupp, La'ona DeWilde, and
    Rosamund Naylor 2008 Increasing Wildfire in Alaska's Boreal Forest: Path-
    ways to Potential Solutions of a Wicked Problem. *BioScience* 58(6):531–540.
Cochran, Patricia, Orville Huntington, Caleb Pungowiyi, Stanley Tom, F. Stuart
    Chapin III, Henry Huntington, Nancy Maynard, and Sarah Trainor 2013
    Indigenous Frameworks for Observing and Responding to Climate Change
    in Alaska. *Climatic Change* 120(3):557–567.
Coulthard, Sarah 2012 Can we be Both Resilient and Well, and What Choices do
    People Have? Incorporating Agency into the Resilience Debate from a Fisher-
    ies Perspective. *Ecology and Society* 17(1):4.
Damas, David 1972 Central Eskimo Systems of Food Sharing. *Ethnology*
    11(3):220–240.
Eakin, Hallie, and Luis Bojorquez-Tapia 2008 Insights into the Composition of
    Household Vulnerability from Multicriteria Decision Analysis. *Global Envir-
    onmental Change* 18(1):112–127.
Eakin, Hallie, and Amy Luers 2006 Assessing the Vulnerability of Social-environ-
    mental Systems. *Annual Review of Environment and Resources* 31(1):365.
Ericksen, Polly 2008 What is the Vulnerability of a Food System to Global Environ-
    mental Change? *Ecology and Society* 13(2):14.
Feit, Harvey 1995 Hunting and the Quest for Power: The James Bay Cree and
    Whitemen in the Twentieth Century. In *Native Peoples: The Canadian
    Experience*, 2nd edition, edited by R. Bruce Morrison and C. Roderick Wilson,
    pp. 171–207. McClelland and Stewart, Toronto.
Ford, James, Barry Smit, and Johanna Wandel 2006 Vulnerability to Climate
    Change in the Arctic: A Case Study from Arctic Bay, Canada. *Global Environ-
    mental Change* 16(2):145–160.
Forbes, Bruce, Florian Stammler, Timo Kumpula, Nina Meschtyb, Anu
    Pajunen, and Elina Kaarlejärvi 2009 High Resilience in the Yamal-Nenets

Social–ecological System, West Siberian Arctic, Russia. *Proceedings of the National Academy of Sciences* 106(52):22041–22048.

Harder, Miriam, and George Wenzel 2012 Inuit Subsistence, Social Economy and Food Security in Clyde River, Nunavut. *Arctic* 65(3):305–318.

Hinzman, Larry, Neil Bettez, Robert Bolton, F. Stuart Chapin III, Mark Dyurgerov, Chris Fastie, Brad Griffith, Robert Hollister, Allen Hope, Henry Huntington, Anne Jensen, Gensuo Jia, Toree Jorgenson, Douglas Kane, David Klein, Gary Kofinas, Amanda Lynch, Andrea Lloyd, David McGuire, Frederick Nelson, Walter Oechel, Thomas Osterkamp, Charles Racine, Vladimir Romanovsky, Robert Stone, Douglas Stow, Mathew Sturm, Craig Tweedie, George Vourlitis, Marilyn Walker, Donald Walker, Patrick Webber, Jeffrey Welker, Kevin Winker, and Kenji Yoshikawa 2005 Evidence and Implications of Recent Climate Change in Northern Alaska and other Arctic Regions. *Climatic Change* 72(3):251–298.

Janssen, Marco, John Anderies, and Elinor Ostrom 2007 Robustness of Social-Ecological Systems to Spatial and Temporal Variability. *Society and Natural Resources* 20(4):307–322.

Janssen, Marco, and John Anderies 2007 Robustness Trade-Offs in Social-Ecological Systems. *International Journal of the Commons* 1(1):43–66.

JTC (Joint Technical Committee of the Yukon River US/Canada Panel) 2013 Yukon River salmon 2012 season summary and 2013 season outlook. Alaska Department of Fish and Game, Division of Commercial Fisheries, Reg. Info. Rep. 3A13-01, Anchorage.

Kofinas, Gary, Shauna BurnSilver, Jim Magdanz, Rhian Stotts, and Marcy Okada 2015 "Subsistence Sharing Networks and Cooperation: Kaktovik, Wainwright, and Venetie Alaska." BOEM Report 2015-023. Published by University of Alaska Fairbanks.

Kruse, Jack 1991 Alaska Inupiat Subsistence and Wage Employment Patterns: Understanding Individual Choice. *Human Organization* 50(4):317–326.

Kruse, Jack, Judith Kleinfeld, and Robert Travis 1982 Energy Development on Alaska's North Slope: Effects on the Inupiat Population. *Human Organization* 41(2):96–107.

Kruse, Jack, Robert White, Howard Epstein, Billy Archie, Matthew Berman, Stephen Braund, F. Stuart Chapin III, Johnny Charlie Sr., Colin Daniel, Joan Eamer, Nick Flanders, Brad Griffith, Sharman Haley, Lee Huskey, Bernice Joseph, David Klein, Gary Kofinas, Stephanie Martin, Stephen Murphy, William Nebesky, Craig Nicolson, Don Russell, Joe Tetlichi, Arlon Tussing, Marilyn Walker, and Oran Young 2004 Modeling Sustainability of Arctic Communities: An Interdisciplinary Collaboration of Researchers and Local Knowledge Holders. *Ecosystems* 7(8):815–828.

Lambden, Jill, Olivier Receveur, Joan Marshall, and Harriet Kuhnlein 2006 Traditional and Market Food Access in Arctic Canada is Affected by Economic Factors. *International Journal of Circumpolar Health* 65(4):331–340.

Lake, Bryce, Mark Bertram, Nikki Guldager, Jason Caikoski, and Robert Stephenson 2013 Wolf Kill Rates Across Winter in a Low-density Moose System in Alaska. *The Journal of Wildlife Management* 77(8):1512–1522.

Langdon, Stephen 1991 The Integration of Cash and Subsistence in Southwest Alaskan Yup'ik Eskimo Communities. *Senri Ethnological Studies* 30:269–291.

Loring, Phil and S. Craig Gerlach 2009 Food, Culture, and Human Health in Alaska: An Integrative Health Approach to Food Security. *Environmental Science and Policy* 12(4):466–478.

Magdanz, James, Charles Utermohle, and Robert Wolfe 2002 The Production and Distribution of Wild Food in Wales and Deering, Alaska. Division of Subsistence, Alaska Department of Fish and Game. Technical Paper 259. Juneau, Alaska.

McCarthy, James 2001 Climate Change 2001: Impacts, Adaptation, and Vulnerability: Contribution of Working Group II to the Third Assessment report of the Intergovernmental Panel on Climate Change. Cambridge University Press, Oxford.

McCarthy, James, Marybeth Long Martello, Robert Corell, Noelle Seli, Shar Fox, Grete Hovelsrud-Broda, Svein Mathiesen, Colin Polsky, Henrik Selin, and Nicholas Tyler 2005 Climate Change in the Context of Multiple Stressors and Resilience. In *Arctic Climate Impact Assessment*, Cambridge University Press, Cambridge, pp. 945–988.

Natcher, David 2009 Subsistence and the Social Economy of Canada's Aboriginal North. *Northern Review* 30:83–98.

Nelson, Richard 1982 *Make Prayers to the Raven: A Koyukon View of the Northern Forest*. University of Chicago Press, Chicago.

Nymand Larsen, Joan, and Lee Huskey 2010 Material Well-being in the Arctic. In *Arctic Social Indicators - a follow-up to the Arctic Human Development Report*, edited by Joan Nymand Larsen, Peter Schweitzer, and Gail Fondahl, pp. 47–66. Nordic Council of Ministers, Copenhagen.

Nymand Larson, Joan, Gail Fondahl, and Henriette Rasmussen (editors) 2014 Arctic Human Development Report: Regional Processes and Global Linkages Nordic Council of Ministers: Denmark. TemaNord. pp. 567. Electronic Document, http://dx.doi.org/10.6027/TN2014-567.

O'Brien, Karen 2009 Do Values Subjectively Define the Limits to Climate Change Adaptation? In *Adapting to Climate Change: Thresholds, Values and Governance*, edited by W. Neil Adger, Irene Lorenzoni, and Karen O'Brien, pp. 255–268. Cambridge University Press, Cambridge.

Peterson, David, Jane Wolken, Teresa Hollingsworth, Christian Giardina, Jeremy Littell, Linda Joyce, Christopher Swanston, Stephen Handler, Lindsey Rustad, and Steven McNulty 2014 Regional Highlights Of Climate Change. In *Climate Change and United States Forests*. pp. 113–148. Springer Netherlands, Houten.

Plattner, Stuart 1989 Introduction. In *Economic Anthropology*, edited by Ed Plattner, pp. 1–21. Stanford University Press, Stanford.

Poppel, Birger, and Jack Kruse 2010 The Importance of a Mixed Cash and Harvest Herding Based Economy to Living in the Arctic – An Analysis on the Survey of Living Conditions in the Arctic (SLiCA). In *Quality of life in the New Millennium: Advances in Quality-of-life Studies, Theory and Research*, edited by Valerie Møller and Denis Huschka, pp. 27–42. Social Indicators Research Series. Springer Netherlands, Houten.

Reynolds, Robert, Tim Kohler, and Zaid Kobti 2003 The Effects of Generalized Reciprocal Exchange on the Resilience of Social Networks: An Example from the Prehispanic Mesa Verde Region. *Computational and Mathematical Organization Theory*, 9(3):227–254.

Sen, Amartya 1982 *Poverty and Famines: An Essay on Entitlement and Deprivation.* Oxford University Press.

Smit, Barry, and Johanna Wandel 2006 Adaptation, Adaptive Capacity and Vulnerability. *Global Environmental Change*, 16(3):282–292.

Slobodin, Richard 1981 *Kutchin Handbook of North American Indians: The Subarctic 6: 514-532.* Smithsonian Institute, Washington.

Soja, Amber, Nadezda Tchebakova, Nancy French, Michael Flannigan, Herman Shugart, Brian Stocks, Anatoly Sukhinin, E.I. Parfenova, F. Stuart Chapin III, and Paul Stackhouse Jr. 2007 Climate-induced Boreal Forest Change: Predictions versus Current Observations. *Global and Planetary Change* 56(3):274–296.

Schweitzer, Peter, Peter Skold, and Olga Ulturgasheva 2014 Cultures and Identities. In *Arctic Human Development Report: Regional Processes and Global Linkages*, edited by, Joan Nymand Larson, Gail Fondahl, and Henriette Rasmussen, pp. 104–149. Denmark. TemaNord, Nordic Council of Ministers. Electronic Document. http://dx.doi.org/10.6027/TN2014-567.

Stevens, Carrie, Caroline Brown, and David Koster 2012 *Subsistence Land Mammal Harvests and Uses, Yukon Flats, Alaska: 2008-2010 Harvest Report and Ethnographic Update*: Alaska Department of Fish and Game, Division of Subsistence.

Taras, Mike, and Laura McCarthy 2011 *Interior Alaska Moose News. Alaska Department of Fish and Game*, Fairbanks, Alaska.

Trainor, Sarah, Monika Calef, David Natcher, F. Stuart Chapin III, A. David McGuire, Orville Huntington, Paul Duffy, T. Scott Rupp, La'Ona DeWilde, Mary Kwart, Nancy Fresco, and Amy Lovecraft. 2009 Vulnerability and Adaptation to Climate-related Fire Impacts in Rural and Urban Interior Alaska. *Polar Research* 28(1):100–118.

Turner, Billy, Roger Kasperson, Pamela Matson, James McCarthy, Robert Corell, Lindsey Christensen, Noelle Eckley, Jeanne Kasperson, Amy Luers, Marybeth Martello, Colin Polsky, Alexander Pulsipher, and Andrew Schiller. 2003 A Framework for Vulnerability Analysis in Sustainability Science. *Proceedings of the National Academy of Sciences* 100(14):8074–8079.

Usher, Peter, Gérard Duhaime, and Edmund Searles 2003 The Household as an Economic Unit in Arctic Aboriginal Communities, and its Measurement by Means of a Comprehensive Survey. *Social Indicators Research* 61(2):175–202.

Walker, Donald, Patric Webber, E.F. Binnian, Kaye Everett, N.D. Lederer, E.A. Nordstrand, and Marilyn Walker 1987 Cumulative Impacts of Oil Fields on Northern Alaskan Landscapes. *Science* 238(4828):757–761.

Wheeler, Polly, and Tom Thornton 2005 Subsistence Research in Alaska: A Thirty-Year Retrospective. *Alaska Journal of Anthropology* 3(1):69–103.

Wolfe, Robert, and Robert Walker 1987 Subsistence Economies in Alaska: Productivity, Geography, and Development Impacts. *Arctic Anthropology* 24(2):56–81.

4

Trading off Food and Military Security in Contact-Era New Guinea

PAUL ROSCOE

The tradeoff case study that I contribute in this chapter examines what, relative to most other studies in this volume, was something of a success story in maintaining two critical components of human well-being without degrading biodiversity. Drawing on a database that refers to food production and military security in ninety-eight contact-era New Guinea societies and an ethnographic record that includes about another fifty, it examines the tradeoffs that these small-scale societies made between defensive military capacity and food security and their effect (or rather lack of effect) on the natural resources on which they depended.

The term *tradeoff* can be defined in several different ways (Hegmon, Chapter 1, this volume). In discussing these military/food security tradeoffs in New Guinea, I shall mean, "a *balancing* of factors all of which are not attainable at the same time" (Merriam-Webster 1984:1250, emphasis added). In this sense, a tradeoff is the particular *solution* involved in trading factors off against one another – what some might refer to as "optimal" or "satisficing" solutions. Safety from violence and access to food are among the most critical of all imperatives to human well-being, but to achieve acceptable levels of both in New Guinea required several intricate tradeoffs between military defense and food security, along with further tradeoffs in terms of labor. Ultimately, the labor costs that New Guineans were willing to tolerate determined just how far above these minimal levels defensive military capacity and food security rose. The case is of particular interest because population density affected the tradeoff calculus in a novel way, precipitating a kind of state transition in settlement patterns, from nucleation to dispersal at densities above about 40 people/sq. km.

The success of this military defense-and-food-security system can be attributed to the existence of tight feedback loops that engaged support for the tradeoffs involved, kept local population levels within sustainable limits, and redistributed population when it threatened to exceed those limits.

Sustainability: The New Guinean View

As Hegmon reviews in Chapter 1, the overarching goals of sustainability are to improve people's lives and alleviate poverty in today's world, without sacrificing the chances of future generations. Researchers in the developed world are still struggling with how to achieve this ideal. New Guineans, however, had a different perspective. For them, sustainability was conceived as a very local goal. Rather than an ideal to be extended to the planet and humanity as a whole, sustainability was to be secured for one's own community and specifically denied to one's enemies. Survival and prosperity for oneself, one's community, and one's descendants derived from an overarching ethic or aesthetic of maximal individual and community "strength" (Roscoe 2001). Strength referred to the overall *physical* strength of the community's members – that is, their numbers; their physical health, strength, and endurance; and their ability to work together as a unit. But it also had a psychological dimension, referring to the mental acuity of the group's members, and a suite of psychological dispositions such as assertiveness, courage, and generosity. Finally, there was a spiritual dimension to the concept, an idea that supernatural forces had, or could be, enlisted to support the community's efforts to maintain and manifest its strength. Initiation rites and other ritual procedures were a major means by which a community could make its members physically and psychologically strong and guarantee their fertility and hence its numbers. But spiritual help could also work in veiled ways, invigorating the soil, fattening pigs, drawing game onto human arrows, and so on.

New Guineans were as concerned with sustainability as we are, but their views of what ensured it differed considerably. Survival and prosperity in the present demanded an ongoing curation of strength, and the same activities were considered crucial to the sustainability of future generations. By maintaining the community's strength in the present, there was a presumption that its descendants would be as strong or stronger in the future. They would be just as numerous, just as physically and psychologically fit, just as capable of functioning as a well-oiled unit . . . if not more so. Equally, if the present generation attended to its strength, its descendants would have as many if not more material resources in the future. This view of the underpinnings of long-term sustainability, of course, do not recognize the effects of humans on the environment, but this makes sense within the New Guinean world view; for them, environmental degradation was the product not of human to resource ratios but of moral or ritual failings. Accordingly, their responses were ritual rather than profane – pig sacrifice, wealth payments, ritualized head-hunting, and so on (e.g., Allen and Frankel 1991:95–97; Bateson 1958:139–141; Roscoe 2004:178–180).

There is a sense, nonetheless, in which New Guineans were right to assess strength as critical to the sustainability of themselves and their communities, present and future. Before European contact, every New Guinea community was permanently or episodically at war with at least one of its neighbors, though the level of threat appears to have varied considerably. In the highlands, war mortality varied from about 11 percent in the Mae Enga region to perhaps around 50 percent in the Eastern Highlands (Roscoe 2009:82). War mortality rates in the lowlands were likely lower, though we have very few data on which to base an opinion. Whatever the local mortality rate was, however, the military threat was significant enough that every political community felt it necessary to take defensive measures, and the strength that so absorbed New Guinean interest was seen as the foremost means of combatting the risk. If a community did not maintain its strength in the present, it would lose its claims to the environment from which it drew sustenance. There would be nothing left to sustain its descendants in the future. Indeed, in a worst case scenario, there would be no descendants at all. In the hostile landscapes of New Guinea, communities needed "to remain strong in order to remain at all" (Watson 1983:193).

The Logic of Military Defense

Anthropology has only begun to pay serious attention to the importance of war in the last couple of decades, recognizing that, in the context of a significant and enduring military threat, demographic sustainability depends above all on military security. A lapse in food production or other material manufacture may endanger demographic sustainability over time, but a lapse in military security can jeopardize it instantly.

Ever since humans first became their own predators and prey – their own hunters and hunted according to Richard Alexander (1979:222) – their polities have been trapped in "balance-of-power races." Each community must try to ensure that its fighting capacity never falls below – and ideally is superior to that of – its neighbors. Since their neighbors subscribe to the same logic, the result is a perpetual struggle to maintain and augment military capacity. Military capacity, though, has two dimensions – offensive and defensive capacity – and in an environment of military threat the key to military security is defensive capacity, the ability of an individual or community to withstand an attack. Offensive capacity can enhance people's defensive capacity in so far as it enables them to deter or wipe out a military threat, but this is a derivative of defensive capacity. A group that is unable to withstand attack is unlikely to deter or to launch one for very long. One consequence of Alexander's balance-of-power races, therefore, is that a community is always motivated to augment its defensive capacity. The greater its defensive strength, the more secure its demographic sustainability.

Defensive strength is a complex product of many factors: natural and artificial defenses, weaponry, warrior numbers, the distribution of warriors across space, the individual fighting capacity and commitment of those warriors, their ability to submerge their individual agencies in that of the force and act cohesively as a defensive force, and so on (Roscoe 2009:90–94). To augment any one of these components, however, is to generate costs, tradeoffs. In the case of contact-era New Guinea, some tradeoffs were of little analytical interest. Weaponry – the spear, bow-and-arrow, and club – was about as effective as it could be absent a technological revolution, and its costs were straightforward: a modest quantity of material resources and the labor invested in its manufacture. Likewise, warrior training, discipline, and commitment were about as good as male initiation rites and a lifetime of training from childhood onward could make them (see Figure 4.1), but again the costs were uncomplicated: a fair amount of pain and/or labor. Some components of defensive strength, though, are analytically more interesting because they demanded more intricate and consequential tradeoffs. Here, I focus on those involved in two components of defensive military capacity: warrior numbers and the spatial arrangement of warriors and those they protect.

The Costs and Benefits of Defensive Military Capacity I: Warrior Numbers

In small-scale societies like those of contact-era New Guinea, defensive military capacity depended heavily on both the number of armed defenders that could muster to the site of an attack and the speed with which they could reach the site. The logic of warrior numbers all but explains itself:

FIGURE 4.1. Warrior dress in a Walahlia pig-exchange ceremony, Womeina Village, 1981. Photo by Paul Roscoe.

the more warriors a community can draw on to repulse an attack, the greater its defensive capacity. Warrior numbers, though, do not come without costs. Warriors, along with their families, must be fed; so to increase the number of its warriors a community must either intensify its food production, increase the area of its exploitable food resources, or both. Whichever strategy it chooses, however, requires increased work inputs. Subsistence intensification – increasing the amount of food raised per unit area of land – commonly demands increased work for mounding, manuring, more diligent weeding, and so on. Likewise, increasing the area of exploitable land requires that community members travel farther on average between their settlements and their food resources. In sum, increasing defensive capacity by increasing community numbers involved trading the benefits of military protection against increased energy expenditures.

The Costs and Benefits of Defensive Military Capacity II: Organizing People in Space

In themselves, warrior numbers are of little use unless, as noted already, they can also rally to the site of an attack in time to render effective military aid. The more rapidly they can so muster, the greater the defensive capacity; at a minimum, they must be able to reach the site before the attack is over. In small-scale societies in which mobility is mostly on foot, the main strategy to achieve a rapid defensive response is for warriors to remain close to one another as they move through their daily routines. The tradeoff for proximity is increased travel times to resources – though, as we shall see, these costs vary markedly with the diurnal cycle and population density.

Low-density Communities

Let us begin with low population density communities and the routines of night, when people are typically asleep and at their most vulnerable. In low-density New Guinea communities, the defensive strategy was to nucle-ate warriors against the threat of enemy attack that came at night or dawn. The logic is straightforward: sleeping has a small areal footprint, so at night warriors (and their families) can cluster near to one another and muster quickly to the site of an attack when the alarm is raised.

The costs of settlement nucleation, however, parallel those of increasing warrior numbers. Nucleation increases travel times to food and other material resources (see Figure 4.2), and the larger a community and the tighter its nucleation, the greater these travel-times and, hence, labor costs are likely to be (Figure 4.3). Since humans are incapable of expanding their physical energy expenditures to infinity, it follows that the size and degree of nucleation of a small-scale community will be limited by the labor its members are willing to invest in commuting to their food and other material resources. The evidence we have on maximum commutes in small-scale societies is rudimentary, but it suggests that people are reluctant to tolerate a one-way commute of more than about 45–70 min-utes/day, a travel time that converts into community territories on the order of 16–72 sq. km, with a midpoint of about 40 sq. km (Roscoe 2016).

Nucleation for security at night, in sum, imposed labor costs on the food quest during the day. Reciprocally, the food quest imposed costs on defen-sive security. This is because the *per capita* area that people require for sleeping is usually considerably smaller than the area of land they require

FIGURE 4.2. Women crossing an old battlefield as they return from the gardens, Sima Village, 1980. Photo by Paul Roscoe.

FIGURE 4.3. Nucleated settlements in the Ommura region, Eastern Highlands, where the estimated contact-era population density was 14.1 people per square kilometer (Mayer 1987:88; Pataki-Schweizer 1980).

for subsistence (Roscoe 2009:85–86, 2016). In a nucleated community, people must disperse as they leave their settlements for their subsistence patches, and to the degree they do, they degrade the proximity of other warriors and hence their capacity to muster quickly to the site of an attack.

In addition to forcing a degree of warrior dispersal during the day, the food quest imposed a second defensive cost: it drove people outward toward enemy borders. At night, nucleation at the center of a territory increased defensive capacity because, in addition to facilitating a rapid military response, it maximized the distance an enemy force had to cover to launch its attack and then escape. This, in turn, raised the chances that it could be detected before it could attack or be cut off and annihilated as it tried to escape through foreign terrain after the strike (Roscoe 2008). The routines of day, though, obliged community members to move out into the countryside, closer to their borders and more exposed to enemy assault. This vulnerability likely explains why, on some New Guinea terrains, the favored mode of war was a surprise attack on parties working distant gardens (e.g., Forge 1970:5; Newman 1962:2; Tuzin 1976:47; Watson 1983:31).

High Density Communities

Early European visitors to the highlands of New Guinea were puzzled to observe a curious switch in settlement patterns as they moved westward. Eastern Highlands settlements were everywhere nucleated and, in many places, palisaded villages. On entering the more densely populated valleys of the Central and Western Highlands, however, the pattern changed to a hamlet system. "The most interesting feature of these people," James Taylor wrote as he trekked into Chimbu territory, "are [sic] that they make the chess-board type of garden, and that they do not build villages but live in small farm houses instead. When one crosses the Chimbu River the change is immediate, and from then on to Mt. Hagen this type of garden and manner of living persist" (1933:53; also Hide 1981:210). "About 10 km east of the Chimbu river," the missionary, William Bergmann, observed, "is the borderline for villages and from there on towards Mt. Hagen one finds only the hamlet system" (1971:2:1; also 1971:1:13, 28). Bergmann was puzzled by the transition, and he wondered whether Central Highlanders were "somewhat more 'individualists'" (1971:2:2) than those to the East.

The idea that people would abandon the defensive benefits of settlement nucleation challenges conventional anthropological wisdom. It is puzzling because it suggests these groups were less concerned with defense than were those who nucleated their settlements. It is as though their "individualism" somehow led them to set the tradeoff between defensive strength and the costs of commuting to their subsistence resources at a different point. On closer inspection, though, it transpires that the homestead pattern of the Central and Western Highlands had nothing to with individualism and everything to do with how population density affects the tradeoff between defensive costs and energetic benefits.

As population density rises, the average distance among people and houses necessarily decreases. This increased proximity, in turn, accelerates the scale and rapidity with which members of a polity can muster a defensive response in the event of an attack. Figure 4.4 illustrates the point by plotting the time it would take a hundred warriors distributed homogenously across a firm, flat, open landscape to assemble at the site of an attack against population density. At densities below two people per square kilometer, the force would need more than half an hour to assemble fully, leaving an attacking force ample time to wreak large-scale damage before having to flee or fight a rear-guard action. At these densities, in other words, nucleation has considerable defensive value. At high densities, by contrast, an attacking force has no option but to hit and run. Above 40 people/sq. km, for instance, attackers would have no more than seven minutes to inflict harm before having to confront a hundred defenders.

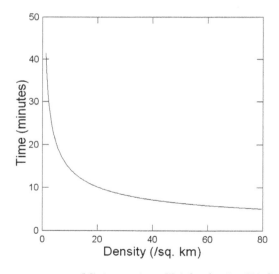

FIGURE 4.4. Minimum time (T_N) by density (D) for 100 dispersed defenders on firm, flat, open terrain to rally to site of an attack. Assumes mean running speed of 16.7 km/hr. and that warriors comprise 20 percent of population. Equation is $T_N = (1/16.7) \times \sqrt{100/(0.6284D)}$.

Given this relationship, people will find that above a certain density they can radically reduce commuting costs to their material resources at no more than a marginal cost to their defensive capacity by abandoning nucleation and dispersing into small subsistence units located at the center of the subsistence patches that support them (Figure 4.5). The genius of this solution is that, in contrast to a nucleated community, people remain almost as safe during the day as they do at night because, with their subsistence patches located immediately around their homesteads, daytime routines require only marginal dispersal.

To summarize: as population density rises, so too does the capacity of a dispersed population to muster a large and rapid military response, and at some point the defensive advantages of nucleation over dispersal cease to outweigh the commuting advantages of dispersal over nucleation. It is then

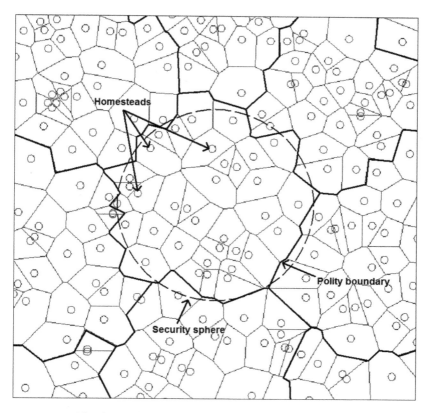

FIGURE 4.5. The dispersed settlement pattern, in which each homestead is surrounded by its own subsistence patches.

in agents' interests to reorganize their housing, abandoning residential nucleation in favor of dispersal into subsistence units surrounded by their subsistence resources. In so doing, they trade some defensive capacity for a reduction in the energy they must invest in daily commutes to their material resources, but the former sacrifice is so small and the latter advantage so great that the tradeoff becomes quite rational.

Since this transition from a nucleated to a dispersed settlement pattern greatly reduced subsistence travel costs, should we not expect the population and territory of these dispersed polities to explode in size? After all, if defensive capacity depends on numbers, and if commuting costs no longer constrain the number of people who can combine for defensive purposes, it would make sense for large swathes of these small residential units to unite into one gigantic, all but invulnerable community. The ethnographic record tells us that this did not happen: dispersed communities were among the more populous New Guinea polities, but their territorial sizes were actually among the smallest (Roscoe 2016)! Central Chimbu, Mae Enga, and Central Melpa clan polities, for instance, numbered between 260 and 645 people yet their territories were no more than 3.1 to 8.4 square kilometers in size. This is because, freed of subsistence-commute constraints, their territorial boundaries fall under the control of a second constraint: military response times.

For a community to function as a defensive unit, warriors must be located close enough together to be able to render one another effective defensive support. If they are too far apart their mutual interest in defense evaporates. Under this new calculus, a defensive community's territorial area is defined by a security circle, the diameter of which is the maximum distance that a warrior can be from the point of an attack and still arrive in time to render effective military aid. Beyond that distance, mutual defensive aid is impossible, no bonds of defensive mutuality exist to unite people, and the result is a political fault line (Roscoe 2013). Order of magnitude calculations of New Guinean response times indicate that, for a dispersed community, this territorial area is indeed smaller than that of a nucleated community (Roscoe 2013; 2016). Assuming, for instance, a firm, flat, open terrain across which warriors can run at an average speed of about 17 km/hour, the sphere within which people in a high-density, dispersed community can provide mutual defensive aid is between about 6 to 14 square kilometers in area, depending on whether attacks average 10 or 15 minutes. This compares to the territorial sizes of lower-density, nucleated cultivators, which range between about 12 and 27 square kilometers (Roscoe 2016).

Defensive Security and the Impact on the Food Quest

Defensive security imposed one further cost on the food quest. It will be remembered from earlier in the chapter that food production became increasingly perilous the closer it occurred to territorial borders. In low density, nucleated communities, where residents commuted out to their subsistence patches each day, the threat was shared equally. Consequently, everyone had an incentive to farm or forage close to their settlement. Doing so allowed them to more rapidly muster a large military response or to make it back behind the defenses of the settlement itself. In high density, dispersed homestead systems, the same threat was not equally shared: farms closest to a community's territorial border were more exposed to enemy attack than those toward its center.

This threat topology affected food production in two ways. First, it resulted in a heterogeneous exploitation of subsistence resources. As some scholars have pointed out (De Boer 1981; Martin and Szuter 1999), an environment of military threat creates minimally exploited buffer regions between potential enemies where wild resources can flourish. This was true of many New Guinea communities, but the proposition needs to be elaborated. First, there is a corollary: because people prefer to avoid subsistence resources distant from home, they are obliged to farm or forage more intensively those resources closer to their settlements. Thus, Bena Bena villages "were fortified, the gardens immediately outside the fences" (Langness 1973:315, fn.5). "Descending steep grass slopes" in Kamano territory, a 1933 Australian patrol "reached a swamp. Passing through the swamp, we entered the village of Fura. ... The village was entirely sur-rounded by large gardens which had been made in the swamp" (Bates 1933:24; also Watson 1983:85).

This heterogeneous exploitation pattern was more pronounced in low-density, nucleated systems than in high density, dispersed systems. The latter systems were not immune to the border-threat problem. Although characterized as dispersed, they were, in fact, modestly nucleated in so far as border regions tended to have lower homestead densities than more central regions and to be used for pig-foraging rather than farming. In times of heightened threat, moreover, members of more peripheral regions would evacuate to stay with more centrally located kin and friends (Brown 1972:62; Meggitt 1977:80; Vicedom and Tischner n.d.:302). Nonetheless, in the normal course of events, subsistence exploitation patterns appear to have been more homogenous in these high density, dispersed systems than in their low density, nucleated counterparts.

The second way in which the spatial contours of military threat affected food production came in times of heightened tensions, when people temporarily reset the balance between defensive capacity and food production to favor the former over the latter. In areas where the principal mode of war was surprise attack – a large-scale raid or small-scale ambush – people were inclined to stay at or close to home during the day rather than risk exposure in traveling to more distant subsistence resources. To the extent that a community depended on foraging rather than farming, people could achieve this rebalance without a significant drop in food production. Communities dependent primarily on cultivation, however, could go hungry if military tensions lasted long enough to exhaust harvests close to home.

In areas where open battle was the primary mode of war, hunger was a more pronounced threat. Many gardens would fall into disrepair because women, the principal labor force in the gardens, and their children, would commonly take refuge with kin farther afield for the duration of the conflict. Meanwhile, their menfolk were in little position to fill the subsistence void as they sallied out every few days, over a period of several months to a year or more, to do battle against an enemy bent on destroying their settlements and gardens. Indeed, hunger was one of the main motives for concluding a drawn-out war. Among the Huli, "shortage of food may eventually force both sides to press for a truce" (Glasse 1968:98). If the number of dead in a Chimbu war "was fairly even on both sides or close to even, and when they were tired of warfare, and also the food became scarce, because they cold [sic] not make gardens or not at the right time, or not enough gardens then they agreed to come to terms and make peace" (Bergmann 1971:1:192). Among the northern Tairora: "A conflict of interest between horticulture and warfare seems clear, and informants often refer to the sad state into which their gardens sometimes fell in consequence of fighting" (Watson 1983:47).

Enacting Tradeoffs: Feedback Loops and Biodiversity Conservation

The strategy that New Guineans deployed to achieve defensive military capacity and food security was no win-win solution but instead involved a number of tradeoffs. How was it, then, that they were able to enact a solution that was not only workable but, to judge from its prevalence across New Guinea, also highly resilient? The answer would appear to be the set of tight and fast feedback loops that characterized the system, a concept derived from the work of Simon Levin (1999:142–143, 149–150, 190, 196; 2003).

A feedback loop exists where the output of one process directly or indirectly influences its input. So, for instance, humans make a decision to drive a car, one effect of which is to increase atmospheric pollution. If that pollution generates a signal that humans can monitor such as generating smog or increasing greenhouse gas emissions, and if they adapt their behavior in response to that signal by, for instance, increasing the fuel efficiency of their vehicles, then a feedback loop exists.

Feedback loops are metaphorically referred to as "tight" or "loose" (or sometimes as "fast" or "slow"). A loose feedback loop is one in which linkages among processes are tenuous, weak, and/or slow acting. Systems characterized by such loops generally have low resilience: they are poorly structured to withstand or adapt to threats. In coupled natural-human systems, they impede cooperative solutions to a challenge, and climate change provides a case in point. The relationship between adaptive action and readily detectable results is slow: decisions about driving fossil-fueled vehicles today, for instance, will not have detectable climatic and environmental effects for years or even decades. Greenhouse gases are invisible, so they do not generate a readily detectable signal. Furthermore, those suffering the consequences are not those causing the problem: although the developed world was and remains the main driver of climate change, the lesser developed world – Pacific Islanders, Africans, the Inuit, and others – will suffer most under its effects. The result is a world doing far too little to mitigate the problem. In some of the developed nations most responsible for the problem, there is widespread skepticism or outright rejection that a problem actually exists, while some developing nations that are starting to exacerbate the problem reject the idea that they should bear the costs of mitigating it.

Tight feedback loops, conversely, are those in which linkages among component processes are durable, direct, and fast acting. Systems characterized by tight feedbacks can have either low or high resilience. In coupled natural-human systems, they can promote selfish, antagonistic, or counter-productive behavior, but they can also promote cooperative solutions to a challenge (Levin 1999:149–150, 190; 2003). Britain's 1956 Clean Air Act furnishes an example. In the 1930s and 1940s, a rapid rise in the population of London and of domestic coal-fires resulted in pea-souper smogs, culminating in the Great Smog of 1952 that killed thousands and made another hundred thousand ill (Bell et al. 2004). In this case, the link between cause (coal burning in hundreds of thousands of houses) and effect (days of reduced visibility and elevated illness and death) were obvious and immediate. Those suffering the consequences, moreover, were those who caused the problem. This tight feedback loop fostered a rapid cooperative response (it probably helped that Britain's government was located in London): The Clean Air Act was passed in 1956, and London rarely again saw the smog for which it was once famous.

Like the London fog example, New Guinea's defense-food-labor system represented a tight feedback loop – likely the tightest of all discussed in this volume – that, despite the tradeoffs involved, fostered a cooperative response to threat. The presence of enemies no more than a few kilometers away was obvious to every knowledgeable and competent agent. The consequences of defensive failure were equally obvious: most every New Guinean beyond childhood in every polity had seen or heard of someone being killed in an attack. They also knew that the consequences of a breakdown in defense could be immediate. Likewise, though it might not be as immediate as a defensive failure, every knowledgeable and capable agent knew the consequences of going without food for an extended period, and each was well able to recognize the physical demands of labor. Finally, deaths in war or from hunger are arguably the greatest existential challenges to human life, and every knowledgeable and competent agent could recognize the tradeoffs that would be required to sustain a workable solution.

As the climate change/smog examples indicate, though, it is not sufficient to recognize a workable solution; cooperation is also needed to implement it. In these small-scale societies, people cooperated because everyone who stood to bear the costs in labor, food production, and security also stood to reap the benefits. The result was a highly resilient cooperative system that surmounted the tradeoffs involved because it was grounded in a set of tight feedback loops. These loops also promoted a rapid adaptation to fluctuation, though of course historical contingency could always interfere. In particular, a sharp drop in polity population due to demographic fluctuation, disease, or some other misfortune could take time to remedy and might even block an adaptive response altogether. It could take a generation or more to overcome the deficit through natural increase; and if the drop were large, immigrants – the more rapid means of making up the shortfall – might decline offers of resources in return for becoming members, knowing that enemies of the polity were likely to capitalize on their sudden military superiority while they had the chance.

While limiting human losses to war and food shortages, the system also worked in a way that sustained the environmental biodiversity on which people relied for their material well-being. This property is all the more remarkable because of the existential priority that defensive security has over resource conservation and food security: humans can degrade their environment over a lifetime and suffer little in consequence; they can go several weeks without food and many more on reduced rations; but lapses in defensive security can be fatal within moments.

The system did not owe its environmental sustainability to any homeo-static mechanism of the mysterious kind that Rappaport (1968) claimed somehow kept Maring populations in balance with their environment. This and other neofunctionalist claims have been roundly and rightfully rejected (Vayda 1989). Nor is there any reason to believe that the humans involved designed the system to be sustainable: such a goal is difficult enough to implement in the politically centralized, developed nations of the world; it would be an even greater challenge for decentralized, trans-egalitarian societies like those in New Guinea. Rather, environmental sustainability seems to have been epiphenomenal to the system in place, a fortunate by-product of the tradeoffs that it enshrined.

At first blush, it might seem that the system could hardly avoid degrading its material environment. A community's interest in maximizing its popu-lation for defensive security would eventually drive population growth and population densities beyond prevailing carrying capacities. The tradeoffs in the system, though, exerted a brake on population density. Recall that to feed a growing population required rising labor investments and increased military exposure during the daytime. People thus had a competing interest in capping local population once labor demands and daytime military risk reached the outer limits of the tolerable. As a result, polity population and population density could be expected to rise rapidly through natural growth or by incorporating immigrants (Roscoe 2009:90–91) until it reached an optimum dictated by these conflicting interests and then stabilized.

Once a community has achieved an optimum population and density, what keeps it there? Reproductive decisions are driven by a variety of considerations beyond those of defensive and food security, so we would expect population levels frequently to exceed the optimum. In the absence of reliable diachronic information about the development of New Guinea society, we can only hypothesize, but given the resilience of the system in place, there are only two possible pathways. First, the community absorbs the excess population, a strategy that requires it to increase its labor invest-ments beyond what it considers desirable at a potential cost of degrading its subsistence resources. This fate, anthropologists and geographers once thought, had befallen the ancestors of a dense band of lowland population in the Sepik that lies between Yangoru and Dreikikir (e.g., Forge 1965; Tuzin 1976). Further research has shown, however, that what had been taken as evidence of prehistoric environmental degradation – the barren grasslands of the North Sepik Plains – was probably nothing of the sort; instead, the grasslands were poor in fertility and deficient in water (Allen 2005; Roscoe 2011).

The other possible pathway, strongly suggested by the resilience of the defensive capacity and food security system described in this chapter, is that beyond the desirable optimum, the excess population relocates to an area where resources are available. If the excess population leaves the area entirely, fission obviously follows. But if the community attacks and displaces or destroys a weaker neighbor, fission must still follow because territorial borders are determined by subsistence labor inputs or military response times. As a result, the community cannot simply expand to fill the territory left vacant; rather, it must fission into parent and daughter communities.

Living the Defensive Capacity-Food Security Tradeoff

The tradeoffs among defensive military capacity, food production and security, and labor stamped New Guinean lived experience in several ways, none more indelible perhaps than the intense communality and defensive paranoia that it imposed on daily lives. Understanding these experiences is an important part of the archaeology (and ethnography) of the human experience (Hegmon 2013). As noted earlier, every known contact-era New Guinea community was, without exception, either permanently or episodically at war with one or more of its neighbors, and though people might experience occasional periods of formal or comparative peace, these rarely lasted more than a year or two before lethal hostilities again broke out.

This unrelenting threat must have subjected New Guineans to an order of fear that the anthropological imagination can scarcely appreciate. With little cognizance or experience of peace, we must presume, New Guineans were sufficiently adapted cognitively and affectively that they could function capably in the face of the threat. Even so, they must have lived out their lives under anxiogenic circumstances of a magnitude beyond any that, fortunately, we are likely to ever experience. If we try to take the level of their terror into account, though, we can recognize and perhaps better appreciate a couple of profound consequences that the tradeoff between defensive security and the demands of the food quest imposed on their lives.

The first is the spatial propinquity mandated by defensive military capacity: If people were to maintain their military strength against an attack, both warriors and those they defended had to remain in exceptionally close proximity to one another, *all the time*. In high-density communities, military threat required aggregation and, with their gardens immediately surrounding their homesteads, people could cluster almost as tightly during the day as they could at night. In low-density communities, people dispersed to some degree as they commuted out to their subsistence resources, but they still sought to move around the landscape in groups that were as large as the demands of subsistence exploitation allowed (Roscoe 2009:85–87).

This physical aggregation conferred a level of collectiveness, sociability, and monitoring quite foreign to Western experience. From birth to death, people spent just about every waking moment – for that matter, every hour asleep – in the company of others, more often than not a lot of others. This experience might seem no different to that of city residents in the developed world. The crucial difference, though, is the size of the community and its implications for surveillance. In contrast to the anonymity of cities, there were no opportunities in small-scale communities to escape the collectivity, to spend time alone or with one or two favored others. On the positive side of the ledger, the social isolation and anomie that many city dwellers experience were foreign to New Guinean experience. On the other hand, there was no privacy. There was nowhere in a New Guinea society where the individual could escape intense monitoring by others or control the flows of information that shaped his or her social identity and relationships. To apply a metaphor that is otherwise inappropriate to non-literate societies, people's lives were open books to just about everyone in their social universe.

The close and enduring proximity that defensive capacity demanded also had implications for conflict in New Guinea societies. Partly because people were in constant and close contact with one another, and partly because they could not readily relocate, the potential for interpersonal conflict was high. Conflict, though, was antithetical to the cooperation required among people dependent on one another for protection in the event of an attack. The only way to resolve this Hobson's Choice was to place a high premium on ethics of harmony and on social mechanisms that facilitated and enforced it. Anthropologists make a lot from the fact that small-scale societies have human (or gift) economies, in which goods or assistance are not commoditized for trade and profit but conferred as gifts to meet moral expectations, a kind of "baseline communism" (Graeber 2012:95–96). The contradiction between the potential for conflict and the harmony that proximity and defensive security demand in these communities may go some way to explaining the origins of these human economies.

A second, largely unrecognized, experiential feature of small-scale social life stems from the tradeoff cost that the food quest forced on defensive capacity: the chronic need, during the routines of day, to monitor the environment for enemy encroachments. To anthropologists familiar with the film *Dead Birds*, the tall watchtowers erected by the Dugum Dani to surveil the no-man's land between them and the Widaia will immediately spring to mind. Elsewhere in the highlands, sentries monitored their gardens not from towers but from high points on the landscape (e.g., Criper 1967:86–87; Watson 1983:31). In most of lowland New Guinea, though, surveillance from above was of little use because the land was carpeted in dense vegetation. People therefore resorted to more subtle clues. One was a sudden silence in the ambient buzz of insect life, which might signal an enemy presence. Others included footprints, damaged vegetation, and other evidence that an enemy had passed by earlier. Whatever the method, the need for vigilance was chronic, but it took an immense toll on daily life. As the leader of a Nimo-speaking lowland settlement observed when asked by a patrol officer how he felt about the colonial presence: it was "good to be able to walk about with one's head in the air instead of continually looking at the ground for the footprints of enemies as formerly" (MAY 3–62/63:14).

Conclusion

I have sought in this paper to trace out the principal tradeoffs that characterized New Guinean attempts to ensure both their defensive military capacity and their food security. In short, each imposed costs on the other, and both imposed costs on human labor. Defensive capacity eroded food production, especially in times of heightened tensions or extended periods of open battle. Food production reduced daytime defensive capacity because subsistence routines forced people to disperse across the landscape, taking them closer to enemy borders. Together, defensive capacity and food security imposed substantial labor costs on people. Defensive capacity depended on numerical strength, which in turn required subsistence intensification, extended commutes to subsistence resources, or both – levies of labor over and above those that would be required had war not existed and people could arrange themselves optimally on the landscape to exploit their subsistence resource.

An important characteristic of defensive military capacity is that demand is insatiable: no community with potentially hostile neighbors can ever have enough. Because humans do not have infinite amounts of energy to invest, however, labor costs must eventually place limits on a community's defensive capacity. In other words, it is the daily time budgets and/or human energy reservoirs that a community is willing to devote to defense that ultimately limit the level of its defensive capacity – that is, its numerical size and, at low densities, its levels of nucleation.

Although contact-era New Guinea is now remote in time, the case study in this chapter underscores the importance of three obvious facts along with a conclusion that is sometimes overlooked. First, humans are dedicated above almost anything else to demographic sustainability, that is to the survival of themselves and (in varying degrees also) their close kin and allies. Second, war is a particular challenge to demographic sustainability, not least because of the immediacy of the mortal threat it can pose. Third, demographic sustainability involves tradeoffs against all sorts of other goals. Where tradeoffs have to be made, therefore, concerns with defensive capacity will usually trump other concerns such as environmental, economic, and social sustainability. It makes limited sense to invest resources in environmental conservation, for instance, unless one can be sure of surviving to reap the benefits.

This conclusion highlights two weaknesses in current thinking about sustainability in the contemporary world. First, although the concepts of human security and sustainability exist within a framework that includes military security, which includes defensive capacity, sustainability research and policy prescriptions derived from it usually assume a context of peace. Second, most of the sustainability literature focuses on developed nation-states, in particular the United States and those of Europe, and its policy prescriptions assume the presence of institutions with a sophisticated capacity to monitor, detect, and respond to challenges (e.g., Olsson et al. 2004). By comparison, the literature is less preoccupied with the post-colonial nations of the world – the remnants of Euro-American empires. This is important because these post-colonial nations are currently the sites of most of the world's lethal conflict.

The quandary for these post-colonial states is their hybrid structure. Prior to colonialism, their members were distributed among numerous autonomous indigenous polities ranging from the egalitarian to the politically developed, which were usually at war with their neighbors on a periodic or permanent basis. New Guinea is a case in point: prior to contact and its division among various European powers, New Guinea comprised thousands of small, autonomous polities that ranged from egalitarian forager groups through trans-egalitarian cultivators to fisher-forager petty chiefdoms. With colonization, however, these polities found themselves abruptly grouped together as a single polity – a "colony" – within borders arbitrarily defined by accidents of geography and history. Even under the control of a hierarchical apparatus imposed by the politically centralized, colonizing power, this act of political bricolage was usually only modestly successful at maintaining peace among these component sovereignties and the stability of the whole. It is hardly surprising therefore that once Empire withdrew after a few generations, and having hastily installed an indigenous political elite, many of these hybrid, post-colonial entities proved chronically unstable. To begin with, the hierarchical Euro-American superstructures grafted onto these egalitarian, erstwhile sovereign worlds had limited political control. As Strathern (1993:719) has noted of post-colonial Papua New Guinea:

> When populations of this kind are introduced first to colonial and then to post-colonial power, we cannot expect them to invent overnight a respect for hierarchical authority. They obeyed the colonial power out of a combination of fear and self-interest. When fear is no longer there, they will continue to pursue the self-interest part of the equation unless curbed. In short, the national government, inheriting the colonial state apparatus in 1975, was not initially equipped with automatic legitimacy in the people's eyes.

Second, the wand of "independence" proved to have limited influence in persuading scores if not hundreds or thousands of "us's" and "thems" to lay aside their erstwhile enmities without rancor and become a single united "us." Third, these us's and thems were seldom pre-adapted for easy communication. In contrast to their erstwhile overlords, whose political objectives were facilitated by unilingualism, colonized polities rarely spoke a single language. (Depending on definitions, the number of languages in Papua New Guinea governance is at least 600; the Democratic Republic of the Congo has at least 215.) To add insult to injury, the common failure of these post-colonial states to live up to the ideals of other nation-states is commonly attributed to "tribalism," corruption, or incompetence – facile charges that obscure the historical, exogenously determined origins and structures of these polities (Roscoe 2004; 2013; 2014).

   None of this is to deny that multiple agents and processes are at work in post-colonial nations, attempting to mediate or broker the contradictions between colonial and local structures. Developments in transportation and communication technologies and the expansion of *lingua francae*, for instance, link people together to a degree that was impossible in the past, innovations that both enable and are driven by other developments. Political relations expand in scale, offering local politicians and leaders novel opportunities to mediate the imposition of state forms and altering, in turn, the scale of people's political models. Economic developments and expansions of communication motivate and facilitate modernist cultural processes that recruit advertising (Foster 1995), national sports, the artwork on postage stamps and public buildings, and so on to the job of forging a national identity.

Nevertheless, where environmental sustainability and systemic resilience are concerned, it is obvious that post-colonial nations must be approached and analyzed as very different structural entities than nations of the type that colonized them. The tendency in global policy, for obvious diplomatic reasons, is to treat all nations alike and to equate their policy making capacity to that of their political elites. In the case of post-colonial nations, this has not worked well (arguably it has fared not all that much better in the case of developed nations), but the response has been a rather naïve focus on strengthening "governance," conceived of primarily as a nation's political elite. In thinking about sustainability, I suggest, it is equally, if not more, useful to think of post-colonial nations in terms of component communities that are still significantly subject to much the same reckonings as those of contact-era New Guinea. Seen from this perspective, the encouraging message of this case study might be that, in these nations, even (or especially) during times of civil war, defensive capacity, food security, and sustainability might take better care of themselves than we might have hoped.

Acknowledgments

Warmest thanks for suggestions and comments on previous drafts to Colin Grier, Terry Hays, Michelle Hegmon, and Ann Kinzig, none of whom are in any way culpable for the results.

References

Alexander, Richard D. 1979 *Darwinism and Human Affairs*. University of Washington Press, Seattle and London.
Allen, Bryant J. 2005 The Place of Agricultural Intensification in Sepik Foothills Prehistory. In *Papuan Pasts: Cultural, Linguistic and Biological Histories of Papuan-Speaking Peoples*, edited by Andrew Pawley, Robert Attenborough, Jack Golson, and Robin Hide pp. 585–623. Pacific Linguistics, 572. Australian National University, Research School of Pacific and Asian Studies, Canberra.
Allen, Bryant J., and Stephen Frankel 1991 Across the Tari Furoro. In *Like People You See in a Dream: First Contact in Six Papuan Societies*, edited by Edward

L. Schieffelin and Robert Crittenden, pp. 88–124. Stanford University Press, Stanford.

Bates, C. D. 1933 *Ramu Govt. Post to Purari Govt. Post. 15/5/33 to 24/5/33*. File Q. 836/3 – External Territories. CRS A7034, Item No.170. Australian Archives, Canberra.

Bateson, Gregory 1958 *Naven: A Survey of the Problems Suggested by a Composite Picture of the Culture of a New Guinea Tribe Drawn from Three Points of View*. 2nd edition. Stanford University Press, Stanford.

Bell, Michelle L., Devra L. Davis, and Tony Fletcher 2004 A Retrospective Assessment of Mortality from the London Smog Episode of 1952: The Role of Influenza and Pollution. *Environmental Health Perspectives* 112:6–8.

Bergmann, W. 1971 *The Kamanuku: The Culture of the Chimbu Tribes*. 4 Vols. H.F.W. Bergmann, Harrisville, Qld.

Brown, Paula 1972 *The Chimbu: A Study of Change in the New Guinea Highlands*. Schenkman, Cambridge, Massachusetts.

Criper, Clive 1967 *The Politics of Exchange*. Unpublished PhD dissertation. Department of Anthropology, Australian National University, Canberra.

De Boer, Warren 1981 Buffer Zones in the Cultural Ecology of Aboriginal Amazonia: An Ethnohistorical Approach. *American Antiquity* 46:364–377.

Forge, Anthony 1965 Art and Environment in the Sepik. *Proceedings of the Royal Anthropological Institute of Great Britain and Ireland* 1965:23–31.

_____ ca. 1970 Violence among the Abelam. MSS 411, B19, F21. San Diego: Mandeville Special Collections Library, University of California, San Diego.

Foster, Robert 1995 Print Advertisements and Nation Making in Metropolitan Papua New Guinea. In *Nation-Making: Emergent Identities in Postcolonial Melanesia*, edited by Robert Foster, pp. 151–184. University of Michigan Press, Ann Arbor, Michigan.

Glasse, Robert M. 1968 *Huli of Papua: A Cognatic Descent System*. Mouton and Co., Paris.

Graeber, David 2012 *Debt: The First 5,000 Years*. Melville House, Brooklyn and London.

Hegmon, Michelle 2013 The Archaeology of the Human Experience. *The SAA Archaeological Record* 13(15):16–19.

Hide, Robin Lamond 1981 *Aspects of Pig Production and Use in Colonial Sinasina, Papua New Guinea*. PhD Dissertation. Department of Anthropology, Columbia University, New York. University Microfilms, Ann Arbor.

Langness, Lewis L. 1973 Bena Bena Political Organization. In *Politics in New Guinea: Traditional and in the Context of Change: Some Anthropological Perspectives*, edited by Ronald M. Berndt and Peter Lawrence, pp. 298–316. University of Western Australia Press and University of Washington Press, Nedlands and Seattle.

Levin, Simon A. 1999 *Fragile Dominion: Complexity and the Commons*. Perseus, Cambridge, Massachusetts.

_____ 2003 Complex Adaptive Systems: Exploring the Known, the Unknown, and the Unknowable. *Bulletin of the American Mathematical Society* 40:3–19.

Martin, Paul S., and Christine R. Szuter 1999 War Zones and Game Sinks in Lewis and Clark's West. *Conservation Biology* 13:36–45.

MAY 3–62/63 1962/63 May River Patrol Report No.3–62/63. East Sepik: May River Patrol Reports, Microfiche 1. National Archives and Public Records Service, Boroko, Papua New Guinea.

Mayer, Jessica R. 1987 *Sickness, Healing and Gender in Ommura, Central High-lands, Papua New Guinea.* Unpublished PhD Dissertation, Department of Anthropology, University of Sussex, Sussex.

Meggitt, Mervyn J. 1977 *Blood Is Their Argument: Warfare among the Mae Enga Tribesmen of the New Guinea Highlands.* Mayfield Publishing Company. Palo Alto, California.

Merriam-Webster Inc. 1984 *Webster's Ninth New Collegiate Dictionary.* Merriam Webster, Springfield, Massachusetts.

Newman, Philip Lee 1962 *Supernaturalism and Ritual among the Gururumba.* PhD Dissertation, Department of Anthropology, University of Washington, Seattle. University Microfilms, Ann Arbor.

Olsson, Per, Carl Folke, and Fikret Birkes 2004 Adaptive Comanagement for Building Resilience in Social–Ecological Systems. *Environmental Management* 34:75–90.

Pataki-Schweizer, K. J. 1980 *A New Guinea Landscape: Community, Space, and Time in the Eastern Highlands.* Anthropological Studies in the Eastern Highlands of New Guinea, 4. University of Washington Press, Seattle.

Rappaport, Roy A. 1968 *Pigs for the Ancestors: Ritual in the Ecology of a New Guinea People.* Yale University Press, New Haven.

Roscoe, Paul 2001 Strength and Sexuality: Sexual Avoidance and Masculinity in New Guinea and Amazonia. In *Gender in Amazonia and Melanesia: An Exploration of the Comparative Method,* edited by Thomas A. Gregor and Donald Tuzin, pp. 279–308. University of California Press, Berkeley.

2004 Crime and "Tribal" Warfare in Contemporary Papua New Guinea. In *Globalization and Culture Change in the Pacific Islands,* edited by Victoria S. Lockwood, pp. 59–71. Pearson Prentice Hall, Upper Saddle River, New Jersey.

2008 Settlement Fortification in Village and "Tribal" Society: Evidence from Contact-era New Guinea. *Journal of Anthropological Archaeology* 27:507–519.

2009 Social Signaling and the Organization of Small-Scale Society: The Case of Contact-Era New Guinea. *Journal of Archaeological Method and Theory* 16:69–116.

2011 The Abelam "Invasion" and the Rise of Ilahita Revisited. In *Echoes of the Tambaran: Masculinity, History and the Subject in the Work of Donald F. Tuzin,* edited by David Lipset and Paul Roscoe, pp. 25–43. ANU e-Press, Canberra.

2013 War, Collective Action, and the "Evolution" of Polities. In *Cultural and Evolutionary Dynamics of Cooperation,* edited by David M. Carballo, pp. 57–82. Colorado University Press, Boulder, Colorado.

2014 The End of War in Papua New Guinea: "Crime" and "Tribal Warfare" in Post-colonial States. *Anthropologica* 56:327–339.

2016 War and the Food Quest in Small-Scale Societies: Settlement-Pattern Formation in Contact-era New Guinea. In *The Archaeology of Food and*

Warfare: Food Insecurity in Prehistory, edited by Amber Vanderwarker and Gregory Wilson, pp. 13–39. Springer, New York and Philadelphia.

Strathern, Andrew 1993 Violence and Political Change in Papua New Guinea. *Bijdragen tot de Taal-, Land- en Volkenkunde* 149:718–736.

Taylor, J. L. 1933 *Mount Hagen Patrol, March–October, 1933. CRS A7034, Item 218.* Australian Archives, Canberra.

Tuzin, Donald F. 1976 *The Ilahita Arapesh: Dimensions of Unity.* University of California Press, Berkeley.

Vayda, Andrew P. 1989 *Explaining Why Marings Fought. Journal of Anthropological Research* 45:159–177.

Vicedom, Georg F., and Herbert Tischner. ca. 1960 *The Mbowamb: The Culture of the Mount Hagen Tribes in East Central New Guinea, Vol.2. I. Social Organisation. II. Religion and Cosmology.* Translated by F. E. Rheinstein and E. Klestadt. Menzies Library, Australian National University, Canberra.

Watson, James B. 1983 *Tairora Culture: Contingency and Pragmatism.* University of Washington Press, Seattle.

5

Will Agricultural Technofixes Feed the World?

Short- and Long-Term Tradeoffs of Adopting High-Yielding Crops

AMANDA L. LOGAN

How will we feed a growing population projected to reach 10 billion by 2050? Agricultural scientists estimate that we need to double our current food supply to meet growing demand. Based on the successes of the Green Revolution, many claim that matching this target is possible through improved agricultural technologies, yet there is little agreement on how to meet these goals in a sustainable manner (Godfray et al. 2010; Pretty and Bharucha 2014). In an ideal scenario, high yields could be maintained with negligible environmental impacts even in the face of major shocks. This scenario presents a daunting challenge because of complex and inevitable tradeoffs between competing economic, environmental, and social goals (Tilman et al. 2002:672). In this paper, I consider this conundrum by evaluating the tradeoffs involved in adopting high-yielding crops over the short and long-term.

The development and adoption of high-yielding cultigens is framed as a key strategy in the fight against current and future hunger. This is especially the case in the African continent, where the impact of the early Green Revolution was minimal, and consequently the greatest future increases in crop production are projected (Evenson and Gollin 2003). Crop techno-fixes are often framed as win-win situations, where higher levels of production help alleviate food shortages by increasing the actual supply of food, which results in feeding more individuals and ensures a higher income for subsistence farmers. Such arguments align neatly with the goals of large biotechnology companies, who disseminate their products as development aid in the form of agricultural improvement technologies (Patel 2012). The costs and benefits of such interventions are often framed quite narrowly in terms of optimizing yields in the immediate term, but do not take into account the diversity of tradeoffs involved for individual farmers, particularly over the long-term.

Archaeology provides an important lens on how and why people adopted new crops in the past and a means by which to evaluate the long-term tradeoffs of such decisions. Since the majority of farmers in the past operated in non-market settings, archaeology can facilitate understanding of motivations in settings where the market does not always reign supreme. This perspective is critical since the vast majority of subsistence farmers today employ a mix of market- and non-market-based strategies to weather the vagaries of environmental change and economic deprivation (e.g., food sharing; Mandala 2005). These strategies may provide alternative means of coping that are overlooked by yield-centric, market-derived analyses (see Spielmann and Aggrawal (Chapter 11), as well as BurnSilver (Chapter 3), this volume, for additional examples). Understanding non-market approaches to agricultural production are also critical for situating market-based development interventions today. Market logics are often ill-equipped to deal with the challenges people face in resource-poor areas, and do not capture the variation in hierarchies of need as defined in different cultural settings (e.g., see De Waal 1990). In addition, archaeology is uniquely able to access the *long-term* impacts of crop adoptions over generations, centuries, and even millennia. Many translocations of high-yielding crops have occurred since the beginnings of food production. While often interpreted as a means to optimize yields, recent research demonstrates that the potential to increase production is often merely a tertiary concern in farmers' initial decision to adopt new crops (Boivin et al. 2012). This may relate to the perceived tradeoffs of adopting high-yielders, perceptions that are often based on an analysis of short-term, and therefore visible, costs and benefits. Archaeology allows us to make both predictable and unintentional long-term tradeoffs visible.

I begin by examining the tradeoffs involved in adopting high-yielding crops generally. To address short-term tradeoffs, I explore the process of and motivations behind new crop adoptions in the present and the past, drawing largely on anthropological and archaeological approaches. I tackle long-term tradeoffs through an archaeological case study from Ghana that details how high-yielding maize was adopted and the associated long-term costs. By focusing our lens of analysis on tradeoffs, we can empirically evaluate progressive and modernist "produce more" narratives, populating them with human experiences: decisions made, lives lived, and costs paid over the long term.

Tradeoffs of High-Yielding Crops

A tradeoff is the idea that when some things are gained, other things are lost (see Hegmon, Chapter 1 for a more detailed definition). These gains and losses may not be immediately evident, but displaced in time or over social or geographical space (McShane et al. 2011:968). This broad view of tradeoffs problematizes the narrow focus on yield optimization for high-yield crops in two important, interrelated ways. First, yield is not necessarily the central concern of farmers, who actually consider a much wider range of factors in deciding to adopt new crops. Do higher yields expose farmers to greater risk? Or, are the risks worth it because the new crop is imbued with high prestige value? Does the new crop require additional processing technologies, along with associated labor and material costs? While industrial agriculture may privilege yield at the expense of social and environmental sustainability, the priorities of subsistence farmers are often very different. Tradeoffs are perspectival; what is a tradeoff to one person may not be to others, a point made throughout this volume. It is therefore necessary to examine tradeoffs in their spatial, social, and historical contexts. Second, timing is everything; farmers may assess the costs and benefits with an eye to the short- and long-term consequences, but short-term effects are more readily observed and experienced, as discussed by Roscoe (Chapter 4), this volume. The intended reasons why a farmer may adopt a new crop may be very different than the outcomes of such a decision over the long term.

Here I review some of the known tradeoffs of adopting high-yielding crops. The most significant short-term benefit to adopting a high-yielding crop is an increase in productivity. In market-based economies, improved productivity increases the amount of marketable surplus (see Spielmann and Aggarwal (Chapter 11), this volume), potentially resulting in a greater food supply and higher incomes. New species may also be used to extensify agricultural production into previously marginal niches, as was the case with maize in areas too dry for rice cultivation in China, or too wet for wheat in southern Europe (Boivin et al. 2012; Crosby 2003[1972]). However, productivity has several associated costs, including losses in biodiversity, skills, and culinary identity.

The environmental costs of adopting high-yielding cultivars are related to reductions in the biodiversity of cultigens and their associated agroecologies, especially when the new cultivars are non-native. While extensification of agriculture through the addition of new cultigens may increase productivity, such practices may alter the ecology of marginal zones, potentially decreasing overall biological diversity (Boivin et al. 2012; Boserup 1965). These zones may support plant life that is used for human and livestock consumption, even if crops are not cultivated there. Interviews from the Banda, Ghana case indicate the shrinking of these useful plant zones coincident with the application of pesticides and herbicides that increase the productivity of cash crops. Another biodiversity-related cost concerns the genetic diversity of new cultigens themselves; typically a single or a limited number of new varieties is introduced, creating a genetic bottleneck and thus higher susceptibility to pests and disease. The classic case is the Irish potato famine. Potatoes were introduced to Europe in the sixteenth century, and by the 1800s much of the Irish poor were dependent on a single potato variety. When the potato blight arrived from the Americas in 1845, the effects were disastrous, in part due to low genetic diversity of the potato crop (Fraser 2003). This bottleneck of genetic diversity may also negatively impact farmers' ability to weather environmental shocks. Multiple varieties of native cultigens are often cultivated as a risk reduction strategy, in the hope that at least some varieties will produce harvests, even if not in large quantities (e.g., pearl millet varieties in the African continent, National Research Council 1996). Finally, high-yielding cultigens are often cultivated as monocrops, rather than as part of multi-cropping systems strategies that are more suited to tropical environments in particular. This practice may lead to accelerated declines in soil fertility, requiring the use of inputs like fertilizer, and increasing the monetary costs associated with agriculture. Such inputs are commonly included as part of development projects such as One Acre (Thurow 2012), who supply farmers with improved seed stock, fertilizers, and pesticides. These inputs act to increase productivity in the short-term, but have long-term costs including decreased soil fertility and the continued need to purchase inputs.

There are also social costs associated with the adoption of high-yielding cultivars, particularly if the rate of adoption is too fast. Glenn Stone (2007) documents processes of farmer de-skilling in India associated with the rapid adoption of GMO (Bt) cotton. The rate at which new cotton varieties are adopted is too quick for farmers to acquire a working knowledge of how the crops perform in their specific field environments, leading to farmer de-skilling. Taste and local culinary identity may also be sacrificed in exchange for increased yields, and are often costs too high to merit adoption. Rogers (2003:241–242) gives the example of a high-yielding rice variety introduced in Asia that tripled yields over some traditional varieties. While the rice had superior yield ability and pest resistance, it did not have the same taste characteristics as local varieties. Even decades later, farmers in India continued to grow small amounts of local rice for their own consumption, and the quick-growing rice for sale. The improved variety still sold for considerably less than local varieties because of reduced local demand. Finally, increased yields can act to exacerbate existing structural inequalities. In West African examples, Carr (2008) shows how men claim ownership over the cultivation of introduced crops that produce big yields, while women are often relegated to subsistence crop production. Higher yielding crops may act to increase the income gap between men and women, bringing existing tensions to the surface.

Why Do People Choose to Adopt New Crops?

Short-term tradeoffs are those costs and benefits that can be perceived most easily because they occur within months, years, or decades – time scales observable to farmers and policy makers. They are thus among the easiest to document both by farmers and by agricultural researchers, and play an important role in the initial adoption of new cultivars. However, as I detail here, a historical lens illustrates that such decisions may have much less to do with a crop's yield potential, and much more to do with social and economic factors external to the cultivar itself.

The movement and adoption of new crops in the past has been a perennial interest amongst archaeologists and historians. Two major translocation events have received considerable attention: the Columbian Exchange, which moved crops between the Eastern and Western Hemispheres after 1492; and earlier food globalizations such as the Trans-Eurasian Exchange, which involved the introduction of European crops to Asia and vice versa. Previous scholars, including environmental historian Alfred Crosby (2003[1972]), tended to frame new crop adoption in terms of ecological or economic opportunism. New crop species are able to take advantage of specific agroecological niches to which native crops were not adapted or were considered marginal. Populations who adopted these crops were able to extensify production in the face of population, dietary, or economic stressors. For many scholars, the greater caloric return that resulted was a primary motivator for ancient farmers (e.g., see Jones et al. 2011). However, Boivin and colleagues (2012), among others (see Logan 2012), have critiqued this model on the grounds that most new species did not become staples until centuries or even millennia after their initial adoption. "If the production of more calories had been a goal of acquiring new crops, we would expect rapid uptake and large-scale consumption of novel staples. Instead there was often a delay ... That the transformation of native agricultural systems did not occur until later periods indicates that it was an outcome rather than a goal of crop translocations" (Boivin et al. 2012:455–456). This important point shows that there is often considerable slippage between the reasons for *initial* adoptions versus the *long-term* effects of such choices. I suggest that initial adoption decisions are based on farmers' analysis of short-term tradeoffs – between yield and taste, for example. The tradeoffs considered by farmers at the beginning of the adoption process may also be quite different than the long-term, less visible tradeoffs that occur over time.

Considerable evidence confirms that initial adoptions are often motivated by social reasons, rather than purely economic motives. Beyond anthropology, one of the dominant models for understanding crop adoption is innovation diffusion theory, which was based on an initial study of the adoption of hybrid maize among Iowan farmers (Rogers 2003; Ryan and Gross 1943 [cited in Stone 2007]). Ryan and Gross identified four stages in farmers' adoption process, including learning about the new crop, being persuaded to try it, deciding to give it a go, and evaluating the performance of the new addition. Not all farmers accomplish this process with the same rapidity, with farmers labeled as ranging from early adopters, early majority, late majority, to laggards. Importantly, the perceived benefits in adopting new innovations was often defined more strongly based on local cultural practices and beliefs rather than empirical observations of crop performance (Ryan and Gross 1943 in Stone 2007:70–71). Knowledge of these social determinants of crop adoption has been utilized by biotechnology companies in India to promote GMO crops. New seed varieties are often given to leaders or "big farmers" first, since other farmers seek to emulate those individuals. In this situation, the decision to adopt a new crop variety is less about its performance in agricultural fields and more about the association of new crops with successful individuals (Stone 2007:72). The perceived tradeoff in this case is the social capital gained from "joining the club," despite the possibility that the crop itself may not be successful.

Other motivations for adopting or not adopting new cultigens may have even less to do with their performance in the field. While some cultures may value novelty in both the field and cooking pot, and quickly select new cultigens over old ones, the opposite is also true. Preference for existing crops often prevents people from adopting new crops, even when the new species is more productive, as is the case for my study of maize adoption in West Africa. If new crops require additional processing technologies, people are frequently slow to incorporate them into their subsistence regimes (Boivin et al. 2012). For example, cassava or manioc, a root crop from the Americas, seems to have been incorporated slowly in West Africa, in part because it required additional processing steps for detoxification (Van Oppen 1999). Using examples drawn from Europe, China, and India, Boivin et al. (2012) show that most new crops were adopted in small quantities as luxuries or curiosities, only to become staples many centuries or millennia later. Maintaining existing crop repertoires also takes work – and is an active choice (Logan 2012). The tradeoffs perceived by the farmer may vary, and include balancing culinary preferences with yield, or risk with yield. Whatever the primary motivation for adopting new crops or maintaining old ones, farmers go through an active deliberation of the costs and benefits. These costs and benefits may be defined by the farmers' priorities or motivations, be they cultural or symbolic, economic, or ecological.

Assessing the Long-Term Tradeoffs of Maize Adoption in Ghana

Over the long-term, the core tradeoffs in adopting high-yielding cultivars are improved productivity at the expense of environmental sustainability, culinary identity, and/or social equity. Here, I briefly consider an example of how these conflicting benefits and costs unfold over time through a case study of maize adoption in Banda, west central Ghana (Figure 5.1). Domesticated in Mexico, maize is a tropical plant that is well-suited to cultivation in the African tropics. Its success is also due to its ability to produce high yields, and the short time required for the plant to reach maturity (Miracle 1965; McCann 2005). Maize was introduced to West Africa in the 1500s as part of Atlantic trade networks, which sought to acquire gold and later slaves to supply burgeoning European and American economies. Early scholars proposed that maize was adopted because of its ability to produce faster and in larger quantities than local grains sorghum and pearl millet (Crosby 2003 [1972]:188), an interpretation that continues to have currency in more recent investigations (McCann 2005). Maize adoption has thus been framed as a win-win situation, much in the same vein that adoption of

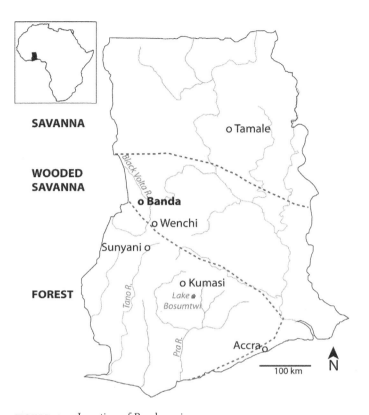

FIGURE 5.1. Location of Banda region.

high-yielding crops is championed by development experts today. Here, I trouble this perspective by considering the tradeoffs associated with choosing maize over local grains, and by investigating how farmers' motivations changed over the last five centuries, as maize transformed from a curiosity to a staple crop.

Tradeoffs in Switching to Maize

Here I outline potential tradeoffs in switching to maize, based on what we know in the present, in order to frame some of the "hard choices" (McShane et al. 2011:968) that farmers may have faced in the past. Maize would have yielded several benefits in the short-term. In today's modern market economy, maize fetches a much higher price at market due to global and local demand, although we need not assume that it was as highly valued in the past. Much like the rice variety example mentioned earlier in the chapter, local cultigens may have been favored in terms of taste and thus been more valuable. Maize is easier to process (remove seed from cob) than native grains millet or sorghum, decreasing requisite time and labor costs. Perhaps the most significant benefits relate to maize's high-yielding potential and short maturity time. In Ghana today, maize is a high-yielding crop par excellence, particularly with the application of fertilizers (350–800 lb. /acre). Native grains pearl millet (*Pennisetum glaucum*; 200–600 lb. /acre) and sorghum (*Sorghum bicolor*; 300–700 lb. /acre) yield consistently less, and respond less well to fertilizer (Staff of the Division of Agriculture 1962:369–372). Synthetic fertilizers would not have been available at the time of maize's introduction several centuries ago, but its ability to produce a crop more quickly (3–4 months) relative to pearl millet and sorghum (5–6 months) would have been highly advantageous. In tropical West Africa, this short maturity time lines up perfectly with the dominant two-peak rainfall pattern, so that two harvests can be grown per year rather than just one, potentially doubling yields. In terms of food security, the timing of maize's maturity is critical: It is ready to harvest as early as July/August, which falls during a period of food shortage known as the hungry season gap (McCann 2005; Miracle 1965). The hungry season gap is created in part by the maturity schedule of indigenous cultigens like yams, which are not ready until August or September, while sorghum and millet are usually harvested in November and December. The first crop of maize is ready precisely when people need it most, in July, when previous grain stores are running low prior to the maturity of indigenous staples.

However, there are short- and long-term costs associated with choosing maize over native grains. Maize is prone to more storage loss than pearl millet or sorghum due to its high moisture content. It is also highly susceptible to loss due to insect and pest damage (Forsyth 1962:394–396). Because pearl millet and sorghum have long coevolved with local pests, these crops may be better suited to pest management, although improved maize varieties may have some of the same qualities. Maize is highly demanding of soil fertility, especially in settings where fertilizers are inaccessible; over the long-term, significant investment in maize production could have serious consequences on land fertility. Finally, one of the more serious long-term tradeoffs of maize adoption is its susceptibility to drought at key points in its life cycle, particularly during tasseling. Indigenous crops like pearl millet and sorghum, on the other hand, are well-known for their drought resilience.

Archaeological Evidence

I turn now to a brief examination of maize adoption over a longer time period, in order to evaluate when and why maize was adopted, and whether the costs of such adoptions were displaced over time. My focus is a region in west central Ghana called Banda, which lies approximately 400 km inland from the Ghanaian coast, where historical sources document the introduction of maize in the 1550s–1590s. Banda is the only region in West Africa where systematic sampling and analysis of plant remains dating to the period of maize adoption have been conducted. Our archaeological record extends from 1000 CE until the 1920s (Stahl 2001, 2007), and is supplemented by ethnoarchaeological research on food security and crop introductions in living memory (Logan 2012; Logan and Cruz 2014). This time frame encompasses the time prior to the introduction of maize, as well as the transition to a market economy.

Archaeobotanical evidence suggests that two indigenous African grains – pearl millet and sorghum – were the primary staples for much of the last millennium, even after maize was introduced in the sixteenth and seventeenth centuries. Maize was first introduced in the archaeological Kuulo phase (1450–1650 CE), a time when people were heavily involved in craft production and long-distance trade, as focus began to shift from northward-looking trans-Saharan networks to southward-directed Atlantic networks. Our first evidence of maize was directly dated to 1484–1660 calibrated years CE; combined with historical sources that suggest maize's first introduction along the coast in 1555 CE (Alpern 1992:25), we can surmise that maize was introduced to the region between 1555–1660s CE, indicating a rapid movement of this crop inland. Despite this early introduction, maize does not appear to have been adopted as a staple crop. A handful of maize kernels and cupules was discovered in one residential structure (Mound 118) at the site of Kuulo Kataa, but maize was absent in three other structures tested, as well as over one hundred samples derived from garbage deposits at multiple sites in the region. Instead, pearl millet was common across all of these contexts. These data indicate that maize was adopted rapidly, but as a minor curiosity or luxury crop. Indeed, maize did not supplant pearl millet, either in quantity or ubiquity, for many centuries. This pattern is very common in other world regions as well, such as eastern North America, where maize remained a minor crop for several centuries after its introduction (Fritz 1990; Hart and Lovis 2013).

Why was maize not adopted with gusto at its first introduction, despite its high-yielding qualities? Elsewhere I have interpreted this hesitancy as a preference for local foods like pearl millet (Logan 2012; 2016), but I also think this relates to environmental conditions during the Kuulo phase – a factor that has not been considered in the historical studies noted in this chapter. Oxygen 18 isotope data from Lake Bosumtwi (~200 km south of Banda) indicates a severe, multi-century drought from about 1400–1650 CE (Shanahan et al. 2009). Maize is quite sensitive to drought, whereas pearl millet is one of the most drought-resistant crops in the world. While pearl millet is much lower yielding, in arid conditions it would have been optimal for insuring harvests even in the driest of times. What is interesting is that this risk-averse strategy allowed Banda to weather a severe drought, maintain high economic productivity (Logan 2016a,b; Stahl and Logan 2014), and retain what appears to be a higher density of settlement than is evident in all other archaeological periods (Smith 2008:548). Furthermore, there is no evidence of wild famine foods or economic insecurity, which characterize later phases. This has some interesting implications for the enduring focus on yield-maximizing crops to solve food security crises in modern day Africa, particularly as a means by which to prevent drought-induced food shortage (Logan 2016a,b). To learn from the decisions made by Kuulo phase farmers, it appears that maize is not an ideal choice for coping with drought, something we might consider more seriously given the projected impacts of global warming in the future (e.g., Lobell et al. 2008).

Maize remained a minor crop well into the nineteenth century, even after a return to wetter conditions after 1700 CE, supporting the thesis that people retained local culinary preferences for pearl millet and sorghum. We only see a shift to maize in the late nineteenth and early twentieth centuries, after decades of dislocation and violence and the imposition of British rule. To date, there is no evidence that the British imposed or encouraged the cultivation of maize, especially in peripheral regions like Banda, over which they had little involvement or control. What does seem to be the case is that Banda farmers – who may have been increasingly composed of women as men were called up to fill colonial labor quotas (Stahl and Cruz 1998) – made the hard choice to cultivate maize during a time of food shortage, when its fast producing and high-yielding qualities would have been needed (Logan and Cruz 2014).

Maize has now become the most preferred staple crop in the region, and is preferentially grown whenever possible. Sorghum is still cultivated, but pearl millet production has ceased altogether over the last three decades. In Banda, several reasons are given for the abandonment of pearl millet, even though it retains much ritual importance. The first is that pearl millet is sensitive to too much rainfall at particular points in its lifecycle (during flowering), and that unpredictable rainfall today results in lower productivity. The second is that there are a host of cultural taboos surrounding the cultivation and harvesting of millet, which aim for more equitable distribution, reducing the amount an individual farmer has at his/her disposal. For example, multiple people are needed to take part in onerous millet processing, and tradition dictates that everyone involved receives a share of the crop, even unborn children; such reciprocities are apparently not mandated for other crops. Third, millet is especially time consuming and difficult to process into clean grain, a process that has not yet been mechanized. Finally, pearl millet fetches a much lower price at market than maize or sorghum. Combined with lower pre- and post-harvest yields, pearl millet is no longer an economically viable option for farmers today. Banda is not unique; pearl millet abandonment is widespread across Africa, aided by development dollars that ignore millet in favor of maize (National Research Council 1996).

I suggest that the reasons why maize was adopted slowly initially were related to the tradeoffs perceived by farmers at the time. At maize's initial introduction, dry conditions may have been a sufficient reason to reject maize as a staple; however, even following a return to wetter conditions in Early Makala times (c. 1725–1820s CE), people continued to rely on native staples, suggesting the importance of these grains in social and culinary identity. Pearl millet in particular appears to be the site of several highly ritualized meanings that people may have been hesitant to abandon. The rejection of maize as a staple grain may have been because the costs – losing ritual and culinary identity and increasing vulnerability to drought – outweighed the yield-maximizing benefits. At some point in the late nineteenth and early twentieth centuries, the need for a fast-producing grain outweighed the potential risks in adopting drought-sensitive maize. Based on precipitation records, conditions were wet and may have been ideal for maize cultivation; in the short-term, the benefits of maize may have outweighed the costs, at least at the time. Unfortunately, the long-term costs are now becoming visible. Drying trends since the 1970s have severely impacted harvests of many crops in the Banda area, especially maize. After nearly a century of reliance on maize, people now prefer its taste over pearl millet or sorghum. Sorghum, which continues to produce reliably under variable conditions, is sold on the market, in part to acquire money to purchase maize, further indebting people to the market economy.

Toward Conceptualizing Tradeoffs over the Long Term

In the case of Banda, using high-yielding maize as a staple in the late nineteenth and early twentieth centuries made sense at the time, but had the effect of "kicking the can down the road" – costs were displaced until much later in time. Under different economic and environmental conditions in the sixteenth to seventeenth centuries, maize did not make sense as a staple. In many ways, these costs were in part predictable; we know, as farmers likely did in the past, that maize is susceptible to drought. But the growing preference for maize, and associated burdens to produce enough to meet local demands as well as to sell to the market, may not have been predictable. This suggests that time can function to not only displace but also exacerbate costs down the line. Fundamentally, these costs result from the abandonment of diverse and culturally meaningful cultigens, which reduces the options people have in times of stress, and locks them into a marriage with maize that is beneficial only when environmental conditions and land access are optimal. Economic and environmental changes are something of a constant, though the directions in which they change are not always predictable. Some effects may become more pronounced as time wears on. We see this in at least two ways. First, in the case of maize, preference increased over time, meaning that returning to other staples like sorghum, which is a more reliable producer in variable precipitation regimes, is no longer favored; new tastes are hard to undo. Second, declines in harvest during drought may actually be more costly to farmers under market conditions, which today require they sell off a good portion of their harvests to earn much needed cash income.

Archaeology provides a long-term view of tradeoffs that helps us evaluate costs and benefits under a much wider range of possibilities – of terrible drought, violence, tyranny, or even just normal background climatic variability – that may help us model temporal effects. Narrow market-centric analyses that assume yield is always top priority obscure the complex decision making of farmers, and may leave them more susceptible to down the line, temporally displaced costs. These costs are not always predictable precisely because some effects are exacerbated over time, and because we cannot always reconstruct alternate, non-market rationalities. Tradeoffs are thus a moving target, and this is something we need to capture without necessarily assuming directionality or currency. One way forward is to model long-term costs and benefits with the help of computer-based modelling, as chapters by Freeman and colleagues (Chapter 2) and by BurnSilver (Chapter 3) (this volume) illustrate. Here, archaeology can serve as a means to ground-truth and contextualize long-term costs and benefits. Local context is especially important for documenting people's rationalities, and costs that may be unevenly distributed across social groups. In any analysis, decisions about what is traded off, and for whom, are politically situated, underscoring the need to understand local contexts. Finally, conceptualizing how tradeoffs play out over the long-term raises questions regarding the nature of "balance" that is core to the concept of tradeoffs itself. Balance today between economic, cultural, and environmental factors may lead to costs tomorrow, which raises the question of whether or not "balance" is ever really achievable, or is always itself a moving target that is constantly being redefined. While agricultural technofixes may contribute to solving food insecurity in the present, they may do so at the expense of the future.

References

Alpern, Stanley 1992 The European Introduction of Crops in West Africa in Precolonial Times. *History in Africa* 19:13–43.

Boivin, Nicole, Dorian Q. Fuller, and Alison Crowther 2012 Old World Globalization and the Columbian Exchange: Comparison and Contrast. *World Archaeology* 44(3):452–469.

Boserup, Ester 1965 *The Conditions of Agricultural Growth*. Aldine, Chicago.

Carr, Edward R. 2008 Men's Crops and Women's Crops: The Importance of Gender to Understanding Agricultural and Development Outcomes in Ghana's Central Region. *World Development* 36(5):900–915.

Crosby, Alfred 2003 [1972] *The Columbian Exchange: Biological and Cultural Consequences of 1492*. Praeger, Westport, CN.

De Waal, Alex 1990 A Re-Assessment of Entitlement Theory in the Light of Recent Famines in Africa. *Development and Change* 21(3):469–490.

Evenson, R.E., and D. Gollin 2003 Assessing the Impact of the Green Revolution, 1960-2000. *Science* 300:758–762.

Forsyth, J. 1962 Major Food Storage Problems. In *Agriculture and Land Use in Ghana*, edited by J. Brian Wills, pp. 394–401. Oxford University Press, London.

Fraser, Evan D.G. 2003 Social Vulnerability and Ecological Fragility: Building Bridges between Social an Natural Sciences Using the Irish Potato Famine as a Case Study. *Conservation Ecology* 7(2):9.

Fritz, Gayle J. 1990 Multiple Pathways to Farming in Precontact Eastern North America. *Journal of World Prehistory* 4(4):387–435.

Godfray, H. C. J, J. R. Beddington, I. R. Crute, L. Haddad, D. Lawrence, J. F. Muir, J. Pretty, S. Robinson, S. M. Thomas, and C. Toulmin 2010 Food Security: The Challenge of Feeding 9 Billion People. *Science* 327:812–818.

Hart, John P., and William A. Lovis 2013 Reevaluating What We Know about the Histories of Maize in Northeastern North America: A Review of the Evidence. *Journal of Archaeological Research* 21:175–216.

Jones, M., H. Hunt, E. Lightfoot, D. Lister, X. Liu, and G. Motuzaite-Matuzeviciute 2011 Food Globalization in Prehistory. *World Archaeology* 43(4):665–675.

Lobell, David B., Marshall B. Burke, Claudia Tebaldi, Michael Mastrandrea, Walter Falcon, and Rosamond Naylor 2008 Prioritizing Climate Change Adaptation Needs for Food Security in 2030. *Science* 319 (5863):607–610.

Logan, Amanda L. 2012 *A History of Food Without History: Food, Trade, and Environment in West-Central Ghana in the Second Millennium AD.* PhD Dissertation, Department of Anthropology, University of Michigan, Ann Arbor.

2016a An Archaeology of Food Security in Banda, Ghana. In *Archaeology of the Human Experience*, edited by M. Hegmon. *Archaeological Papers of the American Anthropological Association* 27: 106–119.

2016b "Why Can't People Feed Themselves": Archaeology as Alternative Archive of Food Security in Banda, Ghana. *American Anthropologist* 118 (3):508–524.

Logan, Amanda L., and M. Dores Cruz 2014 Gendered Taskscapes: Food, Farming, and Craft Production in Banda, Ghana, in the 18th to 21st centuries. *African Archaeological Review* 31(2):203–231.

Mandala, Elias 2005 *The End of Chidyerano: A History of Food and Everyday Life in Malawi, 1860–2004.* Heinemann, Portsmouth, NH.

McCann, James 2005 *Maize and Grace: Africa's Encounter With A New World Crop, 1500–2000.* Harvard University Press, Cambridge.

McShane, T. O., P. D. Hirsch, T. C. Trung, A. N. Songorwa, A. Kinzig, B. Monteferri, D. Mutekanga, H. Van Thang, J. L. Dammert, M. Pulgar-Vidal, M. Welch-Devine, J. P. Brosius, P. Coppolillo, and S. O'Connor 2011 Hard Choices: Making Trade-offs Between Biodiversity Conservation and Human Well Being. *Biological Conservation* 14:966–972.

Miracle, Marvin P. 1965 The Introduction and Spread of Maize in Africa. *The Journal of African History* 6(1):39–55.

National Research Council 1996 *Lost Crops of Africa: Grains.* National Academy Press, Washington D.C.

Patel, Raj 2012 *Stuffed and Starved: The Hidden Battle for the World Food System.* Melville House, Brooklyn.

Pretty, Jules, and Zareen P. Bharucha 2014 Sustainable Intensification in Agricultural Systems. *Annals of Botany* 114:1571–1596.

Rogers, Everett M. 2003 *Diffusion of Innovations.* Free Press, New York.

Shanahan, T. M., J. T. Overpeck, K. J. Anchukaitis, J. W. Beck, J. E. Cole, D. L. Dettman, J. A. Peck, C. A. Scholz, and J. W. King 2009 Atlantic Forcing of Persistent Drought in West Africa. *Science* 324:377–380.

Smith, J. N. Leith 2008 *Archaeological Survey of Settlement Patterns in the Banda Region, West-Central Ghana: Exploring External Influences and Internal*

Responses in the West African Frontier. PhD Dissertation, Department of Anthropology, Syracuse University, NY.

Stahl, Ann 2001 *Making History in Banda: Anthropological Visions of Africa's Past.* Cambridge University Press, Cambridge.

2007 Entangled Lives: the Archaeology of Daily Life in the Gold Coast Hinterlands, AD 1400-1900. In *Archaeology of Atlantic Africa and the African Diaspora*, edited by Toyin Falola and Akin Ogundiran, pp. 49–76. Indiana University Press, Bloomington.

Stahl, Ann B., and M. Dores Cruz 1998 Men and Women in a market economy: gender and craft production in west central Ghana ca. 1775-1995. In *Gender in African Prehistory*, edited by S. Kent, pp. 205–226. Rowman and Littlefield, Landham, Maryland.

Stahl, Ann B., and Amanda L. Logan 2014 Resilient Villagers: Eight Centuries of Continuity and Change in Banda Village Life. In *Current Perspectives in the Archaeology of Ghana*, edited by J. Anquandah, B. Kankpeyeng, and W. Apoh, pp. 44–63. Sub-Saharan Publishers, Accra.

Staff Division of Agriculture 1962 Crops other than Cocoa and the Diseases and Pests which Affect Them. In *Agriculture and Land Use in Ghana*, edited by J. B. Wills, pp. 353–393. Oxford University Press, London.

Stone, Glenn D. 2007 Agricultural Deskilling at the Spread of Genetically Modified Cotton in Warangal. *Current Anthropology* 48(1):67–103.

Thurow, Roger 2012 *The Last Hunger Season: A Year in an African Farm Community on the Brink of Change*. Public Affairs, New York.

Tilman, D., K. G. Cassman, P. A. Matson, R. Naylor, and S. Polasky 2002 Agricultural Sustainability and Intensive Production Practices. *Nature* 418:671–677.

Van Oppen, Achim 1999 Cassava, "The Lazy Man's Food"? Indigenous Agricultural Innovation and Dietary Change in Northwestern Zambia (ca. 1650-1970). In *Changing Food Habits: Case Studies from Africa, South America and Europe*, edited by Carola Lentz, pp. 43–71. Harwood Academic Publishers, Amsterdam.

6

Tradeoffs in Pre-Columbian Maya Water Management Systems

Complexity, Sustainability, and Cost

CHRISTIAN ISENDAHL AND SCOTT HECKBERT

> "If you don't like the effects, don't produce the cause"
> (George Clinton and Garry Shider; *Funkadelics: America Eats its*
> *Young*, Westbound Records, 1972)

Sustaining water security is a key global challenge for humanity. Water security can be defined as the situation whereby people have physical and economic access to water of sufficient quality and quantity to meet their physiological needs, including drinking water, water for food production and processing, and water for sanitation (Barthel and Isendahl 2013:224). Given that we may have entered a global "post-peak-water scenario" with rapidly inflating costs for meeting rising demands on a diminishing supply, this is a challenge that will require foresight in planning to develop hydro-technological solutions that respond to current and future socio-ecological needs and conditions. Leaving no stone unturned, water security is a challenge that begs learning from past experiences of the long-term function of water management systems. Water management systems can be considered as the sequence of actions that links water "production, processing, distribution, consumption, and waste management, as well as all the associated regulatory institutions and activities" (Pothukuchi and Kaufman 2000:113). Archaeology can potentially offer a range of insights on the long-term aspects of the efficacy, resilience, and sustainability of water management institutions to this body of knowledge. These insights are relevant beyond their particular historical context, and can inform water security issues today. Archaeology can also provide unique insights into the long-term function and efficacy of water management systems. At the most general level, the demand for water security has been central in the social negotiation of resource management institutions and a catalyst for cooperation as well as a source of conflict throughout history, thus forming a key theme in archaeological research on social change and socio-ecological system dynamics (Scarborough 2003). In managing social-hydrological systems to provide water security (or inversely to mitigate vulnerability or water insecurity), there are inherent tradeoffs that affect system resilience and manifest themselves over time.

Archaeological data are particularly appropriate for analyzing certain kinds of tradeoffs because enough time has elapsed for evaluating processes with long-term temporal lags. This chapter outlines the relationships between complexity and sustainability from the perspective of Classic Maya water management systems. We focus on how challenges to water security have been met with different strategies and how some of these eroded the long-term sustainability of water management systems and, by extension, undermined economic and political foundations. We conclude that management of water systems involves intertemporal tradeoffs in water security, as evidenced by case studies of the pre-Columbian Maya described in this chapter. Maintaining physical and economic access to water is an adaptive process that occurs as social, ecological, and biophysical conditions change. Water management in the present may in some cases reduce options available in the future, and hence an intertemporal tradeoff occurs between current and future water security.

The Maya Lowlands is a particularly interesting case since archaeological research demonstrates that water management systems in this region were multi-componential, diverse across space, and shifted over time (Isendahl et al. 2016). The region has a highly heterogeneous environment and presents different challenges to water security under which the Maya developed a variety of strategies to manage water security.

Here we take a bi-scalar approach to demonstrate both regional variation and local diversity. The first section takes a comparative look at Classic Maya water management in three physiographic sub-regions: the Yalahau, Péten Karst Plateau, and Belize River Valley sub-regions. We describe the environmental conditions framing water security, summarize the main management practices employed in each sub-region, link these practices to their contextual socio-political and economic institutions, and trace tradeoffs in water security that are generated as a result. The second section focuses on one sub-region, the Puuc-Nohkakab, to detail two concomitant water management technologies and their roles in the long-term historical

trajectory of agro-urban development in that area. Although the archaeological literature presents several different aspects of Maya water management systems (technical, economic, political, symbolic, etc.), few examples
have explicitly focused on how strategies to manage water security involved
intertemporal tradeoffs in water security that eroded long-term
sustainability.

The Lowland Maya and Their Environments

The Maya Lowlands are a 250,000 km² region within present-day Mexico,
Guatemala, Belize, and Honduras (Figure 6.1). The development of Lowland Maya society unfolded over several millennia and with significant
regional differences, resulting in the emergence of state polities, urban
settlements, long-distance economic and social networks, innovative technologies, and diverse resource management systems in place by the first
millennium BCE. The long-term history of the Lowlands suggests a series
of regional and sub-regional cycles of growth, decline, and reorganization

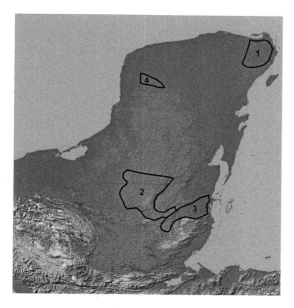

FIGURE 6.1. The Maya Lowlands with the physiographic sub-regions discussed in the
text indicated: (1) Yalahau, (2) Petén Karst Plateau, (3) Belize River Valley, and (4) Puuc-
Nohkakab. Plotted by Christian Isendahl on a modified map from NASA available
online: www2.jpl.nasa.gov/srtm/central_america.html (accessed on 22 November 2011).

during the course of the Preclassic (1000 BCE–250 CE), Classic (250–1000 CE), and Postclassic periods (1000–1500 CE), in which long- and short-term rainfall variations seem to have played an important role (e.g., Kennett et al. 2012). Sub-regional chronologies may divert slightly from this general chronological framework, as indicated in some cases outlined later in the chapter.

Although set in a heterogeneous tropical environment with respect to rainfall timing and volume, topography, geology, vegetation, and soil type, the hydrological regimes of the Lowlands share two basic characteristics: a tropical climate with a pronounced dry season (from October to May) and karst limestone geomorphology. In terms of water security, water supply is limited by the naturally low water retention capacity of the geology, and the timing of the onset of the wet season. Precipitation generally follows a southeast to northwest gradient of decreasing rainfall, with almost arid conditions (<500 mm) on the northwest coast of the Yucatán Peninsula and averages of 1,500–3,500 mm in eastern and southern regions. Similarly, there are regional differences in topography and depth to the water table, arising from karstic geology of the limestone bedrock. These factors affect the supply of surface and sub-surface fresh water and pose challenges to accessing and storing water. These factors provided different opportunities and challenges for people with respect to water security, and the pre-Columbian Maya developed a series of water management systems address-ing the particulars of local social-hydrological conditions.

Intertemporal Tradeoffs in Water Security

Our examination of intertemporal tradeoffs in water security of the Classic Maya takes a theoretical point of departure from a body of work linking sustainability, problem-solving, and complexity (Allen et al. 2003; Tainter 2006; Tainter and Taylor 2014; Tainter et al. 2003), work also discussed in Hegmon's analysis of Mimbres history (Chapter 7, this volume). Complexity has many ad hoc understandings, and here we follow Tainter's conceptualization of complexity in social systems as "differentiation in both structure and behavior, and/or degree of organization or constraint" (2006:92). The main line of reasoning is that (1) sustainability emerges from success at solving problems, (2) technological and institutional com-plexity is a powerful tool for problem-solving, but (3) complexity requires resources and carries a cost to be maintained. In requiring resources, increasing complexity means that people need to work harder. Following from that premise, we suggest that some tradeoffs in water security can be directly associated with the burden of costs that complexity-fostered sustainability generates.

Costs come in different forms. Considering water security at a system level there can be direct costs, such as increased difficulties in access to water, and opportunity costs, such as loss of agricultural production; these are costs of foregone benefits that cannot be achieved in a water insecure situation. The complexity of the water management system carries an institutional cost, which is larger for more management-intensive hydro-technological solutions. Institutions themselves are a solution to excessive transaction costs, but institutional change is expensive and incremental, producing the "sunk-cost effect," that is, decisions are based on past investments rather than future returns, which leads to a reluctance to abandon something (e.g., an institution) that has been heavily invested in, despite poor expectations (Janssen and Scheffer 2004).

In other words, the solutions applied to build secure water management systems from increasing technological sophistication and involving complex forms of management organization may be highly effective for a time, but have tradeoffs: they require resources, for instance up-front investment and ongoing maintenance costs that carry with them a long-term series of inbuilt costs that can limit the future capacity to adapt. More complex hydro-technological solutions may be best suited and least vulnerable in predictable social-hydrological conditions, and in this case large-scale engineering and hierarchically managed systems potentially generate immense benefits. However, when conditions change or are unpredictable, the costs of the system may quickly outweigh the benefits of maintaining it. Our understanding of tradeoffs in water security suggests there is a path dependency in achieving water security over time, in which institutions (complex water management systems in this case) have high start-up costs, but once in place have prohibitively large transaction costs to fundamental change, even under increasing inefficiency (see Pierson 2000).

These investments in water security are played out over a heterogeneous set of biophysical conditions that change over time. The pathway that a social-hydrological system takes along this complex timeline can lead it to achieve sustainable development, or alternatively it can be grasped by a so-called poverty trap, that is, "any self-reinforcing mechanism which causes poverty to persist" (Azariadis and Stachurski 2005:326), and end in failed investment.

A key anthropological issue to which archaeologists ideally should be able to contribute some insights is the extent to which people considered costs and tradeoffs in past decision making processes. There is a need to unfold the string of motivations that guided decisions that led to the trajectory that is observed for each social-hydrological system. Which awareness did people have of the full scheme of potential tradeoffs, the extent to which tradeoffs were internalized in the decision making process, and how were these insights balanced against the desired goal of problem-solving? However, in the absence of textual evidence directly detailing such considerations in the past, archaeological data are, at best, inconclusive or, at worst, unsuitable for deducing intent, and interpretations are probably best modeled from ethnographic analogies of economic decision making and tested against archaeological data.

The potential of archaeology to generate important insights on the tradeoffs in system sustainability have remained largely uncharted until recently (Nelson et al. 2010). The many limitations of the archaeological record notwithstanding, archaeologists are well positioned to evaluate tradeoff effects in multiple social and ecological realms and at different temporal and spatial scales. Suggesting that policy makers draw from a wide range of examples, archaeological data sets can be used to identify factors that have established water security sustainably in the past, as well as to trace complex causation and the full tradeoff effects of decisions. These are processes frequently concealed from current planners and policy makers because of the limitations of enough elapsed time for evaluation. In addition, a long-term perspective on the links between complexity, sustainability, and tradeoffs will be helpful to problematize the common but misguided simplification of sustainability as an attainable epitome end-product of ideal planning.

A Sample of Lowland Maya Water Management Systems

This section takes a comparative look at Classic Maya water management, contrasting three physiographic sub-regions: the Yalahau, Petén Karst Plateau, and Belize River Valley sub-regions. Summarizing data discussed in Isendahl et al. (2016), the small number of cases reported here draws from among the twenty-seven physiographic sub-regions in the Maya Lowlands that Dunning and Beach (2010) identify, outlining the environmental conditions framing water security, the main management practices employed, and their contextual socio-political and economic institutions, and trace generated tradeoffs in water security and their impact on system resilience and vulnerability.

The Yalahau Sub-Region

Covering about 134 km² of the northeast Yucatán Peninsula, the Yala-hau sub-region encompasses the most extensive inland wetland system in the Maya Lowlands. The wetlands are associated with a system of fracture depressions in the limestone bedrock and represent the exposed surface of the aquifer. The annual average rainfall is ca. 1,200 mm, but frequent storms often raise annual precipitation above 2,000 mm. During the dry season the water level drops but most wetland areas contain moist soil and open water all year round (Fedick and Morrison 2004). With surface water available in all seasons and the water table at a depth of less than 5 m the Yalahau wetland environment provided opportunities for water security, with few, if any, challenges to access water of sufficient quality and quantity, and there is no clear evidence of water management institutions above the household level. Prehistoric populations excavated wells in the relatively soft limestone bedrock, which provided an easily managed source for household consumption, including pot irrigation of home gardens (Winzler and Fedick 1995). The aquifer was also accessed by natural sinkholes (cenotes, formed by dissolution of karstic limestone by surface or ground water) (Fedick and Morrison 2004).

In addition to surface water, cenotes, and dug wells, archaeological mapping of the wetlands has documented an extensive system of con-structed rock-alignment features that probably served to manage water (overland flow) and soil movement (sediment transport) in the agro-system (Fedick and Morrison 2004). In addition, Fedick and colleagues argue that pre-Columbian Yalahau farmers practiced a form of precision agriculture, targeting karst cavities in the bedrock that hold deep pockets of thick, nutrient-rich soil with high organic content that retain moisture over the dry season and that sometimes provided direct access to the aquifer (Fedick and Morrison 2004; Flores-Delgadillo et al. 2011).

Available archaeological settlement data indicate that the Yalahau landscape had quite high population numbers during the Late Preclas-sic and beginning of the Early Classic periods (ca. 100 BCE–350 CE), but there are no indications, such as monumental public architecture, of strong centralized authority in the area. When water is available to all with minimal investment, hierarchical institutions appear to not have formed. Thus, according to our description of costs, the transaction costs of accessing water are low, so institutional investments to reduce these transaction costs are not needed. Given high levels of water security with low investment costs, it is puzzling that settlement in the Yalahau was relatively brief: the region appears to have been abandoned already during the course of the Early Classic, with limited reoccupation not until the Late Postclassic, at around 1250 CE (Fedick and Morrison 2004). Water security was clearly not the only key variable for sustainability, and abandonment may have been related to the growth of the northwest regional center at Cobá (Fedick and Morrison 2004).

The Petén Karst Plateau Sub-Region

The Petén Karst Plateau in the elevated interior of the southern Maya Lowlands forms a physiographic sub-region of uplifted karst terrain essentially devoid of perennial surface water and accessible groundwater (Dunning et al. 2012). Through the Late Classic period (ca. 600–800 CE) the plateau was one of the most densely populated regions of the pre-Columbian Maya Lowlands and numerous cities had emerged in this area, including two of the largest, both in terms of monumental construction in the civic-ceremonial centers and the area of the extending agro-urban landscape: Tikal and Calakmul. The annual average rainfall on the plateau is around 1,500–2,000 mm, but to support agro-urban populations the Maya developed a water management system based on the capture and storage of rainwater in large open reservoirs (Isendahl et al. 2016).

The Tikal water management system consisted of prepared catchment areas and elevated reservoirs within the city center and in surrounding extensive agro-urban areas. A series of large reservoirs were created by damming the uppermost reaches of seasonal streams draining the ridge upon which the monumental civic-ceremonial core was constructed. These dams were progressively remodeled to increase water-holding capacity. Further reservoirs were constructed along the lower margins of the ridge, facilitated by the natural slope of the landscape. These reservoirs were located within the residential zone and in proximity to local areas of particularly productive soil in the agro-urban landscape, suggesting their use in field irrigation (Scarborough and Gallopin 1991; Scarborough et al. 2012). Further afield from the city center the agro-urban extension areas of Tikal extended to include more low-lying terrain (Puleston 1983) with numerous reservoirs, often near parcels with particularly productive soils and terraced fields (Fialko 2005). Water storage features were not confined to urban space, and reservoirs, albeit of lesser grandeur, were also constructed in smaller fringe settlements. In addition, households utilized tanks to store water for domestic consumption and pot irrigation of kitchen gardens (Akpinar et al. 2012; Weiss-Krejci and Sabbas 2002).

The elaborate, extensive, and complex hydro-technological system of the greater agro-urban landscape at Tikal was a creative solution to the challenges to water security presented by the hydrological regime of the sub-region, with little access to natural surface or sub-surface water sources. The emerging complex reservoir system took advantage of landscape-specific opportunities to collect and store large volumes of rainwater, thus allowing sustainable livelihoods of large agro-urban populations for centuries.

Although the chronology of the reservoir system is not fully understood, components of the central reservoir system were constructed to collect and store water from a small natural spring early in the Late Preclassic (500 BCE–100 CE) (Scarborough et al. 2012). Scarborough and colleagues (2012) further suggest that the spring may have formed an important locational factor for the city center. The transition between the Late Preclassic and Early Classic (200–600 CE) periods was marked by significant social crises on the Péten Karst Plateau, including temporary abandonment of several urban centers (Grube 1995), which may have been related to the vulnerability of the water management system to increasing drought frequency and severity (Dunning et al. 2014a; Hansen et al. 2002; Wahl et al. 2007). Dunning and colleagues (2014a) suggest that increasing regional aridity at this point in time was a particularly important stimulus for the development of the reservoir system at Tikal, thus developing largely as an adaptive response to escalating climatic stress on water security. Reservoir construction continued through the Classic periods, with new reservoirs established, existing ones elaborated and augmented in capacity, and continuous maintenance work as population levels peaked in the Late Classic (ca. 600–800 CE). Toward the end of the Late Classic, however, the sub-region went through a more severe crises from which it could not recover, and monumental and reservoir construction came to a halt, the political system collapsed, and the city was largely abandoned as part of the Classic Maya Collapse, the intense debate over which we will not enter here. As part of these processes, however, economic downturn made reservoir maintenance costs difficult to meet, ultimately limiting their efficacy. Further, uncertainty regarding access to sufficient water made these urban systems further susceptible to environmental and political perturbations (Dunning et al. 2012).

In the case of Tikal and other large cities that became subject to the Classic Maya Collapse, water insecurity at the beginning of development meant that transaction costs of institutional change and direct costs of investment and maintenance of complex and hierarchical systems would have been worth the investment. These hydro-technological systems yielded great benefits until the system became unstable and/or unpredictable both in terms of social and environmental conditions, and/or they were not maintained. Regardless of the reason for discontinuing the use of large-scale, hierarchical water management systems, a significant investment in maintaining the system would have been needed for it to continue to provide water security. The breakdown of hydro-technological systems could have immediately reduced carrying capacity of cities as the system crossed a non-linear threshold where water went from a secure resource to an unmanageable insecure resource in very short time frames. The costs of changing the system from an institutional and economic perspective become prohibitive at this point. The sunk costs and high ongoing maintenance requirements resulted in a loss of adaptiveness available in the water management system, presenting only two options: continue large-scale investment, or abandon the hydro-technical system.

The Belize River Valley Sub-Region

The Belize River Valley sub-region forms an interesting counter-image to the Petén Karst Plateau. The Belize River Valley is located to the east of the latter region and receives somewhat higher annual average precipitation (2,160 mm). The most important difference in environmental conditions framing water security, however, is that the elevated interior provides surface runoff that flows into the Belize River Valley, supplying water as well as nutrient-rich clay sediments (Lucero et al. 2004). Since water was an abundant, readily available year-round resource there was no need for complex reservoir systems to provide for water security (Isendahl et al. 2016).

The pre-Columbian Maya settlements of the Belize River Valley form a similar contrast to the mega-cities of the Petén Karst Plateau, especially in terms of water and political systems. At Saturday Creek, for instance, Lucero and colleagues (Lucero 2006; Lucero et al. 2004) show that this minor agro-urban landscape, dating from at least 900 BCE through to 1500 CE, had a minor elite segment based on wealth, who nevertheless lacked the ability (or need) to extort tribute payments to fund conspicuous consumption such as royal palaces and hieroglyph inscriptions. Recent mapping shows a high density of farmsteads interspersed with ceremonial cores with temple complexes, ball courts, and elite residences (Harrison-Buck et al. 2014), suggesting a differential but heterarchical organization of settlement of commoners and elites that lacks central authority. Lucero and colleagues (2014) suggest that the sheer abundance of water and fertile farmland effectively prevented aspiring leaders from acquiring political power by gaining control over key resources, similar to conditions in the Yalahau sub-region and in great contrast to Tikal.

A sustainable local resource base, independence from construction and maintenance costs of landesque capital such as reservoirs, a less complex form of social organization, and relative political and economic autonomy from regional cities such as Tikal provided Belize River Valley settlements with high capacity to adjust to external stress factors such as increasing drought frequency and severity in the ninth century (Medina Elizade et al. 2010) or to the political collapse of the Péten Karst Plateau that hit Tikal (Lucero 2002; Lucero et al. 2011). Thus, the Belize valley settlements were resilient to changes occurring around them, and their supporting water management system maintained its adaptive capacity to adjust and continue to provide water resource benefits without interruption.

When compared to Tikal, the case of Saturday Creek seems to emphasize the interpretation that in situations where water security does not require significant economic investments in hydro-technology or complex institutions for management, vulnerability to perturbations is low. The decentralized system of water management is resilient to shock, but does not necessarily generate the same scale of benefits from water resources during normal functioning. There are few intertemporal tradeoffs in water security in decentralized water management systems, and tipping points can be avoided.

Lowland Maya Water Management: A Closer Look at the Puuc-Nohkakab Sub-Region

In this section we focus in more detail on one sub-region, Puuc-Nohkakab, to discuss the use of two hydro-technologies and their role in the long-term historical trajectory of the sub-region. Here, the agro-urban settlement economy depended on maintained growth, with consequences for long-term sustainability (Isendahl et al. 2014). Puuc-Nohkakab is perhaps particularly interesting since these cities were established relatively late, in the Late Classic period (600–800 CE), and rapidly gained large populations, flourished briefly, then with a halt in major building construction were depopulated in the Terminal Classic (800–1000). The boom-and-crash character of Puuc-Nohkakab settlement history follows a series of opportunities, challenges, and problem-solving with varying efficacy for sustainability. The argument pursued here is based on a recent analysis of economic growth and decline in the sub-region (Isendahl et al. 2014), but furthers those lines of reasoning to connect to the tradeoffs of building water security on systems dependent on continued investments.

The Puuc-Nohkakab sub-region covers about 1,300 km² and forms a wedge-shaped zone of very gently folded, bedded limestone on the northwest Yucatán Peninsula. The soilscape is diverse, but some dominating soils are deep, well-drained, and permeable nutrient-rich soils with relatively high organic content that rank among the most productive in the Maya Lowlands (Dunning 1992). Ethnohistoric sources indicate that the Maya thought of the region as *Nohkakab*, "the place of good earth" (Dunning 2008), and Dunning (1992) suggests that it may have formed a regional bread basket.

While offering good soils for agriculture, water security is a major limiting factor for settlement. At 1,150 mm, annual average precipitation is nearly half that of the sub-regions discussed in the previous section, and in addition to the prolonged dry season there are a string of geophysical conditions affecting water security (Isendahl 2011): (1) a common midsummer dry spell putting stress on the initial wet season planting in May; (2) a hurricane season during August to October potentially ruining harvests (Dunning and Houston 2011); (3) a fractured and permeable limestone bedrock checking the development of perennial water bodies and rivers; (4) an absence of water-bearing landscape features formed by karst solution processes, such as *cenotes* or caves; and (5) an inaccessible water table.

The Puuc-Nohkakab Maya addressed these challenges to water security by developing a water management system with two main hydrotechnological components: small, underground water cisterns (*chultuns*) and large, open still-water reservoirs. Most Puuc-Nohkakab Maya household-based agro-urban farmsteads are associated with one or several *chultuns* providing stored rainwater for domestic consumption, probably including pot irrigation of home gardens, and were managed at the household level. *Chultuns* were fashioned, commonly on the residential platform, by excavating a ca. 50 cm wide channel through the platform and into the subsoil, in which a storage chamber was constructed. The size of these chambers varies considerably; currently available data indicate capacities to store from 5,000 to 100,000 liters of rainwater (McAnany 1990:268). The ground surface around the *chultun* opening was swept to not let rubbish contaminate stored water, and chamber surfaces were plastered to avert seepage (Zapata Peraza 1989).

Reservoirs with the capacity to capture and store much greater volumes of water than the average *chultun* are widespread in the sub-region, occurring in most – but not all – agro-urban landscapes of the Puuc-Nohkakab sub-region (Dunning 2008; Isendahl et al. 2014). Water reservoirs were clearly managed at levels above the household in the socio-administrative organization of Puuc-Nohkakab cities – at the urban neighborhood, city, or polity leadership level – depending on their location in the agro-urban landscape, the amount of labor invested in their construction and continued maintenance, and their storage capacities (Dunning 2008; Isendahl 2011; Isendahl et al. 2014; see also Davis-Salazar 2003; Lucero 2006; Scarborough 1998). The formation of Puuc-Nohkakab water reservoirs is a long process involving geomorphological processes and hydro-technological engineering (Dunning 2008; Isendahl 2011). Reservoirs were modified from topographic flatland depressions in the regional landscape mosaic that form in association with structural fracturing in the limestone bedrock underlying the soil cover (Dunning 1992:22). In regional geomorphology, large structural fractures enable karst solution processes of the bedrock, producing vertical conduits that connect the surface with the aquifer. These geological conduits may function as swallow-holes through which hydrostatic pressure during the wet season creates a draw, draining surface runoff that carries dirt and organic materials to the aquifer (Siemens 1978:136–137). Repeated over time, subsurface transport of matter excavates the flatlands and produces depressions in the landscape. When plugged to prevent water from washing out, the depression will fill to form bodies of water. Water reservoirs were constructed by modifying these depressions to control seepage and enhance storage capacities. At Xuch, for instance, up to 10,000m³ of soil was moved from the depression floor to construct a berm on the perimeter of a reservoir that may have held 100,000m³ of water (Isendahl 2011). Puuc-Nohkakab reservoirs clearly played an important role for community water security, probably in the pot irrigation of nearby fields and to refill household water cisterns (Dunning et al. 2014b), but also functioned in political activities as a place for large-scale public ceremonies and as key nodes in the cosmological understanding of landscape (Isendahl 2011).

Sixteenth-century ethnohistoric data suggest a four-tiered social-administrative model of polity, city, neighborhood, and household in the northern

Maya Lowlands (Okoshi Harada 1992; Quezada 1993, Roys 1957), which also seems to fit well with archaeological settlement patterns (McAnany 1995; Prem and Dunning 2004; Williams-Beck 1998). Applying this model to the Puuc-Nohkakab offers some leads for interpreting how soil and water resources were managed and distributed in the pre-Columbian period (Isendahl and Smith 2013; Isendahl et al. 2014). The model indicates that the neighborhood lineage-based leadership was in a key management position, supervising agro-production, organizing labor, distributing resource rights to households, and controlling and coordinating the flow of tribute to the city leadership and, ultimately, polity leadership (McAnany 1995).

When large-scale agro-urban settlement in Puuc-Nohkakab took off in the sixth century CE, initial conditions offered a significant reserve of under-exploited soil resources that with measures taken for water security presented an opportunity for highly productive farming (Isendahl et al. 2014). This situation can be analyzed in terms of transitions in the net energy gain of the agricultural economy over the long term, again building on a theoretical framework that Joseph Tainter has introduced to archaeology, applying an ecological approach to socioeconomic analysis (Hall et al. 1992) of transformations in the long-term sustainability of the Roman imperial economy (e.g., Allen et al. 2003; Tainter 1988; Tainter et al. 2003). The approach examines patterns of large-scale social change and their linkages to transitions in net energy gain, and the consequences of such transitions for the sustainability and resilience capacity of social-ecological systems. The key concept in this model is energy gain, or energy returned on energy invested, tracing how societies deal with transitions between phases of high-gain and low-gain energy returns.

In the competitive agricultural economy of the Maya Lowlands, taking control over previously under-exploited productive soil resources in Puuc-Nohkakab, which an efficient strategy to water security made possible, yielded high returns on investments and ultimately financed the establishment of central institutions and associated urban services and functions. Evidence of conspicuous consumption in the form of elaborate monumental construction and ceremonialism indicates that the high-gain phase was accompanied by political integration and economic maximization (Isendahl et al. 2014). For instance, at the Puuc-Nohkakab polity capital of Uxmal, monumental construction works, such as the House of the Governor and the Nunnery Quadrangle, demanded enormous resource investments at the end of the ninth century (Kowalski and Dunning 1999). In Tainter's model, high-gain phases are usually of relatively short duration since an initially abundant key resource is typically inefficiently managed and rapidly depleted, which seems largely to hold true in Puuc-Nohkakab (Andrews 2004; Dunning 1992).

Energy gain in Puuc-Nohkakab seems to have climaxed during the ninth century, and a transition from high- to low-gain followed as a response to the synergetic effects of increasing regional population, diminishing available farmland per capita, intensified cropping, and decreasing surplus production, while costly pressure to maintain central institutions and water reservoirs remained. Once the agro-system had been pushed into producing maximum yields, soils could not maintain production levels indefinitely – no more than seventy-five years before crashing, according to one estimate (Andrews 2004). Tainter's model suggests that in phases of low-gain the key resource is usually scarce, dispersed, produces little surplus per capita, and requires efficient management that often increases costs. In this view, urban depopulation in the tenth century CE (Braswell et al. 2011; Carmean et al. 2004; Simms et al. 2012) may indicate that dwindling returns to water security investments prompted institutional change. Increasing drought frequency and severity at this time (Medina Elizade et al. 2010) may have affected the Puuc-Nohkakab socio-ecological system.

Puuc-Nohkakab water security depended on landscape modifications that required upfront and continuous maintenance investment. Once a high- to low-gain transition occurred as regional population levels and resource extraction increased, the balance may have shifted from achieving a positive return on water security investment given maintenance costs of hydro-technologies and their institutions. Water security slipped, past the point when maintenance of the large-scale system was not done: reduced population-carrying capacity to non-irrigated levels and depopulation followed.

Sizeable reoccupation would have necessitated another upfront investment to restore water reservoirs (Dunning et al. 2012), which may be part of the explanation why Puuc-Nohkakab was not reoccupied with large urban settlements after the economic and organizational crises (Isendahl et al. 2014). Investing in reservoirs had significant economic implications with start-up and maintenance costs. While these investments in hydro-technological infrastructure clearly increased water security for a time, these were long-term high-risk ventures that generated dependency on continued future investments, thereby transmitting the tradeoff of dependence on continued economic growth across generations. Paradoxically, the water security that reservoirs initially helped to build ultimately produced high social and political dependencies and economic vulnerability (Isendahl et al. 2014).

How do *chultuns*, the small, underground water cisterns, fit into this scheme? The *chultuns* offered autonomous sources of water to households, but it seems these hydro-technologies were not sufficient for supporting the broader social system. Managed, constructed, and maintained by householders, these self-organized, locally managed hydro-technologies may, in conjunction with residential gardens, have offered a capacity of resilience to form flexible units that could function independently from social-administrative hierarchies. They could reorganize into less complex forms of settlements, and buffer themselves from higher-level political turmoil. At the level of the city and polity the importance of the reservoir component of the water system certainly overshadowed that of the *chultun*; effective household strategies to water security may have mattered little in contributing to the sustainability of the overall political system.

Concluding Discussion

The four examples of Maya water management systems discussed here show that in these cases there is a tendency for more complex and hierarchical forms of socio-political organization, where water is a scarce resource and water security depended on large-scale reservoirs. In contrast, where water was a relatively abundant resource, water security required less investment in water storage technology and there were less pronounced hierarchical forms of political organization. Four case studies is clearly an inadequate sample for making any nomothetic statements on the relationship between resource scarcity and the emergence of social complexity in a Wittfogelian sense, and this is not our point either, as there are several other cases in the Lowlands where this tendency is less obvious and even clearly erroneous. The cases nevertheless provide an interesting observation that we can think of in a slightly different manner and without any pretense of universal laws on social change. With the vantage point in Tainter's model on the relationship between sustainability, problem-solving, and complexity and keeping in mind that social complexity and state-level agro-urban societies existed in the Lowlands at an earlier stage than our case studies, it does seem that, in the two water-deficient sub-regions, water security on a level that could support heavily populated agro-urban landscapes was a challenge that required problem-solving at a fairly sophisticated hydro-technological level, which only complex organizations could address. In this view, the organization needed to develop large-scale water reservoir systems was not the root of social complexity. Instead, departing from a purely local or sub-regional perspective on internal processes, we suggest that only existing or emerging complex social infrastructures could muster the means and resources to solve these problems in this particular way, the high levels of upfront investments considered. That water reservoirs were important for water security as well as being associated with economic, social, religious, and political dimensions of control that served to manifest and reinforce power structures only seems to underline this point. In this sense, the relationship between complex water management systems and complex social organization may possibly be thought of as co-evolutionary, in a loose sense, with problem-solving as the key social action.

In this contribution we have associated intertemporal tradeoffs in water security with certain kinds of costs. As we have argued, costs in relation to water security come in different forms. In a water-deficient environment, costs may, for instance, be energetic costs to access and transport water, and indirect costs such as the human hardships of not meeting water security in all its dimensions. In the cases discussed here, the tradeoffs we see are those that directly follow from increased institutional costs of management-intensive hydro-technological solutions such as water reservoirs, for instance upfront and continuous maintenance investments. But we also extend the scope of tradeoffs to include the path dependency that these investments stimulated. In this perspective, landesque capital such as water reservoirs had initial economic benefits in elevating agricultural productivity and increasing the number of people that could be fed and watered, but as the agricultural economy entered a low-gain phase the benefit/cost ratio leveled out, and the social-hydrological system became less sustainable. Investments that once might have been worthwhile resulted in an altered trajectory in terms of the intertemporal tradeoffs in wealth and water security. Adapting to decreasing returns would have required significant institutional change in the upper tiers of the social-administrative hierarchy, involving a range of costs and requiring a political readiness for social change that may not have existed. Hence the attraction into a so-called poverty trap as a result of not being able to adapt sufficiently to regain momentum toward sustainable development.

To support agro-urban landscapes, water security on the Péten Karst Plateau and in Puuc-Nohkakab depended on elaborate water management systems that not only required high upfront costs for their construction but also longer-term maintenance investment that was difficult to sustain in periods of economic decline. This interpretation fits well with the proposition that complexity arises from problem-solving that increases water security, with the tradeoff being high costs and thus increased vulnerability to economic fluctuations.

An important point in comparing these cases is to indicate just how diversified Maya water management systems were, and the range of challenges they had to address and opportunities they took advantage of. Some environmental challenges to sustainable water security required higher-level management institutions, sophisticated hydro-technological infrastructure, and upfront investments, while other opportunities were basically there for the taking, with few technological and economic investment requirements. In the socio-ecological climate of today, those opportunities are increasingly rare. Given that water security is currently a key global challenge for humanity, and will remain so, we must develop hydro-technological solutions that respond to current and future socio-ecological needs and conditions. The long-term archaeological perspective provides insight into the tradeoffs involved in contemporary water security concerns. Given the set of hydro-technological management systems available today, and our understanding of institutional co-evolution with water systems, the archaeological record reminds us that achieving water security involves tradeoffs, and long-term sustainability requires flexibility under changing conditions. This flexibility must come in both engineered solutions and institutional arrangements, and both have costs to develop, maintain, and most importantly change within the context of dynamic social and environmental conditions.

Acknowledgments

Parts of this contribution build on collaborative work within the IHOPE-Maya group, and we thank Nicholas Dunning, Scott Fedick, Joel Gunn, Gyles Iannone, Lisa Lucero, Jeremy Sabloff, and Vernon Scarborough for previous input. We are particularly grateful to Michelle Hegmon for inviting us to the Amerind tradeoff seminar (at which regrettably only the senior author could attend), thus prompting us to write this paper, and to fellow seminar participants for stimulating discussions. We are indebted to

Frances Hayashida, Lisa Lucero, Peggy Nelson, and Joseph Tainter for their sharp and helpful comments on an earlier draft.

References

Akpinar-Ferrand, Ezgi, Nicholas P. Dunning, David Lentz, and John G. Jones 2012 Aguadas as Water Sources at Southern Maya Lowland Sites. *Ancient Mesoamerica* 23:85–102.

Allen, T. F. H., Joseph A. Tainter, and Thomas W. Hoekstra 2003 *Supply-Side Sustainability*. Columbia University Press, New York.

Andrews, Bradford W. 2004 Sayil Revisited: Inferring Terminal Classic Population Size and Dynamics in the West-Central Yucatan Peninsula. *Human Ecology* 32:593–613.

Azariadis, Costas, and John Stachurski 2005 Poverty Traps. In *Handbook of Economic Growth*, Vol. 1A, edited by Phillipe Aghion and Steven N. Durlauf, pp. 295–384. Elsevier, Amsterdam.

Barthel, Stephan, and Christian Isendahl 2013 Urban Gardens, Agriculture, and Water Management: Sources of Resilience for Long-Term Food Security in Cities. *Ecological Economics* 86:224–234.

Braswell, Geoffrey E., Iken Paap, and Michael D. Glascock 2011 The Obsidian and Ceramics of the Puuc Region: Chronology, Lithic Procurement, and Production at Xkipche, Yucatan, Mexico. *Ancient Mesoamerica* 22:135–154.

Carmean, Kelli, Nicholas P. Dunning, and Jeff K. Kowalski 2004 High Times in the Hill Country: A Perspective from the Terminal Classic Puuc Region. In *The Terminal Classic in the Maya Lowlands: Collapse, Transition, and Transformation*, edited by Arthur A. Demarest, Prudence M. Rice, and Don S. Rice, pp. 424–449: University Press of Colorado, Boulder.

Davis-Salazar, Karla L. 2003 Late Classic Maya Water Management and Community Organization at Copan, Honduras. *Latin American Antiquity* 14:275–299.

Dunning, Nicholas P. 1992 *Lords of the Hills: Ancient Maya Settlement in the Puuc Region, Yucatán, Mexico*. Monographs in World Archaeology Vol. 15. Prehistory Press, Madison.

    2008 Hill Country Chronicles: Puuc Landscapes as Texts. Paper presented at the 6th Annual Mesa Redonda de Palenque, Palenque, Mexico.

Dunning, Nicholas P., and Timothy Beach 2010 Farms and Forests: Spatial and Temporal Perspectives on Ancient Maya Landscapes. In *Landscapes and Societies I*, edited by Peter Martini and Ward Chesworth, pp. 369–389. Springer, Berlin.

Dunning, Nicholas P., Timothy Beach, and Sheryl Luzzadder-Beach 2012 Kax and Kol: Collapse and Resilience in Lowland Maya Civilization. *Proceedings of the National Academy of Sciences of the United States of America* 106:3652–3657.

Dunning, Nicholas P., and Stephen Houston 2011 Chan Ik': Hurricanes as a Destabilizing Force in the Pre-Hispanic Maya Lowlands. In *Ecology, Power, and Religion in Maya Landscapes*, edited by Christian Isendahl and Bodil Liljefors Persson, pp. 57–67. Acta Mesoamericana 23. Verlag Anton Saurwein, Markt Schwaben.

Dunning, Nicholas P., David Wahl, Timothy Beach, John G. Jones, Sheryl Luz-
     zadder-Beach, and Carmen McCane 2014a The End of the Beginning:
     Drought, Environmental Change, and the Preclassic to Classic Transition in
     the East-Central Maya Lowlands. In *The Great Maya Droughts in Cultural
     Context: Case Studies in Resilience and Vulnerability*, edited by Gyles Ian-
     none, pp. 107–126. University Press of Colorado, Boulder.
Dunning, Nicholas P., Eric Weaver, Michael Smyth, and David Ortegón 2014b
     Xcoch: Home of Ancient Maya Rain Gods and Water Managers. In *The
     Archaeology of Yucatan*, edited by Travis Stanton, pp. 65–80. Archaeopress
     Pre-Columbian Archaeology Vol. 1. Archaeopress, Oxford.
Fedick, Scott. L., and Bethany A. Morrison 2004 Ancient Use and Manipulation of
     Landscape in The Yalahau Region of the Northern Maya Lowlands. *Agricul-
     ture and Human Values* 21:207–219.
Fialko, Vilma 2005 Diez años de investigaciones arqueológicas en la Cuenca del
     Río Holmul, region norteste del Petén. In *XVIII simposio de investigaciones
     arqueológicas en Guatemala, 2004*, edited by Juan Pedro LaPorte, Bárbara
     Arroyo, and Héctor E. Mejía, pp. 244–260. Museo Nacional de Arqueología e
     Etnología, Guatemala City.
Flores-Delgadillo, Lourdes, Scott L. Fedick, Elizabeth Solleiro-Rebolledo, Sergio
     Palacios-Mayorga, Pilar Ortega-Larrocea, Sergey Sedov, and Esteban Osuna-
     Ceja 2011 A Sustainable System of Traditional Precision Agriculture in
     a Maya Homegarden: Soil Quality Aspects. *Soil & Tillage Research*
     113:112–120.
Grube, Nikolai 1995 Transformations of Maya Society at the End of the Preclassic:
     Processes of Change between Predynastic and Dynastic Periods. In *The Emer-
     gence of Lowland Maya Civilization*, edited by Nikolai Grube, pp. 1–5. Acta
     Mesoamericana 8. Verlag Anton Saurwein, Möckmühl.
Hall, Charles A. S., Cutler J. Cleveland, and Robert Kaufmann 1992 *Energy and
     Resource Quality: The Ecology of the Economic Process*. University Press of
     Colorado, Niwot.
Hansen, Richard D., Steven Bosarth, John Jacob, David Wahl, and Thomas
     Schreiner 2002 Climatic and Environmental Variability in the Rise of Maya
     Civilization: A Preliminary Perspective from the Northern Peten. *Ancient
     Mesoamerica* 13:273–295.
Harrison-Buck, Eleanor, Marieka Brouwer-Burg, Mark Willis, Chet Walker,
     Satoru Murata, Brett Houk, and Astrid Runggaldier 2014 Drones, Mapping,
     and Excavations in the Middle Belize Valley: Research Investigations of the
     Belize River East Archaeology (BREA) Project. Paper presented at the 11th
     Annual Belize Archaeology and Anthropology Symposium, San Ignacio,
     Belize.
Isendahl, Christian 2011 The Weight of Water: A New Look at Prehispanic Puuc
     Maya Water Reservoirs. *Ancient Mesoamerica* 22:185–197.
Isendahl, Christian, Nicholas P. Dunning, and Jeremy A. Sabloff 2014 Growth and
     Decline in Classic Maya Puuc Political Economies. In *The Resilience and
     Vulnerability of Ancient Landscapes: Transforming Maya Archaeology through
     IHOPE*, edited by Arlen F. Chase and Vernon L. Scarborough, pp. 43–55.
     AP3A, Arlington.

Isendahl, Christian, Vernon L. Scarborough, Joel D. Gunn, Nicholas P. Dunning, Scott L. Fedick, Gyles Iannone, and Lisa J. Lucero 2016 Applied Perspectives on Prehispanic Maya Water Management Systems: What Are the Insights for Water Security? In *Handbook of Historical Ecology and Applied Archaeology*, edited by Christian Isendahl and Daryl Stump. Oxford University Press, Oxford, in press.

Isendahl, Christian, and Michael E. Smith 2013 Sustainable Agrarian Urbanism: The Low-Density Cities of the Mayas and Aztecs. *Cities* 31:132–143.

Janssen, Marco A., and Marten Scheffer 2004 Overexploitation of Renewable Resources by Ancient Societies and the Role of Sunk-Cost Effects. *Ecology and Society* (9)1:6.

Kennett, Douglas J., Sebastian F. M. Breitenbach, Valorie V. Aquino, Yemane Asmerom, Jaime Awe, James U. L. Baldini, Patrick Bartlein, Brendan J. Culleton, Claire Ebert, Christopher Jazwa, Martha J. Macri, Norbert Marwan, Victor Polyak, Keith M. Prufer, Harriet E. Ridley, Harald Sodemann, Bruce Winterhalder, and Gerald H. Haug 2012 Development and Disintegration of Maya Political Systems in Response to Climate Change. *Science* 338:788–791.

Kowalski, Jeff K., and Nicholas P. Dunning 1999 The Architecture of Uxmal: The Symbolics of Statemaking at a Puuc Maya Regional Capital. In *Mesoamerican Architecture as a Cultural Symbol*, edited by Jeff K. Kowalski, pp. 274–297. Oxford University Press, London.

Lucero, Lisa J. 2002 The Collapse of the Classic Maya: A Case for the Role of Water Control. *American Anthropologist* 104:814–826.

　2006 *Water and Ritual: The Rise and Fall of Classic Maya Rulers.* University of Texas Press, Austin.

Lucero, Lisa. J., Scott L. Fedick, Andrew Kinkella, and Sean M. Graebner 2004 Ancient Maya Settlement in the Valley of Peace Area, Belize. In *Archaeology of the Upper Belize River Valley: Half a Century of Maya Research*, edited by James F. Garber, pp. 86–102. University Press of Florida, Gainesville.

Lucero, Lisa J., Joel D. Gunn, and Vernon L. Scarborough 2011 Climate Change and Classic Maya Water Management. *Water* 3:479–494.

McAnany, Patricia A. 1990 Water Storage in the Puuc Region of the Northern Lowlands: A Key to Population Estimates and Architectural Variability. In *Precolumbian Population History in the Maya Lowlands*, edited by T. Patrick Culbert and Don S. Rice, pp. 263–284. University of New Mexico Press, Albuquerque.

　1995 *Living with the Ancestors: Kinship and Kingship in Ancient Maya Society.* University of Texas Press, Austin.

Medina Elizade, Martín, Stephen J. Burns, David W. Lea, Yemane Asmerom, Lucien von Gunten, Victor Polyak, Mathias Vuille, and Ambarish Karmalkar 2010 High Resolution Stalagmite Climate Record from the Yucatan Peninsula Spanning the Maya Terminal Classic Period. *Earth and Planetary Science Letters* 298:255–262.

Nelson, Margaret C., Keith W. Kintigh, David R. Abbott, and John M. Anderies 2010 The Cross-Scale Interplay between Social and Biophysical Context and the Vulnerability of Irrigation-Dependent Societies: Archaeology's Long-Term Perspective. *Ecology and Society* 15(3):31.

Okoshi Harada, Tsubasa 1992 Los Canules: análisis etno-histórico del Codice de Calkiní. Unpublished PhD dissertation, Instituto de Investigaciones Antropológicas, Universidad Nacional Autónoma de México, Mexico City.

Pierson, Paul 2000 Increasing Returns, Path Dependence, and the study of Politics. *The American Political Science Review* 94(2):251–267.

Pothukuchi, Kameshwari, and Kaufman, Jerome L. 2000 The Food System: A Stranger to the Planning Field. *APA Journal* 66:113–124.

Prem, Hanns J., and Nicholas P. Dunning 2004 Investigations at Hunto Chac, Yucatan. *Mexicon* 26:26–36.

Puleston, Dennis E. 1983 *The Settlement Survey of Tikal.* The University Museum, University of Pennsylvania, Philadelphia.

Quezada, Sergio 1993 *Pueblos y casiques yucatecos: 1550–1580.* El Colegio de México, Mexico City.

Roys, Ralph L. 1957 *The Political Geography of the Yucatán Maya.* Carnegie Institution of Washington Publ. 613. Carnegie Institution, Washington, D.C.

Scarborough, Vernon L. 1998 The Ecology of Ritual: Water Management and the Maya. *Latin American Antiquity* 9:135–159.

    2003 *The Flow of Power: Ancient Water Systems and Landscapes.* School of American Research Press, Santa Fe.

Scarborough, Vernon L., Nicholas P. Dunning, Kenneth B. Tankersley, Christopher Carr, Eric Weaver, Liwy Grazioso, Brian Lane, John G. Jones, Palma Buttles, Fred Valdez, and David L. Lentz 2012 Water and Sustainable Land Use in an Ancient Tropical City: Tikal, Guatemala. *Proceedings of the National Academy of Sciences of the United States of America* 109:12408–12413.

Scarborough, Vernon L., and Gary G. Gallopin 1991 A Water Storage Adaptation in the Maya Lowlands. *Science* 251:658–662.

Siemens, Alfred H. 1978 Karst and the Pre-Hispanic Maya in the Southern Lowlands. In *Pre-Hispanic Maya Agriculture*, edited by Peter D. Harrison and Billy Lee Turner II, pp. 117–143. University of New Mexico Press, Albuquerque.

Simms, Stephanie R., Evan Parker, George Bey III, and Tomas Gallareta Negrón 2012 Evidence from Escalera al Cielo: Abandonment of a Terminal Classic Puuc Maya Hill Complex in Yucatan, Mexico. *Journal of Field Archaeology* 37:270–288.

Tainter, Joseph A. 1988 *The Collapse of Complex Societies.* Cambridge University Press, Cambridge.

    2006 Social Complexity and Sustainability. *Ecological Complexity* 3:91–103.

Tainter, Joseph A., T. F. H. Allen, Amanda Little, and Thomas W. Hoekstra 2003 Resource Transitions and Energy Gain: Contexts of Organization. *Conservation Ecology* 7(3):4.

Tainter, Joseph A., and Temis G. Taylor 2014 Complexity, Problem-Solving, Sustainability and Resilience. *Building Research & Information* 42:168–181.

Wahl, David, Roger Byrne, Thomas Schreiner, and Richard Hansen 2007 Paleolimnological Evidence of Late-Holocene Settlement and Abandonment in the Mirador Basin, Peten, Guatemala. *The Holocene* 17:813–820.

Weiss-Krejci, Estella, and Thomas Sabbas 2002 The Potential Role of Small Depressions as Water Storage Features in the Central Maya Lowlands. *Latin American Antiquity* 13:343–357.

Williams-Beck, Lorraine A. 1998 *El dominio de los batabob: el área Puuc Occidental campechana*. Universidad Autónoma de Campeche, Campeche.

Winzler, Susan, and Scott L. Fedick 1995 Ancient Wells and Water Resources of Naranjal and the Yalahau Region. In, *The View from Yalahau: 1993 Archaeological Investigations in Northern Quintana Roo, Mexico*, edited by Scott L. Fedick and Karl A. Taube, pp. 101–113. Latin American Studies Program, Field Report Series, No. 2. University of California, Riverside.

Zapata Peraza, René L. 1989 *Los chultunes: sistemas de captación y almacenamiento de agua pluvial*. Instituto Nacional de Antropología e Historia, Mexico City.

7

Growth and Inter-Generational Tradeoffs

Archaeological Perspectives from the Mimbres Region of the US Southwest

MICHELLE HEGMON

In the early 1960s, about a thousand people a day moved to California, which became the most populous state in the United States in 1962. That great achievement was cause for a four-day long celebration, presided over by Governor Edmund G. (Pat) Brown, Sr. Pat Brown was an unabashedly pro-growth governor whose administration built new highways and universities to support the growing population. His crowning achievement was the construction of an enormous water distribution network that made possible the expansion of agriculture in the central valley and population growth in the arid south (Rarick 2006). The verb "to grow" of course, means to become larger, but it also means to become "better or improved in some way" (www.merriam-webster .com/dictionary/grow). By the standards of the day (before conservation or the environment were of widespread concern) California truly was becoming better as well as bigger. The infrastructure it created in the 1960s to support the growth made it a more attractive place, which led to more growth, etc.

Now, in 2015, the state continues to prosper in many ways but it is also facing a drought of unprecedented severity and the likelihood of long-term water shortages linked to global climate change. The current governor Edmund G. (Jerry) Brown Jr. (Pat's son) is working to manage those shortages and has instituted restrictions on water usage for some segments of the population and economy. A recent news analysis points out that, more than fifty years after the "aggressive growth policies advocated by his father," Governor Jerry Brown and the state of California are now "confronting fundamental questions about its limits and growth" (Nabourney 2015). The California political dynasty is just one well-known example of a basic issue: The intergenerational and other tradeoffs inherent in growth.

In today's world, informed by everything from *The Limits to Growth* (Meadows et al. 1972) to recent work on global food (in)security (Ash et al. 2010; FAO 2014), it is easy to see the problems engendered by growth. A recent analysis has even revisited the anthropological concept of "limited good" to describe the uneven benefits and unsustainable trajectory of growth in the contemporary world (Trawick and Hornborg 2015). Yet many people in the world today want growth so that they too will have running water, electricity, and internet. Curbing growth in order to help the future may further disadvantage the already disadvantaged. As I reviewed in Chapter 1 (this volume) these are some of the key tradeoffs that confront sustainability policy and research: How do we improve people's lives today without sacrificing the future? One poignant example is the rapidly changing lives of Punan hunter-gatherers in Indonesia, who do not want to choose between the advantages of growth and their traditional life: "They want ... to enjoy both free forest products and the positive aspects of modern life, to go wild boar hunting in the morning and watch television in the evening" (Levang et al. 2007). But it is unfortunately clear that they cannot have both, especially not over the long term.

At a global scale, the rate and impact of growth have increased exponentially in the past few centuries, as a result of industrialization and capitalism. But the general issue – the tradeoffs inherent in growth – has a deep history that extends back at least to the beginning of food production in the early Holocene, about 12,000 years ago. Archaeology has documented hundreds, possibly thousands, of sequences of growth, which are often followed by times that must face the consequences of growth. My goal in this chapter is to use one well-documented archaeological example, from the Mimbres region of the US Southwest, to investigate some of the tradeoffs of growth.

Drawing on multiple lines of evidence, I consider intergenerational tradeoffs through the Mimbres sequence in the tenth to twelfth centuries CE. Within this broad view, I also consider specific tradeoffs involved in social inequality and the varying experiences of the people whose lives were parts of these processes. The approach, which involves tacking between a developmental sequence and a more particular view of people's experiences in that sequence, is in part inspired by recent archaeological approaches that link big histories and human lives (Robb and Pauketat

2013), as well as recent efforts by myself and colleagues to focus on the archaeology of the human experience (Hegmon 2016a). This chapter also sets the stage for the subsequent Chapter 8 (by Nelson and colleagues), which considers tradeoffs regarding vulnerability in several cases, including the end of the Mimbres Classic.

Mimbres is not California. As is detailed in the next section, there are many differences between the societies of Neolithic times and those of today's industrial and post-industrial age. In drawing parallels between Mimbres and California, I do not intend to imply that California faces an abrupt end (or "simplification") similar to that seen in the Mimbres sequence, nor do I suggest that Mimbres had all the options available to California. Rather, the parallel is intended to focus attention on the general issue – applicable to many times and places – of the intergenerational and other tradeoffs inherent in growth. The goal, and one of the strengths of anthropology writ large, is to recognize and learn from both differences and similarities.

Mimbres Background

The Mimbres archaeological region is centered in southwest New Mexico and extends into the surrounding states (it is illustrated further in the map in Figure 7.2). Overviews of Mimbres archaeology are available in a number of sources (Anyon Gilman and LeBlanc 1981; Hegmon 2002; Hegmon et al. 1999). In the center of the region is the Mimbres River Valley, the locus of the densest settlement. The Mimbres region is part of the larger Mogollon tradition, which encompasses much of the southern Southwest, and the Mimbres region was quite similar to the overall Mogollon area during the Early Pithouse period (200–550 CE) and most of the Late Pithouse period (550–1000 CE).

The Mimbres region is defined based primarily on developments that emerged in the tenth century and came to characterize the distinctive Classic period (1000–1130 CE). Population grew and peaked during the Classic, and people resided in above-ground pueblos, some with more than a hundred rooms. They made a spectacular and unique style of black-on-white pottery distinguished by what are known as "representational" paintings of animals and occasionally humans, as well as geometric designs (Figure 7.1; Brody 2004). The pottery was used in an elaborate mortuary tradition, in which the dead were buried under the floors of houses, often with a painted bowl inverted over the skull. The Classic period ended fairly abruptly around 1130 CE. Most people left the large villages and many left

(a)

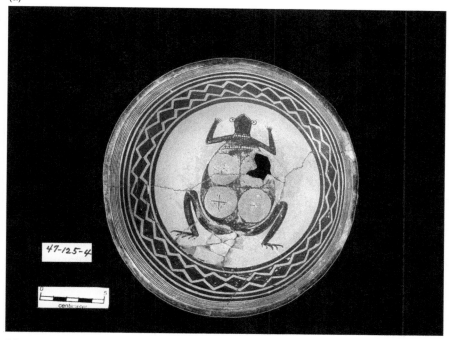

(b)

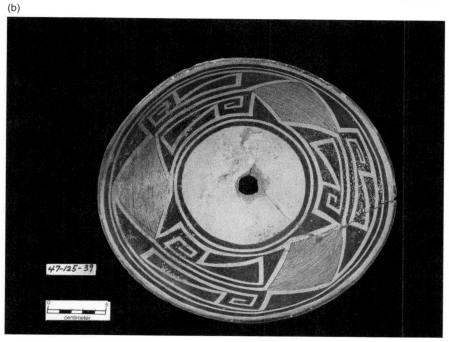

FIGURE 7.1. The spectacular geometric and representational designs on Mimbres Black-on-white pottery, both from the Eby site. Bowls from the University Museum, University of Arkansas collections, photographs by Jane Kellet. (a) Representational design depicting a frog. MimPIDD 4571, museum catalog number 47-125-4. (b) Geometric design. MimPIDD 4588, museum catalog number 47-125-39.

the region, though others stayed and reorganized, moving into smaller residential hamlets (Nelson 1999). After 1130 the distinctive pottery was no longer made and there is no longer any unifying characteristic that defines the region; instead, parts of what had been the Mimbres region were incorporated into other archaeological traditions with different styles of pottery and architecture (Hegmon et al. 1999).

The Big Picture across the Southwest

The eleventh century CE, the time of the Mimbres Classic florescence, was a remarkable period of growth across much of the US Southwest. To the west of Mimbres, in southern Arizona, is the Hohokam region and the largest irrigation system in pre-Hispanic North America. During the eleventh century, that region also saw the development of the complex Hohokam regional economy with market-based exchange (Abbott et al. 2007). To the north of Mimbres, in northern New Mexico, is Chaco Canyon with its massive great houses and cultural influence that reached across much of the northern Southwest. Construction in Chaco Canyon intensified during the eleventh century, and the Chaco World extended its reach, eventually encompassing an area of about 250,000 square kilometers (Kantner 2003: figure 1). Mimbres society appears to have maintained a degree of isolation from Chaco and Hohokam, in that there is little material from either of those expansive traditions in the Mimbres region, and little Mimbres material in either of the other regions. Still, the regions must have influenced each other in some non-material ways: People all across the Southwest would have been aware of goings on in other areas, especially developments as unique as markets, great houses, and a spectacular new style of pottery.

By the middle of the twelfth century, everything had changed. The Hohokam regional economy ended around 1170 CE, and although the reason for the end is not well understood, it is thought to have been a fragile system, sensitive to failure in any one component (Merrill 2014). Growth in Chaco Canyon ended around 1130 CE, after which the center of power moved north but no longer extended its reach across what had been the Chaco World. That date, 1130, also marks the end of the Mimbres Classic period, when people stopped making the spectacular pottery and many moved out of the large villages.

In many ways these pre-Hispanic Neolithic developments are very different from anything in the twenty-first-century world. People in Chaco and Hohokam and Mimbres had only human (and occasional canine) labor and thus limited ability to intensify. Their pre-capitalist economies were not driven by endless accumulation and expansion, and their transportation (they had not invented the wheel) precluded their ability to "fix" problems spatially, by moving the consequences elsewhere. Also, their population densities were low enough that movement to other areas was an option, albeit difficult in many cases. In spite of these differences, there are important similarities between these ancient societies and today's world. There are cycles of growth, often followed by changes that end the growth. And these cycles involve tradeoffs, between those who experience the benefits and those who bear the burdens of growth.

Theoretical Perspectives on Growth and its Consequences:

Complexity, Path Dependence, and the Human Securities

In work that links archaeological, historical, and contemporary cases, Joseph Tainter has developed a useful framework for understanding these processes of growth and change in terms of what he terms "complexity" (Tainter 1990; Tainter and Taylor 2014). His perspective also informs the chapter by Isendahl and Heckbert, (Chapter 6) this volume. Briefly, complexity (by which Tainter means complex technologies and institutions, not necessarily social hierarchies) is developed to solve problems, but complexity is expensive and over time it has diminishing returns. To the extent that complexity contributes to making things both bigger and better, it is an important component of growth. The problems created by complexity can be temporarily mitigated or postponed by what Tainter calls a "reserve problem-solving capacity," but the eventual result is a rapid simplification, a loss of that complexity, which he terms "collapse." Importantly, he uses a precise definition of collapse that is not necessary synonymous with failure, a point I consider in more detail later. Tainter also notes that the costs of complexity require energy input, which (before the advent of fossil fuels) meant that people – or at least some people – had to work harder. In hierarchical societies:

> ... the benefits of complexity often accrue at the top of a hierarchy, while the costs are paid at lower levels. Since benefits and costs do not connect, the costs of complexity often cannot constrain its growth. Anyone who has worked in a large organization will understand this readily (Tainter and Taylor 2014:170).

Tradeoffs are evident at several levels in Tainter's framework. The complexity itself has costs, requiring energy and other resources. There are intergenerational tradeoffs, between people who experience growth and complexity at one time and those who experience simplification and collapse at some time in the future. Finally, as he notes, the benefits and costs of complexity are distributed unevenly.

Implicit in Tainter's framework is the idea of path dependence, which is the sense of becoming increasingly stuck in a particular way of doing things (see Hegmon 2016b for a review of path dependence in archaeology). Often, path-dependent trajectories begin with actions or developments that are helpful at the time but lead to increasingly problematic self-reinforcing and difficult-to-exit trajectories. For example, the creation of a complex technology such as a water-management system might be a good way to grow more crops and feed more people, but once a large population becomes dependent on it, the system is difficult to change.

The concepts discussed so far – growth, complexity, simplification, path dependence – are fairly abstract. In order to understand how they involve tradeoffs, important costs, and benefits, it is necessary to also understand how they affect peoples' lives. One approach utilizes what are known as the dimensions of human security set forth by the United Nations Development Programme in 1994 to focus attention on everyday human life, in the context of growing concerns with national security. The securities – economic, food, health, environmental, personal, community, and political – can be operationalized archaeologically; they have been used in the emerging study of the archaeology of the human experience (Hegmon 2013, 2016a), and are used in the chapters by Logan, Roscoe, and Nelson and colleagues (Chapters 5, 4, and 8, respectively) in this volume. In this chapter I consider three of these: *food security* has to do with the availability and access to food; *environmental security* concerns natural resources and threats to those resources; and *community security* concerns the social, defensive, and other benefits one derives from membership in a (usually residential) community.

Intergenerational Tradeoffs

The Benefits and Costs of Growth in the Mimbres Sequence

The Mimbres sequence fits well with Tainter's framework and the other concepts developed in the previous section. The Mimbres Classic period was a time of growth in both size and complexity. That complexity worked well, for a time, but also created path-dependent feedback processes that led to risky and ultimately unsustainable practices. The tradeoffs (against the benefits of growth) include food and environmental insecurity and eventually community insecurity, as well as social inequality. In this section I focus on the overall sequence and intergenerational tradeoffs; the next section explores issues of social inequality in more detail.

The Sequence in Geographic Context

People began farming in the Mimbres region and larger Mogollon area by the first centuries CE, if not earlier. The Early Pithouse settlements were often in upland locations and farming was part of a mixed economy that included a range of gathered and hunted resources. Reliance on farming increased over time as people settled in more low-lying areas, developed new kinds of grinding technologies, invested more in pithouse construction, and became more residentially stable (Diehl and LeBlanc 2001).

The Mimbres Valley is particularly well-suited for agriculture compared to the surrounding region. Across much of the southern Southwest, the basin and range topography creates mostly small and patchy arable areas. The broad floodplain of the Mimbres River and parts of the Upper Gila River in the western part of the Mimbres region are important exceptions in that they provide large and mostly continuous arable areas. The perennial rivers provided reliable and usually manageable sources of water that could be controlled and enhanced with relatively simple ditch irrigation systems. Throughout much of the Southwest, there is a tradeoff between growing season and water, in that higher elevations are generally colder but receive more precipitation. In contrast, the topography of the Mimbres Valley created a sort of geographic win-win. Because the valley is relatively low in elevation and relatively far south it has a long growing season with little threat of killing frosts. At the same time, orographic flows from the west are blocked by the Black Range that flanks the valley to the east, so the clouds release their moisture and rain on the Mimbres Valley.

This geographic situation is illustrated in Figure 7.2, which displays the result of a model of agricultural suitability. Specifically, each point on the landscape is assessed in terms of its elevation (which affects temperature), slope, proximity to watercourses, and rainfall as estimated for the 1000–1100 period (more technical details are provided in Table 7.1). The Mimbres Valley is among just a handful of places on the landscape with the highest level of suitability. These are locales that are relatively flat, high enough that they get rainfall but low enough that they are not subject to killing frosts, and near water courses. Most of the large Classic

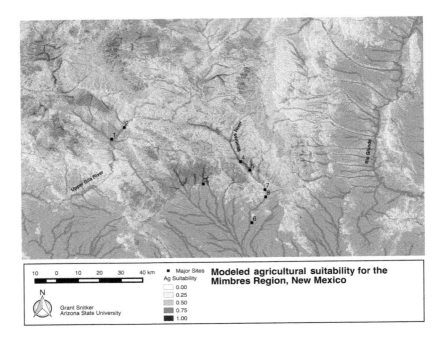

FIGURE 7.2. The suitability of land for agriculture across the Mimbres region, showing the major Classic period villages. 1 = Saige-McFarland, 2 = Woodrow, 3 = Cameron Creek, 4 = Mattocks, 5 = Galaz, 6 = Old Town, 7 = Swarts, 8 = NAN Ranch. Map prepared by Grant Snitker.

Mimbres villages are in or near these locales. The southern part of the Mimbres Valley was rated slightly less suitable, and the large villages along that part of the river were probably irrigating from the river and so less dependent on rainfall.

After centuries of fairly gradual development through the Pithouse periods, a dramatic event or series of events ushered in a time of rapid change. Most pithouse villages had great kivas, a form of communal ritual architecture, and the size of the kivas was roughly proportional to the size of the villages. In the first decades of the tenth century, nearly all of these structures burned, possibly simultaneously. Detailed architectural analysis concluded that the great kivas' destruction was deliberate and in many cases planned in advance (Creel and Anyon 2003), which in turn suggests that it was linked to deliberate and planned institutional change. Soon after, the pithouse villages were transformed into above-ground pueblos, often on the same sites; these were some of the largest and longest-lived sites in the Southwest at the time (outside the Hohokam region). Most of

TABLE 7.1. *Parameters used for the model used to generate the agricultural suitability map in Figure 7.2*

Parameter and weight	Categories and score	Data and justification
Elevation 15%	< 2000m = 3 2000–3000m = 2 > 3000m = 1	Digital Elevation Model (DEM) created from the US Geological Survey 1/3-Arc Second National Elevation Dataset (Gesch 2007). Elevation affects temperature, which in turn affects growth. In the Southwest most maize is grown below 3000m (Perales et al. 2003; Sandor et al. 2007).
Slope 35%	0–10% = 5 10–15% = 4 15–20% = 3 20–30% = 2 > 30% = 1	Slopes calculated based on DEM. Slope is an important factor in non-terraced cultivation. Dryland and semi-irrigated farming relies heavily on low slope contexts (Dorshow 2012; Kirkby 1973).
Hydrology 15%	< 200m from main channel = 5 200-500m from main channel = 4 < 100m from tributary = 3 100-200 from tributary = 2 Not near any watercourse = 0	Stream networks were created using a hydrology module that calculates flow paths using slope and elevation. Proximity to watercourses provides fields with water as a result of the water table and natural floods. Irrigation, known from some parts of the Mimbres region, would only be possible near watercourses.
Precipitation 35%	> 600 mm = 5 400–599 mm = 3 0–399 mm = 1	Precipitation maps generated using a climate retrodiction methodology that utilizes modern PRISM climate data to estimate past precipitation (Bocinsky and Kohler 2014; PRISM 2004). Estimates of annual precipitation requirements for maize based on research in New Mexico (Rhode 1995; Sandor et al. 2007). Data used here are the average annual precipitation from 1000–1100 CE, an interval of generally good and reliable precipitation, in contrast to the dry periods beginning ca. 1120.

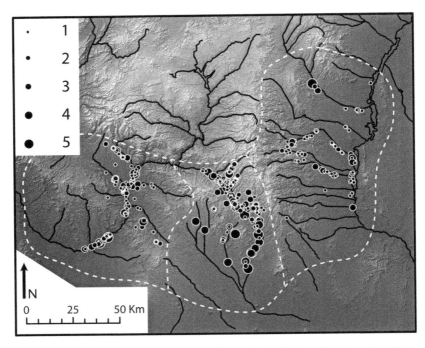

FIGURE 7.3. Distribution of settlements during the Mimbres Classic period. Size classes (in number of rooms) are as follows Class 1 = 3–10, Class 2 = 11–25, Class 3 = 26–50, Class 4 = 51–125, Class 5 = 126+. Figure prepared by Matthew Peeples.

the large villages were located on benches along the arable floodplain, and in some areas their fields were watered by ditch irrigation systems.

Population growth was an important part of these processes. Population generally increased over time, but it peaked during the Classic period as a result of both natural growth and substantial in-migration (Cordell et al. 1994:127). Recent estimates conclude that there were 2,737 people resident in the Mimbres Valley and 5,577 in the region as a whole during the Classic (Peeples 2010). These estimates assume sites were used for forty years, but if some were occupied for longer – likely for the larger villages especially in the Mimbres Valley – the actual population would have been higher. Settlement pattern maps (Figure 7.3) show the distribution of sites across the Mimbres region and the concentration of population in the Mimbres Valley.

Complexity: Technologies and Social Institutions
The burning of the great kivas began an era of demographic growth and increasing complexity in the Mimbres region, continuing through much of

the Classic period. This complexity took the form of intertwined new technologies and institutions. In Tainter's terms, the complexity might have addressed some of the challenges of in-migration and population growth by contributing to social integration and organizing access to land. At the same time, the complexity attracted more people, thus creating new challenges, a feedback process that is explored mathematically by Anderies and Hegmon (2011).

Probably the most visible new technology was the elaborate style of pottery painting illustrated in Figure 7.1. The tradition itself has deep roots: As early as 650 CE people painted red designs on brown pottery, then added a white slip, and established a black-on-white style by about 750 CE. Although the early designs were similar to those seen in other areas, the tenth century was a period of rapid innovation (Hegmon and Kulow 2005) roughly contemporaneous with the burning of the great kivas. In the eleventh century the designs, especially the representational tradition, become increasingly distinct from those seen in other regions (Hegmon and Nelson 2007). The elaborate design tradition of the Classic period (known as Mimbres Style III) is unlike anything else in the Southwest and is a product of a unique set of social institutions. Mimbres artists developed individually recognizable painting styles (LeBlanc 2006; Russell and Hegmon 2015) and emphasized creativity as they taught their craft to children (Crown 2001). LeBlanc (2010) suggests that these social institutions encouraged creativity and help explain why the art is so elaborate and stunning.

The painted pottery was also part of new institutions of marking graves and organizing multi-generational social units. Although the pottery was widely used in various contexts, many unbroken bowls were eventually deposited in burials. This mortuary complex is characteristic of the Classic period and is also unlike anything known from other parts of the Southwest. Mimbres roomblocks were often founded with a small set of rooms and then expanded over time. As later rooms were added, the earlier core rooms were used for burial; in some cases more than thirty interments – often with painted bowls placed over the skulls – were placed under the floors. Ethnographic comparisons suggest that the mortuary practices were a means of establishing ancestral claims to land through a heritable land tenure system (Shafer 2006). This interpretation is strengthened by the observation that this burial tradition is most evident in the large sites located near the arable floodplains. It is also linked to growing evidence of social inequality, which is discussed in more detail later.

The pottery was part of region-wide social institutions. Some components of the design tradition, including the representational designs as well as the layout, are quite homogenous across the region and thus symbolized a shared identity. As people migrated into the region, they maintained some of their former ways of doing things but they adopted the Mimbres style of pottery. This interpretation is supported by analyses that show considerable diversity in some realms (such as household organization) but strong homogeneity in the pottery designs (Hegmon 2010). This shared identity would have been reinforced by institutions such as feasting and exchange that distributed the pottery widely (Shafer 2013). Up and down the Mimbres Valley, every site has the same kinds of designs in roughly the same proportions (Hegmon et al. 2016). Studies of production and distribution show that some of the larger southern sites such as Old Town (which would have enjoyed long growing seasons but had less fuel for pottery making) imported all of their painted pottery (Creel et al. 2016), and some of the more northern sites such as Galaz controlled much of the pottery production. However, the distribution of the pottery had clear boundaries that separated the Mimbres region; during the Classic period sites within the region had almost no decorated pottery other than Mimbres, and very little Mimbres Style III pottery is found outside the region.

Intergenerational Tradeoffs: Food, Environmental, and Community Insecurity

People moved into the region attracted by both the good farming conditions and the emerging social institutions. The arrival of more people in turn led to the development and reinforcement of the social institutions in part as a means of managing access to land. The environmental conditions through much of the eleventh century would have encouraged this cycle. Specifically, a period of relatively higher and consistent rainfall during much of the eleventh century made it possible for people to expand into and farm upland areas (Minnis 1985). However, upland fields were watered only by direct rainfall or runoff from rainfall; they were vulnerable to changes in weather patterns and to the period of below-average rainfall that began around 1120 CE. In Tainter's terms, this expansion – both of the population and the settlement distribution – would have eroded the problem-solving capacity.

Early analyses, based on what were probably unreasonably large population estimates, concluded that the early twelfth century – the latter part of the Mimbres Classic period – was a time of food shortages and environmental degradation (Minnis 1985), although recent research has tempered this picture somewhat. Upland soils were degraded in some locales (Sandor et al. 1990) and floodplain vegetation was depleted (Minnis 1985).

However, there is no evidence that the agricultural potential of the flood-plain itself was degraded, especially since floodplains are replenished by periodic floods. Similarly, analyses of population and resources indicate that farming would have become more difficult and people may have had to work harder by utilizing less desirable areas or traveling further to fields (Pool 2002; Schollmeyer 2011). However, there is no evidence of actual food shortages or increasing nutritional problems.

The concepts of food and environmental insecurity are applicable to understanding these developments in the latter part of the Mimbres Classic. People were not starving, but the food quest was becoming more difficult; in addition to farming less productive fields, people were also eating less desirable foods (Minnis 1985). Pueblo farmers typically try to keep two to three years' worth of corn in storage (Burns 1983; see also Spielmann and Aggarwal, (Chapter 11) this volume), but this would likely have been impossible with the worsening conditions in the twelfth century. Also, because the floodplain was depleted, people would have had to use alternative resources for firewood and construction or travel further to gather resources. Cultural perceptions might have exacerbated the difficulties. In many non-Western societies, including those known in the Southwest, proper ritual maintains balance in the universe, causing the clouds and rain to come or sun to move through its cycle (Titiev 1992). Thus climatic downturns such as dry periods are interpreted as moral or cultural failures (see Lucero and Kinkella 2015).

Around 1130 CE, many people left the Mimbres villages, and the complex institutions that characterize the Mimbres Classic period came to an end. This is "simplification" in Tainter's terms. Some people left the region entirely; others moved to other parts of the region and established new residential hamlets. The reasons for the change are much debated and probably include the worsening food insecurity as well as events in other parts of the Southwest. What is clear is that the depopulation of long-lived villages would have eroded community security. Those who remained in the area would have seen many of their neighbors and relatives leave. Nelson and colleagues (Chapter 8, this volume) explore the compounding of vulnerabilities in this case: Not only could people no longer rely on some of their fields; they also could no longer depend on their social ties across the region.

Growth has tradeoffs that develop over time and cross generations. Some people, mostly those who lived in the early part of the Classic period, experienced more of the benefits of the growth and complexity including productive agricultural practices and flourishing cultural institutions.

Artists who lived at that time could establish individual traditions and would have seen their work traded and used across the region. Young people born at that time could have established new fields and attracted mates from other areas. Others, born a few generations later, bore the burdens as conditions became more difficult; they were the ones who had to grapple with the food and environmental insecurities. Ultimately, they, or their descendants, experienced the community insecurity as many people left the villages and the region.

This tradeoff in the Mimbres case provides an interesting comparison to and contrast with the Maya developments in the Puuc-Nohkakab sub-region analyzed by Isendahl and Heckbert (Chapter 6, this volume). In the Mimbres case, growth was in a particularly well-watered area, while in the Maya case the growth was in an area that needed considerable investment to capture and manage water. Both experienced similar cycles of growth and complexity followed by simplification, but the growth seems to have had different root causes.

Social Inequality: More Tradeoffs in the Mimbres Sequence

Anthropological and archaeological work in the US Southwest is expanding social scientists' understanding of social inequality (Hegmon 2005). On the one hand, in many Southwestern cultures, there is a strong egalitarian ethos, dislike of ostentatious display, and few overt material differences such as rich and poor houses or stores of wealth (Levy 1992; Ware 2014). On the other hand, there are clear social strata, often based on unequal access to knowledge and ritual (Brandt 1980, 1994). Although the differences are materially subtle, they have very real consequences. Drawing on his work with the Hopi, Levy (1992) argues that hierarchy was about the control of scarcity rather than wealth, and when times were bad, the high ranking clans determined who had food and who had to leave. In other words, there is a tradeoff in that food security for those at the top of the hierarchy came at the expense of food security for those lower in the hierarchy. (A contrasting situation, in which food security was widespread but participation in other aspects of social life was restricted, is described in Brewington's chapter on the Faroe Islands (Chapter 10, this volume.)

There is evidence that these kinds of inequality tradeoffs in ritual and food security developed in the Mimbres Classic period. The great kivas in the preceding Late Pithouse period were evenly distributed, suggesting that access was also fairly even and unrestricted. In contrast, the smaller kivas and other ritual spaces in the Classic are associated with only some roomblocks, suggesting there were inequalities in ritual access (Clayton 2006). There are no large differences in material wealth found in Classic burials (Gilman 1990), but some residential architecture is more substantial than others (Shafer 2003). Russell's ongoing research is exploring these issues in more depth (2016).

Across the Southwest, hereditary land tenure systems were an important component of social inequality. Some higher ranking people or corporate groups had privileged access to land, giving them a better subsistence base that in turn attracted followers and reinforced their status. In the archaeological record, multi-generational occupation of particular places, evidenced through architectural sequences and chronological dates, is interpreted as evidence for heritable land tenures systems (Adler 1996; Schriever 2012; Varien 1999). In the Mimbres region, the architectural and mortuary sequences indicate that the first-comers and their descendants controlled access to the best land (Shafer 2006). Patterns of architectural growth show that many roomblocks grew over time as people added on to initial core rooms. Through this process, they buried their dead in the core rooms thus marking their longstanding claims to land with their ancestors. Both cross-culturally and in other archaeological contexts, these kinds of practices are associated with "house societies," which tend to form at times of emerging social inequalities and emphasize differences among houses based on access to power (Plog and Heitman 2010).

The inequality can be understood as involving tradeoffs, in at least two senses. The first is inequality in general as a cost, a tradeoff against the benefits of growth and complexity. It is possible this tradeoff was perceived by some of the people who experienced it, who might have viewed inequality as an unwelcome development. As was discussed earlier, there is a strong egalitarian ethos in many Southwestern societies, despite the evidence of actual inequalities. Furthermore, in several cases, traditional histories view the rise of powerful people who tried to dominate others as a social aberration. For example, Lekson (2006:29) reports that Pueblo people view Chaco Canyon as a place where "people got power over people;" people today reject that way of life and do not want anything like Chaco ever again. Similar accounts are reported regarding Mesa Verde (Ortman 2012) and the great houses of the Hohokam Classic (Teague 2009). Building on these and similar insights, Arakawa (2012) views cycles of growth and decline in the Southwest as representing the emergence of and then resistance to social hierarchies.

At another level, there are also tradeoffs inherent in a system of social inequality, in that (as Tainter notes) the benefits of the cultural institutions are not enjoyed equally. The land tenure system might have provided necessary structure to land use, not unlike the Sheep Letter in the Faroes described by Brewington (Chapter 10, this volume). However, by its nature, a land tenure system assures access to land for some, while denying it to others. Those at the top of the hierarchy – the first-comers and their descendants – maintained food security at the expense of food insecurity for others who lacked privileged access to land. Here, as in many other examples in this volume, the gains and losses that comprise tradeoffs are distributed unevenly.

The Importance of Perspective: The Human Experience of "Simplification"

Life in the Mimbres region changed in many ways at around 1130 CE. Most of the large villages were partially or totally depopulated, many people left the region, and the spectacular pottery was no longer made. These events can reasonably be described as a "rapid simplification" and thus fit Tainter's definition of "collapse" (though see Torvinen et al. 2015). However, at least in this case, these changes do not indicate the end of a people or abandonment of the region (Nelson and Schachner 2002). This is one reason many researchers (e.g., McAnany and Yoffee 2009) are wary of the term collapse and its implications of disaster or failure. As Margaret Nelson and I have argued in a number of publications (e.g., Hegmon et al. 2008; Nelson 1999; Nelson et al. 2006;), the simplification that marks the end of the Mimbres Classic is best understood as a "regional reorganization:" a type of "social transformation" (see also B. Nelson et al. 2014). People changed their styles and some of them left the region, but others stayed in their homeland, building new residences in other parts of the region. People also returned to the large villages, sometimes burying their dead there in post-Classic times. We have also argued that the Mimbres transformation was relatively mild in comparison to social transformations that ended periods of growth in other areas, where there is evidence of violence, large-scale migrations, or rapid population decline (Hegmon et al. 2008).

It is possible to see all kinds of tradeoffs in the events that end a period of growth, and the nature of those tradeoffs depend very much on one's perspective. A dominant assumption in most historical sequences, including most of what has been presented so far in this chapter, is that growth is a positive development, and the end of growth (whether it is called simplification or collapse or reorganization or social transformation) is negative. This perspective informs the concept of an intergenerational tradeoff in which earlier generations reap the benefits and later generations bear the costs. Mimbres art grew – in both frequency and design elaboration and quality – early in the sequence and its disappearance after 1130 would have been a loss for people who participated in the cultural and mortuary tradition involving that pottery. The decline of the land tenure system would also have been a loss by those whom it privileged. However, from the perspective of other members of society, specifically those marginalized by the land tenure system, the simplification would have relieved them of the hierarchy and given them access to previously restricted resources. It could even be understood as a social rejection of hierarchy and inequality similar to that seen in other parts of the Southwest (Arakawa 2012). The simplification also relieved pressure on the local environment, allowing the floodplain vegetation and local fauna to recover (Minnis 1985; Schollmeyer 2011) and eventually increasing food security (Nelson et al., Chapter 8, this volume). In other words, a different perspective also sees tradeoffs, but with gains and losses reversed.

Conclusions and Implications

The general topic of this chapter is growth and the intersecting series of tradeoffs that result from growth. These issues are examined and illustrated with the archaeological example of the emergence and eventual end of the Mimbres Classic period (1000–1130 CE) in the US Southwest. Growth involves becoming larger and also better or improved, and both meanings apply to some of the developments in the Mimbres Classic. People moved into the ecologically attractive area and developed new social and artistic institutions that prompted more people to move in. The benefits of growth were probably experienced more, and more evenly, in the early part of the Classic. These benefits included the flourishing artistic tradition, social interactions and ritual participation, and opportunities to expand agriculture into new areas.

The growth was not sustainable, however. In this case, as in many others discussed in this volume, the downsides – tradeoffs – were mostly experienced by those who did not reap the benefits. The hereditary land tenure system would have provided food security for some at the expense of food insecurity for others. The challenges became more serious near the end of the Classic period, resulting in intergenerational tradeoffs. Those who lived during the last decades of the Classic would have experienced the brunt of the environmental and food insecurity, and ultimately community insecurity as people left their villages and some left the region.

This chapter perhaps illustrates why the field of sustainability was originally wary of considering tradeoffs (a point I discuss in more detail in
Chapter 1, this volume). The Mimbres Classic was mostly a good era, with
no evidence of violence or unusual nutritional problems compared to the
rest of the Southwest: Mimbres artists created a marvelous and unique
design style, and the end of the Classic was relatively mild. Enumerating
the tradeoffs implicated in all these accomplishments seems like such a
negative, even churlish view. Some perspective can be gained by returning
to the story of California and the Governors Brown, which opened this
chapter. Although he is a strong believer in "small is beautiful" (Schumacher 1973), Governor Brown, Jr. (Jerry) "said he would have done what his
father did if he had been governor" in that era, in those different times
(Nagourney 2015). It's true that neither Governor Brown, Sr. (Pat) nor the
people who lived early in the Mimbres Classic period created perfect win-
win situations. The point is not to somehow find fault with them, but to
understand their decisions, including the consequences and tradeoffs that
resulted from those decisions, and to learn from them. To that end, I close
with several general implications:

(1) *Inequality is a key issue in tradeoffs.* One of the tradeoffs of Mimbres
growth was increasing social inequality. And other tradeoffs that
eventuated, especially food insecurity, were unevenly distributed
across the social hierarchy. Social inequality is a key issue in archaeology and the world today, and an understanding of tradeoffs should
be an important component of research on inequality.

(2) *Perspective matters.* The insights gained by considering social
inequality make clear that how we see tradeoffs is very much a matter
of perspective. From an analytical perspective, growth involves tradeoffs – benefits for some, losses for others – but from the perspective of
some of the people involved, there might have been only benefits or
only losses. Explicit concern with perspective should be central to
any consideration of tradeoffs, and will provide meaningful insights
into the human experience of the tradeoffs.

(3) *Some tradeoffs are better than others.* As I said in Chapter 1 (this
volume) and as I have illustrated in this chapter, there are always
tradeoffs that can be seen as gains for some, losses for others. But this
realization should not lead to the conclusion that "anything goes."
There are better and worse, more and less equitable, more and less
painful tradeoffs. The more we understand them, an understanding
that can come from history, the more we are likely to be able to

make good decisions about them. In the parlance of path dependence, this is called "anticipatory governance."

Acknowledgments

This research is part of the Long Term Vulnerability and Transformation Project, which has been supported by NSF Dynamics of Coupled Natural and Human Systems (CNH) BCS-1113991 and NSF Biocomplexity BCS-0508001. I am grateful to Peggy Nelson and Frances Hayashida for specific comments on this chapter and to all the seminar participants for their many ideas and open minds. Mary Suter arranged for the photographs used in Figure 7.1. Grant Snitker did the analysis that resulted in Figure 7.2, which he prepared. Matt Peeples did the analysis that resulted in Figure 7.3, which he prepared.

References

Abbott, David R., Alexa M. Smith, and Emiliano Gallaga 2007 Ballcourts and Ceramics: The Case for Hohokam Marketplaces in the Arizona Desert. *American Antiquity* 72(3):461–484.

Adler, Michael A. 1996 Land Tenure, Archaeology, and the Ancestral Pueblo Social Landscape. *Journal of Anthropological Archaeology* 15(4):337–371.

Anderies, John M., and Michelle Hegmon 2011 Robustness and Resilience across Scales: Migration and Resource Degradation in the Prehistoric U.S. Southwest. *Ecology and Society* 16(2):22.

Anyon, Roger, Patricia A. Gilman, and Steven A. LeBlanc 1981 A Reevaluation of the Mogollon-Mimbres Archaeological Sequence. *Kiva* 46(4):209–225.

Arakawa, Fumiyasu 2012 Cyclical Cultural Trajectories: A Case Study from the Mesa Verde Region. *Journal of Anthropological Research* 68(1):35–69.

Ash, Caroline, Barbara R. Jasny, David A. Malakoff, and Andrew M. Sugden 2010 Introduction to Special Issue: Feeding the Future. *Science* 327(5967):797–797.

Bocinsky, R Kyle, and Timothy A Kohler 2014 A 2,000-year Reconstruction of the Rain-fed Maize Agricultural Niche in the US Southwest. *Nature Communications* 5:5618.

Brandt, Elizabeth A. 1980 On Secrecy and the Control of Knowledge: Taos Pueblo. In *Secrecy: A Cross-cultural Perspective*, edited by Stanton K. Teft, pp. 123–146. Human Sciences Press, New York.

1994 Egalitarianism, Hierarchy, and Centralization in the Pueblos. In *The Ancient Southwestern Community*, edited by W. H. Wills and Robert D. Leonard, pp. 9–24. University of New Mexico Press, Albuquerque.

Brody, J. J. 2004 *Mimbres Painted Pottery*, Revised Edition, School of American Research Press, Santa Fe.

Burns, Barney T. 1983 *Simulated Anasazi Storage Behavior Using Crop Yields Reconstructed from Tree Rings: A.D. 652-1968*. PhD dissertation, Department of Anthropology, University of Arizona, Tucson.

Clayton, Sarah C. 2006 Ritual and Residence: The Social Implications of Classic Mimbres Ceremonial Spaces. *Kiva* 72(1):71–92.

Cordell, Linda S., David E. Doyel, and Keith W. Kintigh 1994 Processes of Aggregation in the Prehistoric Southwest. In *Themes in Southwest Prehistory*, edited by George J. Gumerman, pp. 109–134. SAR Press, Santa Fe.

Creel, Darrell, and Roger Anyon 2003 New Interpretations of Mimbres Public Architecture and Space: Implications for Cultural Change. *American Antiquity* 68(1):67–92.

Creel, Darrell, and Robert J. Speakman 2016 Mimbres Pottery: New Perspectives on Production and Distribution. In *New Perspectives on Mimbres Archaeology: Three Millennia of Human Occupation in the Desert Southwest*, edited by Patricia Gilman, Roger Anyon, and Barbara Roth. University of Arizona Press, Tucson. In preparation.

Crown, Patricia L. 2001 Learning to Make Pottery in the Prehispanic American Southwest. *Journal of Anthropological Research* 57:451–470.

Diehl, Michael W., and Steven A. LeBlanc 2001 *Early Pithouse Villages of the Mimbres Valley and Beyond: The McAnally and Thompson Sites in Their Cultural and Ecological Contexts*. Papers of the Peabody Museum of Archaeology and Ethnology Vol. 83. Harvard University, Cambridge.

Dorshow, Wetherbee Bryan 2012 Modeling Agricultural Potential in Chaco Canyon during the Bonito Phase: A Predictive Geospatial Approach. *Journal of Archaeological Science* 39:2098–2115.

Food and Agriculture Organization of the United Nations 2014 *The State of Food Insecurity in the World: Strengthening the Enabling Environment for Food Security and Nutrition*. FAO, Rome.

Gesch, D. B. 2007 The National Elevation Dataset. In *Digital Elevation Model Technologies and Applications: The DEM Users Manual*, edited by D. Maune, pp. 99–118. American Society for Photogrammetry and Remote Sensing, Bethesda, Maryland.

Gilman, Patricia A. 1990 Social Organization and Classic Mimbres Period Burials in the SW United States. *Journal of Field Archaeology* 17:457–469.

Hegmon, Michelle 2002 Recent Issues in the Archaeology of the Mimbres Region of the North American Southwest. *Journal of Archaeological Research* 10 (4):307–357.

2005 Beyond the Mold: Questions of Inequality in Southwest Villages. In *North American Archaeology*, edited by T. R. Pauketat and D. DiPaolo Loren, pp. 212–234. Blackwell Publishing, Malden, MA.

2010 Mimbres Society: Another Way of Being. In *Mimbres: Lives and Landscapes*, edited by Margaret C. Nelson and Michelle Hegmon, pp. 39–45. School of Advanced Research Press, Santa Fe.

2013 The Archaeology of the Human Experience. *The SAA Archaeological Record* 13(5):16–19.

2016a (editor) *The Archaeology of the Human Experience*. Archaeological Papers of the American Anthropological Society. Volume 27.

2016b Path Dependence: Approaches in and for Southwest Archaeology. In *The Oxford Handbook of the Archaeology of the American Southwest*, edited by B. J. Mills and S. Fowles. Oxford University Press. Volume 27.

Hegmon, Michelle, and Stephanie Kulow 2005 Painting as Agency, Style as Structure: Analyses of Mimbres Pottery Designs from Southwest New Mexico. *Journal of Archaeological Method and Theory* 12(4):313–334.

Hegmon, Michelle, and Margaret C. Nelson 2007 In Sync, but Barely in Touch: Relations between the Mimbres Region and the Hohokam Regional System. In *Hinterlands and Regional Dynamics in the Ancient Southwest*, edited by Alan P. Sullivan and James Bayman, pp. 70–96. University of Arizona Press, Tucson.

Hegmon, Michelle, Margaret C. Nelson, Roger Anyon, Darrell Creel, Steven LeBlanc, and Harry Shafer 1999 Scale and Time-Space Systematics in the Post-A.D. 1100 Mimbres Region of the North American Southwest. *Kiva* 65:143–166.

Hegmon, Michelle, Margaret C. Nelson, and Karen Gust Schollmeyer 2016 Experiencing Social Change: Life during the Mimbres Classic Transformation. In *The Archaeology of the Human Experience*, edited by M. Hegmon. Archaeological Papers of the American Anthropological Association. Volume 27, 54–73.

Hegmon, Michelle, Matthew Peeples, Ann Kinzig, Stephanie Kulow, Cathryn M. Meegan, and Margaret C. Nelson 2008 Social Transformation and Its Human Costs in the Prehispanic U.S. Southwest. *American Anthropologist* 110(3):313–324.

Kantner, John 2003 Preface: The Chaco World. *Kiva* 69:83–92.

Kirkby, A. 1973 *The Use of Land and Water Resources in the Past and Present Valley of Oaxaca, Mexico*. Memoirs of the Museum of Anthropology No. 5. University of Michigan, Ann Arbor.

LeBlanc, Steven A. 2006 Who Made the Mimbres Bowls? Implications of Recognizing Individual Artists for Craft Specialization and Social Networks. In *Mimbres Society*, edited by Valli S. Powell-Martí and Patricia A. Gilman, pp. 109–150. University of Arizona Press, Tucson.

2010 The Painters of the Pots. In *Mimbres: Lives and Landscapes*, edited by Margaret Nelson and Michelle Hegmon, pp. 74–81. SAR Press, Santa Fe.

Lekson, Stephen H. (editor) 2006 *The Archaeology of Chaco Canyon: An Eleventh Century Pueblo Regional Center*. SAR Press, Santa Fe.

Levang, Patrice, Soaduon Sitorus, and Edmond Dounias 2007 City Life in the Midst of the Forest: A Punan Hunter-gatherer's Vision of Conservation and Development. *Ecology and Society* 12(1):18.

Levy, Jerrold E. 1992 *Orayvi Revisited: Social Stratification in an "Egalitarian" Society*. School for Advanced Research Press, Santa Fe.

Lucero, Lisa J., and Andrew Kinkella 2015 Pilgrimage to the Edge of the Watery Underworld: An Ancient Maya Water Temple at Cara Blanca, Belize. *Cambridge Archaeological Journal* 25:163–185.

McAnany, Patricia A., and Norman Yoffee (editors) 2009 *Questioning Collapse: Human Resilience, Ecological Vulnerability, and the Aftermath of Empire*. Cambridge University Press, Cambridge.

Meadows, Donella H., Dennis L. Meadows, Jorgen Randers, and Williams W. Behrens 1972 *The Limits to Growth*. Universe Books, New York.

Merrill, Michael 2014 *Increasing Scales of Social Interaction and the Role of Lake Cahuilla in the Systemic Fragility of the Hohokam System (A.D. 700-1100)*. Unpublished PhD dissertation in Anthropology, Arizona State University.

Minnis, Paul E. 1985 *Social Adaptation to Food Stress: A Prehistoric Southwestern Example*. University of Chicago Press, Chicago.

Nagourney, Adam 2015 Brown's Arid California, Thanks Partly to His Father. *New York Times*, May 16.

Nelson, Ben A., Adrian S.Z. Chase, and Michelle Hegmon 2014 Comparative Landscapes: Transformative Relocation in the American Southwest and Mesoamerica. In *The Resilience and Vulnerability of Ancient Landscapes: Transforming Maya Archaeology through IHOPE*, edited by Arlen F. Chase and Vernon L. Scarborough. Papers of the Archaeology Division of the American Anthropological Association, Vol 24, pp. 171–182. Washington, DC.

Nelson, Margaret C. 1999 *Mimbres During the Twelfth Century: Abandonment, Continuity, and Reorganization*. University of Arizona Press, Tucson.

Nelson, Margaret C., and Gregson Schachner 2002 Understanding Abandonments in the North American Southwest. *Journal of Archaeological Research* 10(2):167–206.

Nelson, Margaret C., Michelle Hegmon, Stephanie Kulow, and Karen Gust Schollmeyer 2006 Archaeological and Ecological Perspectives on Reorganization: A Case Study from the Mimbres Region of the U.S. Southwest. *American Antiquity* 71(3):403–432.

Peeples, Matthew A. 2010 The Demographic Context of Social and Ecological Change: An Example from the Mimbres Region of New Mexico. Manuscript in possession of author.

Perales, Hugo R., S. B. Brush, and C. O. Qualset 2003 Dynamic Management of Maize Landraces in Central Mexico. *Economic Botany* 57(1):21–34.

Plog, Stephen, and Carrie Heitman 2010 Hierarchy and Social Inequality in the American Southwest, AD 800–1200. *Proceedings of the National Academy of Sciences* 107(46):19619–19626.

Pool, Michael David 2002 Prehistoric Mogollon Agriculture in the Mimbres River Valley, Southwestern New Mexico: A Crop Simulation and GIS Approach. Unpublished PhD dissertation, Department of Anthropology, University of Texas, Austin.

PRISM 2004 Climate Group, Oregon State University, http://prism.oregonstate .edu, created 4 Feb 2004.

Robb, John, and Timothy R. Pauketat (editors) 2013 *Big Histories, Human Lives: Tackling Problems of Scale in Archaeology*. SAR Press, Santa Fe.

Rarick, Ethan 2006 *California Rising: The Life and Times of Pat Brown*. University of California Press, Berkeley.

Rhode, D., 1995 Estimating Agricultural Carrying Capacity in the Zuni Region, West-Central New Mexico: A Water Allocation Model. In *Soil, Water, Biology, and Belief in Prehistoric and Traditional Southwestern Agriculture*, edited by H. W. Toll, pp. 85–100. New Mexico Archaeological Council, Albuquerque.

Russell, Will G., and Michelle Hegmon 2015 Identifying Mimbres Artists: A Quantitative Approach. *Advances in Archaeological Practice*. In press.

Sandor, Jonathan A., Paul L. Gersper, and John W. Hawley 1990 Prehistoric Agricultural Terraces and Soils in the Mimbres Area, New Mexico. *World Archaeology* 22:70–86.

Sandor, J. A., Norton, J. B., Homburg, J. A., Muenchrath, D. A., White, C. S., Williams, S. E., Havener, C. I., and Stahl, P. D. 2007 Biogeochemical Studies of a Native American Runoff Agroecosystem. *Geoarchaeology* 22:359–386.

Schollmeyer, Karen Gust 2011 Large Game, Agricultural Land, and Settlement Pattern Change in the Eastern Mimbres Area, Southwest New Mexico. *Journal of Anthropological Archaeology* 30:402–415.

Schriever, Bernard A. 2012 Mobility, Land Tenure, and Social Identity in the San Simon Basin of Southeastern Arizona. *Kiva* 77:413–438.

Schumacher, E. F. 1973 *Small Is Beautiful: A Study of Economics as if People Mattered*. Blond and Briggs, New York.

Shafer, Harry J. 2003 *Mimbres Archaeology at the NAN Ranch Ruin*. University of New Mexico Press, Albuquerque.

2006 Extended Families to Corporate Groups: Pithouse to Pueblo Transformation of Mimbres Society. In *Mimbres Society*, edited by Valli S. Powell-Marti and Patricia A. Gilman, pp. 15–31. University of Arizona Press, Tucson.

2013 Possible Archaeological Evidence for Classic Mimbres use of Tesquino at the NAN Ranch Ruin, Southwest New Mexico. In *Collected Papers of the 17th Biennial Mogollon Archaeology Conference*, edited by Lonnie Ludeman, pp. 109–117. Las Cruces, New Mexico.

Tainter, Joseph 1990 *The Collapse of Complex Societies*. Cambridge University Press, Cambridge.

Tainter, Joseph A., and Temis G. Taylor. 2014 Complexity, Problem-solving, Sustainability and Resilience. *Building Research & Information* 42(2): 168–181.

Teague, Lynn S. 2009 Prehistory and the Traditions of the O'odham and Hopi. *Kiva* 75(2):239–259.

Titiev, Mischa 1992 *Old Oraibi: A Study of the Hopi Indians of Third Mesa*. University of New Mexico Press, Albuquerque.

Torvinen, Andrea, Michelle Hegmon, Ann P. Kinzig, Margaret C. Nelson, Matthew A. Peeples, Karen G. Schollmeyer, Colleen Strawhacker, and Laura Swantek 2015 Transformation Without Collapse: Two Cases from the U.S. Southwest. In *Beyond Collapse: Archaeological Perspectives on Resilience, Revitalization, and Transformation in Complex Societies*, edited by R. K. Faulseit, pp. 262–286. Southern Illinois University Press, Carbondale.

Trawick, Paul, and Alf Hornborg 2015 Revisiting the Image of Limited Good: On Sustainability, Thermodynamics, and the Illusion of Creating Wealth. *Current Anthropology* 56(1):1–27.

Varien, Mark D. 1999 *Sedentism and Mobility in a Social Landscape: Mesa Verde and Beyond*. University of Arizona Press, Tucson.

Ware, John A. 2014 *A Pueblo Social History: Kinship, Sodality, and Community in the Northern Southwest*. SAR Press, Santa Fe.

8

Vulnerability to Food Insecurity

Tradeoffs and Their Consequences

MARGARET C. NELSON, ANN P. KINZIG, JETTE ARNEBORG,
RICHARD STREETER, AND SCOTT E. INGRAM

In this chapter, we are interested in food security – how it is achieved, what tradeoffs are made to achieve it, and how people become vulnerable to shortage, especially under climate challenges. Accomplishing food security involves tradeoffs and creates some degree of vulnerability. And the state of security, or "load of vulnerability" as we describe it in this chapter, is constantly changing as conditions change and people act (IPCC 2012). So there is no perfect, enduring achievement of food security both because conditions change and because any decisions or actions to attain security have tradeoffs.

Nearly all of the decisions we make, as individuals and as societies, involve tradeoffs large and small. Those involving food systems are quite varied. Dearing and colleagues (2014) describe tradeoffs in Chinese agricultural intensification that reduce poverty but increase environmental degradation. They also reference a study by Erb and colleagues (2008) documenting the tradeoff over time in Austria as fossil fuel was substituted for biomass as an energy source. Gains in food supply and forest cover were accomplished while greenhouse gas emissions increased. Turner and colleagues (2003) describe different kinds of tradeoffs in chili farming in southern Yucatan: between raising income and raising vulnerability to variation in yield, between land clearance to create farmland and vulnerability to deforestation and hurricane impacts on forests, between intensification of farming and vulnerability to pests and disease.

These tradeoffs are often not addressed as we make decisions and design policies. Consider an example close to our individual lives. The cell phone has improved communication and access to information, especially in remote areas. But at what cost? Have we considered the environmental, material, and social costs of cordless phones? Are there long-run consequences or vulnerabilities created by our reliance on them? Hurricane Sandy in the New York area made clear our vulnerability to electrical outage when relying on cordless phones for communication (Johnston 2012). When electricity was disabled, communication was disabled. "Attention to the spatial and temporal dynamics of exposure and vulnerability is particularly important given that the design and implementation of adaptation and disaster risk management strategies and policies can reduce risk in the short term, but may increase exposure and vulnerability over the longer term" (IPCC 2012:9).

In this paper we consider how actions that enhance food security in the context of climate challenges have tradeoffs. People create new vulnerabilities or may worsen existing vulnerabilities simply by acting to solve a problem, in this case a food security challenge. We characterize this as the resilience-vulnerability tradeoff[1]. By increasing resilience to food shortage at one point in time, new vulnerabilities can be created about which people may be unaware or inattentive.

In an earlier paper, colleagues and we examined the relationship between vulnerability to food shortfall and the magnitude of impacts of climate challenges over long sequences documented by archaeologists and historians in the US Southwest and the North Atlantic Islands (Nelson et al. 2015). We found a consistent relationship between preconditions of vulnerability and consequences of climate challenges. Our research responded to the call for information on the role of vulnerability in climate related disasters: "Understanding the multi-faceted nature of ...vulnerability is a prerequisite for determining how weather and climate events contribute to the occurrence of disasters, and for designing and implementing effective adaptation and disaster risk management" (IPCC 2012:8).

In this paper, we build on this study and explore two cases of resilience-vulnerability tradeoffs related to food security. In the first, people displaced food provisioning challenges over time. Specifically, Norse Greenlanders

---

[1] The term robustness-vulnerability tradeoff also appears in the literature. Both resilience and robustness have multiple meanings, ranging from an ability to resist change to an ability to maintain function under changing conditions. We are using robustness and resilience interchangeably to mean the ability to maintain essential functions or services under different conditions.

responded to immediate climate challenges by changing their selection of food resources in order to maintain food supplies in the short term. However, these strategies substantially increased their vulnerability to food shortfall, a vulnerability that was later realized when a subsequent climate challenge further reduced access to food resources, which contributed to the final end of the Norse occupation in Greenland. The second tradeoff is across different kinds of human securities rather than time. We refer to the different securities as domains. In this case from the pre-Hispanic Mimbres region of the US Southwest, changes in mobility and changes in settlement allowed people to maintain food security under conditions of climate challenges, However, the changes in mobility and settlement involved major social and demographic changes and thus reduced community security. These cases illustrate the importance of attention to the tradeoffs we make – solving one challenge creates others. While we cannot eliminate vulnerabilities we can endeavor to balance, and minimize, the vulnerabilities we create (Schoon et al. 2011).

Our Approach

In 1994 The United Nations issued the *Human Development Report*, in which it redirected attention from "national security" to "human security," a concept argued to revolutionize society because of its focus on life and dignity (UNDP 1994:22; see also Barnett et al. 2010). "Security in general refers to freedom from the risk of loss or damage to a thing that is important to survival and wellbeing" (Barnett et al. 2010: 5). Among the seven human securities is food security – "physical and economic access to basic food" (UNDP 1994:27). Amartya Sen (1999; 2005), in discussing poverty and inequality, argues that the capability of individuals to function is foundational to such access. Yet that capability can be limited by structural conditions that create vulnerabilities to shortfalls that people are not capable of overcoming. People are agents of change as long as they have the capabilities (Sen 1999) or capacities (Barnett 2010) to plan for and adapt to changing conditions.

   Numerous environmental and social conditions create vulnerabilities to shortfall in food. Neal Adger has offered an excellent review of various uses of the term vulnerability. He defines it as "the state of susceptibility to harm from exposure to stresses associated with environmental and social change and from the absence of capacity to adapt" (Adger 2006:268; see also Turner et al. 2003). Vulnerability to climate challenges does not exist outside the wider political economy and is mediated by institutional structures (Adger 2006:270–271; Burton et al. 1993; Hewitt 1983). That is, people create vulnerabilities, which may be experienced by themselves or by others, through their social and political decision making and through the design of their institutions. In addition, social and environmental interactions are constantly changing and impacting people's capability to avoid declines in food security. The IPCC has argued that "inequalities influence local coping and adaptive capacity, and pose disaster risk management and adaptation challenges" (IPCC 2012:8).

Arguing from a resilience perspective, some authors suggest that efforts to improve resilience of a system always involve tradeoffs. Anderies and others (Anderies 2006; Janssen and Anderies 2007; Anderies et al. 2007; Scheffer et al. 2001) have suggested that resilience, at a particular focal scale, is not an absolute; rather, to understand resilience, we must consider tradeoffs between resilience and vulnerability with respect to different classes of uncertainties. Nelson et al. (2010) have shown how water management systems that increase robustness to fluctuating climate conditions can create vulnerabilities to longer-term processes and rare climate events. Their analysis of three sequences of socio-environmental change, spanning many centuries in the US Southwest, illustrates differences in the robustness-vulnerability tradeoffs across different social-ecological contexts. Anderies and colleagues, evaluating modern fisheries as well as pre-Hispanic water control systems for agriculture, found that for their cases "policies robust to uncertainty in one group of parameters are … vulnerable to uncertainty in another group" (Anderies et al. 2007:15194). Tradeoffs can occur among social groups, between domains, and across temporal and spatial scales (Schoon et al. 2011). The best we can expect to do is to minimize susceptibility to selected vulnerabilities and attempt to manage for general resilience (Schoon et al. 2011). To do this we must be aware that tradeoffs occur and what they might be. One of the key findings of the IPCC in its 2012 Special Report on Climate Change is that "Multi-hazard risk management approaches provide opportunities to reduce complex and compounding hazards … Considering multiple types of hazards reduces the likelihood that risk reduction efforts targeting one type of hazard will increase exposure and vulnerability to other hazards" (IPCC 2012:15).

Dealing effectively with uncertainty and change demands attention to a variety of domains and scales. The long-term record of archaeologically and historically documented cases provides an opportunity to identify where tradeoffs were made, what new vulnerabilities were created, and how these tradeoffs played out over time. Archaeological and historical sequences are not sources of "lessons" as much as they are sources of information on how people's decisions and actions created vulnerabilities and how these vulnerabilities played out under different kinds of challenges. This research posits that addressing vulnerabilities to food shortages at one time and place creates tradeoffs that can lead to unintended consequences. That process in the past can illuminate contemporary decision making by pointing to the importance of recognizing and weighing tradeoffs. This potential for archaeological and historical studies is well-stated by two of our colleagues:

> Today, as in the past, people face major challenges. Some are new (global warming) while others (ethnic conflict) were problems in antiquity. Archaeology's long-term view is helpful because it can examine problems of ancient societies to see how they responded. We can also see how their solutions worked out in the short run and the long run. Engaging the cultural histories of different peoples can help us move beyond the confines of our own reality to consider a broader range of possible solutions and possible futures. (Kintigh and Redman 2013)

As people attempt to cope with variation and vulnerabilities at particular scales and in particular domains, we must be keenly aware of the tradeoffs generated at other scales and in other domains. Lack of such awareness is a recipe for a costly and likely unpleasant transformation. Armed with this awareness, people can better weigh the implications of their decisions, and attempt to build general resilience to respond if and when potential vulnerabilities are realized.

Our Initial Study

An initial study of vulnerabilities to food shortfall from climate challenges examined archaeological and historical information from centuries of occupation on the North Atlantic Islands of Iceland, Greenland, and the Faroes and in the US Southwest pre-Hispanic cultural regions of Zuni, Salinas, Mimbres, and Hohokam (Nelson et al. 2015). Challenges included extreme dry periods in the US Southwest and extreme cold and ice or regime shifts in the North Atlantic Islands. Our current exploration of tradeoffs derives from patterning recognized in that study. Thus, we summarize the study and its outcomes.

Why compare such different parts of the world? The cases we explore are centuries-long occupations of very different regions of the world – the arid

US Southwest and the sub-polar North Atlantic Islands. Patterns in one region or impacts of one type of climate challenge can be interpreted as only regionally informative. In contrast, the cases we consider and compare are from different climate regimes, physiographic regions, cultural traditions, and historical contexts. Patterns evident in this diverse data base indicate relationships between vulnerability and the impacts of climate challenges that have import for resilience planning and disaster management generally.

The three North Atlantic cases include Norse occupations in Iceland (McGovern 2007; Vésteinsson and McGovern 2012; Vésteinsson et al. 2006), Greenland (Arneborg 2008), and the Faroe Islands (Arge 2005; Brewington [Chapter 10, this volume]) beginning in the late ninth and early tenth centuries. Our data extend into the eighteenth century, except in Greenland, which was depopulated by the Norse in the fifteenth century. Data derive from decades of research by the North Atlantic Biocultural Organization (NABO, www.nabohome.org/).

The cases from the US Southwest and Northern Mexico are all indigenous occupations during the tenth to sixteenth centuries, though for this study we use only the US Southwest cases. Data derive from work by the Long-Term Vulnerability and Transformation Project (LTVTP), including field, laboratory, and records research in Zuni (Kintigh et al. 2004; Peeples et al. 2015), Salinas (Spielmann et al. 2011), Mimbres (Hegmon 2002; Nelson et al. 2006), and Hohokam (Abbott 2003; Ingram 2010) archaeological regions.

We began the study by identifying rare climate challenges, events so unusual that they had not been experienced in at least four centuries and had considerable potential to result in disaster (Nelson et al. 2015). The two major regions have quite different climate data and fundamentally different kinds of climate challenges. For the US Southwest, extreme dry periods were identified using tree-ring annual records (Ingram 2010; Nelson et al. 2015). For the North Atlantic, rare events include extreme cold temperatures, sea ice, and/or storminess or regime shifts in these conditions. Because the Norse occupation of the North Atlantic is described in historic documents, these along with proxy records on temperature, sea ice, and storminess were used to identify unprecedented events during the period 900 to 1900 CE (Nelson et al. 2015). Thirteen events were identified for the two regions (Table 8.1).

We then characterized vulnerability to food shortage prior to each of these thirteen climate challenges using eight variables that can potentially impact food security:

(1) Availability of food on the landscape (population-resource balance).
(2) Diversity of food resources.
(3) Health/sustainability of available resources.
(4) Social connections (risk sharing options).
(5) Adequate storage.
(6) Mobility (ability to move away from the problem).
(7) Equal access to resources.
(8) Lack of barriers to resource areas.

To quantify the contribution of each variable to the pre-condition of vulnerability to food shortage, we used a qualitative ranking (1 through 4) to assess each variable's contribution to vulnerability to food shortage. For example, if the resource base is healthy and sustainable, Variable 3 would get a ranking of 1, indicating that it does not negatively impact food security. If resources are mildly depleted, though not permanently degraded, Variable 3 would get a ranking of 2, indicating some negative impact on food security, and if the resources are severely degraded,

TABLE 8.1. *Rare climate challenges: Extremes and climate system regime changes*

Regions	Cases	Initiation date of challenge (CE)	Kind of climate challenge
US Southwest	Zuni	1133	Extreme dry
	Salinas	1335	Extreme dry
	Mimbres 1	1127	Extreme dry
	Mimbres 2	1273	Extreme dry
	Hohokam 1	1338	Extreme dry
	Hohokam 2	1436	Extreme dry
North Atlantic	Greenland 1	1257	Extreme cold
	Greenland 2	ca. 1310	Regime change to colder system with increasing sea ice extent
	Greenland 3	ca. 1421	Regime change to stormier system, Extreme cold
	Iceland 1	1257	Extreme cold shock
	Iceland 2	ca. 1310	Regime change to colder system with appearance of sea ice
	Iceland 3	1640	Extreme cold and greatest extent of sea ice
	Faroes	1257	Extreme cold

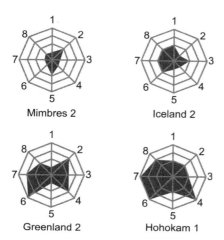

FIGURE 8.1. Vulnerability loads to food shortage for four cases.

Variable 3 would get a ranking of 4, indicating a strong negative impact on food security.

Using this approach we compared the amount of vulnerability prior to each rare, extreme climate challenge. Four of the thirteen cases are shown as spider graphs in Figure 8.1 to illustrate a range of outcomes of this analysis. Each radius in the web represents one of the variables listed above, and the size of the outlined area within the web of each graph represents the vulnerability load and makes comparison visually simple. Mimbres 2 has the least vulnerability to food shortage prior to a rare, extreme climate challenge. Only two variables contribute to that load – lack of diversity of available resources and lack of adequate storage – and their contribution to vulnerability is slight. Hohokam 1 has the greatest vulnerability load of this set of four cases. Every variable impacts the vulnerability to food shortage, especially those in the social domain (Variables 4–8).

Figure 8.2 compares the vulnerability precondition in each case to the scale and degree of social change and food shortage following a climate challenge. The distribution of vulnerability load before each of the thirteen climate challenges is plotted in descending order (i.e., Hohokam 2, at the top of the y-axis, had the greatest vulnerability load, and Mimbres 2, at the bottom, had the least). The right side shows this distribution, with the scale of social change after each climate challenge represented by shapes and tones on a grey scale as indicated on the illustration. Transformation (dark grey triangle) includes both considerable population decline and

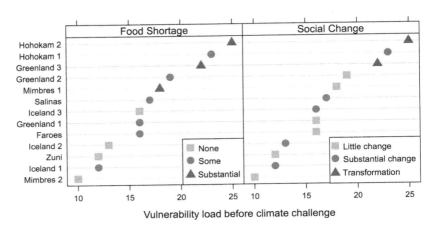

FIGURE 8.2. Social change and food conditions following climate challenges in relation to vulnerability load prior to climate challenges (adapted from Nelson et al. 2015:figure 1).

disappearance of key social institutions and structures (Hegmon et al. 2008; Torvinen et al. 2015). Substantial changes (grey circle) are changes in social institutions and structures without demographic decline. These rankings are based on empirical archaeological and historical evidence documented in Nelson et al. (2015, Supporting Information #3). Those cases with preconditions of relatively low vulnerability are also those with little or no social change following a climate challenge. In contrast, transformations occur in cases with the highest vulnerability load. Not all social changes are bad for people, but they do represent changes in the structural relationships that influence human capability for securing livelihood and they can create uncertainty.

Food shortage is considered on the left side of Figure 8.2. Again the shape and grey scale of the points indicate the extent of food shortage after the climate challenge: a light grey square indicates no shortage, a grey circle indicates either limited shortage experienced by all or extensive shortage by some, a dark triangle indicates extensive shortage for all. This shortage is due most often to access and institutional decline rather than resource shortfalls. The pattern of food shortage does not follow the pattern of preconditions of vulnerability as clearly as social change does, except that substantial food shortage only occurred in the cases with the highest vulnerability load.

This prior research indicates that the vulnerabilities created by human actions and decisions, whether intentional or not, correlate to some extent with the outcomes or impacts following climate challenges. One conclusion of the study supports disaster management recommendations that reducing vulnerability can reduce the scale of impact of climate challenges (Nelson et al. 2015). But all actions and decisions involve tradeoffs. Reducing vulnerability in one arena or at one time may increase it for another.

In this study, our analysis focuses on tradeoffs that created vulnerabilities and resulted in unanticipated outcomes in the Greenland and Mimbres cases. Note that the left side of Figure 8.2 shows that from Greenland 2 (ca 1310 CE) to Greenland 3 (ca 1421 CE), vulnerability to food shortage became larger prior to the climate challenge. The right side shows that social change following the climate challenge became more dramatic, ending in the total depopulation of Norse Greenland in the late fifteenth century. The Mimbres example follows an opposite pattern in that vulnerability to food shortage and scales of subsequent social change following climate challenges improved from Mimbres 1 (1127 CE) to Mimbres 2 (1273 CE). But the transformation following Mimbres 1 involved substantial depopulation of the region and transformation in major social institutions. Greenland 3, the third climate challenge, was followed by severe limitations on access to food. In Mimbres no shortage was experienced even though vulnerability to food shortfall was high before Mimbres 1. We return to these cases below to examine how tradeoffs were integral to these outcomes.

Kicking the Can Down the Road: Tradeoffs between Immediate and Future Food Challenges in Norse Greenland

> "The most effective adaptation and disaster reduction actions are those that offer development benefits in the relatively near term, as well as reductions in vulnerability over the long term (high agreement, medium evidence). There are tradeoffs between current decisions and long-term goals."
>
> (IPCC 2012: 18 Key finding).

The case of Norse occupation of Greenland (Figure 8.3) offers a view of the complex interaction between human decisions in the socioeconomic realm and climate conditions. Greenland was first occupied by the Norse in the ninth century and the last Norse settlement ended in the mid-fifteenth century. Figure 8.4 shows the setting of a Norse farm in the

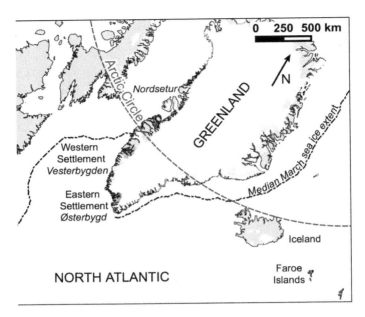

FIGURE 8.3. North Atlantic Islands of Greenland, Iceland, and the Faroes. Figure prepared by Richard Streeter.

Eastern Settlement. Climate factors and social factors together played a role in the end of the Norse occupation. For this study we are focused exclusively on decisions regarding food security. The tradeoff develops over time: a decision that addressed the potential for shortfall under a challenging climate regime increased vulnerability to shortfall later in time. The vulnerability was realized when a rare climate challenge further impacted food security.

Figure 8.5 illustrates estimated changes in the vulnerability load in Greenland from the mid-thirteenth century to the early fifteenth century. The greater the darkened area the greater the vulnerability load. This spider graph also shows the extent to which eight variables contribute to the vulnerability to food shortfall (these are described earlier in the chapter). Of particular interest to this discussion of tradeoffs is the gradual decline in resource diversity, which is indicated by an increase in the value of variable 2. Looking across the three time blocks in Figure 8.5, variable 2 increasingly contributes to vulnerability load, as indicated by the higher value along that radius of the spider graph. In the mid-thirteenth century (left side of Figure 8.5), farming decreased while seal hunting increased (Arneborg et al. 2012; Bichet et al. 2014; Enghoff 2003; McGovern 1985),

FIGURE 8.4. A Norse farm in the Eastern Settlement of Greenland. Photo by Jette Arneborg.

mildly impacting the diversity of food resources. By the early fourteenth century (center of Figure 8.5), a change in climate regime to a colder system made grazing even more difficult than it had been in the mid to late thirteenth century. People responded by decreasing their investments in domesticated animals and focusing on marine resources to an even greater extent (Arge et al. 2005; Arneborg et al. 2012; Enghoff 2003). This strategy addressed the challenges posed by the extreme cold, but reduced the diversity of food resources and increased vulnerability to food shortage (indicated by the size of the shaded area in Figure 8.5), especially to conditions of sea ice and storminess. In addition, people had to travel from mid- to inner-fjord settlements to outer coast to obtain their reliable marine food resources, a dangerous journey in open boats (Dugmore et al. 2007).

Other major contributors to vulnerability of food shortage that developed in the fourteenth century were difficulty with mobility (radius 6 in Figure 8.5) and decline in social connections (radius 4 in Figure 8.5) resulting from the isolation of the Norse settlements. In the thirteenth century, Greenland had been relatively well-connected to northern Europe, especially because of Norwegian control of the Greenland Norse

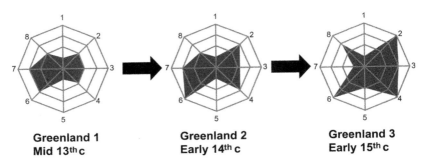

Greenland 1   Greenland 2   Greenland 3
Mid 13th c   Early 14th c   Early 15th c

FIGURE 8.5. Changes in vulnerability load over time in Greenland. The final stage ended in the abandonment of Greenland by the Norse.

settlements. In the early and mid-fourteenth century, Greenland still had a Bishop and a valuable ivory trade, but by the end of the fourteenth century contact with Norway had declined (Arneborg 1991). Additionally, contact with the Inuit had complicated assess to resource areas (radius 8 in Figure 8.5), and harbor seals had been depleted (radius 3 in Figure 8.5), reducing potential food. In the early to mid-fifteenth century, another rare climate challenge hit Greenland – a regime shift to extreme storminess. This event compromised access by people to the marine food base, which was the primary food resource. Though we have no data on starvation conditions or precisely what happened to the Norse in Greenland, most experts agree that they moved away from the problem by leaving Greenland for other islands or for northern Europe (Arneborg 2008; Dugmore et al. 2012). Whatever the specific outcome, the Norse settlement of Greenland ceased.

Many factors contributed to this end. Deterioration of relations with northern Europe and potential contestation with Inuit indirectly and unintentionally influenced vulnerability to food shortfall. The decision in early mid-fourteenth century to focus the food base on marine resources addressed the climate challenges to food supply at that time but increased vulnerability by reducing the diversity of food resources used. That vulnerability, created by relying on a limited resource base at a distance from Norse settlements, was realized following another climate challenge roughly a century later and contributed to the end of Norse occupation in Greenland.

Could the Norse Greenlanders have done otherwise? Kept domestic animals? Engaged in other networks with Norse in Iceland or northern Europe? Avoided the shift to a marine-focused diet? Certainly, their departure was not inevitable, as the Inuit, with whom they had contact by at least the fifteenth century, were present at the time of their departure.

The Inuit would have needed an adequate food supply. Perhaps the perspective the Norse had on their landscape, their technology, and/or their society made their end inevitable. We should ask these questions of the Norse case, and also of our own actions. Can we avoid increasing vulnerability by considering the potential long-term consequences of solving immediate concerns? And what are our range of options and the vulnerabilities created by them?

Tradeoffs between Human Securities: The Mimbres Case

> "Actions are framed by tradeoffs between competing prioritized values and objectives, and different visions of development that can change over time"
>
> (IPCC 2012: 18)

The Mimbres case (Figure 8.6; see also the discussion and photos in the preceding Chapter 7) illustrates a different kind of tradeoff. Rather than a tradeoff between immediate needs and later consequences, as in Norse Greenland, the tradeoff is between different kinds of human securities. Focusing on one human security can be shortsighted and limit our understanding of the impacts of achieving security in one domain while decreasing it in another. Our analysis of vulnerability to food shortage indicated that following the climate challenge that began in 1127 CE (Mimbres 1 in Table 8.1), people decreased their vulnerability to food shortage to such an extent that when a second climate challenge began just over a century later (Mimbres 2 in Table 8.1), no social changes or food shortages were evident archaeologically following that challenge. At what cost? What other securities were traded off? That is what we explore here.

The rare, extreme dry period that began in 1127 CE is associated with the transformation referred to as the end of the Classic Mimbres period, which took place around 1130 CE. We have described this change as "transformative relocation" because of the substantial population shifting and organizational changes that occurred (B. Nelson et al. 2014; Torvinen et al. 2015). All major villages (settlements having more than fifty domestic structures) throughout the Mimbres region were substantially or completely depopulated. Researchers have estimated that the regional population declined by 75–80 percent due to out migration (Nelson and Hegmon 2001).

While many people left the region, some remained, either occupying small segments of their previous villages in the Mimbres Valley (Hegmon et al. 1999), or forming new hamlet settlements in the eastern Mimbres

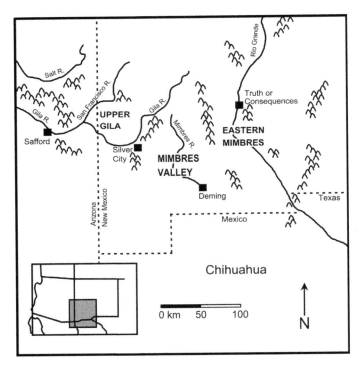

FIGURE 8.6. The Mimbres Region in southwest New Mexico.

area (Nelson 1999). For the eastern Mimbres area, we have referred to this as the Reorganization phase of the Postclassic period (Hegmon et al. 1999). Part of this reorganization involved people from other regions and traditions moving into the region, joining the remnant local population and forming new settlements (Hegmon et al. 2000; Nelson 1999). The Mimbres black-on-white pottery tradition of the Mimbres periods was entirely replaced with several different decorated ceramic wares brought in from surrounding regions (Nelson 1999).

The spider graphs in Figure 8.7 illustrate the load of vulnerability to food shortage prior to 1127, during the Classic Mimbres period, and prior to 1270s CE, the early Postclassic period. Again, the radii indicate the variables that contribute to vulnerabilities, listed above, and the size of the shaded area indicates the overall estimated vulnerability load to food shortage during each period. The decrease in size of shaded area shows a decrease in vulnerability to food shortage from the early 1100s to the mid-1200s, that is, from the Classic Mimbres period to the Reorganization phase

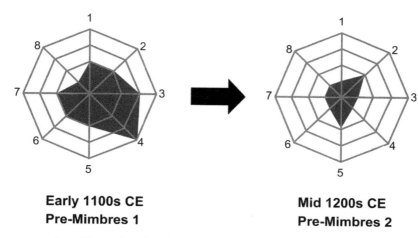

Early 1100s CE
Pre-Mimbres 1

Mid 1200s CE
Pre-Mimbres 2

FIGURE 8.7. Change in vulnerability to food shortage in the Mimbres region. The difference in size of the darkened polygon is indicative of the difference in estimated vulnerability load.

of the Postclassic. This appears on the surface to be an excellent outcome when we focus only on food security. But we can understand tradeoffs in achieving this low level of vulnerability by looking at all seven human securities – economic, food, health, environment, personal, community, political (UNDP 1994) – rather than food security alone. These dimensions of human security identified by the UNDP are, of course, modern constructs, so our use transforms each in a way that can be assessed archaeologically (see Hegmon 2016 for more discussion of how the human securities can be operationalized archaeologically).

Here we characterize the change in securities from Classic Mimbres to Reorganization phase of the Postclassic to consider how people experienced the change and what securities were traded off. Table 8.2 lists these changes, with the strongest indicated with italics.

Economic security – assured basic income and work including equal access to income and work (UNDP 1994). For pre-Hispanic occupants of southwestern New Mexico, who were primarily maize farmers, access to arable land would have been a primary factor in economic security. Some have argued that the first occupants of Mimbres Classic villages and their descendants had access to the best farmland (Shafer 2006), which may be evident in the unequal distribution of storage areas across residential units. Hegmon et al. (2006) document considerable difference in household size and amount of storage area within Classic Mimbres villages. Thus the

TABLE 8.2. *Changes in conditions for each of seven securities across the Classic Mimbres to Reorganization phase transformation*

Securities	Change from Classic Mimbres to Postclassic Phase
Economic	Possible minor improvement
Food	*Major improvement in vulnerability to shortage*
Health	No evident change, little evidence of poor health in either phase
Environment	Some improvement in portion of region
Personal	No evident change, little evidence of violence in either phase
Community	*Major decline in conditions of membership and identity*
Political	Possibly some improvement with increased autonomy

Note: Postclassic data are usually but not always from Reorganization phase. Rows in italics are those with greatest change.

inequality may have created some degree of economic insecurity during the Classic period. However, in the subsequent Reorganization phase settlements, residential units are similar in size with no difference in storage area. This pattern indicates a shift toward more economic equality, although limited storage for Reorganization phase households may counterbalance this security. This possible improvement would not have been substantial because, as Schollmeyer (2009) demonstrated, there was plenty of farming land even at the highest population levels in the Classic Mimbres period. Overall, economic security was relatively good through the Mimbres sequence and may have improved slightly in the Reorganization phase of the Postclassic period.

Food security – physical and economic assess to food (UNDP 1994). This paper and an earlier one by Nelson et al. (2015) have devoted considerable time to documenting both the vulnerability to food shortage and any actual experience of shortage. Based on the data and patterns discussed above we have established that vulnerability to food shortage was quite high in the Classic Mimbres period (preceding the climate challenge labeled Mimbres 1) and decreased considerably from the Classic Mimbres period to the later Postclassic, which includes the Reorganization phase (preceding the climate challenge labeled Mimbres 2). Even with considerable vulnerability in the Classic Mimbres period, people did not suffer from food shortage as evident in the analysis of human remains (Lippmeier 1991).

Health – conditions and access to care (UNDP 1994). For this region there is currently only one systematic study that includes skeletal analysis from the Classic Mimbres and Postclassic, done by Lippmeier (1991). That study includes human skeletons from villages in the Mimbres valley dated to the Classic Mimbres period and the Black Mountain and Cliff phases of the Postclassic. She found no significant differences in health between these periods. Thus, we have no evidence of change in health insecurity between these periods.

Environment – conditions for healthy ecosystems (UNDP 1994). These conditions are accessible from archaeological materials through the analysis of plant and animal remains. Based on pollen and paleoethno-botanical remains, Minnis (1985) argued for decline in the riparian zone of the Mimbres Valley in southwest New Mexico during the Classic Mimbres period, yet Schollmeyer (2009) found no such pattern in the eastern Mimbres area. Minnis (1985) also found recovery of the riparian zone following the Classic Mimbres period. In addition, large animal populations were depleted well before the Mimbres period (Schollmeyer 2009). Minnis (1985) suggests some recovery in the Postclassic in Mimbres valley, but Hegmon and colleagues (2006) see no recovery in the small samples from Reorganization phase hamlets in the eastern Mimbres area. Thus, there was mixed evidence for improvement in environmental security in the region.

Personal – protection from bodily harm resulting from violence or dangerous activities (UNDP 1994). Archaeological indicators of violence and harm are available through analysis of human skeletons as well as through practices of burning and destruction of property. No evidence has been found of systematic accident or violence (Lippmeier 1991), although analysis of human skeletons is limited. In addition, evidence of burning or property destruction is rare. That said, room burning is relatively more frequent in the Reorganization settlements than in the earlier Classic Mimbres villages. Fourteen of the twenty excavated Reorganization phase rooms in the eastern Mimbres area were burned to some extent. Burning can occur intentionally for reasons of conflict, ritual, and closure due to disease. Four of the fourteen Reorganization phase rooms were disman-tled before burning, indicating acts of closure rather than conflict. It can also occur unintentionally due to house fires created by indoor cooking. The causes of burning in Reorganization phase hamlet rooms is not definitive, but the burning is clustered and in some cases the fires were quite hot, as if intentionally started with fuel. Thus, burning could indicate some increase in personal insecurity but the evidence is not strong.

Community – practical support from group membership and source of identity (UNDP 1994). Communities can offer security of membership among a known group, but security is complicated because "communities can also perpetuate oppressive practices" (UNDP 1994: 31). For the Mimbres case, changes in population size, settlement size, pottery wares, and community structures are all indirect indicators of changes in community organization. The end of the Classic Mimbres period was marked by the depopulation of all villages, the end of production and use of the only decorated pottery made and distributed through the Mimbres region, and the end of multi-roomblock villages with below ground ceremonial rooms (kivas). Reorganization phase settlements were single blocks of rooms occupied by people who acquired and used many different styles of decorated pottery, and had no evident community structures (Nelson 1999). These changes could have had implications for leadership, access to land and resources, connections to others, religious practices, support relationships, among other aspects of daily life. Thus the scale of changes from Classic Mimbres to Postclassic indicate a dramatic shift, which might have been a relief to some and a concern to others but to all it was a major shift in group membership and composition, which contributed to decreased community security.

Political – honoring basic human rights, lack of oppression, allowing for autonomy (UNDP 1994). Our archaeological evidence cannot allow direct assessment of human rights in the Mimbres region, but we can make inferences about autonomy. The single, fairly standardized, decorated pottery ware used by all people in the Mimbres Classic period has been interpreted as evidence for a kind of social conformity (Nelson et al. 2011). The presence of kivas and kiva rooms as community gathering spaces in Classic Mimbres villages also may indicate some control or lack of autonomy; these are absent in the Reorganization phase settlements. These two indirect indicators of sources of conforming behavior in the Classic Mimbres that are absent in the Reorganization phase suggest increased autonomy in the latter phase, which may be interpreted as increased political security.

Thus, human securities were either unchanging or improved for nearly all domains, except community security, from the Classic Mimbres to the Postclassic (Table 8.2). The securities with greatest change were the improvement in food security and the decline in community security. Food security is evident in decreased size of the vulnerability load indicated by the decreased size of the shaded area in Figure 8.7. Community security was deeply affected by the transformation from Classic Mimbres to Reorganization phase. Residential communities disintegrated, as did the regional system that was defined by the single decorated pottery – Classic Mimbres black-on-white – that characterizes the Mimbres region during the Classic Mimbres period. The Classic Mimbres period ended with considerable out migration, increase of outside influence, and change in household and community organization (Nelson 1999). All point to a high level of community insecurity for people.

The lived experience of people during the twelfth century shifted such that vulnerability to food shortfall was decreased to an extremely low level – everyone had the means to secure food and enough food was available on the landscape on a consistent basis – but daily community experiences were not at all secure. People were encountering foreign ways of "making" and "doing," as evident in the changes of ceramic ware and village form that potentially made life unpredictable (Nelson et al. 2011). For example, the many new decorated wares were made with new materials and designs and new ways of forming and painting. Encountering such new practices can create uncertainty about how people may behave (Wiessner 1983).

Achievement of food security (or the reduction in vulnerability to shortfall) could be thought to have been the outcome solely of the substantial decline in population due to out-migration. But vulnerability to food shortfall before the end of the Classic Mimbres period was not based on a population-resource balance. There is strong evidence that food was available on the landscape, indicated by the small values for radius 1 in Figure 8.7, both before Mimbres 1, which represents the Classic Mimbres period, and before Mimbres 2, which represents the Postclassic period. In both cases population-resource balance contributed little or not at all to vulnerability. The key differences between the two times were improvement in condition of some resource areas (radius 3 in Figure 8.7) and increase in external connections (radius 4 in Figure 8.7). This kind of analysis allows us to get beyond a simple population-based argument about vulnerability to food shortage.

The tradeoff between food security and community security that followed the Classic Mimbres period and the extreme dry period beginning in 1127 CE probably was not an intentional decision or planned strategy. Many people left the region, new and diverse exchange relations were established, and social relations within the region were reorganized from the household to the settlement to the regional level. Those changes reduced vulnerability to food shortfall, but increased community insecurity. This possibly unintended consequence impacted the human experience. The decline in population marking the end of the Classic Mimbres period was never reversed. Food security was stronger but the Mimbres region never returned to be a center of an integrated regional community.

Discussion

Decisions that address challenges or issues always have consequences or tradeoffs. A perfect solution is doubtful. Here we looked at outcomes from climate challenges, the actions taken, and the tradeoffs experienced.

In the case of Norse Greenland, decisions were made to narrow the resource base, focusing on marine resources. The narrowing eventually led to difficulty obtaining food. Settlements were far from the key marine resource, and repeated climate challenges made getting to that food increasingly difficult. We cannot say what would have happened if the food resource base had not been narrowed, but we can say that Norse Greenlanders may have had more and more easily accessed food if they had not narrowed their food base to sea mammals. Perhaps this was their only option, but, again we do not know. The example does illustrate, however, that there are costs to narrowing options. Today we rarely consider those costs.

In the case of Mimbres, depopulation improved food security for the remaining population but created challenges to community security. People were faced with reorganizing locally and regionally and creating new connections. The Mimbres region never returned to be a population center, although the landscape offered adequate food. The tradeoff of food security against community security was not intentional, nor are many of the tradeoffs we make today, but they have consequences that if considered could be evaluated before they are experienced.

The key to considering tradeoffs is not that we can avoid them but that, by recognizing they exist, we can look for them in every decision we make or pathway we take. What are the tradeoffs for building less porous national borders? What is gained and lost in online education? What are the benefits and costs of current farming practices? The answers are complicated but if we maintain a focus on tradeoffs we may be able to reduce the costs borne by our actions.

Acknowledgments

Credit to all team members contributing to this research: LTVTP: M. Nelson, Scott Ingram, Matt Peeples, Michelle Hegmon, Colleen Strawhacker, Keith Kintigh, Kate Spielmann, Andrea Torvinen. NABO:

Andrew Dugmore, Seth Brewington, Tom McGovern, Richard Streeter, Jette Arneborg, Ian Simpson, Christian Madsen, Laura Comeau, George Hambrecht. Grant support: NSF Dynamics of Coupled Natural and Human Systems (CNH) BCS-1113991; NSF Arctic Social Science RCN ARC-1104372; NSF Polar Programs Science, Engineering, & Education Research Coordination Network RCN-1140106.

References

Abbott, David R. (editor) 2003 Centuries of Decline during the Hohokam Classic Period at Pueblo Grande. University of Arizona Press, Tucson.

Adger, W. Neal 2006 Vulnerability. Global Environmental Change 16(3):268–281.

Anderies, John M. 2006 Robustness, Institutions, and Large-Scale Change in Socio-ecological Systems: The Hohokam of the Phoenix Basin. Journal of Institutional Economics 2(2):133–155.

Anderies John M., A. A. Rodriguez, Marco A. Janssen, and O. Cifdaloz 2007 Panaceas, Uncertainty, and the Robust Control Framework in Sustainability Science. Proceedings of the National Academy of Sciences 104(39):15194–15199.

Arge S. V., G. Sveinbjarnardóttir, K. J. Edwards, and P. C. Buckland 2005 Viking and Medieval Settlement in the Faroes: People, Place, and Environment. Human Ecology 33(5):597–620.

Arneborg, Jette 1991 The Roman Church in Norse Greenland. The Norse of the Norse Atlantic. Acta Archaeologica 61(1990):142–150.

2008 The Norse Settlements in Greenland. In The Viking World, edited by S. Brink and N. Price, pp. 588–597. Routledge, New York.

Arneborg Jette, N. Lynnerup, and J. Heinemeier 2012 Human Diet and Subsistence Patterns in Norse Greenland AD c.980–AD c.1450: Archaeological Interpretations. Journal of the North Atlantic. Special Volume 3:119–133.

Barnett Jon, Richard A. Matthew, and Karen L. O'Brien 2010 Global Environmental Change and Human Security: An Introduction. Global Environmental Change and Human Security, edited by R. A. Matthew, J. Barnett J, B. McDonald, and K. L. O'Brien, pp. 3–32. MIT Press, Cambridge.

Bichet V, E. Gauthier, C. Massa, and B. Perren 2014 Lake Sediments as an Archive of Land Use and Environmental Change in the Eastern Settlement, Southwestern Greenland. Journal of the North Atlantic. Special Volume 6:47–63.

Burton I., R. W. Kates, and G. F. White 1993 The Environment as Hazard. Guilford, New York.

Dearing, John A., Rong Wang, Ke Zhang, James G. Dyke, Helmut Heberl, Md Sarwar Hossain, Peter G. Langdon, Timothy M. Lenton, Kate Raworth, Sally Brown, Jacob Carstensen, Megan J. Cole, Sarah E. Cornell, Terence P. Dawson, C. Patrick Doncaster, Felix Eigenbrod, Martina Flörke, Elizabeth Jeffers, Anson W. Mackay, Björn Nykvist, and Guy M. Poppy 2014 Safe and Just Operating Spaces for Regional Social-Ecological Systems. Global Environmental Change 28:227–238.

Dugmore Andrew J., Christian Keller, and Thomas H. McGovern 2007 Reflections on Climate Change, Trade, and the Contrasting Fates of Human Settlements in the North Atlantic Islands. *Arctic Anthropology* 44(1):12–37.

Dugmore Andrew J., Thomas H. McGovern, Orri Vésteinsson, Richard Streeter, and Christian Keller 2012 Cultural Adaptation, Compounding Vulnerabilities, and Conjunctures in Norse Greenland. *Proceedings of the National Academy of Sciences* 109(10):3011–3016.

Enghoff, I. B. 2003 Hunting, Fishing and Animal Husbandry at the Farm Beneath the Sand, Western Greenland. *Man & Society* 28. Danish Polar Center, Meddelelser om Grønland, Copenhagen.

Erb, K-H, S. Gringrich, F. Krausman, and H. Haberl 2008 Industrialization, Fossil Fuels, and the Transformation of Land Use. *Journal of Industrial Ecology* 12:686–703.

Few R., H. Osbahr, L. M. Bouwer, D. Viner, and F. Sperling 2006 *Linking Climate Change Adaptation and Disaster Risk Management for Sustainable Poverty Reduction: Synthesis Report*. For Linking Climate Change Adaptation and Disaster Risk Management for Sustainable Poverty Reduction, European Commission on behalf of the Vulnerability and Adaptation Resource Group (VARG).

Hegmon, Michelle 2002 Recent Issues in the Archaeology of the Mimbres Region of the North American Southwest. *Journal of Archaeological Research* 10:307–357.

— 2016 The Archaeology of the Human Experience: An Introduction. In *Archaeology of the Human Experience*, edited by M. Hegmon. Archaeological Papers of the American Anthropological Association, forthcoming.

Hegmon, Michelle, Jennifer A. Brady, and Margaret C. Nelson 2006 Variability in Classic Mimbres Room Suites: Implications for Household Organization and Social Differences. In *Mimbres Society*, edited by V. S. Powell-Martí and P. A. Gilman, pp. 45–65. University of Arizona Press, Tucson.

Hegmon, Michelle, Margaret C. Nelson, Roger Anyon, Darrell Creel, Steven A. LeBlanc, and Harry Shafer 1999 Scale and Time-Space Systematics in the Post-A.D. 1100 Mimbres Region of the North American Southwest. *Kiva* 65(2):143–166.

Hegmon, Michelle, Margaret C. Nelson, and Mark J. Ennes 2000 Corrugated Pottery, Technological Style, and Population Movement in the Mimbres Region of the American Southwest. *Journal of Anthropological Research* 56:217–240.

Hegmon, M., M. C. Nelson, K. G. Schollmeyer, M. Elliott, and M. Diehl 2006 Agriculture, Mobility, and Human Impact in the Mimbres Region of the US Southwest. In *Managing Archaeological Data and Databases: Essays in Honor of Sylvia W. Gaines*, edited by J. L. Hantman and R. Most, pp. 105–119. Anthropological Research Paper #55, Arizona State University, Tempe.

Hegmon Michelle, Matthew A. Peeples, Ann P. Kinzig, Stephanie R. Kulow, Cathryn M. Meegan, and Margaret C. Nelson 2008 Social Transformation and Its Human Costs in the Prehistoric US Southwest. *American Anthropologist* 110(3):313–324.

Hewitt, K. 1983 The Idea of Calamity in a Technocratic Age. *Interpretations of Calamity: From the Viewpoint of Human Ecology*, edited by K. Hewitt, pp. 3–32. Allen & Unwin, Boston.

Ingram, Scott E. 2010 *Human Vulnerability to Climatic Dry Periods in the Prehistoric U.S. Southwest*. PhD dissertation, Arizona State University, Tempe.

IPCC 2012 Summary for Policymakers. In *Managing the Risks of Extreme Events and Disasters to Advance Climate Change Adaptation: A Special Report of Working Groups I and II of the Intergovernmental Panel on Climate Change*, edited by C. B. Field, V. Barros, T. F. Stocker, D. Qin, D. J. Dokken, K. L. Ebi, M. D. Mastrandrea, K. J. Mach, G-K. Plattner, S. K. Allen, M. Tignor, and P. M. Midgley, pp 1–19. Cambridge University Press, Cambridge.

Janssen, Marco A., and John M. Anderies 2007 Robustness-tradeoffs in Social-ecological Systems. *International Journal of the Commons* 1(1):77–99.

Johnston, David C. 2012 12 Ways to Avoid the Next Catastrophe. *Newsweek*, Nov 28 and Dec 3, pp 27–33.

Kintigh Keith W., Donna M. Glowacki, and Deborah M. Huntley 2004 Long-Term Settlement History and the Emergence of Towns in the Zuni Area. *American Antiquity* 68(4):432–456.

Kintigh Keith W., and Charles L. Redman 2013 *Looking for the Future in the Past: Archaeology's Long-Term View*. Exhibit, Anthropology Museum at School of Human Evolution and Social Change, Arizona State University, Tempe.

Kinver, M. 2013 Chatham House Report: Famine Risks Are Badly Managed. *BBC News Science & Environment* April 5, 2013.

Lippmeier, Heidi S. 1991 *A Preliminary Assessment of the Relative Health Status between Classic and Post-Classic Populations of Southwestern New Mexico*. MA thesis, State University of New York, Buffalo.

McGovern, Thomas H. 1985 Contributions to the Paleoeconomy of Norse Greenland. *Acta Archaeologica* 54: 73–122.

McGovern, Thomas H., Vésteinsson, Orri, Adolf Fridriksson, Mike Church, Ian Lawson, Ian A. Simpson, Arni Einarsson, Andy Dugmore, Gordon Cook, Sophia Perdikaris, Kevin J. Edwards, Amanda M. Thomson, W. Paul Adderley, Anthony Newton, Gavin Lucas, Ragnar Edvardsson, Oscar Aldred, and Elaine Dunbar 2007 Landscapes of Settlement in Northern Iceland: Historical Ecology of Human Impact and Climate Fluctuation on the Millennial Scale. *American Anthropologist* 109(1):27–51.

Minnis, Paul E. 1985 *Social Adaptation to Food Stress: A Prehistoric Southwestern Example*. University of Chicago Press, Chicago.

Nelson, Ben A., Adrian S.Z. Chase, and Michelle Hegmon 2014 Comparative Landscapes: Transformative Relocation in the American Southwest and Mesoamerica. The Resilience and Vulnerability of Ancient landscapes: Transforming Maya Archaeology through/HOPE. *Papers of the Archaeology Division of the American Anthropological Association* 24:171–182. Edited by A. F. Chase and V. L. Scarborough. Washington D.C.

Nelson, Margaret C. 1999 *Mimbres during the 12th Century: Abandonment, Continuity, and Reorganization*. University of Arizona Press, Tucson.

Nelson, Margaret C., and Michelle Hegmon 2001 Abandonment Is Not As It Seems: An Approach to the Relationship Between Site and Regional Abandonment. *American Antiquity* 66(2):213–235.

Nelson, Margaret C., Michelle Hegmon, Stephanie R. Kulow, and Karen Gust Schollmeyer 2006 Archaeological and Ecological Perspectives on Reorganization: A Case Study from the Mimbres Region of the US Southwest. *American Antiquity* 71(3):403–432.

Nelson, Margaret C., Michelle Hegmon, Keith W. Kintigh, Ann P. Kinzig, Ben A. Nelson, John M. Anderies, David R. Abbott, Katherine A. Spielmann, Scott E. Ingram, Matthew A. Peeples, Stephanie R. Kulow, and Colleen A. Strawhacker 2012 Long-term Vulnerability and Resilience: Three Examples from Archaeological Study in the Southwestern US and Northern Mexico. *Surviving Sudden Environmental Change*, edited by J. Cooper and P. Sheets, pp. 193–217. University Press of Colorado, Boulder.

Nelson, Margaret C., Michelle Hegmon, Stephanie R. Kulow, Matthew A. Peeples, Keith W. Kintigh, and Ann P. Kinzig 2011 Resisting Diversity: A Long-Term Archaeological Study. *Ecology and Society* 16(1):25.

Nelson Margaret C., Keith W. Kintigh, David R. Abbott, and John M. Anderies 2010 The Cross-Scale Interplay between Social and Biophysical Context and the Vulnerability of Irrigation-Dependent Societies: Archaeology's Long-Term perspective. *Ecology and Society* 15 (3):31.

Nelson, Margret C, Scott E. Ingram, Andrew J. Dugmore, Richard Streeter, Matthew A. Peeples, Thomas H. McGovern, Michelle Hegmon, Jette Arneborg, Keith W. Kintigh, Seth D. Brewington, Katherine A. Spielmann, Ian A. Simpson, Colleen Strawhacker, Laura E.L. Comeau, Andrea Torvinen, C. K. Madsen, George Hambrecht, and Konrad Smiarowski 2015 Climate Challenges, Vulnerabilities, and Food Security. *Proceedings of the National Academy of Sciences* 113(2):298–303. doi:10.1073/pnas.1506494113.

O'Brien, Karen, Linda Sygna, Robin Leichenko, W. Neil Adger, Jon Barnett, Tom Mitchell, Lisa Schipper, Thomas Tanner, Coleen Vogel, and Colette Mortreux 2008 Disaster Risk Reduction, Climate Change Adaptation and Human Security. Report prepared for the Royal Norwegian Ministry of Foreign Affairs by the Global Environmental Change and Human Security (GECHS) Project. *GECHS Report* 2008:3.

Peeples, Matthew A., Gregson Schachner, and Keith W. Kintigh 2015 The Cibola/Zuni Region. In *The Oxford Handbook of Southwest Archaeology*, edited by B. J. Mills and S. Fowles. Oxford University Press, Oxford, UK, in press.

Scheffer, M., S. Carpenter, J. A. Foley, C. Folke, and B. Walker 2001 Catastrophic Shifts in Ecosystems. *Nature* 413:591–596.

Schollmeyer, Karen Gust 2009 *Resource Stress and Settlement Pattern Change in the Eastern Mimbres Area, Southwest New Mexico.* PhD dissertation. Arizona State University, Tempe.

Schoon, Michael, Christo Fabricius, John M. Anderies, and Margaret C. Nelson 2011 Synthesis: Vulnerability, Traps, and Transformations—Long-term Perspectives from Archaeology. *Ecology and Society* 16(2):24.

Sen, Amartya 1999 *Development as Freedom.* Anchor Books, New York.

2005 Conceptualizing and Measuring Poverty. In *Poverty and Inequality*, edited by D. B. Grusky and R. Kanbur, pp. 30–46. Stanford University Press, Palo Alto.

Shafer, Harry 2006 Extended Families to Corporate Groups. In *Mimbres Society*, edited by V. S. Powell-Martí and P. A. Gilman, pp 15–31. University of Arizona Press, Tucson.

Spielmann Katherine A., Margaret C. Nelson, Matthew A. Peeples, and Scott E. Ingram 2011 Sustainable Small-scale Agriculture in Semi-Arid Environments. *Ecology and Society* 16(1):26.

Torvinen, Andrea., Michelle Hegmon, Ann P. Kinzig, Margaret C. Nelson, Matthew A. Peeples, Karen G. Schollmeyer, Colleen Strawhacker, and Laura Swantek 2015 Transformation without Collapse: Two Cases from the U.S. Southwest. In *Beyond Collapse: Archaeological Perspectives on Resilience, Revitalization, and Transformation in Complex Societies*, edited by R. K. Faulseit, pp.262–286. Southern Illinois University Press: Carbondale, in press.

Turner B.L., III, Roger E. Kasperson, Pamela A. Matson, James J. McCarthy, Robert W. Corell, Lindsey Christensen, Noelle Eckley, Jeanne X. Kasperson, Amy Luers, Marybeth Martello, Colin Polsky, Alexander Pulsipher, and Andrew Schiller 2003 A Framework for Vulnerability Analysis in Sustainability Science. *Proceedings of the National Academy of Sciences* 100(4):8074–8079.

United Nations Development Program (UNDP) 1994 *Human Development Report 1994*. Oxford University Press, New York.

Vésteinsson, Orri, and Thomas H. McGovern 2012 The Peopling of Iceland. *Norwegian Archaeological Review* 45(2):206–218.

Vésteinsson Orri, H. Þorláksson, and A. Einarsson 2006 *Reykjavík 871 ± 2. Landnámssýningin. The Settlement Exhibition*, Anna Yates transl. Reykjavík.

Wiessner, Polly 1983 Style and Social Information in Kalahari San Projectile Points. *American Antiquity* 48(2):253–276.

9

Tradeoffs in Coast Salish Social Action

Balancing Autonomy, Inequality, and Sustainability

COLIN GRIER AND BILL ANGELBECK

In this chapter, we examine the socioeconomic organization of the pre-contact Coast Salish, a mostly marine and riverine-adapted society that has inhabited the southern British Columbia and Washington State coasts throughout the Holocene (Figure 9.1). Over much of their history, local Coast Salish groups retained a high degree of autonomy, which was expressed in their economy, social relations, and political organization, as well as their identity. Ethnographically, Salish groups identified with their local village, household, or kin group more so than any larger scale of identity, such as the region, language group, or pan-Salish ethnicity (Suttles 1958, 1960; Thom 2010).

Despite this emphasis on local autonomy, the Coast Salish coordinated social action across the Salish Sea region, and they did so without employing centralized political authorities. In the Coast Salish world this was accomplished through various highly formalized but decentralized networks. Affinal networks and potlatching connected individuals across landscapes, and, as we discuss later, facilitated information sharing, resource exchanges, and collective action within and across the Salish Sea (Suttles 1958, 1960).

Our central objective is to examine tradeoffs in societies that emphasize autonomy, but in which actors nonetheless engage in structured and coordinated action with other groups across a region. We argue that two fundamental tradeoffs have operated in Coast Salish societies, manifesting in historical processes and tensions over time.

The first tradeoff involves sustainability and inequality. The Coast Salish, unlike most societies that did not practice agriculture, had formal systems of

FIGURE 9.1. Extent of the Coast Salish region in southwestern British Columbia and northwestern Washington state.

ownership (or, as we describe later in this chapter, proprietorship), in which resources and resource areas were controlled and managed by various individuals and local groups. This ownership was tantamount to steward-ship, allowing those closest to the resource to monitor ecological conditions and regulate production cycles. These practices produced sustainability in two ways. First, they prevented the degradation of resources over time, and second, they provided for a level of resource productivity that supported continuity of Coast Salish social practices over the long term. The tradeoff associated with this resource stewardship, and the resulting longer-term sustainability that it promoted, was inequality in access to resources. Over time, ownership led to concentrations of sociopolitical power among an elite class as incipient social inequalities were increasingly formalized into struc-tural, class-based inequalities.

The second tradeoff is between decentralization (the political expression of local autonomy) and the Intricacies of decision making that resulted. Decentralized social networks provided a means of mitigating concentra-tions of economic and political inequality arising from local resource ownership. Decentralized networks provide "richer, more complex infor-mation" for managing local arrangements (Podolny and Page 1998:62–63) and, in the Coast Salish case, for ecological monitoring in complex, diverse environments. Decentralization had important benefits, but also costs.

Decentralized decision making structures, such as the potlatch, required constant input and engagement by various stakeholders and political actors. These structures also involve slower and more cumbersome processes of negotiation toward consensus. When this process breaks down, significant internal conflict can occur. The tradeoff for political autonomy therefore involved the time and effort of many individuals in society to engage in complicated political mechanisms.

The Coast Salish case is important because it highlights that centralization is not an inevitable requirement for action at large regional scales. Hierarchies may provide a high degree of efficiency in controlling information and for decision making (Johnson 1982; Roscoe 2009). However, the tradeoff with hierarchies is that autonomy is surrendered to a centralized and institutionalized authority, producing pervasive structural inequalities. In Coast Salish history, social institutions emerged that connected various autonomous local authorities and other actors, facilitating information sharing and coordinated social action across regions without such hierarchical authorities.

In certain respects, the case we consider can be viewed as a particular expression of the tragedy of the commons (Hardin 1968; Ostrom 1990). A variety of solutions have been proposed to avoid this problem, involving some form of regulation (whether locally based or centrally imposed) over access to resources (e.g., Adams et al. 2003; Kranich 2007; Milinski et al. 2002; Ostrom 2010; Santos and Pacheco 2011). On the Northwest Coast, several researchers have argued that the institution of ownership/proprietorship and restrictions on access to resource locations prevented overexploitation (e.g., Cannon 2011; McLaren et al. 2015; Trosper 2009).

However, as we make clear, the Coast Salish approach was clearly not a win-win scenario, but rather involved tradeoffs. Decisions and practices that promoted sustainability had negative consequences for human well-being when measured in terms of inequality. Brewington (this volume, Chapter 10) makes a similar point for the hierarchical society in the Faroe Islands. For the Coast Salish case, the autonomy provided by decentralized, local ownership acted as a brake on the level of inequality that could emerge. The Coast Salish case provides an example of how we might manage the tradeoff of simultaneously promoting sustainability while mitigating inequality, now and into the future. Their particular strategy of meshing ecological stewardship, economics, social practices, and politics is an instructive lesson in the organizational possibilities of human societies at any scale.

Decentralization, Autonomy, and Authority in Coast Salish Practices

Many decentralized societies of the recent and distant past can be described as anarchies, as they operate without formal, hierarchical institutions of government. In a previous work, we considered the nature of anarchic political organization (Angelbeck and Grier 2012). One objective was to break out of past constraints for envisioning how complex sociopolitical action can occur without centralization. Our research was driven by the specific need to account for the complex social and political networks of Coast Salish societies. Previous conceptual frameworks, including notions of egalitarianism, transegalitarian societies, and chiefdoms, did not sufficiently characterize Coast Salish sociopolitical organization. Neither egalitarian nor centralized, they constituted an exception to most state-focused anthropological typologies (e.g., Fried 1967, Sahlins and Service 1960).

Our study drew on the body of theory in anarchism. Popular conceptions cast anarchism as social chaos or disorder, as with the bomb-throwers of the early 1900s, the nihilist elements of 1970s punk rock, or glass-breaking factions of recent globalization protests. However, contrary to such notions, the theory of anarchism describes a form of social order, based in several foundational organizational elements including individual and local autonomy, voluntary association, mutual aid, network (rather than hierarchical) organization, decentralization, and justified (rather than arbitrary) authorities (Angelbeck and Grier 2012).

These elements are interrelated, and together allow for individuals and local groups to remain autonomous but also voluntarily associate with others. Through these associations, actors collaborate in mutual aid and develop networks of cooperation. Such networks are decentralized in structure, but allow for authorities within their structure. These authorities are justified, in that their authority stems from their knowledge, skill, or experience in specific contexts. This justified authority contrasts with the more arbitrary authority typically imposed in centralized societies. Anarchic societies are therefore not ungoverned, but rather are self-governed, maintaining the autonomy of local groups while facilitating interaction at multiple scales.

Our previous analysis of Coast Salish sociopolitical structures indicated that their practices were organized around anarchic principles in many respects, and that these principles were contested and renegotiated over time. This contestation has produced complex but discernible patterns in the archaeological record as people challenged the concentration of sociopolitical power by asserting local autonomy (Angelbeck and Grier 2012; Kropotkin 1987 [1898]). Here, we move beyond an analysis of political dynamics to consider anarchic elements in the ecological realm and the organization of production. We frame our analysis in terms of the tradeoffs involved in Coast Salish practices and the consequences of those practices, in order to further develop an anthropological perspective on both tradeoffs and sustainability.

Historical Context

An important objective of our analysis is to treat the dynamics of tradeoffs and their consequences in historical context. Significant change has occurred in Coast Salish societies over the last 3,500 years, and it is helpful to outline the chronology of these changes as a long-term framework for our analysis. This also serves to emphasize that some consequences of decisions play out over long time scales, with the costs and consequences of tradeoffs displaced in time (see papers by Logan and Roscoe, this volume). These consequences may be unintended and unforeseen.

The last 3,500 years of the Coast Salish past consists of three main periods (Table 9.1). The earliest, the Locarno Beach period (3,500 to 2,500 years ago), represents a time of seasonal sedentism following greater mobility in the earlier Archaic period. There are indications of social differentiation, including some elaborate burials and feasting items (e.g., Carlson and Hobler 1993). These data suggest inequality was limited but present and likely consisted of achieved (rather than inherited) social status. Overall, the Locarno Beach period is thought to reflect relatively low population levels and a mobile and fluid society antecedent to the iconic large, permanent cedar plankhouse village societies of later cultural periods (Matson and Coupland 1995:154–176).

Subsequently, between 2,500 and 1,000 years ago, the features and characteristics associated with ethnographic Northwest Coast societies are fully represented in the archaeological record. This period, called Marpole, includes widespread evidence of permanent villages, multifamily households, large plankhouses, an economic focus on harvesting salmon and other productive coastal resources, ascribed hereditary social inequalities, and resource ownership (Grier 2014). Matson and Coupland (1995:200–224) have called this set of features the "Developed Northwest Coast Pattern" to characterize cultural complexity in the Coast Salish region.

TABLE 9.1. *Cultural chronology for the Salish Sea region from 3,500 years ago.*[*]

Years ago	General Northwest Coast chronology	Salish Sea period	Description
225–0	Postcontact	Postcontact	Contact at 1790 CE with Spanish; 1792 CE with British; period of warfare ensues after contact; firearms introduced
550–225	Late Pacific	Sí:yá:m	Rise of powerful chiefs on the mainland Fraser River area
1,000–550	Late Pacific	Late	Shift to above ground mortuary structures by 1,000 years ago
1,600–1,000	Middle Pacific	Late Marpole (Garrison)	Period of warfare; bow and arrow introduced ca. 1,600 years ago; defensive sites and large burial features constructed
2,000–1,600	Middle Pacific	Middle Marpole (Beach Grove)	Permanent winter plankhouse villages and markers of hereditary status appear
2,500–2,000	Middle Pacific	Early Marpole (Old Musqeuam)	Continuation of Locarno Beach practices
3,500–2,500	Middle Pacific	Locarno Beach	Semisedentary populations with signs of differences in achieved status

[*] General Northwest Coast chronology from Ames and Maschner (1999); Salish Sea chronology synthesized from Angelbeck and Grier (2012), Matson and Coupland (1995), Mitchell (1971) and Schaepe (2009). Years ago indicates approximate years before now, not 1950CE as used for radiocarbon ages BP.

The Late period spans from 1,000 years ago to European contact, with contact occurring in the late eighteenth and early nineteenth century in the Coast Salish region. The Late period has been viewed as a continuation of the level of complexity that first emerged in the Marpole period. Plankhouses organized into substantial villages remain in use. Increased evidence of landscape modification in the service of large-scale resource production is evident (Grier 2014; Lepofsky et al. 2015). The economies of the Late period are clearly diverse and productive and population densities high. A significant shift away from the use of mounds and cairns for elites in Marpole to primarily above-ground burial (e.g., suspension in trees or placement in caves) suggests a transformation of the way in which hereditary elites expressed their status (Angelbeck and Grier 2012).

The last 3500 years was a time of significant transformation of the social order in Coast Salish societies (Grier 2014). Increased population, intensive resource production, and the emergence of hereditary elites brought issues of sustainability to the fore, since these changes placed significant pressure on resources. However, despite increasing populations and elevated social demands on resources, Coast Salish economies exhibit a strong degree of continuity over this extended period, suggesting that they achieved some level of long-term sustainability (Butler and Campbell 2004; Campbell and Butler 2010; Grier 2014).

Taking a regional view, Butler and Campbell (2004) find no evidence of resource depression in the Salish Sea region, arguing for stability with only minor shifts in resource use over the last 7000 years. While their data are relatively course-grained, more contextualized site-focused studies support the interpretation of continuity in Coast Salish economies in the Strait of Georgia region (e.g., Bilton 2013; Hopt 2014).

Such findings contrast sharply with earlier interpretations of resource intensification on the Northwest Coast. Croes and Hackenberger (1988) and Matson and Coupland (1995) predicted shifts in focal resources over the Holocene due to populations reaching carrying capacity at various junctures. These models predicted that strong reliance on abundant and storable Pacific salmon would be the ultimate result. However, while salmon are clearly important to Coast Salish economies (Coupland et al. 2010; Grier et al. 2013), the faunal record shows that they are represented in lesser and more variable quantities than was predicted by the economic models.

Overall, Coast Salish economies show considerable diversity and stability despite the dramatic changes seen in the social and political spheres from Locarno Beach times onward. This suggests that Coast Salish people were actively strategizing to feed more mouths and retain an inherent flexibility and sustainability in their economies (Moss 2012). As we argue later in the chapter, this sustainability in Coast Salish organization was not without tradeoffs.

Tradeoff 1: Sustainability and Inequality

The first tradeoff we consider is between sustainability and inequality. The key connection between the two lays in resource ownership systems.

Resources areas and collectively built mass-harvesting facilities (e.g., fish weirs, clam gardens) were owned mostly by noble, high-class individuals. Cross-culturally, ownership is not typical in small-scale societies that did not rely on agricultural production. This pervasive ownership is often cited as one of many ways in which Northwest Coast societies constitute exceptions to common hunter-gatherer models (Matson and Coupland 1995:1–9).

But, as we have argued elsewhere, these ownership practices seem unusual primarily because they have been interpreted through inappropriate social evolutionary frames. Coast Salish ownership protocols contrast sharply with notions of "ownership" in modern, private property-based systems, and also with territoriality-based anthropological explanations for how ownership emerges (e.g., Acheson 2015; Dyson-Hudson and Smith 1978). As such, it is useful to provide a brief recounting of ethnographically described Coast Salish ownership protocols, which likely developed over several millennia (Grier 2014).

Many aspects of the world were owned in Coast Salish societies, including resource-harvesting locations such as salmon fishing spots, berry patches, shellfish beaches (Figure 9.2), and upland hunting areas (Deur and Turner 2005; Richardson 1982; Turner 2014). Furthermore, human-made infrastructure such as fish weirs, clam gardens (Figure 9.3), and reef net salmon fishing systems were owned or highly restricted in their use (Grier 2014; Suttles 1951). The resources obtained from these locations were also owned, and distributed according to ownership and status. Improved places such as house sites had owners or owning groups, which were often lineage or household-based. In addition to material things, stories, knowledge, songs, and histories were also owned and could be transferred or given away in ritual contexts.

Ownership was claimed in prominent ceremonies, such as in potlatches, in which attendees witnessed the proceedings and validated claims through public acknowledgment. Social witnessing without challenge constituted acceptance. Locations could be claimed and owned by a variety of social entities including individuals, kin or corporate groups, or communities (Richardson 1982:96). Ownership was connected with social status. Elites typically owned the most productive resource locations (Suttles 1951:56). Specific locations and owners were associated with ancestral names that were passed on through lines of high-status individuals, often inherited over many generations.

Access to owned locations was granted by the owner under conditions that preserved the resource and respected the title of its owners (Grier 2014).

FIGURE 9.2 Beach and (behind) intertidal lagoon areas at Montague Harbour, Galiano Island. These locations were typically owned by individuals, households, or kin groups in Coast Salish territory. Photo by Colin Grier.

An important way of securing access to resources outside of one's own local context was to establish kinship (primarily affinal) ties. For instance, groups based in the islands of the Salish Sea would seek and maintain reciprocal kin ties with groups on the mainland. As a result, individual island groups might have rights of access to mountain goat hunting areas or alpine berries, while mainland groups would have access to clamming beaches or other marine resources (Blukis Onat 1984:92–94). These kin-based networks were extensive and multifaceted. In this way ownership actually facilitated access to diverse resources for a broad suite of society in a highly structured way.

Ronald Trosper has argued that "proprietorship" rather than property better describes the indigenous Northwest Coast concept of ownership:

> To distinguish the idea from that of property, I shall call their territorial system one of proprietorship. The distinction is necessary because the person with the rights of proprietorship was not able to sell the land. He was also obligated to share some of the land's products. Neither of these conditions is typical of 'property' in the European sense [Trosper 2009:14].

FIGURE 9.3. View of a clam garden at Shingle Point, Valdes Island. This feature, which is a roughly 800 meter-long linear arrangement of rocks in the lower intertidal zone, was constructed sometime after 2500 years ago and likely owned by the residents of Shingle Point. Photo by Colin Grier.

Proprietorship, Trosper (2009:14–15) emphasizes, was dependent upon proper management and stewardship of resources, which included monitoring for sustainability for future generations. Also, noble and titled proprietors were obligated to redistribute the resources they managed through the public potlatch and frequent gifting to extended kin and other allies. As Trosper (2009:23) notes, "reciprocity provided incentives for titleholders to share knowledge about salmon management, and the system of inheriting titles provided ways for knowledge to pass among generations." Moreover, significant social sanctions could be laid on individuals who did not act in the spirit of reciprocity (Suttles 1958).

In this way, ownership systems promoted sustainability by allowing for the local control of access to key resources, avoiding resource degradation over the short and long term. First, local knowledge was privileged, allowing for more fine-grained monitoring of resources. Second, the information from such monitoring provided a richer and broader basis for decision making about how to sustainably utilize local ecologies.

An important aspect of our analysis is to contextualize the historical development of these practices and protocols in the Coast Salish archaeological record. Status systems have changed over time, and ownership systems developed in concert with resource intensification and increasingly formalized status differences (Grier 2014). The archaeological record indicates that the tradeoff for the sustainability imparted through ownership was inequality. Inherent in the system of ownership were differences in access to resources. Over time, these differences produced increasing disparities in wealth and status, ultimately resulting in a class system in which access to resources was inherited and ownership became the privilege of a hereditary elite (or noble) class (Matson 1985).

The archaeological expression of these processes is complex, but several patterns are indicative of the ownership/inequality tradeoff. Achieved status is evident in burials across the Coast Salish region between roughly 3,500 and 2,500 years ago, as indicated by the unequal distribution of exotic goods and status markers (e.g., labrets, which were decorative inserts in the lip that signaled high status). The achieved nature of status suggests that inequalities in the region were fluid and limited prior to 2,500 years ago. For example, on the northern coast, egalitarian corporate villages appear to have controlled resource areas during this time, as seen in the placement of villages with similarly sized houses near important salmon fishing locations around 4,000 years ago (Coupland 1985, 1988; Matson and Coupland 1995:148–150).

In the Marpole period, a much more formalized and status-structured system of ownership of resources was in place, emerging in concert with the appearance of a hereditary class by approximately 1,600 years ago. These elites differentiated themselves through cranial deformation (a life-long marker of status) and the use of burial mounds and cairns (Burley 1980:60; Matson and Coupland 1995:215, Mitchell 1971:49). Again, this is the time period of construction of substantial villages and large-scale production features (Grier 2014), suggesting elites were increasingly in control of access to much of the wealth evident in Marpole-period Coast Salish societies.

Toward the end of the Marpole period, those who lacked hereditary status and preferential control of resources challenged increasingly restricted and inherited authority. The mortuary record reveals that the practice of cranial deformation, initially a sign of eliteness, was expanded to include a much wider segment of the population. It is likely that ownership privileges expanded as well. We have interpreted this pattern as evidence of challenges to the accumulation of wealth and concentration of social power (Angelbeck and Grier 2012). This challenge is also signaled by elevated levels of conflict, as outlined by Angelbeck (2009).

Ownership, control over resources, and the construction of social inequalities developed in a dynamic fashion over several millennia. This long-term process can be viewed as an example of how an initial tradeoff (sustainability for inequality) can have unintended and dramatic consequences down the road. Practices that promoted sustainability over time resulted in more formal systems that increasingly restricted ownership and resource access. At first, these inequalities went unchallenged, but resistance emerged with greater inequalities.

Tradeoff 2: Decentralization (Autonomy) and Messy Decision Making

The second tradeoff we consider concerns the complex sociopolitical dynamics inherent in maintaining local autonomy and the Complications that result from consensus-based decision making. Local autonomy was stridently maintained by Coast Salish peoples, and has been a key element of Coast Salish political organization ethnographically and in modern political negotiations (Thom 2010). The specific tradeoff is that the decentralized decision making that maintained local autonomy and ownership required a high investment by many individuals in sociopolitical life, and, when the system failed, conflict could readily emerge.

As we have described, autonomous actors (whether individuals, households, or kin groups) in the Coast Salish world were linked through broader local and regional sociopolitical, or kin-based, associations (Suttles 1951, 1958, 1960). These associations were not the hierarchical, regionally centralized relationships typical of chiefdom societies. Instead, Coast Salish groups were heterarchical. As defined by Crumley (1995:3), heterarchies involve relations among actors or elements that are not ranked or can be ranked differently depending on context. Heterarchy also describes social structures with numerous centers or nodes of authority, each of which has differing realms of influence. Coast Salish sociopolitical organization was a heterarchy of autonomous political actors with flexible degrees of authority in different situations.

Within heterarchical, decentralized, or as we argue, anarchic societies, political actors engage in complex negotiations to make decisions, and foster cooperation locally or regionally. This kind of engagement and direct action is costly in terms of the time, effort, and resources required to get things done. As discussed in part by Johnson (1982) and Roscoe (2009), reaching decisions under such conditions is hindered by the potential breakdown of attempts to forge consensus and the need to reconcile disparate interests. Heterarchies can be messy, stemming from the need to work through negotiation to arrive at consensus among autonomous actors, true even when the objectives may be clear and shared.

In contrast, in centralized hierarchies, responsibility for political action and decision making flows down the hierarchy. This frees up many from the responsibilities of direct engagement. As outlined by several researchers, the advantage of centralized control hierarchies is that they provide top-down clarity of purpose and action (Johnson 1982; Scott 1998, 2009). Dissent and resistance are typically overcome through institutionalized authority and domination. In these respects, hierarchy and centralization offer an advantage relative to decentralized networks (at least for those at its center) in that they create predictability within interactions, make coordination at larger scales more efficient and less costly, and clarify where authority lies.

Though decision making hierarchies may obviate the messy negotiations often required to get things done in heterarchical, decentralized systems, the Coast Salish resisted enduring forms of centralization (Angelbeck and Grier 2012:553–554). In fact, active resistance to such centralized decision making has been a strong current in historic and recent narratives. As Thom (2010) illustrates, for contemporary Coast Salish peoples the centralized and hierarchical administrative units imposed by the nation state of Canada for land claim negotiations often are short-lived and ultimately dissolve; they represent an imposed and centralized hierarchical structure and authority, rather than the justified authority typical of Coast Salish society.

It is clear that the Coast Salish could mobilize at large scales, and that short-term authorities emerged for the purpose and limited time they were needed. Angelbeck and McLay (2011) show that regional-scale decision making emerged in the context of conflict, as with the historic-period battle at Maple Bay off the east coast of Vancouver Island. In this battle, Coast Salish peoples from across the region came together to defeat an external enemy. Large-scale cooperation and coordination was therefore possible, but broad-scale coalitions dissolved afterwards, because their purpose was temporary and situational.

While effectively staving off centralization, this Coast Salish approach to politics came with costs and consequences. While not everyone participated in decision making (household leaders were primarily involved in such actions), the process required household heads and their factions to be regularly involved in politicking. Providing input into decision-making processes involved regular and cumbersome engagement, and demanded resources be expended in such contexts as potlatches. Moreover, when the decision-making process broke down, conflict could result. Both internal social tension and outright physical conflict are evident in the recent and distant Coast Salish past. Evidence of conflict has been attributed to raiding and other forms of status competition through violence; however, it is evident from oral histories that political leveling was an important objective of violence (Angelbeck 2009:227–229). Conflict often emerged between households, particularly when certain individuals overstepped their authority or disrespected the authority of others. Conflict was aimed at correcting the problem of over-ambitious individuals. Wars in the past, as told in Coast Salish oral traditions, were often framed as battles waged to "make the world right" (Angelbeck and McLay 2011:365, 383). Similar processes have been noted in other societies, including the US Southwest, as discussed by Hegmon in Chapter 7, this volume.

The moral imperative in such conflict is expressed in transformer stones recorded in the Coast Salish area. These stones are geological prominences regarded as individuals turned to stone by the spirit Xe:xáls during the Time of Transformation. One transformer stone represents a person with "greed for power" (Miller 2001:142) who was turned to stone. This geological feature now serves as a landmark and a reminder for all Coast Salish that greed results in violent misfortune. The associated oral traditions serve as a warning against efforts to centralize control over resources and pursue unjustified power and privilege.

From this we can glean that the tradeoff for maintaining equality and autonomy was first and foremost the requirement that actors consistently engage the political system. However, political actors also had to bear the costs of pursuing conflict as a mechanism for confronting those who pursued the centralization of social power. The long-term interplay between autonomy, inequality, and decentralization underscores the historical nature of tradeoffs, specifically that the consequences of tradeoffs can play out differently for various sub-groups of society over long periods of time.

Archaeologically, this relationship between power and conflict over the long term is that warfare increased after periods characterized by evidence for the increasing power of elites or chiefs (Angelbeck and Grier 2012). The substantial record of elite burial cairns and mounds dating to the Marpole period suggests elites had significantly concentrated their wealth and social power at this time. Starting around 1,600 years ago, elevated levels of

warfare are indicated by the construction of trench-embankment fortifica-
tions throughout Coast Salish territory. Many of these are small, appropriate for several allied households rather than large-scale regional defense,
suggesting a rise in internal conflict after 1,600 years ago (Angelbeck
2009:265–266).

This period of escalated warfare and construction of defensive features
was followed by a period of decreased visibility of inequality overall. The
burial mounds of the Marpole period, used to inter high-status individuals,
disappear by around 1,000 years ago (Thom 1995). In the transition to the
subsequent Late Period (i.e., after 1,000 years ago) there also appears to be a
broadening of elite status to a majority of the population, producing what
Suttles describes as an "inverted pear" status demographic (Suttles 1958).
This pattern suggests that increasing concentrations of power were contested and successfully countered.

Another period of increased inequality and concentration of wealth in
the hands of fewer individuals occurs after roughly 550 years ago in the
Fraser River region of the mainland. Characterized by Schaepe (2009) as
the period of the Sí:yá:m (great chiefs), during this time both intra-
settlement (house size differences) and intersite hierarchies become
increasingly evident. Schaepe (2009) argues this represents a significant
increase in chiefly power. This concentration of power initiates a period of
intra-Salish warfare that erupted after the time of European contact.

The Coast Salish peoples used other mechanisms to ensure that power
was not overly concentrated in particular individuals. As described by
Wayne Suttles ethnographically (1990:151), certain aspects of their subsistence activities were typically conducted in small teams – as individuals,
two-person teams, or nuclear families – that did not engender hierarchical
relations. These individualistic activities worked to counter the advantage
held by higher status individuals in communal realms of production:

> There certainly were elements that strengthened the power of leaders—
> the ownership or management of resources and equipment, including
> houses and canoes. But from the number of one-person and two-person
> activities, it seems that a family not in control of such property could still,
> most of the time, do fairly well with their own equipment and small
> canoe. I say 'most of the time' because there were failures of fish runs,
> periods of bad weather, and other calamities that would have made long-
> term independence hazardous. But if our family also had, as most did, kin
> ties in other villages and the option of changing residence [as they did
> with bilateral kin reckoning], they could still have been pretty independ-
> ent of any would-be powerful chief in their own village. It is my guess that

for people living like the Central Coast Salish to have become docile followers of powerful chiefs, there would have to have been greater rewards for organized activities [run by title-owners] and an increase in the hazards of independence [Suttles 1990:151].

Here, Suttles highlights an important tension between managerial authority and autonomy, framing the need to tolerate some authorities (typically elites in society) as a tradeoff. Certain individuals achieved control over a resource (or the equipment to harvest it, as is required with reef-netting operations for mass-harvesting salmon, for instance), or to organize these activities. This was tolerated as long as the distribution of benefits was greater than those acquired through more autonomous pursuits.

Social Institutions in Decentralized Networks

We have made the case that Coast Salish peoples engaged in efforts to maintain autonomy and stave off centralization over the last 1,600 years. We have also argued that Coast Salish practices, specifically the decentralized form of resource ownership that emerged, promoted sustainability over time despite increased demands on resources (e.g., from increasing populations, to finance elite activities such as potlatching). It is clear from the previous discussion that the two tradeoffs we have discussed are not independent, but are embedded in a complex system of social networks. At the core of these networks were what we call "network institutions" – enduring arrangements and highly structured sets of practices that existed in Coast Salish societies to manage these tradeoffs. It is useful to characterize these network institutions in order to understand how the specific tradeoffs we have analyzed were part of a larger, complex and uniquely Coast Salish set of practices.

A salient example of a network institution on the Northwest Coast is the renowned potlatch. Many ethnographers have addressed the function of potlatching, and varying explanations for the institution have been offered. For example, Codere (1950) and Boas (1897) interpreted the practice among north coast groups as primarily an institution of power construction and surplus-fueled status competition. But potlatching had a much broader role in Northwest Coast economic, social, and political life, and the practice as recorded ethnographically is a product of a long history (Suttles and Jonaitis 1990:84–86).

Among the Coast Salish, potlatching encompassed multiple important objectives, such as the redistribution of resources, collective witnessing of assertions of social status, communication of information, and alliance building. The Coast Salish potlatch emphasized witnessing (Carlson 1997). Most individuals participated in potlatch and similar ceremonies in which social and political relationships were asserted, reconfigured, or renewed. This had the important result of making a broad array of members of society the holders and protectors of the social order.

The potlatch developed within and expressed the dialectics of a heter-archical, decentralized society rather than a centralized authority. While archeological evidence for pre-contact potlatching is limited, several researchers have argued for the time-depth of this important institution (e.g., Ames 1995; Suttles 1958, 1960), linking its development with the emergence of elite strategies of status and wealth production. The potlatch also likely relates to the development of more formalized (possibly affinal) regional networks (Suttles 1960). Through these networks, autonomous individuals and groups could coordinate and create shared practices across large regional scales. Archaeological evidence suggests such formalized networks emerged after 2500 years ago (Burley 1980; Grier 2003). The potlatch can therefore be seen as a long-term focal institution that provided a forum for collective action, for the social production and reproduction of ownership systems and their prerogatives, and for the circulation of eco-logical knowledge.

Similar notions concerning the centrality of the potlatch have been advanced by Trosper (2002, 2003, 2009), who argues that the potlatch institution of the Northwest Coast allowed for a remarkably flexible and locally situated management practice for environmental resources and their sustainability. Through the potlatch, and its publicly negotiated system of rights and access, stewardship of local resources was orchestrated in ways that were beneficial in the long run. Potlatches provided ways to buffer ecological and social disturbances, with the sharing of resources and ecological knowledge through gift exchanges. Trosper (2003:6) emphasizes that these were also managed by the local community, in that a "system that can self-organize establishes itself without external guidance or direc-tion," indicating the bottom-up organization characteristic of decentralized and anarchic approaches.

In a series of papers, Trosper (1998, 2002, 2003, 2009) argues specifically that potlatching practices facilitated and supported enduring forms of resiliency and sustainability, and that Northwest Coast approaches to the local management of resources are an important example of ensuring sustainability while maintaining benefits for the majority of peoples: "the example of the Northwest Coast suggests ... [how it is] relevant to the solution to problems of institutionalizing sustainability. The indigenous people of the Northwest Coast have demonstrated that sustainability was feasible in wealthy societies" (Trosper 2002:341).

Potlatches also helped to regulate and resolve conflicts, which typically arose from political leveling strategies. They created a venue for the transfer of titles to particular resources as compensation payment for a murder after a feud, for example. In this way, the potlatch and its public assertions "provided a way for the consequences of violent conflict to be ratified by other titleholders" (Trosper 2003).

In these realms of practice – ownership, sustainability, decentralization, and conflict – the potlatch served as a Focal institution. It is critical to note, however, that the potlatch had costs. It could also be a source of conflict, as, for example, when the attendees rejected claims of status and ownership, as potlatches and related ceremonies were often subject to political manipulations and the machinations of aspiring elites. The potlatch also was a costly mechanism in that substantial material and social resources were consumed during these events, and in the preparations for them. As such, it should not be viewed solely as a system-serving institution. Rather, the potlatch itself crystallizes the notion of tradeoffs; it was a costly and unwieldy mechanism to sustain desired outcomes and practices in other realms.

Conclusions: Implications for Conceptualizing Tradeoffs

In the preceding sections we have outlined two specific tradeoffs in Coast Salish society: (1) the ownership protocols that promoted sustainability of resource production also promoted inequalities, and these inequalities were amplified over time, and (2) the form of decentralized decision making that maintained autonomy and local ownership required a high investment by many individuals in sociopolitical life, and held the potential for conflict when the system broke down.

Analysis of these Coast Salish tradeoffs provides several specific observations with respect to tradeoffs in general. First, ownership and inequality are linked, since any form of ownership or restriction of access to resources has the potential to concentrate resources into the hands of certain individuals and groups at the expense of others. However, it is important to note that these inequalities can be challenged and mitigated through actions that promote autonomy and maintain decentralized, local decision making, as they were in the Coast Salish case.

Second, decentralized autonomous politics can work effectively to manage ecologies at the local scale, but decentralization itself involves a tradeoff in terms of the complexity of political dynamics required to maintain it. In turn, conflict can emerge, but may act as a political leveling mechanism by preventing resources and authority over them from becoming too concentrated in the hands of any one group or individual.

Our analysis and discussion represents a starting point for exploring the complexities of decentralized organizations and the tradeoffs they entail. Our initial foray into decentralized networks and anarchist theory was fueled by an attempt to address and resolve some inadequacies in existing anthropological theory to account for Coast Salish sociopolitical life. In particular, we were unsatisfied with the egalitarian/hierarchy dichotomy. But pursuing this avenue of analysis has, we feel, led to a more informed perspective on tradeoffs and their consequences. In this sense we are using tradeoffs as an analytical lens through which we may conduct better anthropology, and using anthropology to better articulate how tradeoffs operate.

From a broader perspective, spatially extensive, decentralized networks have been part of the past in many areas of the world. The Coast Salish case is a relatively well-documented ethnographic and archaeological case study, and provides a means to understand the dynamics of such organizations. Moreover, analysis of the tradeoffs that come with the historical process of negotiating local autonomy and coordinated regional action provides a fresh lens through which we might consider ecological and social action in the present (Thom 2010). Many resources in our modern world are managed by highly centralized, hierarchical nation state institutions. The tradeoff for their efficient management is often the degradation of resources, as is the case with many fisheries in Coast Salish territory today (McKechnie et al. 2014). Effecting organizational change and working toward a more sustainable set of tradeoffs is critical to the future of the Salish Sea socially and ecologically.

Viewing the Coast Salish case through the lens of tradeoffs therefore provides a fertile framework for addressing the sociopolitical negotiations and actions of societies in the past and present. Anarchic networks are not specifically solutions to the problems generated by the negative consequences of large-scale and institutionalized political hierarchies, such as overexploitation and lack of local control over ecologies. All social life inherently involves tradeoffs, and exploring tradeoffs provides a basis for theorizing and analyzing social contexts vastly different than our own. Accordingly, such an analysis may illuminate alternatives that have and can exist in human societies, and to understand how we may engage in tradeoffs that we can live with in the present and the future.

Acknowledgments

Discussions with colleagues at the Amerind Tradeoffs Seminar greatly facilitated the production of this manuscript. In addition, several aspects of this paper were developed with funding assistance (to Grier) by the Center for Resilient Communities at the University of Idaho and the Research Institute for Humanity and Nature in Kyoto, Japan. Helpful comments on this paper were provided by Michelle Hegmon, Paul Roscoe, and Shauna BurnSilver.

References

Acheson, James M. 2015 Private Land and Common Oceans: Analysis of the Development of Property Regimes. *Current Anthropology* 58(1):28–55.

Adams, William H., Dan Brockington, Jane Dyson, and Bhaskar Vira 2003 Managing Tragedies: Understanding Conflict over Common Pool Resources. *Science* 302:1915–1916.

Ames, Kenneth M. 1995 Chiefly Power and Household Production on the Northwest Coast. In *Foundations of Social Inequality*, edited by T. Douglas Price and Gary Feinman, pp. 155–187. Plenum Press, New York.

Ames, Kenneth M., and Herbert D. G. Maschner 1999 *Peoples of the Northwest Coast: Their Archaeology and Prehistory*. Thames and Hudson, London.

Angelbeck, Bill 2009 "They Recognize No Superior Chief": Power, Practice Anarchism and Warfare in the Coast Salish Past. Unpublished PhD Dissertation, University of British Columbia, Vancouver.

Angelbeck, Bill, and Colin Grier 2012 Anarchism and the Archaeology of Anarchic Societies: Resistance to Centralization in the Coast Salish Region of the Pacific Northwest Coast. *Current Anthropology* 53(5):547–587.

Angelbeck, Bill, and Eric McLay 2011 The Battle at Maple Bay: The Dynamics of Coast Salish Political Organization through Oral Histories. *Ethnohistory* 58(3):359–392.

Bilton, David 2013 Northern, Central, Diversified, Specialized: The Archaeology of Fishing Adaptations in the Gulf of Georgia (Salish Sea), British Columbia. Unpublished PhD Dissertation, University of Toronto.

Blukis Onat, Astrida R. 1984 Interaction of Kin, Class, Marriage, Property Ownership, and Residence with Respect to Resource Locations among the Coast Salish of the Puget Lowland. *Northwest Anthropological Research Notes* 18(1):86–96.

Boas, Franz 1897 *The Social Organization and the Secret Societies of the Kwakiutl Indians*. Report of the U.S. National Museum for 1895, pp. 311–738. Washington, D.C.

Burley, David 1980 *Marpole: Anthropological Reconstructions of a Prehistoric Northwest Coast Culture Type*. Archaeology Press, Department of Archaeology, Simon Fraser University, Burnaby, BC.

Butler, Virginia L., and Sarah K. Campbell 2004 Resource Intensification and Resource Depression in the Pacific Northwest of North America: A Zooarchaeological Review. *Journal of World Prehistory* 18:327–405.

Campbell, Sarah K., and Virginia L. Butler 2010 Archaeological Evidence for Resilience of Pacific Northwest Salmon Populations and the Socioecological System over the Last 7500 years. *Ecology and Society* 15(17)1–34.

Cannon, Aubrey 2011 Cosmology and Everyday Perception in Northwest Coast Production, Reproduction, and Settlement. In *Structured Worlds: The Archaeology of Hunter-Gatherer Thoughts and Action*, edited by Aubrey Cannon, pp. 54–68. Equinox, Sheffield.

Carlson, Keith Thor (editor) 1997 *You are Asked to Witness: The Stó:lō in Canada's Pacific Coast History*. Stó:lō Heritage Trust, Chilliwack, BC.

Carlson, Roy L., and Philip M. Hobler 1993 The Pender Canal Excavations and the Development of Coast Salish Culture. *BC Studies* (99):25–52.

Codere, Helen 1950 *Fighting with Property: A Study of Kwakiutl Potlatching and Warfare, 1792–1930*. Monographs of the American Ethnological Society, XVIII. J. J. Augustin, New York.

Coupland, Gary 1985 Restricted Access, Resource Control and the Evolution of Status Inequality among Hunter-Gatherers. In *Status, Structure, and Stratification: Current Archaeological Reconstructions*, edited by M. Thompson, M. T. Garcia, and F. J. Kense, pp. 217–226. University of Calgary Archaeological Association, Calgary.

1988 Prehistoric Cultural Change at Kitselas Canyon. In *Research in Economic Anthropology*, supplement 3, *Prehistoric Economies of the Pacific Northwest*, edited by Barry L. Isaac, pp. 211–243. JAI Press, Greenwich, Connecticut.

Coupland, Gary, Kathlyn Stewart, and Katherine Patton 2010 Do You Ever Get Tired of Salmon? Evidence for Extreme Salmon Specialization at Prince Rupert Harbour, British Columbia. *Journal of Anthropological Archaeology* 29:189–207.

Croes, Dale R., and Stephen Hackenberger 1988 Hoko River Archaeological Complex: Modeling Prehistoric Northwest Coast Economic Evolution. In *Prehistoric Economies of the Pacific Northwest Coast*, edited by B. L. Isaac, pp. 19–85. Research In Economic Anthropology Supplement 3. JAI Press, Greenwich.

Crumley, Carole 1995 Heterarchy and the Analysis of Complex Societies. *Archeological Papers of the American Anthropological Association* 6(1):1–5.

Deur, Douglas, and Nancy J. Turner (editors) 2005 *Keeping It Living: Traditions of Plant Use and Cultivation on the Northwest Coast of North America*. University of Washington Press, Seattle.

Dyson-Hudson, R., and Eric B. Smith 1978 Human Territoriality: An Ecological Reassessment. *American Anthropologist* 80:21–41.

Fried, Morton H. 1967 *The Evolution of Political Society: An Essay in Political Anthropology*. Random House, New York.

Grier, Colin 2003 Dimensions of Regional Interaction in the Prehistoric Gulf of Georgia. In *Emerging from the Mist: Studies in Northwest Coast Culture*

History, edited by R. G. Matson, Gary Coupland, and Quentin Mackie, pp. 170–187. University of British Columbia Press, Vancouver.

2014 Landscape Construction, Ownership and Social Complexity in the Southern Gulf Islands of British Columbia. *Canadian Journal of Archaeology* 38(1):211–249.

Grier, Colin, Kelli Flanigan, Misa Winters, Leah G. Jordan, Susan Lukowski, and Brian M. Kemp 2013 Using Ancient DNA Identification and Osteometric Measures of Archaeological Pacific Salmon Vertebrae for Reconstructing Salmon Fisheries and Site Seasonality at Dionisio Point, British Columbia. *Journal of Archaeological Science* 40(1):544–555.

Hardin, Garrett 1968 The Tragedy of the Commons. *Science* 162:1243–1248.

Hopt, Justin 2014 Fish and Complexity: Faunal Analysis at the Shell Midden Component of Site DgRv-006, Galiano Island, B.C. Unpublished Masters Thesis, Washington State University.

Johnson, Gregory 1982 Organizational Structure and Scalar Stress. In *Theory and Explanation in Archaeology: The Southampton Conference*, edited by C. Renfrew, M. Rowlands, and B. A. Segraves-Whallon, pp. 397–421. Academic Press, New York.

Kranich, Nancy 2007 Countering Enclosure: Reclaiming the Knowledge Commons. In *Understanding Knowledge as a Commons: From Theory to Practice*, edited by Charlotte Hess and Elinor Ostrom, pp. 85–122. MIT Press.

Kropotkin, Peter 1987 [1898] *The State: Its Historic Role*. (Originally, *L'Etat—Son Role Historique*) Free Press, London.

Lepofsky, Dana, Nicole F. Smith, Nathan Cardinal, John Harper, Mary Morris, Gitla (Elroy White), Randy Bouchard, Dorothy I.D. Kennedy, Anne K. Salomon, Michelle Puckett, and Kirsten Rowell 2015 Ancient Shellfish Mariculture on the Northwest Coast of North America. *American Antiquity* 80(2):236–259.

Matson, R. G. 1985 The Relationship between Sedentism and Status Inequalities among Hunter-Gatherers. In *Status, Structure, and Stratification: Current Archaeological Reconstructions*, edited by M. Thompson, M. T. Garcia, and F. J. Kense, pp. 245–252. Proceedings of the Seventeenth Annual Conference of the Archaeological Association of the University of Calgary. The University of Calgary Archaeological Association, Calgary.

Matson, R. G., and Gary Coupland 1995 *The Prehistory of the Northwest Coast*. Academic Press, New York.

McKechnie, Iain, Dana Lepofsky, Madonna L. Moss, Virginia L. Butler, Trevor J. Orchard, Gary Coupland, Fredrick Foster, Megan Caldwell, and Ken Lertzman 2014 Archaeological Data Provide Alternative Hypotheses on Pacific Herring *(Clupea pallasii)* Distribution, Abundance, and Variability. *Proceedings of the National Academy of Sciences* 111(9):E807–E816.

McLaren, Duncan, Farid Rahemtulla Gitla (Elroy White), and Daryl Fedje 2015 Prerogatives, Sea Level, and the Strength of Persistent Places: Archaeological Evidence for Long-Term Occupation of the Central Coast of British Columbia. *BC Studies* 187:155–191.

Milinski, Manfred, Dirk Semmann, and Hans-Jurgen Krambeck 2002 Reputation Helps Solve the "Tragedy of the Commons." *Nature* 415:424–426.

Miller, Bruce G. 2001 *The Problem of Justice: Tradition and Law in the Coast Salish World*. University of Nebraska Press, Lincoln.

Mitchell, Donald H. 1971 Archaeology of the Gulf of Georgia Area, a Natural Region and Its Culture Types. *Syesis* 4:1–228.

Moss, Madonna L. 2012 Understanding Variability in Northwest Coast Faunal Assemblages: Beyond Economic Intensification and Cultural Complexity. *Journal of Island and Coastal Archaeology* 7(1):1–22.

Ostrom, Elinor 1990 *Governing the Commons: The Evolution of Institutions for Collective Action*. Cambridge University Press.

2010 Polycentric Systems for Coping with Collective Action and Global Environmental Change. *Global Environmental Change* 20:550–557.

Podolny, Joel M., and Karen L. Page 1998 Network Forms of Organization. *Annual Review of Sociology* 24:57–76.

Richardson, Allan 1982 The Control of Productive Resources on the Northwest Coast of North America. In *Resource Managers: North American and Australian Hunter-Gatherers*, edited by Nancy Williams and Eugene Hunn, pp. 93–112. Westview Press, Boulder, Colorado.

Roscoe, Paul 2009 Social Signaling and the Organization of Small-Scale Society: The Case of Contact-Era New Guinea. *Journal of Archaeological Method and Theory* 16(2):69–116.

Schaepe, David 2009 Pre-Colonial Stó:lō Coast Salish Community Organization: An Archaeological Study. Unpublished PhD Dissertation, University of British Columbia, Vancouver.

Sahlins, Marshall, and Elman Service 1960 *Evolution and Culture*. University of Michigan Press, Ann Arbor.

Scott, James C. 1998 *Seeing Like a State: How Certain Schemes to Improve the Human Condition Have Failed*. Yale University Press, New Haven, Connecticut.

2009 *The Art of Not Being Governed: An Anarchist History of Upland Southeast Asia*. Yale University Press, New Haven, Connecticut.

Santos, Francisco C., and Jorge M. Pacheco 2011 Risk of Collective Failure Provides an Escape from the Tragedy of the Commons. *Proceedings of the National Academy of Sciences of the United States of America* 108:10421–10425.

Suttles, Wayne 1951 The Economic Life of the Coast Salish of Haro and Rosario Straits. Unpublished PhD Dissertation, University of Washington, Seattle.

1958 Private Knowledge, Morality, and Social Classes among the Coast Salish. *American Anthropologist* 60:497–507.

1960 Affinal Ties, Subsistence, and Prestige among the Coast Salish. *American Anthropologist* 62(2):296–305.

1990 Central Coast Salish Subsistence. *Northwest Anthropological Research Notes* 24:147–152.

Suttles, Wayne, and Aldona C. Jonaitis 1990 History of Research in Ethnology. In *Handbook of North American Indians, vol. 7: Northwest Coast*, edited by Wayne Suttles, pp. 73–87. Smithsonian, Washington, D.C.

Thom, Brian 1995 The Dead and the Living: Burial Mounds and Cairns and the Development of Social Classes in the Gulf of Georgia Region. Unpublished Master's Thesis, University of British Columbia.

2010 The Anathema of Aggregation: Toward 21st-Century Self-Government in the Coast Salish World. *Anthropologica* 52(1):33–48.

Trosper, Ronald L. 1998 Incentive Systems that Support Sustainability: A First Nations Example. *Conservation Ecology* 2(11) www.consecol.org/vol2/iss2/art11.

2002 Northwest Coast Indigenous Institutions that Supported Resilience and Sustainability, *Ecological Economics* 41(2)329–344.

2003 Resilience in Pre-contact Pacific Northwest Social Ecological Systems. *Conservation Ecology* 7(3):6.

2009 *Resilience, Reciprocity and Ecological Economics: Northwest Coast Sustainability*. Taylor & Francis, New York.

Turner, Nancy J. 2014 *Ancient Pathways, Ancestral Knowledge: Ethnobotany and Ecological Wisdom of Indigenous Peoples of Northwestern North America*. McGill-Queens University Press, Montreal.

10

Tradeoffs and Human Well-Being

Achieving Sustainability in the Faroe Islands

SETH D. BREWINGTON

Ecosystem managers and environmental-policy makers are increasingly coming to recognize not only that achieving sustainable resource use requires tradeoffs, but also that these tradeoffs can have negative impacts on human well-being (Cavender-Bares et al. 2015). As a result, considerable effort has been made to develop environmental policies that promote resource conservation while at the same time maintaining the welfare of local communities (e.g., Adams et al. 2014; Butler and Oluoch-Kosura 2006; Millennium Ecosystem Assessment 2005). As McShane and colleagues (2011) note, however, win-win outcomes are unfortunately rare. Instead, a variety of factors – such as unforeseen costs, competing goals of different stakeholders, and faulty assumptions underlying management schemes – can complicate efforts to promote both sustainability and human well-being. Rather than win-win scenarios, we are most often left with "hard choices" (McShane et al. 2011).

In this chapter, I take these arguments one step further. It is not enough to simply recognize that management for sustainability involves tradeoffs. Truly effective and socially responsible sustainability initiatives also must recognize the significant impacts their policies have on human well-being. Furthermore, policy makers must consider that these impacts on human well-being are often complex, operating at different scales, and not immediately obvious. Crucially, because different groups within a community are often disproportionately impacted, sustainability initiatives can exacerbate social inequality (Kusters et al. 2006). While there are numerous ways to define and quantify well-being, I employ here what is called a "social conception of well-being" (Armitage et al. 2012; Deneulin and McGregor 2010), and argue that this perspective is useful for its emphasis on the societal context of individual freedom and welfare.

My focus is on a historical case study from the Faroe Islands. In the twelfth and thirteenth centuries, the community of this small archipelago, located midway between Norway and Iceland (Figure 10.1), underwent a period of significant social, economic, and environmental transformation. Several of these changes represented real threats to the long-term viability of the social-ecological system. Though the Faroese successfully navigated these challenges, and did so while avoiding destruction of their limited natural resources, the social costs of sustainability were considerable.

Case Study: Medieval-Period Faroe Islands

The Faroe Islands were settled in the early ninth century CE, during the Viking Age migration of Norse populations from Norway and the Northern

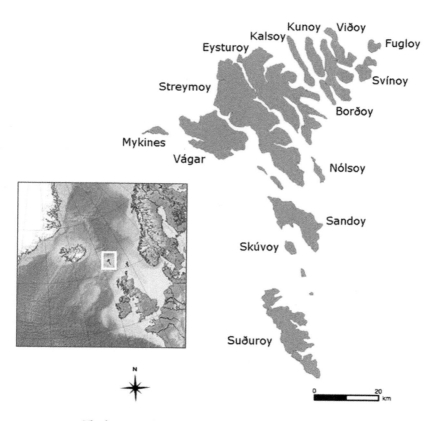

FIGURE 10.1. The location of the Faroe Islands in the North Atlantic.

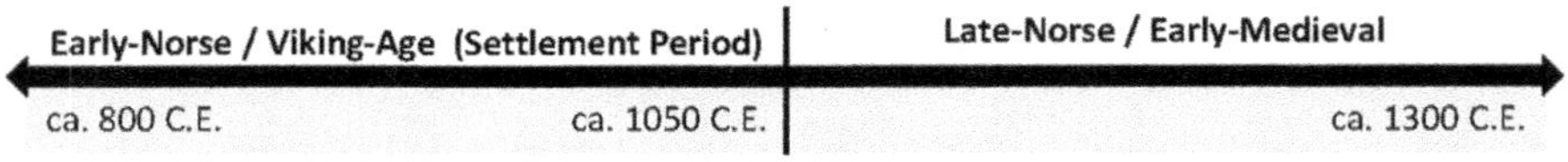

Early-Norse / Viking-Age (Settlement Period)	Late-Norse / Early-Medieval
ca. 800 C.E. ca. 1050 C.E.	ca. 1300 C.E.

FIGURE 10.2. Basic timeline of the historic periods mentioned in this chapter.

and Western Isles of Britain (Arge et al. 2005) (Figure 10.2). Though the Faroes are today a semi-autonomous nation within the Danish Realm, the modern population, numbering nearly 50,000, are direct descendants of the Norse colonizers, and the Faroese language – like modern Norwegian and Icelandic – is descendant from Old Norse. Little is known about the initial settlement (landnám, "land-taking"), though the available archaeological and paleoenvironmental evidence suggests that the settlers imported domesticated animals (cattle, sheep, goats, pigs, and horses) and cereal crops (barley), none of which were available in the islands prior to human settlement (Church et al. 2005). These subsistence staples, together with a rich material culture assemblage, comprised the so-called landnám package that marks the archaeological records of initial Norse settlements throughout the region, including in Iceland and Greenland (Amorosi et al. 1997).

The colonizers of the Faroe Islands faced a number of environmental challenges. First, none of the eighteen islands that make up the archipelago are very large (the biggest, Streymoy, is only around 373 sq. kilometers in size) and all are generally mountainous; the availability of flat, arable land is consequently quite limited. In addition, much of the coastline consists of either tall sea cliffs or very steep slopes (Figure 10.3), severely limiting the options for safe boat landing. Because of these topographic constraints, the settlers of the Faroes established their farmsteads in the relatively few locations offering suitable access to the sea, arable land, and grazing pastures (Arge et al. 2005; Small 1969). Climate presented additional challenges. Cool, wet, and windy, and with a short growing season, the Faroes are marginal for cereal production. Documentary evidence for the later historic period indicates that weather-related failures of barley production in the islands were relatively common (Guttesen 2004). The frequently stormy weather also makes for extremely hazardous boat travel, particularly in the autumn and winter months when the gales are at their fiercest.

Resilience, Sustainability, and the Role of Natural Resources

Despite these challenges, the evidence suggests that the Norse settlers of the Faroe Islands quickly adapted to the islands' limitations, cultivating at

FIGURE 10.3. The rugged coastline typical of much of the Faroe Islands. Photo by Seth Brewington.

least some barley and managing herds of domesticated sheep, cattle, and pigs (Church et al. 2005). The nascent Faroese society was also successful, however, because the settlers made the most of two key natural resources: grazing lands and wild animals. Despite the oceanic climate and short growing season, the grasslands that cover much of the islands are productive and relatively robust to grazing pressure (Lawson et al. 2005, 2008; Mairs 2007:25; Thomson et al. 2005). The rich pastures were an invaluable asset in what was otherwise a very limited terrestrial resource base, and, since the settlement period, the Faroese have relied heavily on these grasslands, particularly those in the uplands, for summertime grazing of sheep and cattle.

Archaeofaunal evidence indicates that the settlers supplemented their agro-pastoral economy by exploiting a variety of wild animal species. The Faroese fished for cod and other marine species, hunted seals, captured seabirds, collected limpets, and exploited whales (Brewington 2011, 2014, 2015; Church et al. 2005). Historically, people welcomed the springtime arrival of migratory seabirds as a much-needed supplement to dwindling winter food supplies, and while some of the birds and their eggs were consumed immediately, much of the catch was preserved with salt or by air drying for use throughout the year (Baldwin 1994; Williamson 1970:145–148). Fowling was a significant subsistence activity in the settlement period (Brewington 2011, 2014, 2015; Brewington and McGovern 2008; Church et al. 2005), and it – along with whaling (Joensen 1976, 2009; Nauerby 1996; Sanderson 1994; Williamson 1970; Wylie and Margolin 1981) – have been important components of the Faroese subsistence economy and cultural identity until modern times (Baldwin 1994; Nørrevang 1979, 1986; Williamson 1970).

Medieval Period Challenges

During the settlement period, the Faroese successfully overcame the challenges posed by climate, topography, and limited natural resources, developing and maintaining a sustained regime of natural resource exploitation. By the twelfth and thirteenth centuries, however, a number of social and economic transformations began to alter the settlement-period landscape management practices. Many of these changes reflected the increasing influence of the Norwegian Crown and the Church in Faroese affairs. Over the course of the twelfth and thirteenth centuries, the law of the Norwegian Realm came to supersede the indigenous judicial-political system in the Faroes. In the early 1270s, King Magnús Hákonarson of Norway extended the Norwegian Gulating Law to the Faroes, greatly diminishing the authoritative power of the *Løgting*, the native legislative-judicial body (Wærdahl 2011; Wylie 1987:11–17; Young 1979:51). At approximately the same time, the local Church, under Bishop Erlendur, also began asserting more political and economic authority (Wylie 1987:10–13).

At the beginning of the thirteenth century, slavery was legally abolished in the Faroes (Young 1979:50). Though we lack good evidence for how prevalent the practice had been in the Faroe Islands prior to this, slaves (or thralls) are believed to have been a feature of Viking-Age Norse societies throughout Scandinavia and the North Atlantic (Brink 2008). In any case, there is some evidence that, following the ending of the practice in the Faroes, some of the former slaves began establishing their own farmsteads (Young 1979:101).

The ending of slavery came during a period of changing landscape management practices in the islands. Prior to about the twelfth century, Faroese communities managed the upland pastures as common-pool resources (Mahler 1998). These commons areas, which were generally located some distance inland from the primary settlements on the coast, were dotted with shielings, small farms occupied only in the summer months and used as bases for seasonal activities such as sheep and cattle herding, milking, and peat cutting (Arge et al. 2005). Archaeological evidence suggests the Faroese began phasing out the use of these shielings by the end of the twelfth century (Arge et al. 2005). With the end of the shielings came a larger restructuring of landscape-management regimes, one in which landowners transformed the upland pastures from commons to "outfield," resulting in a greater privatization of property and resource ownership. In this system, access to resources in the uplands (the outfield) was directly tied to ownership of a farmstead in the primary settlement areas (the infield) (Arge et al. 2005; Mahler 1998). Figure 10.4 shows the line between infield and outfield in the contemporary settlement of Hestur.

The move to an infield/outfield system of landscape management roughly coincided with an increased emphasis on sheep farming. The Crown imposed trade restrictions on the Faroes in the late 1200s (Arge and Mehler

FIGURE 10.4. Hestur Village, showing the demarcation between infield and outfield. Photo by Seth Brewington.

2012), and while this placed control of foreign trade entirely in the hands of Norway, it at least ensured regular trade connections between the Faroes and Europe (Wylie 1987:17). The Faroese population greatly relied on trade imports of basic necessities like grain and timber (Jacobsen 2006; Thorsteinsson 2008). Lacking much of value for export aside from wool (Thorsteinsson 2008), Faroese landholders intensified their focus on sheep farming (Mahler 1998). This twelfth to thirteenth century increase in sheep farming is reflected in the archaeofaunal data (Brewington 2011, 2015).

The social and economic transformations of the twelfth and thirteenth centuries presented Faroese landholders with significant challenges. Modeling of rangeland biomass suggests that although the Faroese landscape overall was likely to have remained relatively robust to grazing pressure, the changes to landscape management initiated with the transition to the infield/outfield system probably had negative impacts on biomass in some areas (Thomson et al. 2005). Early documentary evidence clearly shows that livestock managers in the Faroes (Mahler 1998; Young 1979:147–148), and their contemporaries in Iceland (Dugmore et al. 2007), were acutely aware of the hazards of overgrazing, which in the North Atlantic can easily result in severe landscape degradation. The danger of overgrazing, particularly in the more vulnerable upland pastures, would have risen significantly during the twelfth and thirteenth centuries, when the increased emphasis on wool production led to greater demands on grazing pastures (Mahler 1998; Øye 2005).

Managing seabird nesting sites required additional consideration. Prior to the medieval period, when the Faroese population is believed to have been quite small (Arge et al. 2005), human predation is not likely to have represented a significant threat to seabird populations in the Faroes. Hundreds of thousands of these birds arrive in the islands each spring, staying only three or four months before returning to sea for the remainder of the year (Olsen and Nørrevang 2005). By the twelfth and thirteenth centuries, however, increased hunting pressure did likely pose a significant danger to seabird colonies (Nørrevang 1986). Threats included not only overpredation, but also degradation of the local nesting sites, particularly the rich puffin colonies tunneled into the easily accessible upper slopes of the sea cliffs (Nørrevang 1986).

Responses and Outcomes

Centuries of community-level environmental management expertise were arguably threatened by the application of Norwegian Gulating Law in the Faroes, starting in the 1270s. However, in 1298, following successful petitioning to the Crown by landholders, the Faroese were allowed an exception to the agricultural guidelines dictated by the Gulating Law in the form of a royal decree, the so-called Sheep Letter (*Seyðabrævið*) (Wærdahl 2011:132; Wylie 1987:13; Young 1979:52–53). The Letter dealt primarily with issues of livestock management, land rights, and natural resource owner-ship. Though it likely codified much of the hitherto-unwritten Faroese domestic law (Wylie 1987:13; Thorsteinsson 2008; Young 1979:53), the decree also served to reinforce and legitimize the rights of the elite land-holders to control access of natural resources. In many respects, the Sheep Letter suggests an effort by landholders to enforce restricted access to property and terrestrial resources. The Letter, for example, barred former slaves and other low-status individuals from establishing their own farms, requiring anyone wishing to do so to first own at least three head of cattle (Thorsteinsson 2008; Young 1979:53). Furthermore, the decree made it illegal for any man to marry and start a family unless he was also able to establish his own farm (Wylie 1987:14). In the Faroe Islands (as elsewhere in the Norse world [Brink 2008]), rights of access to resources and social power were fundamentally tied to land ownership (Mahler 1998, Thor-steinsson 2008). As such, the elite effectively held control of not only land, but also access to key resources located in the outfield (grazing pastures, peat fields) and even along the shoreline (fowling cliffs, shellfish, drift-wood, stranded whales).

The Sheep Letter helped preserve community-level management of natural resources in the Faroes, drawing on centuries of ecological know-ledge, even if this control lay ultimately in the hands of the elites. In so doing, the decree contributed to the sustainability of important resources, particu-larly those more vulnerable to overexploitation. A key criterion for successful long-term management of common-pool resources is the ability to restrict access (Ostrom 2007, 2009, 2010). Indeed, it is the ability to regulate the exploitation of common-pool resources that makes it possible to avoid the "tragedy of the commons" scenario (Hardin 1968) to which open-access resources are so vulnerable (Dietz et al. 2003; Ostrom 2007, 2009, 2010; Smith and Wishnie 2000). A number of features of medieval Faroese landscape management practice acted to effectively limit access to critical natural resources. These included restrictions on rights of outfield owner-ship and use, the right to establish farms, and the right to marry and start a family. Because rights of resource ownership were directly tied to land ownership, restrictions on settlement and marriage diminished demand on resources in two primary ways: (1) by limiting the numbers of individuals legally allowed access to resources, and (2) by slowing population growth.

By maintaining tight control of resources, landowners were able to manage sustained exploitation of key common-pool resources for both the short and long term. This is not necessarily to say, however, that medieval Faroese landowners had long-term conservation in mind; it seems more likely that the elites were simply interested in ensuring the sustained availability of the limited and vulnerable resources to which they were legally entitled. Regardless of the exact motivation, the effect of adaptive local management, coupled with policies that strictly limited rights of access, arguably represented at least "epiphenomenal" conservation (*sensu* Hunn [1982]). Indeed, despite a restructuring of landscape management practices, an intensification of pasture use, and what was likely an increase in population, the Faroese do not appear to have significantly degraded their natural resources during the twelfth and thirteenth centuries. Though medieval-period archaeofaunal data are limited, the available evidence suggests that the Faroese sustainably exploited seabird colonies from initial settlement up to the modern period (Brewington 2015; Brewington and McGovern 2008; Brewington et al. 2015). Likewise, paleoenvironmental evidence indicates that human impact on upland pastures – such as overgrazing-induced soil erosion – was relatively minor (Lawson et al. 2005, 2008; Mairs 2007:245–253).

Analysis: Human Well-Being in the Faroe Islands

The Faroese social-ecological system proved resilient to the various challenges faced during the twelfth and thirteenth centuries. The successfully sustained exploitation of key natural resources was a significant factor in this resiliency. Despite the introduction of significant changes to management practices over the course of the medieval period, the Faroese were able to maintain sustainable use of key natural resources, some of which – such as the upland pasture and fowling cliffs – were particularly vulnerable to loss.

Neither resilience nor sustainable resource use are necessarily correlated with positive human well-being, however (Armitage et al. 2012). What can we say about well-being in the Faroes during the twelfth and thirteenth centuries? Did maintaining a resilient social-ecological system via sustainable resource management involve significant tradeoffs in terms of human well-being? To answer this question we need to first be explicit about what we mean by well-being in the Faroese case and how we are going to assess it. There has been a considerable amount of debate in recent decades about how best to define and measure human well-being, with differing approaches drawn from a variety of academic fields (Brown and Westaway 2011; Villamagna and Giesecke 2014). Recent work in the Archaeology of the Human Experience (Hegmon 2016) is exploring these issues archaeologically.

Increasingly, researchers are focusing on the relationship between ecosystem dynamics and human well-being, noting that environmental security is one critical factor contributing to overall well-being (Adams et al. 2014; Butler and Oluoch-Kosura 2006; Chapin et al. 2006; Kasperson et al. 2005; Millennium Ecosystem Assessment 2005). In an effort to better understand the dynamics of human-environment relationships, some social and environmental researchers have in recent years turned to a resilience perspective, and its focus on complex adaptive systems (Folke 2006; Gunderson and Holling 2002). However, the resilience framework has received some criticism for its perceived failure to adequately acknowledge the role of human agency and social conflict in social-ecological dynamics (Brown 2014). As a step in that direction, Armitage and colleagues (2012) have argued that studies of social-ecological resilience would benefit from the inclusion of a social conception of well-being. This approach takes into account the dynamic connections between individuals, social groups, and the natural and cultural environments (Armitage et al. 2012; Deneulin and McGregor 2010). Analyses employing a social conception of well-being move beyond a narrow emphasis on individual well-being, recognizing that each of us is inextricably linked to larger social groups, and that each of these stakeholders have their own, often competing, interests and desired outcomes (Deneulin and McGregor 2010; Deneulin and Townsend 2007; Gough and McGregor 2007). In addition, the social conception of well-being approach represents an effort to account for a wide range of social and psychological factors – other than mere income and property ownership – that contribute to overall human well-being. It is in many ways an attempt to build on the important contribution of Sen's capabilities approach (Sen 1992), strongly emphasizing freedom of access to essential needs but acknowledging that these freedoms are defined at least in part by the individual's relationship with his or her society (Deneulin and McGregor 2010). In recognizing that human well-being as a whole is dynamically linked to often-competing individual and community needs, the social perspective explicitly acknowledges that achieving well-being involves freedom tradeoffs (Deneulin and McGregor 2010).

As a conceptual framework, the social well-being approach takes into consideration three primary dimensions of well-being: (1) **material** (e.g., food, health, income), (2) **relational** (e.g., social interactions, political and cultural agency, community engagement), and (3) **subjective** (e.g., freedom of self-expression and identity, freedom of belief and cultural expression) (White 2009, in Armitage et al. 2012). In the following examination of human well-being for the medieval-period Faroe Islands, I have adapted this approach, looking at two of the three dimensions: material and relational. The third dimension, subjective, incorporates phenomena that are generally not approachable archaeologically (and certainly not for the Faroes case). Because data for the medieval period in the Faroes are quite limited (consisting primarily of historical records, though including some archaeological, paleoenvironmental, and modeling results), I focus here on just one key resource for each dimension: For the material, I examine the degree to which people had access to adequate food; for the relational, I look at access to social capabilities (freedom to develop interpersonal relationships, community-level political agency). While human well-being is on the whole influenced by a number of important factors, the two I examine here are nonetheless key components of well-being in general, and are illustrative of the degree to which individuals in the Faroes during the medieval period had access to fundamental resources, both material and social.

In the following assessment of social well-being, I characterize outcomes by social status. Faroese society in the twelfth and thirteenth centuries – and indeed since *landnám* – was constructed around a rigidly stratified social system, one shared with its Norse contemporaries (Øye 2005). This system included roughly three social classes, characterized here as high, medium, and low status. High-status individuals owned land, and some were well-connected to the Crown or the Church. The middle-status segment of society comprised tenant farmers, who did not own the land they farmed. Those with the lowest status were primarily servants, former slaves, and the truly destitute. Degree of access to key resources differed not only by social status (for one of the dimensions examined) but also between dimensions (Table 10.1).

The Material Dimension of Well-being: Adequate Food

The Faroese were likely to have had adequate access to food regardless of their social status. As noted previously, the initial settlers of the Faroe Islands quickly adapted their settler-kit subsistence economy to better meet both the limitations and opportunities they faced. Among the important strategies was a heavy exploitation of wild animal resources

TABLE 10.1. *Access to material and relational dimensions of well-being*

Dimension	Resource	High-Status	Medium-Status	Low-Status
Material	Adequate food	Yes	Yes	Yes
Relational	Social capabilities	Yes	Some	No

and extensive use of upland pastures. These resources – particularly the wild animals such as seabirds – greatly contributed to the resilience of Faroese society, particularly in periods of domestic food stress, such as crop or livestock failure.

Though the high-status members of society ultimately held rights to these key resources, many parts of the privately owned landscape (e.g., outfield pastures, fowling cliffs, shorelines) could be used by others, so long as the land owner received their legally defined payment (e.g., a share of the catch, in the case of fowling) (Thorsteinsson 2008). Furthermore, it appears there were attempts to provide at least a basic level of care for the poorest members of society. That is, although we lack direct evidence for resource distribution mechanisms in the medieval period, later sources indicate that a portion of the Church tax (tithing) went toward assistance for the poor (Guttesen 2004). Also, the Sheep Letter explicitly authorizes the truly destitute to beg for food and other assistance (Wylie 1987:216; Young 1979).

Thus, it appears that while the developments of the twelfth and thirteenth centuries may have placed significant strains on key resources, the Faroese populace is likely to have maintained adequate access to food. Importantly, people probably had access to sufficient nutrition irrespective of their social status. By this one metric, then, well-being was maintained in the medieval period across social boundaries. In part, this was made possible by the relative robustness of key natural resources in the Faroes. To a large extent, though, it is a testament to the Faroese and their successful management of natural resources. Arguably, this management regime was effective because it allowed a segment of Faroese stakeholders – the land-owning elite – to control access to these resources. Grier and Angelbeck (Chapter 9, this volume) similarly conclude that, among the Coastal Salish, private management of resources promoted ecological sustainability. A significant difference with the Faroese case, however, was that Salish resource management was more local and decentralized in its organization.

The Relational Dimension of Well-being: Social Capabilities

Outcomes regarding well-being are more varied when measured in terms of access to social capabilities. Unsurprisingly, high-status individuals leveraged the greatest amount of social freedom, with opportunities for social, political, and economic advancement (particularly for those well-connected to the Church and Crown). Middle-ranking individuals held considerably less socio-economic clout, though they were legally entitled to marry and have children. It is the lowest demographic, the servant laborers and the indigent, who lacked any meaningful social capability; these individuals did not have the right to marry, start families, or establish small holdings of their own. Without land, the poor lacked rights of access to key natural resources and subsequently any economic independence (middle-status tenant farmers, it should be noted, also lacked a great deal of economic independence, since they did not own the land they worked). In the relational dimension, therefore, one's social status had a lot to do with one's level of well-being.

Summary: Tradeoffs and Social Well-Being

In the Faroes case, a positive outcome in well-being in the material dimension was to a large extent made possible by inequality in the relational dimension; inequality of social capabilities was a tradeoff for food security. From the perspective of those individuals most affected by the restrictions on social freedom, however, the actual impact of this tradeoff on *overall* well-being is perhaps not as easy to characterize as it might first appear. Arguably, restrictions on social freedom had a negative impact on the well-being of the lowest – and even middle-ranking – members of society. We can imagine this was true even if inequality was intrinsic to the larger social system. At the same time, it is also arguably true that social inequality – insofar as it worked to conserve important resources – actually contributed to well-being for every member of society. Because natural resource use served a vital role in maintaining social-ecological resilience, well-being at the community level (i.e., the continued viability of Faroese society) necessarily translated into the individual well-being – in at least some realms – for members of the community. This is not to say that social inequality was the only option for achieving sustainability – modern Faroese resource management has proven that successful long-term exploitation of natural resources can be accomplished with equitable distribution of costs. Rather, the point is that the medieval-period Faroese managed to achieve sustainable use of limited, vulnerable, common-pool resources, and did so through social measures that limited access by social class. Because of the importance of sustainability for the overall well-being of Faroese society, the impacts of the tradeoffs on individual social capabilities were both negative and positive.

This points to a key feature of such tradeoffs: impacts on human well-being are often complex, operating at a variety of different scales (Armitage et al. 2012). While there were certainly real differences in social well-being in the Faroes, expressed most clearly along class lines, the sorts of tradeoffs in well-being we identify will depend in part on our level of analysis and perspective (see also Freeman and colleagues, Chapter 2, this volume) and theoretical framework. As discussed in Hegmon's introductory Chapter 1 (this volume) our understanding of tradeoffs is inexorably linked to the perspectives we bring to our analyses.

In the case of the medieval-period Faroes, there are two scales in particular worth noting: the social and temporal. The tradeoff between societal and individual well-being, for example, illustrates outcomes that differed according to social scale. As just noted, the implications for individual well-being are complex; poor people lacked many social capabilities, which diminished their well-being, but aspects of this inequality – specifically the restrictions on resource access – in essence paid for the conservation of critical resources, thereby increasing food security and contributing to well-being. Social status can also be a dimension of social scale. There is, in the Faroes case, a tradeoff between the high degree of overall well-being for the elites relative to that of the middle- and especially low-status members of society. Because the medieval Faroese socioeconomic system hinged on land ownership, high-status individuals benefited most from social measures that contributed to sustainability.

Other tradeoffs are expressed at a temporal scale. In the Faroes case, conservation efforts carried out in the past – and particularly at vulnerable junctures such as the transformative twelfth and thirteenth centuries – made possible the long-term exploitation of key natural resources. Indeed, the legacy of past resource management regimes continues to benefit the Faroese people to this day. As Deneulin and McGregor (2010:511–512) note, however, "The freedoms and well-being of one group of people in the present are often founded on the ill-being and struggles of others before them." Medieval-period Faroese landholders achieved sustainable resource exploitation in large part by restricting access to vulnerable resources such as fowling cliffs and grazing lands. These restrictions most impacted those with the least socioeconomic power; it was these individuals who carried the cost of long-term food security.

The case study presented here highlights a number of key points about tradeoffs and human well-being:

- *Sustainable resource use – particularly in marginal environments – inevitably requires tradeoffs.* Managing for sustainability most often fails to result in win-win scenarios (McShane et al. 2011). The difficulty for resource managers is to recognize important tradeoffs at the outset. Though tradeoffs are unavoidable, and true win-win scenarios ultimately unachievable, we can take steps to mitigate the impacts if we have adequately identified key areas of concern.

- *Achieving sustainable resource use does not necessarily contribute to human well-being.* What the Faroes case illustrates is that the tradeoffs associated with maintaining sustainability often have impacts on well-being. These impacts might be positive, negative, or, as noted later, mixed. Furthermore, policies that are beneficial to the community may not necessarily be good for individuals or subgroups within that community (Armitage et al. 2012; Deneulin and Townsend 2007), a point also made in several other chapters in this volume, including Grier and Angelbeck (Chapter 9) regarding the Coastal Salish and Hegmon (Chapter 7) regarding the Mimbres. It is critically important that policy makers carefully consider what the costs (broadly defined) of sustainability programs are likely to be, as well as how evenly these will be distributed.

- *Tradeoffs are often complex and not immediately apparent.* Because they may operate at multiple social, temporal, and spatial scales, tradeoffs are often difficult to anticipate or detect. Nevertheless, given the tremendous potential for impact on human well-being, policy makers must take into careful account the scalar nature of possible tradeoffs if they are to adequately mitigate adverse impacts and avoid unintended consequences.

- *The impacts of tradeoffs on human well-being are varied and complex.* As noted in Hegmon's introductory Chapter 1, sustainability is contextual, and defining it for any given case requires us to ask "Of what, for whom, for how long, and at what cost?" (Allen et al. 2003:26). Similar contextually determined variation can be seen in the impacts of sustainability management on human well-being in the twelfth and thirteenth century Faroe Islands. The landholding elite achieved sustainable resource exploitation in large measure because of social practices that excluded access to resources for a sizeable chunk of society. But the impacts of the resulting tradeoffs on human well-being were not always clear-cut; impacts on well-being varied according to social status, most explicitly, but also by social scale (individual vs. "the greater good"), and even between dimensions of overall social well-being. Again, effective and socially responsible sustainability management requires decision makers to identify potentially conflicting outcomes in human well-being among various stakeholders. This is particularly true in marginal environments, and in the case of vulnerable common-pool resources (Adams et al. 2003).

Socially Responsible Sustainability: Lessons Learned from the Faroe Islands

In conclusion, it is worth highlighting what – from the standpoint of present-day resource managers – the medieval-period Faroese got right, and what they got wrong. In terms of the former, the Faroese can be credited with developing a highly effective resource management regime, as exemplified in part by the Sheep Letter. Crucially, the Faroese system was (and is) locally managed and flexible. Outfield use regulations have traditionally been subject to annual revision, at the springtime gathering of the village landowners, lending a high degree of adaptability to the management of the landscape, fowling cliffs included (Mairs 2007:257–259; Nørrevang 1986). This community-level system of management has proven successful at least in part because it effectively incorporates local ecological knowledge, employing a multi-season perspective to gauge the relative vulnerability of various resources. By avoiding the establishment of a top-down, centralized form of resource governance, the Faroese were able to successfully manage the long-term exploitation of key natural resources – particularly those more vulnerable to overuse or degradation, such as fowling cliffs and upland pastures. Effective management of common-pool resources required not only a sophisticated understanding of local ecology, but also the ability to monitor and control exploitation (Ostrom 2007, 2009, 2010). This dynamic, highly regulated, and locally managed system provided the framework for long-term sustainable resource exploitation in the Faroes (several aspects of the Sheep Letter, in fact, serve as the foundation of modern agricultural law [Thorsteinsson 2008]), thereby contributing overall social-ecological resilience.

Though clearly effective in the long-term maintenance of natural resources, the success of the Faroese medieval-period socioeconomic system involved social tradeoffs that were, by today's standards, unacceptable. (Though it could be argued – pointing to the fact that the wealthiest nations have long benefited by displacing environmental tradeoffs on poorer countries [Hornborg 2009] – that our modern standards of equality are not always put into practice.) Achieving sustainability, particularly in a marginal setting such as the Faroes, inevitably involves hard choices; the link between ecosystem health and human well-being is especially acute in such cases. The challenge for modern policy makers is to ensure that the costs associated with resource management are fairly distributed. Given the cultural-historical context, it is unsurprising that the medieval-period Faroese elite achieved conservation in part through social inequality. However, it is important to stress that this was not the only possible path to sustainability in the Faroe Islands. An alternative route would seek to more fairly share the sacrifices required; this is the challenge for present and future socially responsible environmental policy.

Acknowledgments

My sincere thanks to Jacob Freeman, Colin Grier, Michelle Hegmon, and an anonymous reviewer for their thoughtful and helpful comments on previous drafts of this chapter.

References

Adams, Vanessa M., Robert L. Pressey, and Natalie Stoeckl 2014 Navigating Trade-Offs in Land-Use Planning: Integrating Human Well-Being into Objective Setting. *Ecology and Society* 19(4):53.

Adams, William M., Dan Brockington, Jane Dyson, and Bhaskar Vira 2003 Managing Tragedies: Understanding Conflict over Common Pool Resources. *Science* 302:1915–1916.

Allen, Timothy F. H., Joseph A. Tainter, and Thomas W. Hoekstra 2003 *Supply-Side Sustainability. Complexity in Ecological Systems Series.* Columbia University Press, New York.

Amorosi, Thomas, Paul C. Buckland, Andrew J. Dugmore, Jón Haukur Ingimundarson, and Thomas H. McGovern 1997 Raiding the Landscape: Human Impact in the North Atlantic. *Human Ecology* 25:491–518.

Arge, Símun V., and Natascha Mehler 2012 Adventures Far from Home: Hanseatic Trade with the Faroe Islands. In *Across the North Sea: Later Historical Archaeology in Britain and Denmark, c. 1500 – 2000 AD*, edited by Henrik Harnow, David Cranstone, Paul Belford, and Lene Høst-Madsen, pp. 175–186. University Press of Southern Denmark.

Arge, Símun V., Guðrún Sveinbjarnardóttir, Kevin J. Edwards, and Paul C. Buckland 2005 Viking and Medieval Settlement in the Faroes: People, Place, and
Environment. *Human Ecology* 33:597–620.

Armitage, Derek, Chris Béné, Anthony T. Charles, Derek Johnson, and Edward H.
Allison 2012 The Interplay of Well-being and Resilience in Applying a Social-
Ecological Perspective. *Ecology and Society* 17(4):15.

Baldwin, John R. 1994 Sea Bird Fowling in Scotland and Faroe. *Folk Life*
12:60–103.

Brewington, Seth D. 2011 *Fourth Interim Report on Analysis of Archaeofauna from
Undir Junkarinsfløtti, Sandoy, Faroe Islands.* NORSEC Zooarchaeology
Laboratory Report No. 56. CUNY Northern Science and Education Center,
New York.

2014 The Key Role of Wild Resources in the Viking-Age to Late-Norse
Palaeoeconomy of the Faroe Islands: The Zooarchaeological Evidence
from Undir Junkarinsfløtti, Sandoy. In *Climates of Change: The Shifting
Environments of Archaeology*, edited by Sheila Kuluk, Cara G. Tremain,
and Madeleine Sawyer, pp. 297–306. Publication of the 44th Annual
Chacmool Conference. Chacmool Archaeological Association, University
of Calgary.

2015 *Social-Ecological Resilience in the Viking-Age to Early-Medieval Faroe
Islands.* PhD dissertation, Department of Anthropology, Graduate Center of
the City University of New York.

Brewington, Seth, Megan Hicks, Ágústa Edwald, Árni Einarsson, Kesara Anamtha-
wat-Jónsson, Gordon Cook, Philippa Ascough, Kerry L. Sayle, Símun V. Arge,
Mike Church, Julie Bond, Steve Dockrill, Adolf Friðriksson, George Hambrecht, Arni Daniel Juliusson, Vidar Hreinsson, Steven Hartman, Konrad
Smiarowski, Ramona Harrison, and Thomas H. McGovern 2015 Islands of
Change vs. Islands of Disaster: Managing Pigs and Birds in the Anthropocene
of the North Atlantic. *The Holocene* 25(10):1676–1684.

Brewington, Seth D. and Thomas H. McGovern 2008 Plentiful Puffins: Zooarch-
aeological Evidence for Early Seabird Exploitation in the Faroe Islands. In
Símunarbók: Heiðursrit til Símun V. Arge á 60 ára Degnum, edited by Helgi
Michelsen and Caroline Paulsen, pp. 23–30. Fróðskapur. Faroe University
Press, Tórshavn.

Brink, Stefan 2008 Slavery in the Viking Age. In *The Viking World*, edited by Stefan
Brink and Neil Price, pp. 49–56. Routledge, London.

Brown, Katrina 2014 Global Environmental Change I: A Social Turn for Resilience? *Progress in Human Geography* 38(1):107–117.

Brown, Katrina and Elizabeth Westaway 2011 Agency, Capacity, and Resilience to
Environmental Change: Lessons from Human Development, Well-Being, and
Disasters. *Annual Review of Environment and Resources* 36:321–342.

Butler, Colin D., and Willis Oluoch-Kosura 2006 Linking Future Ecosystem
Services and Future Human Well-being. *Ecology and Society* 11(1):30.

Cavender-Bares, Jeannine, Patricia Balvanera, Elizabeth King, and Stephen
Polasky 2015 Ecosystem Service Trade-Offs Across Global Contexts and Scales.
Ecology and Society 20(1):22.

Chapin, F. Stuart, Amy L. Lovecraft, Erika S. Zavaleta, Joanna Nelson, Martin D.
Robards, Gary P. Kofinas, Sarah F. Trainor, Garry D. Peterson, Henry P.
Huntington, and Rosamond L. Naylor 2006 Policy Strategies to Address
Sustainability of Alaskan Boreal Forests in Response to a Directionally
Changing Climate. *Proceedings of the National Academy of Science* 103:
16637–16643.

Church, Mike J., Símun V. Arge, Seth D. Brewington, Thomas H. McGovern,
James H. Woollett, Sophia Perdikaris, Ian T. Lawson, Gordon T. Cook,
Colin Amundsen, Ramona Harrison, Yekaterina Krivogorskaya, and Elaine
Dunbar 2005 Puffins, Pigs, Cod and Barley: Palaeoeconomy at Undir
Junkarinsfløtti, Sandoy, Faroe Islands. *Environmental Archaeology*
10:179–197.

Deneulin, Séverine, and J. Allister McGregor 2010 The Capability Approach and
the Politics of a Social Conception of Wellbeing. *European Journal of Social
Theory* 13:501–519.

Deneulin, Séverine, and Nicholas Townsend 2007 Public Goods, Global Public
Goods and the Common Good. *International Journal of Social Economics*
34(1/2):19–36.

Dietz, Thomas, Elinor Ostrom, and Paul C. Stern 2003 The Struggle to Govern the
Commons. *Science* 302:1907–1912.

Dugmore, Andrew J., Douglas M. Borthwick, Mike J. Church, Alastair Dawson,
Kevin J. Edwards, Christian Keller, Paul Mayewski, Thomas H. McGovern,
Kerry-Anne Mairs, and Guðrún Sveinbjarnardóttir 2007 The Role of Climate
in Settlement and Landscape Change in the North Atlantic Islands: An
Assessment of Cumulative Deviations in High-Resolution Proxy Climate
Records. *Human Ecology* 35:169–178.

Folke, Carl 2006 Resilience: The Emergence of a Perspective for Social-Ecological
Systems Analysis. *Global Environmental Change* 16:253–267.

Gough, Ian and J. Allister McGregor (editors) 2007 *Wellbeing in Developing
Countries: From Theory to Research*. Cambridge University Press, New York.

Gunderson, Lance H. and C.S. Holling (editors) 2002 *Panarchy: Understanding
Transformations in Human and Natural Systems*. Island Press, Washington,
D.C.

Guttesen, Rolf 2004 Food Production, Climate and Population in the Faeroe
Islands 1584–1652. *Geografisk Tidsskrift, Danish Journal of Geography*
104(2):35–46.

Hardin, Garrett 1968 The Tragedy of the Commons. *Science* 162:1243–1248.

Hegmon, Michelle (editor) 2016 The Archaeology of the Human Experience.
Archaeological Papers of the American Anthropological Association, 27.
American Anthropological Association, Arlington.

Hornborg, Alf 2009 Zero-Sum World: Challenges in Conceptualizing
Environmental Load Displacement and Ecologically Unequal Exchange in
the World-System. *International Journal of Comparative Sociology*
50(3–4):237–262.

Hunn, Eugene 1982 Mobility as a Factor Limiting Resource Use in the Colombia
Plateau of North America. In *Resource Managers: North American and*

Australian Hunter-gatherers, edited by Nancy M. Williams and Eugene S. Hunn, pp. 17–43. Westview Press, Boulder.

Jacobsen, Elin Súsanna 2006 The Faroe Islands in the Eighteenth Century. In *Der dänische Gesamtstaat: ein unterschätztes Weltreich? / The Oldenburg Monarchy: An Underestimated Empire?*, edited by Eva Heinzelmann, Stefanie Robl, and Thomas Riis, pp. 91–106. Verlag Ludwig, Kiel.

Joensen, Jóan Pauli 1976 Pilot Whaling in the Faroe Islands. *Ethnologia Scandinavica* 1976:5–42.

    2009 *Pilot Whaling in the Faroe Islands: History, Ethnography, Symbol*. Fróðskapur, Faroe University Press, Tórshavn.

Kasperson, Roger E., Kirstin Dowe, Emma R.M. Archer, Daniel Cáceres, Thomas E. Downing, Tomas Elmqvist, Siri Eriksen, Carle Folke, Guoyi Han, Kavita Iyengar, Coleen Vogel, Kerrie Ann Wilson, and Gina Ziervogel 2005 Chapter 6: Vulnerable People and Places. In *Ecosystems and Human Well-Being: Current Trends and Status*, edited by Rashid Hassan, Robert Scholes, and Neville Ash, pp. 143–164. Vol. 1. Island Press, Washington, D.C.

Kusters, Koen, Ramadhani Achdiawan, Brian Belcher, and Manuel Ruiz Pérez 2006 Balancing Development and Conservation? An Assessment of Livelihood and Environmental Outcomes of Nontimber Forest Product Trade in Asia, Africa, and Latin America. *Ecology and Society* 11(2):20.

Lawson, Ian T., Mike J. Church, Thomas H. McGovern, Símun V. Arge, James Woollett, Kevin J. Edwards, Freddy J. Gathorne-Hardy, Andrew J. Dugmore, Gordon Cook, Kerry-Anne Mairs, Amanda M. Thompson, and Guðrun Sveinbjarnardóttir 2005 Historical Ecology on Sandoy, Faroe Islands: Palaeoenvironmental and Archaeological Perspectives. *Human Ecology* 33:651–684.

Lawson, Ian T., Kevin J. Edwards, Mike J. Church, Anthony J. Newton, Gordon T. Cook, Freddy J. Gathorne-Hardy and Andrew J. Dugmore 2008 Human Impact on an Island Ecosystem: Pollen Data from Sandoy, Faroe Islands. *Journal of Biogeography* 35:1130–1152.

Mahler, Ditlev L. 1998 The Stratigraphical Cultural Landscape. In *Outland Use in Preindustrial Europe*, edited by Hans Andersson, Lars Ersgård, and Eva Svensson, pp. 49–62. Lund Studies in Medieval Archaeology 20. Institute of Archaeology, University of Lund.

Mairs, Kerry-Anne 2007 *Islands and Human Impact: Under What Circumstances Do People Put Unsustainable Demands On Island Environments? Evidence from the North Atlantic*. PhD dissertation, School of Geosciences, University of Edinburgh.

McShane, Thomas O. Paul D. Hirsch, Tran Chi Trung, Alexander N. Songorwa, Ann Kinzig, Bruno Monteferri, David Mutekanga, Hoang Van Thang, Juan Luis Dammert, Manuel Pulgar-Vidal, Meredith Welch-Devine, J. Peter Brosius, Peter Coppolillo, and Sheila O'Connor 2011 Hard Choices: Making Trade-Offs between Biodiversity Conservation and Human Well-Being. *Biological Conservation* 144:966–972.

Millennium Ecosystem Assessment 2005 *Ecosystems and Human Well-Being*. World Resources Institute, Washington, D.C.

Nauerby, Tom 1996 *No Nation is an Island: Language, Culture, and National Identity in the Faroe Islands*. North Atlantic Monographs, 3. SNAI – North Atlantic Publications. Aarhus University Press, Åarhus.

Nørrevang, Arne 1979 Land Tenure, Fowling Rights, and Sharing of the Catch in Faroese Fowling. *Fróðskaparrit* 27:30–49.

1986 Traditions of Sea Bird Fowling in the Faroes: An Ecological Basis for Sustained Fowling. *Ornis Scandinavica* 17:275–281.

Olsen, Bergur, and Arne Nørrevang 2005 Sea-bird Fowling in the Faroe Islands. In *Traditions of Sea-Bird Fowling in the North Atlantic Region*, pp. 162–180. The Islands Book Trust Conference, Sept. 9–11, 2004. The Islands Book Trust, Isle of Lewis.

Ostrom, Elinor 2007 A Diagnostic Approach for Going beyond Panaceas. *Proceedings of the National Academy of Sciences* 104(39):15181–15187.

2009 A General Framework for Analyzing Sustainability of Social-Ecological Systems. *Science* 325:419–422.

2010 The Challenge of Self-Governance in Complex Contemporary Environments. *Journal of Speculative Philosophy* 24:316–332.

Øye, Ingvild 2005 Farming and Farming Systems in Norse Societies of the North Atlantic. In *Viking and Norse in the North Atlantic*, edited by Andras Mortensen and Símun V. Arge, pp. 359–370. Select Papers from the Proceedings of the Fourteenth Viking Congress, Tórshavn, 19–30 July 2001. Annales Soceitatis Scientiarum Færoensis Supplementum XLIV, Tórshavn.

Sanderson, Kate 1994 Grind – Ambiguity and Pressure to Conform: Faroese Whaling and Anti-Whaling Protest. In *Elephants and Whales: Resources for Whom?*, edited by Milton M. R. Freeman and Urs P. Kreuter, pp. 198–201. Gordon and Breach Science Publishers, Basel.

Sen, Amartya 1992 *Inequality Reexamined*. Harvard University Press, Cambridge.

Small, Alan 1969 The Distribution of Settlement of Shetland and Faroe in Viking Times. *Saga-Book of the Viking Society* 17:145–155.

Smith, Eric Alden, and Mark Wishnie 2000 Conservation and Subsistence in Small-Scale Societies. *Annual Review of Anthropology* 29:493–524.

Thomson, Amanda M., Ian A. Simpson, and Jennifer L. Brown 2005 Sustainable Rangeland Grazing in Norse Faroe. *Human Ecology* 33:737–761.

Thorsteinsson, Arne 2008 Land Divisions, Land Rights, and Landownership in the Faeroe Islands. In *Nordic Landscapes: Region and Belonging on the Northern Edge of Europe*, edited by Michael Jones and Kenneth R. Olwig, pp. 77–105. University of Minnesota Press, Minneapolis.

Villamagna, Amy and Craig Giesecke 2014 Adapting Human Well-being Frameworks for Ecosystem Service Assessments across Diverse Landscapes. *Ecology and Society* 19(1):11.

Wærdahl, Randi Bjørshol 2011 *The Incorporation and Integration of the King's Tributary Lands into the Norwegian Realm c. 1195–1397*. Brill Publishers, Leiden.

White, Sarah 2009 Reflecting on Wellbeing and Development. In *Wellbeing and Development in Sri Lanka*. University of Colombo, Sri Lanka.

Williamson, Kenneth 1970 *The Atlantic Islands: A Study of the Faeroe Life and Scene*. 2nd edn. Routledge & Kegan Paul, London.

Wylie, Jonathan 1987 *The Faroe Islands: Interpretations of History*. The University Press of Kentucky, Lexington.

Wylie, Jonathan and David Margolin 1981 *The Ring of Dancers: Images of Faroese Culture*. University of Pennsylvania Press, Philadelphia.

Young, G. V. C. 1979 *From the Vikings to the Reformation: A Chronicle of the Faroe Islands Up to 1538*. Shearwater Press Ltd., Isle of Man.

11

Household- vs. National-Scale Food Storage

*Perspectives on Food Security from Archaeology
and Contemporary India*

KATHERINE A. SPIELMANN AND RIMJHIM M. AGGARWAL

In this chapter we explore the challenges to maintaining food security at the household level in developing countries in the contemporary world, with India as our case study. Following the World Food Summit of 1996, we define food security as existing when all people have access to sufficient quantities of nutritious and culturally appropriate food on a consistent basis. In seeking a new perspective, we emphasize the importance of framing food security as a complex decision problem, which involves tradeoffs at multiple levels across different scales (spatial, temporal, and jurisdictional). Our central argument is that addressing these multiple tradeoffs requires a portfolio of strategies, rather than a single grand strategy. In investigating what this portfolio of strategies should look like, we draw on insights from archaeology to put forth a long durée perspective on a robust set of strategies that have been used to maintain food security by diverse prehistoric societies. We use the term "long durée" to distinguish the multi-century to millennial scale of archaeological information from the "long term" in policy studies, which tends to refer to a few decades.

We draw on the case of India for several reasons. First, being a large country with several agroecological regions and diverse cultures, India exemplifies the complexity of food security challenges at multiple levels (local, state/regional, and national). Second, with its long history of alternative regimes (pre-colonial, colonial, and post-colonial), each of which enacted different food security policies, the case of India presents a vast repository of experiences and lessons to learn from in thinking about future policy. Third, despite India's impressive economic performance in the past two decades, the country continues to struggle with the basic problem of feeding her people. A recent assessment report found India to be one of the fifty-seven countries that has failed to achieve the UN Millennium Development Goal target of halving the proportion of undernourished people by 2015 (FAO, IFAD, and WFP 2014). The report found that the number of undernourished people in India increased by five million in the past five years, with around 15 percent of the population currently classified as undernourished. In the face of this dismal situation, recent press reports about rotting of food held in central government food storage facilities led to a huge public outcry and calls for a fundamental rethinking of the current food policy in India (FAO et al. 2014).

The current food policy of India, as explained in detail later, entails centralized procurement, storage and distribution of food, with a very limited role for households. While such a policy has prevented large-scale famines of the kind faced earlier in the country's history, it has still left millions of people food insecure. For all these reasons, this is an opportune time to examine India's food security policy, specifically focusing on the tradeoffs entailed at multiple levels.

To inform our study we draw on insights from archaeology to document evidence from diverse prehistoric societies, as well as on ethnographic information from India and sub-Saharan Africa, regarding robust portfolios of strategies that have been used for insuring food security at the household level. In comparing this archaeological and ethnographic portfolio of strategies with contemporary settings, we find a critical gap in the realm of household level storage. This strategy was used extensively by households both prehistorically and historically, but has almost disappeared from the portfolio of contemporary farmers.

Prehistoric smallholder farmers in the Southwestern US and elsewhere, and ethnographically documented households from many regions of the world, relied on household storage to increase the resilience of their food supply to inter-annual variation in rainfall and occasionally used this strategy in the face of severe drought. However, in current discussions on food security, attention seems to be devoted almost exclusively to national and regional-level storage, with neglect of the role of household-level storage in maintaining food security. We recognize that smallholder farmers in the twenty-first century face very different conditions than those experienced in smallholder societies in the past. Yet we show how the archaeological and ethnographic records can be helpful in identifying alternative strategies. Such strategies can guide present-day development practitioners in creating a more context-relevant, long-term portfolio of strategies to deal with food security.

We argue that contemporary mental models trap policy makers in a perspective that privileges top-down, highly centralized decision making and management, even in the face of significant failures in that approach over the past several decades. These mental models discount the value and veracity of local knowledge, leaving many smallholder farmers locked in a situation wherein the goals of yield maximization and national-level food security have trumped those of household-level food security. The long durée perspective of archaeological research provides alternative options for policy makers to consider. A long-term perspective also enhances our understanding about the tradeoffs entailed in alternative strategies at different levels (household versus national) and across different spatial and temporal scales. For instance, evidence from prehistoric societies shows how households chose to increase storage space at the cost of sacrificing present living needs, and how this helped them cope with inter-annual variations in food availability to some extent. In many contemporary societies, including the case of India that we discuss here, the national government has taken over the role of managing inter-annual variations in food availability. This shift in roles is at the core of the tradeoffs we consider in this chapter. The state mobilizes food away from households to offset periodic large-scale famines when they occur but may in the process leave households without sufficient food to cover their consumption needs for the year. In the case of India, the central government procures food from farmers right after harvest and stores it in its storage facilities, to be distributed as needed through its retail outlets spread throughout the country. Thus farmers no longer store much food and have to resort to buying food later in the season, either from government distribution outlets or private vendors, often at a higher price. At the same time, as the system currently stands, farmers must sell at harvest to meet urgent cash-based needs. This is the second primary tradeoff in our case study – use of food to maintain household food security vs. selling food to meet household cash needs.

Recent news coverage from India has documented the enormous quantity of food that rots in national storage facilities while the country continues to struggle with problems of hunger and malnutrition (Devraj 2010). This issue became controversial in 2010 when the Supreme Court ordered the government to distribute the surplus free of cost to the hungry and the Prime Minister reacted by accusing the apex court of interfering with policy matters (Devraj 2010). Several proposals have developed since then – including increasing storage space at the state level. We were surprised, as we researched the ongoing policy debates in India, and more generally in the developing world, that there was no discussion regarding improving storage at the household level. Our Indian case study lays out how farmers and policy makers are caught in a system that is failing on multiple levels, what tradeoffs they face, how they navigate these tradeoffs, and what might be the broader lessons that emerge from comparison of the Indian case with other ethnographic and archaeological evidence we present. Although we focus on India as our case study, the issue of food security among smallholder farmers is a global one. Food security is a major sustainability challenge.

We first discuss tradeoffs, our theoretical orientation, and archaeological and ethnographic information on household food storage, and then turn to our case study.

Theoretical Perspectives

We draw on the resilience framework to examine tradeoffs at multiple levels within the food system in our case study, India, and for smallholder farmers more generally. For analytical clarity, we follow Gibson et al. (2000) to define "scale" as the spatial, temporal, quantitative, or analytical dimensions used to measure and study any phenomenon, and "levels" as the units of analysis that are located at different positions on a scale. For example, the spatial or geographical scale has different levels including patches, landscapes, regions, and the globe. Similarly, the temporal scale may describe processes occurring at different levels, such as daily, seasonally, or annually. Of most importance in this chapter is the decision making scale, with different entities – such as nations, states/provinces, counties/districts, localities/communities, and households – making decisions at different levels. Food systems are often quite complex with interactions occurring within or across scales and levels.

The resilience literature emphasizes the need to examine cross-scale and multi-level interactions in building societal resilience to stresses of many kinds, including climate variability and change and food shortage. These interactions provide the basis for understanding tradeoffs, that is, what needs to be given up in order to gain something else (see Hegmon's Chapter 1, this volume).

Tradeoffs

Building food security entails tradeoffs at several levels (household, community, and national) within and across different scales. At the level of household decision making, the primary tradeoff experienced among smallholder households today is between the need for food and the need for cash to meet non-food needs and obligations. In the last several decades, the need for cash to pay school fees, medical expenses, debts, and other cash-focused transactions has trumped the need for the household to maintain food security, and household-level food storage as a mechanism for self-insurance appears to have declined significantly. Given these trade-offs, households are left vulnerable across many human security arenas.

Any solutions to the food security issue would need to address access to other human securities (see Nelson et al., Chapter 8, this volume). The focus of contemporary food management policy, however, has been on short-term, post-disaster management as opposed to building long-term anticipative capacity (Aggarwal 2008; Kapila 2009; Pande and Akermann 2009). Household-level storage is a good example of an anticipative, risk-management strategy.

Another key locus of decision making regarding food security is situated at the national level, where there are multiple tradeoffs between the large-scale mobilization of food and maintaining food security at the household level. Governments in developing countries have a number of reasons to mobilize food away from farming households and into larger markets and central storage facilities. These include maintaining food price stability and food availability at the national level (across different agro-ecological zones), feeding growing urban populations, and insuring income for the country to underwrite industrialization and other growth objectives through the sale of cash crops. In addition, governments use food transfers as a political instrument to gain votes and/or maintain control over their populace. In this cross-scale tradeoff, household-level food security for rural populations is effectively traded off to meet these other objectives. Because tradeoffs often occur across different levels, they involve actors and institutions at these different levels with varied capacities and voice in the decision making process. As Cash et al. (2006:1) observe, "There is a long history of disappointments in policy, management, and assessment arising from the failure to take into proper account the scale and cross-scale dynamics in human-environment systems."

Path Dependence

In examining these multiple tradeoffs, it is clear that path dependence plays a role in shaping the choices that farming households and policy makers in India currently face. In the nineteenth century, British colonists assigned individual rights to land from the communal system that had prevailed earlier and shifted land revenues from payments in kind, which previous rulers had received from farmers, to payments in cash. This began a process that led farmers down the path of commercialization (Raj et al. 1985). Even though land revenue obligations are no longer burdensome in the post-colonial period, other cash needs for purchased inputs have become important. Currently, farm inputs such as herbicides, pesticides, and fertilizers are bought with cash that is obtained through loans. Loan repayments come due at harvest time, compelling farmers to sell off (rather than store) their produce. Later in the year the farmers are obliged to buy food at higher prices, thus deepening the debt cycle (Aggarwal 2008). Farmers are trapped on a path that does not provide a secure and adequate food supply but have few options available for improving their situation. Likewise, policy makers are trapped in a perspective that privileges top-down, highly centralized decision making and management even in the face of significant failures in that approach over the past several decades.

Path dependence clearly plays a role in the top-down, multi-decade emphasis on increasing crop production as a key food security policy. Such policy has focused almost exclusively on (1) the adoption of new technologies coupled with subsidies on inputs to increase farm productivity, (2) the improvement of smallholders' access to markets, and (3) state-supported minimum prices and consumption subsidies. These strategies have led to increased short-term productivity and mobilization of surplus from farm households. However, smallholder households are brought into debt to acquire new technologies and are increasingly exposed to price fluctuations for their goods. Thus, both of these strategies expose households to an unabated risk of food shortfall.

Marketable vs. Marketed Surplus

In order to understand why and how food security at the household level remains problematic, a helpful distinction may be made between "marketable surplus" and "marketed surplus." Marketable surplus for a farm household is theoretically defined as total production minus the amount needed for household consumption during the year and other on-farm needs (e.g., for seeds, feed, and payment in kind for workers). Marketed surplus is the amount of produce that the farm household actually sells on the market. Very often the two terms are confused, leading to considerable misunderstanding about farmer well-being and food security (Government of India 2002).

Marketable surplus is a closer representation of farmers' well-being than marketed surplus. However, most household and market surveys carried out in the developing world report on what farmers end up selling, that is, the marketed surplus. Increases in marketed surplus are often touted as indicators of food security and overall economic development. But this perspective is misleading. In fact, a common trend in recent decades, particularly among smallholders, is for marketed surplus to increase with no increase (or even a fall) in marketable surplus, leaving households less food secure. For example, a study of wheat-growing districts of Rajasthan state in western India reported that 65–92 percent of small farmers have marketed surplus (Upender 1990). The study found that "smaller farmers were forced to sell a major proportion of their marketed surplus in the first quarter immediately after harvest to meet their cash and debt obligations" (Upender 1990:39). Alarmingly, farmers generally pay significantly higher prices later in the crop year to purchase the food needed for household consumption. Often smallholders produce higher quality cereals and sell those while buying lower quality or less culturally appropriate cereals, later in the crop cycle (Shah and Makwana 2013). These forced sales, often also called "distress sales," have become increasingly important among small-holders across the developing world and reinforce the need for household-level storage. Some recent studies on global food security (e.g., Godfray et al. 2010) have acknowledged the need for greater emphasis on household-scale food storage in poorer societies. Although Godfray and co-authors emphasize the need for developing household storage technolo-gies, as we discuss below appropriate technologies already exist for household-scale storage. It is the place of household-scale storage in the overall portfolio of food security strategies that requires revision. To that end we discuss archaeological and ethnographic evidence for the endur-ing, cross-cultural reliance of small-scale farming households on food storage to maintain food security and use these data to make the general case for household storage as part of a portfolio of adaptive strategies needed to improve contemporary smallholder food security and the spe-cific case for its importance in India.

An Archaeological Perspective

One of the challenges in making development experts and national policy makers aware of the tradeoff involved in mobilizing food away from households is their ignorance of households' capacity for food storage to maintain their food security if only marketable surplus was drawn off by the government. There are a few (e.g., Mortimore and Adams 2001), however, who are calling for a long-term perspective on development that focuses on small-scale farmers' adaptive strategies. In a recent publication Spielmann and colleagues (2011a; see also Spielmann et al. 2011b) argued that archaeology's routine engagement with the long term can help provide that perspective by considering vulnerabilities associated with small-scale crop production and the long-term adaptations that have been successfully employed by small-scale farmers for hundreds or thousands of years. These strategies have been particularly well-studied in the Southwestern US.

Given its arid climate, water is the limiting factor in crop production across the US Southwest, and farmers had to deal with extremely high inter-annual variation in precipitation (Figure 11.1). Prehistoric farmers were thus vulnerable to marked variation in crop production from year to year, as many smallholder farmers are today. Figure 11.1 marks periods of drought using lighter and darker bars. Ethnographic and archaeological data (Slatter 1979) document that household storage would not be suffi-cient to cover the needs of families in extended dry periods. In the face of a sequence of extremely dry years, farmers would migrate elsewhere (Spiel-mann et al. 2011a and b). We return to this point of different strategies matching different temporal durations of food insecurity later in our discussion of government and household-level storage in our Indian case study.

The strategies used in the past in the US Southwest to enhance food security included diversifying field locations and crop varieties, concentrating water on agricultural fields, multi-year, household-level storage, inter-household food sharing, and migration. Here we discuss storage.

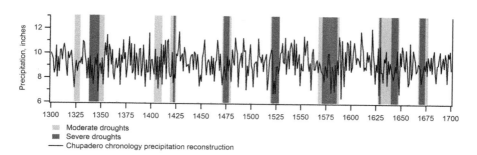

FIGURE 11.1. Annual variability in rainfall in the Salinas region of the US Southwest along with periods of moderate and severe drought.

Prehistoric Household Food Storage in the US Southwest

Prehistoric Southwestern farmers addressed the problem of variation in annual rainfall, and thus crop production, in part through the development of multi-year, household-level storage capacity. The longevity of stored grain in this semi-arid environment helped ameliorate the pattern of high frequency environmental variability and crop production in that an individual poor year or two could be compensated for using the stored products of better years. An emphasis on substantial household-level storage can be seen from the time that corn became a critical staple in the Southwestern diet, by at least 600 CE. Unlike some smallholder farmers today, prehistoric Southwestern farmers did not raise livestock as a potential buffer against a shortfall in grain production. However, in other areas of the world where prehistoric farmers did have livestock such as the Near East, household-scale storage of grains was also a critical strategy for maintaining food security for millennia (Bogaard et al. 2009; Frangipane 2007; Kuijt 2008; Kuijt and Finlayson 2009).

Over the past several decades Southwestern archaeologists (e.g., Burns 1983; Lebo 1991) have conducted a variety of analyses and simulations focused explicitly on the degree to which, over the long durée, household storage of food crops could have maintained food security in the face of shortfalls in crop production during years of low rainfall. These simulations have used annual dendroclimatological data for millennium-long periods, contemporary corn production figures from ethnography or the local region (calibrated to remove the effects of modern fertilizer on crop production), information on the effects of water stress on corn production, estimates of the contribution of corn to prehistoric diets based on a number of bone chemistry analyses, and Pueblo ethnographic information on target amounts of corn in storage. In all cases, researchers concluded that household storage significantly reduced food insecurity and famine. Most recently, Gumerman and colleagues (2003) created a simulation in which farmers made a simple decision – to remain in place when they had two years of corn in storage and move when they did not. They then compared the demographic and settlement outcomes from that model to those of the archaeological record. The match between modeled output and real data was quite close, substantiating the crucial role corn storage played among prehistoric Pueblo households.

Archaeological data also document the critical importance of household-level food storage. Information from a recent review (Spielmann and Nelson 2014) of the association between households and storage facilities (pits, bins, rooms, and granaries) across five Southwestern and northern Mexico case studies provides substantial support for the argument that households relied on food storage over the long term.

The importance of storage for coping with variability in crop production in the past was also recently documented by Jeffrey Dean (2006; Figure 11.2). He analyzed changes in household storage capacity in prehistoric households in Tsegi Canyon, northeastern Arizona, that were occupied between 1250 and 1300 CE. In this case, farmers had developed a strategy that apparently allowed them to cope with inter-annual variation in precipitation. They were then faced with a novel, low frequency process: a marked decline in the water table and a prolonged dry period. Dean documented that in the mid-1200s, as conditions for agriculture worsened, household corn storage rooms (granaries) increased in number and living room space decreased; in the village overall, granary space increased 61 percent at the expense of living area. In effect, households traded off living area for greater food storage capacity. The fact that people chose to

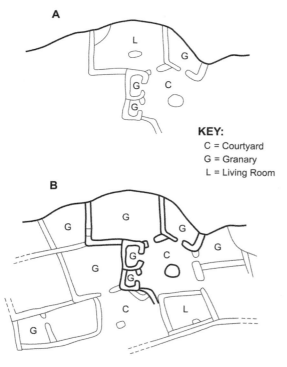

KEY:

C = Courtyard
G = Granary
L = Living Room

FIGURE 11.2. Room Cluster 2 at Kiet Siel, Tsegi Canyon, northeastern Arizona: (A) in 1271 CE with three fairly small granaries and (B) in 1276 CE with eight granaries, note the living room turned into a granary (after Dean 2006:figure 8.3).

increase storage capacity suggests its central function in mitigating the effects of environmental perturbation in the Southwest.

In sum, at the local level, household-based storage was a common and robust adaptation for maintaining a secure food supply through an annual cycle and to mitigate inter-annual variation in crop production. We now turn to ethnographic data from sub-Saharan Africa to document more recent reliance on smallholder household food storage.

Ethnographic Household Food Storage in Sub-Saharan Africa

Inter-annual storage. Storage in the prehistoric Southwest appears especially geared toward alleviating inter-annual fluctuations in the food supply. In Nigeria and Ghana there is also a longitudinal history of multi-year storage of grain that persisted in places into the twentieth century and perhaps into the twenty-first. In the 1820s, explorer Hugh Clapperton (1829) visited the Hausa in what is present-day Nigeria and noted household storage bins holding three to ten tons, in which grain was stored for two to three years. Over a century later, ethnographers conducting research in the 1950s and 1960s also remarked on multi-year storage among the Hausa (Hart 1982; Hill 1972), although they also noted food shortages. Based on data from the 1950s, Forsyth (1962) described maize storage cribs among the Ashanti in Ghana that held on average three to seven tons of maize on the cob. And in the 1960s, William Allan (1965) described the "normal surplus" among small-scale farmers in Kenya that parallels the Southwestern case in that average years produced a surplus that could be stored for consumption during droughts. Mention of multi-year storage largely disappears from ethnographic information after the 1960s; it is not clear if this disappearance reflects an actual change in practices or simply a change in what ethnographers reported.

There is a more recent ethnographic description of multi-year storage in Ethiopia, however, where in the late 1990s sorghum could be stored for up to five years to alleviate famine (Butler 2002), and there are hints that this may also be the case in Sudan and Namibia (Nukenine 2010). We mention these cases because the overall sense of the literature that we have been reading is that a variety of factors preclude the production and thus storage of more than one year's surplus. Key among these factors is one we identified earlier in this chapter: the need to sell crops at harvest for cash to cover other household necessities (Anyango et al. 1989; Armah and Asante 2006; Hill 1982; Kamau et al. 1989; Malambo 1988; Mkandawire 1993; Raynaut 2001; Wolde Mariam 1990).

Current year storage. Sub-Saharan Africa ethnographies also document current year, rather than multi-year, storage of food for household consumption between harvests (Bohannan and Bohannan 1966, 1968; Forsyth 1962; Nukenine 2010; Thamaga-Chitja et al. 2004; Table 11.1). Our sense is that this is the temporal scale of storage that is realistically accessible to most current smallholders. Ethnographers also, however, mention hunger seasons and the fact that current quantities of stored food are insufficient to cover the consumption needs of the family between harvests (Forde and Scott 1946; Hill 1977). This is referred to as an "availability gap" (Armah and Asante 2006). These shortfalls have persistent, critical consequences. As Killick (1978) discusses for Ghana, while starvation was rare in the 1970s, malnutrition was chronic, and Musoke (1990) cites elevated figures of infant mortality in Malawi from the 1980s as evidence of insufficient food availability. Household storage could alleviate availability gaps (Katz 2008; Marchione 2008; Mkandawire and Matlosa 1993; Nustad 2001).

Storage Loss

One of the current impediments to the acceptance of household storage as a viable strategy to improve food security is a widely held (Western) assumption that there are immense losses in traditional household storage. A recent widely cited study from the World Resources Institute on global food wastes and losses, reports that 17 percent of the total food produced in South and Southeast Asia is wasted or lost during the different stages of the value chain (from production to final consumption), and storage losses account for about 6 percent of food produced. That study cites a report from the Food and Agriculture Organization, but in neither of these reports is it clear at what level of storage these losses occur or how these numbers have been calculated (Lipinski et al. 2013). Similarly, Godfray and co-authors (2010) cite an FAO graph of household storage loss that has no associated data. We have found similar problems in the African literature, where one person's (Forsyth 1962) unsubstantiated assertion of large (20 percent) household losses of stored grain was then cited again and again by other researchers.

Actual measurements of household storage loss indicate a general range of from 4 to 10 percent from the 1970s into the 2000s. The efficacy of household-level storage has been emphasized by Greeley (1978), who suggests that post-harvest storage loss is closer to 4–7 percent rather than the 33 percent cited in Indian policy literature (see also Compton et al. 1993; Government of India 2002).

TABLE 11.1. *Ethnographic household storage data for Sub-Saharan Africa*

Location	Form of household storage	Duration	Citation
Ghana	Crib storage for maize	One season for all	Forsyth 1962
	6' diam, 6' tall, circ platform with tin roof for maize		
	1609–3000 cu ft; .65–10.8 tons of maize in sheath; avg capacity 3–7 tons of rice		
	Earth-walled granaries for sorghum, millet, and rice		
	6 × 6' rooms		
	3–4' tall earthen silos for groundnuts		
	Maize		Armah and Asante 2006
Nigeria	11–12' high, 7–8' wide, large urn raised on stones 3' above ground; clay and straw for doura and millet	2–3 years	Clapperton 1829
	"Shacks," on platforms in reception houses for millet	Until yam harvest	Bohannan and Bohannan 1966, 1968
	4–5' sq, 7–8' high outdoor platforms for sorghum	Single season	
	Large baskets for sorghum		
	Pits covered with dried grass matting for yams	Several months	
	Wicker, clay, or grass, off ground for millet, sorghum, other crops	Several months to several years	Hill 1972
	Sacks for threshed grain, husked groundnuts		
	In bags in mud-built room for grains		
Zambia	Conical grass roofs, cylindrical basket on raised platform for maize	At least one year; no more than 2	Malambo 1988
	Kimberley brick, for maize		
Ethiopia	Tall clay or bamboo vessels sealed with dung for grain		Butler 2002
	Sacks		
	Pits for sorghum	up to 5 years	
South Africa	Wattle and daub, metal tank, sack, roof		Thamaga-Chitja et al. 2004

In general, household storage loss has increased due to the introduction of the grain borer in the past twenty years, and in some cases loss can reach 30 percent (Compton et al. 1993; Mutambuki et al. 2010). Storage loss is also significantly greater in introduced high yield varieties of crops than in native varieties due to the new crops' greater susceptibility to pests. For this reason, some farmers grow a mixture of the two.

To the best of our knowledge, there are just a handful of studies assessing the relative costs and benefits of different traditional storage practices. These studies in general show high positive returns to storage techniques that use locally available material and labor. A study carried out in South India in 1976 (Greely 1978) found that an improved bamboo basket (gade) built over a mud platform for outdoor storage of paddy, coupled with periodic fumigation, was a highly effective form of household grain storage. The study found that costs for building household storage facilities vary substantially across regions and depend on the availability of local materials and labor as well as the size of the structure. Thus, for instance, metal bins were found to have a negative return to investment but traditional structures made with locally available paddy straw were found to have a return of 50 percent. Metal bins are generally too expensive for most smallholder farmers to use and it is only the wealthier ones who can afford to purchase them (Gurung 2003; Thamaga-Chitja et al. 2004). Research on the active properties in traditional approaches to pest control has documented their efficacy (Badu-Apraku et al. 2007; Dhaliwal and Singh 2010). These, too, are locally available and safe to use.

Contemporary farmers in sub-Saharan Africa do express concern about loss of stored food through insect and rodent pests, rot, and theft (Kamau et al. 1989; Morton 2007). In India, preventable post-harvest losses of food grains in transit, transportation, handling, and storage are estimated to be roughly 10 percent of the crop, a staggering amount of food in a country in which a significant proportion of the population is undernourished (Basavaraja et al. 2007). In 2009, however, the Indian government's central storage facilities only had the capacity to store 25 of the 55 tons of food the government had collected, and thus 55 percent was not stored securely.

The authors of the ethnographic studies note that more effort and resources spent by the farmer or development agencies in building more secure on-farm storage would ameliorate this problem of storage loss. Household storage is a strategy that draws on local knowledge and locally available materials. Local knowledge in some areas, however, is currently held only by older members of the community and thus is vulnerable to loss.

Case Study: Contemporary India

The case study we focus on for the remainder of this chapter is India, which is home to the largest number of hungry people in the world (Menon et al. 2009). The Indian central government is responsible for the procurement, storage, transportation, and bulk allocation of food grains to the states.

National Indian Food Policy

Since the 1950s, India's food management policy has been motivated by three main objectives: (1) Procure food grains from farmers at remunerative prices to encourage production; (2) Distribute food grains to consumers, particularly the vulnerable urban and rural households, at affordable prices, and (3) Maintain buffer stocks to cope with production uncertainty and maintain price stability (Kapila 2009). The nodal central government agency responsible for the procurement, storage, and distribution of the food stocks is the Food Corporation of India. The two main cereals under the procurement program are wheat and rice.

Figure 11.3 shows the movement of food grains, the main actors involved, and the policy instruments that come into play under this centralized food production and distribution system. The main instruments for implementing this policy are the Minimum Support Price (MSP) and the Central Issue Price (CIP), as shown in Figure 11.3. The MSP for major food grains is announced at the start of the growing season and the government offers to buy all of the produce that comes forth for sale at this price through a vast network of procurement agents. As shown in Figure 11.3, farmers sell almost all of their produce immediately after harvest at the MSP. The Central Government, through the Food Corporation of India, is tasked with managing the purchase, transportation, handling, and storage of this vast stock right after the harvest season. Norms are set for the amount to be stored and the rest of the stock is then distributed to the different states, which, in turn, are responsible for distributing these grains to their rural and urban consumer base through an established network of Fair Price Shops.

The Commission for Agricultural Costs and Prices recommends the levels at which the MSP should be fixed. Their recommendations are based on several considerations that include the cost of cultivation in different agroecological zones, overall shortage of grains as reflected by the trend in wholesale prices, and the need to keep check on the rate of inflation in the country (Kapila 2009). Given the strong farmer lobby in

Public Food Distribution System: India

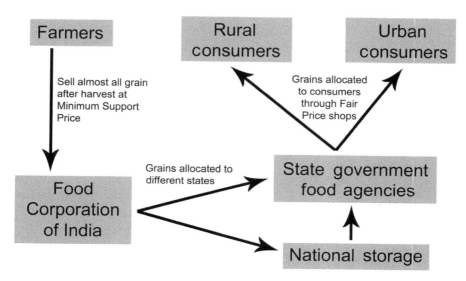

FIGURE 11.3. Public food distribution system in India.

India, MSP tends to be a highly politicized issue, and so the actual MSP is much higher than the recommended levels and above the market price in most years (Kapila 2009). Therefore, farmers – particularly, the small and marginal ones – tend to sell a major proportion of their produce through the government's procurement channels right after the harvest. State governments are responsible for operational tasks including allocation and identification of families below the poverty line, issue of ration cards, and the supervision and monitoring of FPS. The central government has large storage facilities at Delhi and at major regional centers. The state governments have their own storage facilities with smaller capacity.

This centralized system of storage and distribution has failed in three respects: First, it does not address food insecurity at the local level. Recent estimates suggest that the Indian government spent nearly 1 percent of its GDP on its food aid program in the past year, making it one of the largest domestic food aid programs in the world (Tandon and Landes 2012). However, USDA's *International Food Security Assessment, 2013–23* suggests that even under the best-case scenario, nearly 40 percent of India's population is food insecure and India continues to account for the largest share of world population considered to be food insecure (Tandon and Landes 2012). The Public Distribution System (PDS) in particular has encountered huge problems in its goal to feed farmers in need. A recent study commissioned by the Planning Commission of India found that about 58 percent of the subsidized food grains issued from the central pool do not reach the targeted poor families because of identification errors, nontransparent operation, and unethical practices in the implementation of the targeted public distribution system (Planning Commission 2005). The cost of handling food grains by public agencies is also very high. According to the study, for one rupee worth of income transfer to the poor, the Government of India (GoI) spends Rs.3.65. Thus, although the Government of India is making an effort to ameliorate the tradeoff it has created between maintaining food security at the smallholder household level and the national level through a massive food aid bureaucracy, it has failed to do so. Making it possible for farming households to retain food would be a more direct solution to the problem.

The need for this solution is evident in the second major failure in the centralized food storage system: The grain gathered by the system vastly exceeds the available storage capacity. In 2009 the government had a storage capacity of 15 million tons and had rented space to handle another 10 million tons. Against this capacity, 55 million tons were procured in 2008–2009 and ended up being stacked in the open, unprotected from the weather and vermin (Source: ipsnews_net.mht – accessed January 11, 2011).

Third, culturally appropriate food is not routinely supplied from the central storage facilities to the Fair Price Shops. The Planning Commission study also asked the recipients of aid whether the local variety of rice/wheat was strongly preferred to the variety they get through PDS. Around 70 percent of households were found to prefer local varieties (there was a great deal of variation across states, however, with some accounting for as low as 12 percent, while others – largely in remote parts of the country – account for as high as 100 percent). Several households expressed preference for local coarser cereals (such as millets) to the rice and wheat they received through the PDS.

In sum, under the current system, food that has been mobilized away from households at harvest, largely to feed cities and promote industrialization, is often not returned to them in times of food shortfall, and there is a high cost entailed with the current redistribution system in terms of administrative, transport, and energy costs, and storage losses. These problems could be ameliorated through encouraging the storage of food at the smallholder level and only mobilizing the marketable surplus when it is available. If this were to happen, the cross-scale tradeoff in food security would diminish.

Household Storage in India

In this case study it would be helpful to be able to undertake an analysis using archaeological and ethnographic data of whether household-level storage contributed to food security over the very long term. We could then evaluate the degree to which government policies have reduced food security, given the pressure on households to sell food at harvest and then buy it back at higher prices later in the year. Unfortunately these data are not available. The published archaeological record is insufficient from any part of India to make the kind of case for the enduring importance of household storage that we have made from the Southwestern archaeological record. The ethnographic record is also not as rich in terms of household storage information as the sub-Saharan African record we discussed earlier, but existing data (see Table 11.2) highlight the importance of household scale storage.

Part of the challenge in finding even ethnohistoric and ethnographic information on household storage in India are the effects of India's conquest by Britain beginning in the eighteenth century, and Britain's subsequent push to increase the productivity of Indian farms and to shift farm labor from food to cash crops to provide goods for colonists to export to global markets. Davis (2000) has discussed the ways in which food production and distribution changed radically in India after British conquest. He notes myriad means by which rural farmers were protected from famine in pre-colonial times, including the fact that village-level food reserves were larger. British policies, including the appropriation of massive quantities of food for export, demolished these strategies, leading to the worst famines in Indian history. Whitcombe (1972:165–180) discusses farming in northern India in the late nineteenth century, noting that European grain-exporting businesses invested in India in the mid-1800s. Farmers were left with insufficient food to store, causing them to borrow grain at higher prices for sowing or to feed their families during seasons when food stocks were low. They then had to repay these debts at harvest when food prices were low. The pattern of selling low and buying dear thus goes back at least to the 1870s. This early, massive reorganization of small-scale agriculture in India leaves us with no baseline of household risk minimization strategies in the absence of globalization and cash-cropping.

TABLE 11.2. *Ethnographic storage data for India*

Location	Form of household storage	Duration	Citation
S India	Storage pits and rooms	one year?	Ishwaran 1966
Karnataka	Most houses contain a grain storage bin; are also-room-sized bins for rice storage		Singh 1973
NW India	Grain and flour are stored		Mann 1917
Gujarat	Smaller houses may have a large corn bin or clay storage vessels, medium houses have more storage		Glatter 1969
Hyderabad	Wealthier households have a room for storing grain. Smaller households store grain in ceramic or basket containers		Dube 1955

Twentieth-century Indian ethnographies that include descriptions of farming rarely mention food storage, and when they do, the information is generic (Table 11.2), rather than providing a discussion of the scale and importance of storage to household food security. Greeley (1978) makes a sweeping statement that 60–70 percent of food grains are stored at the farm level, with a mean of about one ton in storage overall, roughly enough to last until the next harvest. He notes that this statement is based on his research among farmers in Andhra Pradesh and substantiated by further information from basket makers in south and east India, but the data supporting this statement are not provided. The statement was repeated essentially verbatim in Nagnur et al.'s 2006 article with no further supporting evidence.

It is likely that the rare discussions of household-level food storage (summarized in Table 11.2) in semiarid regions of India hint at much wider practices prior to the spread of green revolution technologies in the 1970s. Around that time, attention shifted to growing a few select cereals supported by government programs that offer to buy major food grains after harvest at pre-announced minimum support prices. Production was emphasized, particularly to support rapidly growing urban populations. It is at this time that traditional storage practices came to be perceived as irrelevant, given that the central government was intent on mobilizing food, storing it at centralized storage facilities and then distributing it across the country (Kapila 2009). In the twenty-first century, Pande and Akermann's (2009) study of how small-scale farmers are dealing with climate change in five Indian states mentions storage only in arid Rajasthan (two of the other loci, in Andhra Pradesh and Maharashtra, produced largely cash crops that were immediately sold). Smallholders in the Rajasthan study each had a small mud granary for storing sorghum, millets, and maize. Although grain can be stored for several years, the farmers in these areas produced only enough for one year's storage.

One of the policy recommendations from Pande and Akermann's (2009) study, based on what the farmers themselves suggested, is to increase household grain and fodder storage capacities to improve food security. Data presented in a recent study by the Indian Ministry of Agriculture (GOI 2002: Annexure 38) concerning paddy storage suggest significant on-farm storage of rice in many states in India, but the data are too coarse-grained to understand how pervasive household-level storage is among smallholders. Interestingly, the researchers note that they were "startled" to find that nearly 74 percent of the storage at the household level was in traditional storage structures (*kutcha* storage) made of locally available materials and only 26 percent was in concrete structures or metal bins (*pucca* storage) (2002:7.1.8). Even with this storage, the amount of crop smallholder households kept for themselves was on average 25 percent below the amount they needed (GOI 2002:Tables 13 and 21). The study estimated storage losses to be around 0.4 percent of total production (GOI 2002:Annexure 38), and attributed these losses to drainage, rodents, infestation, handling, and quality deterioration. We note that this estimate is an order of magnitude lower than Indian ethnographic studies (e.g., Greeley 1978) discussed previously that suggest around 4–6 percent loss. Further information on the nature of household storage across India will be necessary to understand this degree of variation.

Relationships between Household Storage, Malnourishment, and Hunger in India

Given the lack of attention to household-level storage in both contemporary policy discussions as well as development research, routine agricultural surveys do not collect household-level data on storage in India. Thus it is not possible to examine rigorously how the decline in household-level storage has impacted food security. However, as we discussed earlier, there have been quite a few studies on marketed surplus (amount farmer actually sells) and marketable surplus (surplus amount over consumption needs) at the farm household level across India. In Table 11.3 we report results from a government of India study on marketed and marketable surplus for paddy in different states of India (GOI 2002). The last column of the table shows the difference between marketable and marketed surplus. A negative value for this variable (i.e., marketable surplus falling short of marketed surplus) is an indicator of distress sales by farmers. Note that paddy is not a staple crop in some of the states (marked by an asterisk), so this table does not give a complete picture of the food situation. The table also reports results from a recent study on comparison of hunger across different states in India using the Global Hunger Index (Menon et al. 2009).

The table shows that although at the All-India level, marketable surplus exceeded marketed surplus (no distress sales), there is considerable variation across states. There are several states in which distress sales are significant, and states with a high magnitude of distress sales, such as Madhya Pradesh and Bihar in central India, Maharashtra in western India, and Orissa in eastern India, also score high on the hunger index (denoting greater severity of hunger) and calorie malnourishment. This provides indirect support for our argument regarding the relation between the decline of storage at the household level and food insecurity. In future work we hope to collect household-level data on storage and food insecurity to examine this relation more thoroughly.

Implications and Conclusions

The memory of famines during the British colonial period has strongly shaped the narrative, and consequently the mental model, that underlies the framing of food policy in India. Shortly after independence, the import of food (PL-480 packages from the United States) following the severe drought in the mid-1960s was seen as a tremendous embarrassment to the pride of a young nation. Consequently, emphasis was placed on maximizing national production of food by focusing on the most fertile regions of the country, and then distributing surplus food from these regions to those with food deficits through a centralized pubic distribution system. The green revolution in the late 1960s/early 1970s accelerated agricultural growth at the national level and as Sen (1999) argues, "Famines are easy to prevent if there is a serious effort to do so, and a democratic government, facing elections and criticisms from opposition parties and independent newspapers, cannot help but make such an effort." In his opinion the establishment of a multi-party political system and a free press after independence were instrumental in preventing further famines in India. The Indian government has also been able to

TABLE 11.3. *India state hunger index and marketed and marketable surplus*

State	Prevalence of calorie under–nourishment (%)	India state hunger index[a] Score	Rank	Marketed surplus	Marketable surplus	Marketable minus marketed surplus[b]
Punjab[c]	11.1	13.63	1	90.50	93.66	3.16
Kerala	28.6	17.63	2	29.05	27.90	-1.15
Andhra Pradesh	19.6	19.53	3	49.61	50.04	0.43
Assam	14.6	19.83	4	29.05	27.09	-1.96
Haryana[c]	15.1	20.00	5	81.90	88.78	6.88
Tamilnadu	29.1	20.87	6	26.53	11.07	-15.46
Rajasthan[c]	14.0	20.97	7	84.48	88.61	4.13
West Bengal	18.5	20.97	8	47.37	59.92	12.55
Uttar Pradesh	14.5	22.13	9	38.57	40.86	2.29
Maharashtra	27.0	22.80	10	2.73	-56.98	-59.71
Karnataka	28.1	23.73	11	58.92	70.67	11.75
Orissa	21.4	23.80	12	29.37	18.98	-10.39
Gujarat[c]	23.3	24.70	13	57.27	69.2	11.93
Bihar	17.3	27.30	15	18.54	14.15	-4.39
Madhya Pradesh	23.4	30.87	17	54.04	45.80	-8.24
All India	20			43.78	44.99	1.21

Note: Data on hunger index from Menon et al. (2009); data on marketed and marketable surplus from Indian GOI (2002).
[a] Higher number denotes greater severity.
[b] Negative numbers denote distress sales.
[c] Denotes states where paddy is not a staple crop.

shield its population from recent major food crises, such as the global food crisis of 2008, which led to sharp increases in food prices and food riots in several other Asian countries.

Thus, the path that India has followed has allowed her to mobilize and secure food supplies at the national level; however, as we discussed in this chapter, the centralized distribution system also resulted in high levels of food insecurity at the local/household level. This is the central tradeoff that we have emphasized in this chapter. India ranks high on the global hunger index and individual households continue to be highly vulnerable to both intra-annual variations in food access (what we referred to as the availability gap) as well as inter-annual variations.

We argue in this chapter that food security needs to be assured at different levels of decision making. In large countries like China, India, and Indonesia, and even smaller ones such as Ghana, food security is high at the national level but at the household level vulnerabilities remain high (e.g., see Logan, Chapter 5, this volume, on household vulnerabilities to food insecurity). Sufficient food production at the global or national levels has not translated into food security at the household level. Clearly, different strategies are required to address different spatial and temporal scales of food insecurity, necessitating a portfolio of strategies across different levels to achieve food security.

In this chapter we used the resilience framework to better understand these tradeoffs across different decision making levels (national government versus household) and across different scales (temporal and spatial). Although grain storage at the national level helps protect against longer-term shocks and helps smooth out the variability in food production across different agroecological zones of the country, it does not assure food security at the household level. The resilience framework also helps us better integrate lessons from archaeology (the long durée perspective) with more contemporary experience.

Our discussion of the archaeological evidence from the US Southwest further elucidates these shorter and longer-term vulnerabilities to food shortfall, and shows how Southwestern farmers used household storage to cover inter-annual (1–3 years), short-term vulnerabilities to food shortfall, and migration to cope with longer-term vulnerability in the context of drought, when stored food ran out. Contemporary farmers cannot migrate to new farmland (though they do migrate to urban areas) when stored food runs out as there is not much available land for farming. Thus the national system of storage and distribution is helpful to cope with longer-term vulnerability. It is the short-term intra-annual vulnerability to food shortfall that is not alleviated by national storage. In the absence of an appropriately scaled strategy, the problem of chronic food insecurity continues at the household level in India.

This problem of high and chronic food insecurity at the household level is acknowledged and has motivated the passage of major legislation, such as the Food Security Bill of 2013. Instead of thinking differently about food security, however, this Bill seeks solutions in terms of further expanding and better targeting the centralized Public Distribution System. The path dependence associated with the current Indian food distribution system –

the past investments in central storage facilities and the distribution network – have made the system deeply entrenched and difficult to change despite the mounting evidence on rotting of food in central storage facilities and the public outrage against such policy. The solutions being currently proposed focus largely on how central storage facilities can be expanded and made technologically more advanced to decrease losses, instead of thinking about how to increase household capacity to self-insure against short-term vulnerability and chronic food insecurity.

An advantage of our collaboration has been in bringing the household-level and household strategies, which are often the focus of archaeological research in small-scale societies, into an evaluation of contemporary food security strategies. The challenge of ensuring food security in the developing world has largely been framed in terms of how to increase production through technological fixes and then (in the case of India, particularly) how to accumulate and distribute food through a large-scale centralized system. Moreover, the Indian case also reveals that the traditional focus on technological fixes to increase production is both undesirable and infeasible given the emerging evidence of adverse ecological impacts and emerging tradeoffs with scarce water and land resources. Coupled with this, climate change has further challenged us to think more seriously about risks and uncertainties, and how these translate into the need for assuring food security, particularly for smallholders. Given the enormous cost and ineffectiveness of central storage, and yet the ongoing dialogue about improving this approach, it is clear that the current discussions of food security have become locked within a very narrow mental model. It is time to engage with household-level strategies that have proven so effective over the long durée.

References

Aggarwal, Rimjhim 2008 Resource Poor Farmers in South India: On the Margins or Frontiers of Globalization? In *Globalization and the Poor in Asia: Can Shared Growth Be Sustained?* edited by M. Nissanke and E. Thorbecke, pp. 196–220. Palgrave Macmillan, London.

Allan, William 1965 *The African Husbandman*. Oliver and Boyd, London.

Anyango, G., T. Downing, C. Getho, M. Gitahi, C. Kabutha, C. M. Kamal, M. Karanja, S. W. Maghanga, S. K. Mbarire, S. Muene, W. Wainaina, and F. Were 1989 Drought Vulnerability in Central and Eastern Kenya. In *Coping with Drought in Kenya: National and Local Strategies*, edited by T. E. Downing, K. W. Gitu, and C. M. Kamau, pp. 169–210. L. Rienner, Boulder, Colorado.

Armah, Paul W., and Felix Asante 2006 Traditional Maize Storage Systems and Staple-Food Security in Ghana. *Journal of Food Distribution Research* 37 (1):34–39.

Badu-Apraku, B., M. A. B. Fakorede, A. F. Lum, A. Menkir, and M. Ouedraogo 2007 *Demand-Driven Technologies for Sustainable Maize Production in West and Central Africa.* International Institute of Tropical Agriculture, Ibadan, Nigeria.

Basavaraja H., S. B. Mahajanashetti, and N. C. Udagatti 2007 Economic Analysis of Post-harvest Losses in Food Grains in India: A Case Study of Karnataka. *Agricultural Economics Research Review* 20(1):117–126.

Bogaard, Amy, Michael Charles, Katheryn C. Twiss, Andrew Fairbairn, Nurcan Yalman, Dragana Filipovic, G. Arzu Demirergi, Fusun Ertug, Nerissa Russell, and Jennifer Henecke 2009 Private Pantries and Celebrated Surplus: Storing and Sharing Food at Neolithic Catalhoyuk, Central Anatolia. *Antiquity* 83(321):649–668.

Bohannan, Paul, and Laura Bohannan 1966 *A Source Notebook in Tiv Subsistence, Technology, and Economics.* HRAFlex Books, FF57-002, Ethnography Series, New Haven.

   1968 *Tiv Economy.* Longmans, London.

Burns, Barney Tillman 1983 *Simulated Anasazi Storage Behavior Using Crop Yields Reconstructed from Tree Rings: A.D. 652-1968.* PhD dissertation, Department of Anthropology, University of Arizona, Tucson.

Butler, Ann 2002 Sustainable Agriculture in a Harsh Environment. In *Droughts, Food, and Culture*, edited by F.A. Hassan, pp. 171–187. Kluwer Academic, New York.

Cash, D. W., W. Adger, F. Berkes, P. Garden, L. Lebel, P. Olsson, L. Pritchard, and O. Young 2006 Scale and Cross-scale Dynamics: Governance and Information in a Multilevel World. *Ecology and Society* 11(2):8.

Clapperton, Hugh 1829 *Journal of a Second Expedition into the Interior of Africa.* Frank Cass and Co. Ltd, 1966 (first published in 1829).

Compton, J. A. F., P. S. Tyler, P. S. Hindmarsh, P. Golob, R. A. Boxall, and C. P. Haines 1993 Reducing Losses in Small Farm Grain Storage in the Tropics. *Tropical Science* 33(3):283–318.

Davis, Mike 2000 The Origin of the Third World. *Antipode* 32(1):48–89.

Dean, Jeffrey 2006 Subsistence Stress and Food Storage at Kiet Siel, Northeastern Arizona. In *Environmental Change and Human Adaptation in the Ancient American Southwest*, edited by D. E. Doyel and J. S. Dean, pp. 160–179. University of Utah Press, Salt Lake City.

Devraj, Ranjit 2010 Cereals Rot in the Rain While the Poor Stay Hungry. Available at: www.ipsnews.net/2010/09/india-cereals-rot-in-the-rain-while-the-poor-stay-hungry/ (accessed February 1, 2015).

Dhaliwal, R. K., and G. Singh 2010 Traditional Food Grain Storage Practices of Punjab. *Indian Journal of Traditional Knowledge* 9(3):526–530.

Dube, S. C. 1955 *Indian Village.* Routledge and Kegan Paul, London.

FAO, IFAD, and WFP 2014 *The State of Food Security in the World. Strengthening the Enabling Environment for Food Security and Nutrition.* FAO, Rome.

Forde, Daryll, and Richenda Scott 1946 *The Native Economies of Nigeria, Volume 1. The Economics of Tropical Dependency*. Faber and Faber, London.

Forsyth, J. 1962 Major Food Storage Problems. In *Agriculture and Land Use in Ghana*, edited by J. B. Wills, pp. 394–401. Oxford University Press, London.

Frangipane, Marcella 2007 Different Types of Egalitarian Societies and the Development of Inequality in Early Mesopotamia. *World Archaeology* 39(2):151–176.

Gibson, C., E. Ostrom, and T. -K. Ahn 2000 The Concept of Scale and the Human Dimensions of Global Change: A Survey. *Ecological Economics* 32(2):217–239.

Glatter, Augusta 1969 *Contributions to the Ethnography of the Chodhris, Surat District, Gujarat*. Wien, Austria.

Godfray, H. Charles J., John R. Beddington, Ian R. Crute, Lawrence Haddad, David Lawrence, James F. Muir, Jules Pretty, Sherman Robinson, Sandy M. Thomas, and Camilla Toulmin 2010 Food Security: The Challenge of Feeding 9 Billion People. *Science* 327:812–818.

Government of India (GOI) 2002 *Marketable Surplus and Postharvest Losses of Paddy in India*. New Delhi: Ministry of Agriculture.

Greeley, Martin 1978 Appropriate Rural Technology. *Food Policy* (February):39–49.

Gumerman, George, Alan Swedlund, Jeffrey Dean, and Joshua Epstein 2003 The Evolution of Social Behavior in the Prehistoric American Southwest. *Artificial Life* 9:435–444.

Gurung, Astric Bjornsen 2003 The Sacred in Grain Storage. *COMPAS Magazine* 7:40–41.

Hart, Keith 1982 *The Political Economy of West African Agriculture*. Cambridge University Press, Cambridge.

Hill, Polly 1972 *Rural Hausa: A Village and a Setting*. Cambridge University Press, Cambridge.

—— 1977 *Population, Prosperity, and Poverty: Rural Kano 1900 and 1970*. Cambridge University Press, Cambridge.

—— 1982 *Dry Grain Farming Families: Hausaland (Nigeria) and Karnataka (India) Compared*. Cambridge University Press, Cambridge.

Ishwaran, K. 1966 *Tradition and Economy in Village India*. Routledge and Kegan Paul, New York.

Kamau, C., G. Anyango, M. Wainama, T. Downum, and M. Gitahi 1989 Case Studies of Drought Impacts and Responses in Central and Eastern Kenya. In *Coping with Drought in Kenya: National and Local Strategies*, edited by T. Downum, K. Gitu, and C. Kamau, pp. 211–225. L. Rienner, Boulder.

Kapila, Uma 2009 Agriculture: Issues in Development and Policy. In *India's Economic Development Since 1947*, edited by Uma Kapila, pp. 354–403. Academic Foundation, Delhi.

Katz, Solomon 2008 The World Food Crisis: An Overview of Causes and Consequences. *Anthropology News* 49(7):4–5.

Killick, Tony 1978 *Development Economics in Action: A Study of Economic Policies in Ghana*. Heinemann, London.

Kuijt, Ian 2008 Demographic and Storage Systems During the Southern Levantine Neolithic Demographic Transition. In *The Neolithic Demographic Transition and Its Consequences*, edited by J-P. Bocquet-Appel and O. Bar-Yosef, pp. 287–313. Springer, New York.

Kuijt, Ian, and Bill Finlayson 2009 Evidence for Food Storage and Predomestica-
    tion Granaries 11,000 Years Ago in the Jordan Valley. *Proceedings of the
    National Academy of Science* 106(27):10966–10971.
Lebo, Cathy Jean 1991 *Anasazi Harvests: Agroclimate, Harvest Variability,
    and Agricultural Strategies on Prehistoric Black Mesa, Northeastern Arizona.*
    PhD dissertation, Department of Anthropology, Indiana University,
    Bloomington.
Lipinski, Brian, Craig Hanson, James Lomax, Lisa Kitinoja, Richard Waite, and
    Tim Searchinger 2013 *Reducing Food Loss and Waste.* Working Paper, Install-
    ment 2 of Creating a Sustainable Food Future. World Resources Institute,
    Washington, D.C.
Malambo, Lovejoy M 1988 *Rural Food Security in Zambia.* Verlag Weltarchiv,
    Hamburg, Germany.
Mann, Horace 1917 *Land and Labour in a Deccan Village.* Oxford University Press,
    London.
Marchione, Tom 2008 A Time to Rethink the Global Food Regime. *Anthropology
    News* 49(7):5–6.
Menon, Purnima, Anil Deolalikar, and Anjor Bhaskar 2009 *India State Hunger
    Index: Comparisons of Hunger Across States.* International Food Policy
    Research Institute, Washington D.C.
Mkandawire, Richard, and Khabele Matlosa (editors) 1993 Introduction. *Food
    Policy and Agriculture in Southern Africa*, pp. 1–11. Sapes Books, Harare.
Mkandawire, Richard 1993 Agrarian Change and Food Security among Small-
    holder Farmers in Malawi. In *Food Policy and Agriculture in Southern
    Africa*, edited by R. Mkandawire and K. Matlosa, pp. 63–84. Sapes Books,
    Harare.
Mortimore, Michael J., and William M. Adams 2001 Farmer Adaptation, Change,
    and "Crisis" in the Sahel. *Global Environmental Change* 11(1):49–57.
Morton, J. 2007 The Impact of Climate Change on Smallholder and Sub-
    sistence Agriculture. *Proceedings of the National Academy of Sciences*
    104(50):19680–19685.
Musoke, I. K. S. 1990 Approaches to Rural Development and the Food Question:
    Swaziland, Zimbabwe, Malawi. In *African Centre for Applied Research and
    Training in Social Development, Understanding Africa's Food Problems: Social
    Policy Perspectives*, pp. 61–120. Hans Zell Publishers, London.
Mutambuki, K., C. M. Ngatia, and J. N. Mbugua 2010 Post-Harvest Technology
    Transfer to Reduce on Farm Grain Losses in Kitui District, Kenya. 10th
    International Working Conference on Stored Product Protection. *Julius-
    Kuhn-Archiv* 425:984–990.
Nagnur, Shobha, Geeta Channal, and N. Channamma 2006 Indigenous Grain
    Structures and Methods of Storage. *Indian Journal of Traditional Knowledge*
    5:114–117.
Nukenine, E. N. 2010 Stored Product Protection in Africa: Past, Present, and
    Future. 10th International Working Conference on Stored Product Protection.
    Julius-Kuhn-Archiv 425:26–41.
Nustad, Knut J. 2001 Development: The Devil We Know? *Third World Quarterly*
    22(4):479–489.

Pande, Poonam, and Kaspar Akermann 2009 *Adaptation of Small Scale Farmers to Climatic Risks in India*. Sustainet India, New Delhi.

Planning Commission 2005 *Performance Evaluation of Targeted Public Distribution System (TPDS)*. Programme Evaluation Organisation, Planning Commission, Government of India, New Delhi.

Raj, K. N., Neeladri Bhattacharya, Sumit Guha, and Sakti Padhi 1985 *Essays on the Commercialization of Indian Agriculture*. Oxford University Press, Delhi.

Raynaut, Claude 2001 Societies and Nature in the Sahel: Ecological Diversity and Social Dynamics. *Global Environmental Change* 11(1):9–18.

Sen, Amartya 1999 *Development as Freedom*. Oxford University Press, Oxford.

Shah, V. D., and M. Makwana 2013 *Marketed and Marketable Surplus of Major Food grains in Rajasthan*. Agro-Economic Research Centre, Report # 150, Sardar Patel University Gujarat, India.

Singh, Avtar 1973 *Leadership Patterns and Village Structure: A Study of Six Indian Villages*. Sterling Publishers, New Delhi.

Slatter, Edwin Darnell 1979 *Drought and Demographic Change in the Prehistoric Southwest United States: A Preliminary Quantitative Assessment*. PhD dissertation, Department of Anthropology, UCLA, Los Angeles.

Spielmann, Katherine A., and Margaret Nelson 2014 *Vulnerabilities to Food Security: Contributions from the Prehistoric Southwest*. Paper presented at the Society for American Archaeology Annual Meeting, Austin, Texas.

Spielmann, Katherine A., Margaret Nelson, Scott Ingram, and Matthew Peeples 2011a Mitigating Environmental Risk in the US Southwest. In *Sustainable Lifeways: Cultural Persistence in an Ever-Changing Environment*, edited by N. Miller, K. Moore, and K. Ryan, pp. 180–211. University of Pennsylvania Museum of Archaeology and Anthropology, distributed by University of Pennsylvania Press, Philadelphia.

2011b Sustainable Small-Scale Agriculture in Semi-Arid Environments. *Ecology and Society* 16(1):26.

Tandon, Sharad, and Maurice Landes 2012 *Estimating the Range of Food-Insecure Households in India*. USDA, Economic Research Service.

Thamaga-Chitja, Joyce M., Sheryl L. Hendricks, Gerald Ortmann, and Maryann Green 2004 Impact of Maize Storage on Rural Household Food Security in Northern Kwazulu-Natal. *Journal of Family Ecology and Consumer Sciences* 32:8–15.

Upender, M. 1990 *Marketable and Marketed Surplus in Agriculture: A Study at Farm Land*. Mittal Publications, New Delhi.

Whitcombe, Elizabeth 1972 *Agrarian Conditions in Northern India, Volume 1, the United Provinces under British Rule 1860–1900*. University of California Press, Berkeley.

Wolde Mariam, Mesfin 1990 Drought and Famine in Ethiopia: Social Impact and Socio-Economic Development. In *African Centre for Applied Research and Training in Social Development, Understanding Africa's Food Problems: Social Policy Perspectives*, pp. 204–244. Hans Zell Publishers, London.

12

Some Analytical Tradeoffs of Talking about Tradeoffs

On Perspectives Lost in Estimating the Costs and Benefits of Inequality

ALF HORNBORG

The concept of "tradeoffs" raises a number of issues regarding the organization of socioecological systems in the past and present. Most of these issues have been acknowledged and insightfully discussed by the editor in her chapters (Chapter 1 and Chapter 7) in this volume. In this chapter, I will add some further reflections on the tradeoffs represented by the very act of adopting a discourse on tradeoffs, focusing on the risks of subscribing to some of its implicit assumptions drawn from economics and resilience theory. I will be particularly concerned with how the discourse on tradeoffs can be used to rationalize and even justify inequalities in social systems where the most marginalized categories of people have no voice.

Definitions of Tradeoffs and the Implicit Assumptions of Cost-Benefit Analysis

In her introductory Chapter 1, Hegmon quotes a dictionary definition of tradeoffs as "giving up one thing in return for another." In Chapter 4, Roscoe also resorts to a dictionary definition, referring to "a balancing of factors all of which are not attainable at the same time." Logan in Chapter 5 defines a tradeoff as "the idea that when some things are gained, other things are lost," and Spielmann and Aggarwal in Chapter 11 refer to "what needs to be given up in order to gain something else." Such phrasings suggest a single managerial agent consciously deciding which course to follow, based on calculation and optimal balancing of costs and benefits. As all of the contributors to this volume are of course aware, such conditions are rarely – if ever – applicable to socioecological change, and we should keep in mind that adopting the discourse on tradeoffs risks introducing tacit assumptions about the role of rational decision making in such processes.

For several reasons, actual socioecological processes are almost always far removed from rational decision making. First, there is generally very little capacity to predict the long-term consequences of a given strategy, even for the individual or social group who adopts it. Second, choosing a particular course of action is more often a question of yielding to forces or complying with imperatives beyond the agent's control, rather than of rational calculation. Third, social systems rarely constitute a single agent either in terms of objectives or in terms of experiencing negative reper-cussions of a particular strategy. If the negative consequences in the future have been largely unknown and social agency is heterogeneous and contradictory – as exemplified by the dilemma of climate change – it seems misleading to evoke cost-benefit calculation and the rational assess-ment of tradeoffs.

The aspiration to overcome these caveats is a central vision of modern-ity. Not least in the way public deliberations tend to frame the challenges of global climate change, the implicit assumption is that a united human-kind will be able to predict and rationally control the complex webs of causality through which social and ecological systems are intertwined. The idiom of costs and benefits has very palpably come to dominate global negotiations on climate change. I must bluntly declare that I do not share this vision of rational global control. Instead, I view the very discourse on calculation and decision making as a mystification of the possibly disastrous consequences of the current organization of world society. This is not to suggest a simple conspiracy on behalf of the globally most powerful, but to take seriously the fact that, until disaster strikes, the worldviews and narratives that tend to dominate public consciousness are selected less for their accuracy or rationality than for their capacity to provide existential comfort.

Archaeological Studies of Complexity, Collapse, and Resilience

Archaeology offers us appropriate perspectives for assessing the extent to which socioecological change over the past few millennia has been a matter of rational decision making. Tainter (1988) clearly demonstrated how idiosyncratic cultural path dependencies have locked a number of past societies into unsustainable trajectories yielding diminishing returns and, ultimately, collapse. In continuing to invest in the established kind of problem-solving infrastructure (for instance, Roman armies), a previously successful and expansive society may reach a point where new investments will provide declining returns and their costs exceed the benefits. Collections edited by Culbert (1973) and Yoffee and Cowgill (1988) have illuminated the various kinds of circumstances that can precipitate societal collapse. The archaeological evidence suggests that such circumstances include, for instance, agricultural intensification, ecological overshoot, climate change, and disturbances in long-distance trade relations. Analyses of archaeological cases of decline have generally not suggested that conscious decision making was a significant factor in the destinies of these collapsing societies, but simply conclude that factors such as cultural idiosyncrasies, the organization of exchange, or a fragile environment may have been sources of vulnerability.

Diamond (2005) reframed the discourse on collapse in moral and unmistakably modernist terms by attempting to draw conclusions from prehistory for how modern societies might "choose to fail or succeed." His discussion of societal decline introduced a managerial approach that implicitly suggested that the destinies of social systems were contingent on decision making. This approach is cognate to the currently burgeoning discourse on social-ecological resilience – or "robustness," as it is referred to by several of the contributors to this volume (Freeman and colleagues (Chapter 2), BurnSilver and colleagues (Chapter 3), and Nelson and colleagues (Chapter 8)). Resilience is quite simply the capacity to avoid collapse. The discourse on resilience versus collapse, however, raises some analytical issues that are generally not adequately addressed. First, to refer to a condition of "resilience" requires that we specify the goal ranges of that condition, that is, *what* is to be maintained. Which kinds of change are to be classified as radically transformative, and which are merely instances of resilient adaptation? Second, we must define the boundaries of the system to be assessed as resilient. Are we focusing on the resilience of individuals, households, communities, social strata, nations, or the world-system? As Spielmann and Aggarwal emphasize in Chapter 11, for example, the resilience of national food security can be achieved at the expense of food security at the household level. Conversely, we need to agree on what we mean by "collapse," so that, for instance, a sudden loss of sociopolitical complexity in prehistory is not confused with the extinction of a language or ethnic identity (McAnany and Yoffee 2010).

Challenging Economic Reductionism and the Invisibility of the Voiceless

As Hegmon suggests in Chapter 1, anthropology could contribute perspectives and awareness to the concern, within sustainability science, with the notion of tradeoffs. The recognition that disadvantages (or "costs") are borne disproportionately by some social groups is a crucial insight, which tends to be suppressed by the perception of society as a single agent with common interests. The frequent allusions, in this book, to cost-benefit analysis reflect the underlying influence of mainstream economic thought on how socioecological change is currently framed not only in sustainability science, but apparently in archaeology and anthropology as well. Like other concepts imported from economics, the word "costs" evokes monetary expenditures – that is, exchange relations between people – although it is used in this book to cover a wide range of disadvantages that are not easily measured in money, such as environmental degradation, social inequalities, various kinds of vulnerabilities, and even losses of skills and "culinary identity" (Logan, Chapter 5). The problem with a terminology suggesting a single quantitative metric with which all things can be assessed is shared by notions such as environmental "costs," natural "capital," ecosystem "services," and ecological "debt." All these phrases project modern economic categories onto human-environmental relations. They represent the colonization of ecology by economics. The benefit of adopting such a terminology, as in economics itself, is that complex issues are made amenable to calculation, rational decision making, and even simulation (Chapters 2 and 3), but the "cost" may be a loss of awareness of the complexities and contexts from which the calculations have been abstracted. Most importantly, as mentioned, a "cost-benefit" understanding of social change tends to disregard the fact that advantages and disadvantages are frequently very unevenly distributed across social groups.

This point could be illustrated provocatively by considering the British Industrial Revolution in the late eighteenth century in terms of tradeoffs. Using this terminology, the benefits to England in terms of economic growth, imperial expansion, and what Pomeranz (2000) calls "ecological relief" should be balanced against the costs borne by millions of African slaves and the long-term consequences for future generations of the turn to fossil fuel technologies (Malm and Hornborg 2014; Malm 2016). Nelson and colleagues in Chapter 8 mention that the substitution of fossil fuels for biomass may increase food supply and forest cover but also greenhouse gas emissions. The question that must be asked is for *whom* a particular tradeoff appears beneficial or reasonable. The African slaves were not invited to give their opinions on the matter, nor are we currently heeding the anticipated opinions of future victims of climate change.

Hegmon (Chapter 1) pertinently distinguishes between tradeoffs over time and across social space, but the distinction can be problematic. In this volume, straightforward examples of the former include the adoption of maize in Ghana (Logan, Chapter 5), the construction of water management systems in the Classic Maya lowlands (Isendahl and Heckbert, Chapter 6), and the subsistence shifts of the medieval Norse in Greenland (Nelson and colleagues, Chapter 8), but dilemmas such as the current threat of climate change have both temporal and sociospatial aspects. Global warming can be assumed to damage even those populations whose ancestors took the initiative to turn to steam power, which would make it seem a tradeoff over time, but it is likely to be even more damaging to populations and areas that historically have contributed very little greenhouse gas emissions to the atmosphere.

Acknowledging Power, Inequalities, and Contradictions

Whether we consider the damages experienced historically by African slaves or by future victims of climate change, the theoretical framework of world-system analysis (Wallerstein 1974; Hornborg, McNeill, and Martinez-Alier 2007; Hornborg and Crumley 2007) offers an appropriate approach for considering tradeoffs involving inequalities and injustice. The perspective of world-system analysis reminds us to pay attention to how the boundaries of a social system are defined, and to how damages such as environmental degradation and unhealthy working conditions tend to be displaced to other areas and social groups. It is thus germane to discourses on political ecology and environmental justice, but conspicuously absent in the discourse on resilience. Due to its inclination to neglect issues of power, inequalities, and contradictions – as acknowledged by Brewington in Chapter 10 – the basic tenets of resilience theory seem diametrically opposite to those of political ecology. Similarly, to phrase environmental load displacement in the world-system as a "tradeoff" is to suggests that the world-system as a whole is a single agent, the development of which can be assessed in terms of a common set of pros and cons.

From the perspective of contemporary anthropology, a fundamental problem with resilience theory is its revival of the functionalist approach of the school of cultural ecology, which dominated ecological anthropology in the 1960s (Hornborg 2009; Watts 2015). The systems ecology framework underlying resilience discourse tends to reproduce assumptions about the adaptive virtues of various socioecological processes, as when Roscoe in Chapter 4 identifies "tight feedback loops that engaged support for the tradeoffs involved, kept local population levels within sustainable limits, and redistributed population when it threatened to exceed those limits." Although Roscoe emphasizes that environmental sustainability was an epiphenomenal and "fortunate by-product" of local considerations of defense and food security, explicitly rejecting Rappaport's (1968) "neofunctionalist" analyses of Maring ritual, his mention of the role of ritual pig slaughter in feedback loops maintaining sustainable population levels in native New Guinea is indeed reminiscent of early cultural ecology. His comparison of the "tight" feedback loops capable of alleviating London smog and New Guinean insecurities, on the one hand, and the "loose" feedback loops impeding the mitigation of global climate change, on the other, seems an unnecessary application of cybernetic terminology to sociopolitical circumstances that could no doubt readily be grasped through a more familiar idiom.

This is not to propose that resilience theory or a systems ecology approach must necessarily be functionalist in outlook. As illustrated by Redman's (1999) study of *Human Impacts on Ancient Environments*, it is quite feasible to offer cybernetic models of human-environmental relations that acknowledge the negative long-term repercussions of cultural idiosyncrasies. Nevertheless, several of the chapters in this volume suggest that social inequality may be a justifiable "cost" of overall sustainability. This approach recurs in Grier and Angelbeck's study of precontact Coast Salish in British Columbia (Chapter 9), Brewington's study of medieval Faroese (Chapter 10), Hegmon's analysis of Mimbres (Chapter 7), and indirectly also in Isendahl and Heckbert's somewhat Wittfogelian conclusion that, among the Classic Maya, "there is a tendency for more complex and hierarchical forms of socio-political organization where water is a scarce resource and water security depended on large-scale reservoirs" (Chapter 6). The implication in these studies is that inequality can have adaptive advantages. As particularly Hegmon (Chapters 1 and 7) has observed, however, such a conclusion is offensive and would hardly be acceptable to the lower rungs of social hierarchies in the cases mentioned. Again, the question must be to *whom* the impoverishment of some social groups will appear as components in a total cost-benefit analysis. Is it in the interests of all social strata to have an elite? An alternative approach would be to observe that the interests of the elite are ideologically presented as the common interests of society as a whole, and that the opinions of the underprivileged are not counted.

Money, Energy, and Other Metrics

The discipline of anthropology is divided and ambivalent about the virtues of cost-benefit analyses. In a book called *Trade and Trade-offs*, M. Estellie Smith (2000) by and large encourages students of economic anthropology to think in terms of the sociocultural "costs" and benefits that result from making choices, but shows that such calculations very often involve values that cannot be measured in money. The problem, however, is that the phenomenon of money tends to condition our thinking about costs, benefits, and tradeoffs whether we are aware of it or not. Consider, for example, the conundrum of "unequal exchange." Because voluntary market transactions are by definition judged to be fair and reciprocal, mainstream economics cannot conceptualize unequal exchange in any other sense than as the result of distortions of market mechanisms. In neoclassical economics, the material substance of traded commodities is thus completely irrelevant to moral assessments of exchange rates (Hornborg 2016). This should preclude concerns with an exchange partner giving "more than she receives," as envisaged by Freeman and colleagues in their section on unbalanced reciprocity in Chapter 2. If money is believed to make all commodities commensurable, one wonders what alternative metric is applied by Freeman and colleagues when they deliberate on "the act of giving more agave than maize received." It is paradoxical to find archaeologists and anthropologists applying the terminology of cost-benefit analysis to material metrics such as energy, which are axiomatically excluded from the calculations of economists.

In view of the way in which the notion of "costs" – applied throughout the volume – evokes a monetary metric, it is noteworthy to find it explained, for instance, in terms of "increased energy expenditures" or "travel times" (Roscoe, Chapter 4) and even spelled out as "energetic costs" (Isendahl and Heckbert, Chapter 6). Roscoe's reference to the "tradeoff between defensive costs and energetic benefits" recalls Tainter's (1988) understanding of costs and benefits in terms of net energy. Tainter's insights on the increasing burdens of path-dependent energy investments in complexity are explicitly applied by Isendahl and Heckbert in Chapter 6 and by Hegmon in Chapter 7. Water management systems among the Classic Maya are indeed a paradigmatic example of diminishing returns to complexity, and although they refrain from entering the debate on the Maya Collapse, Isendahl and Heckbert's contribution has significant implications for that debate. But their chapter also provides a particularly clear illustration of how a terminology imported from modern economics may shape our understanding of prehistoric processes and considerations that probably had very little in common with the market logic for which that terminology was designed. In their extensive discussion of the "costs" of complexity, they refer to opportunity costs, transaction costs, sunk-cost effects, maintenance costs, start-up costs, direct costs, and other analytical tools of economics, implying that such tools are applicable also in premodern contexts. They similarly speak of "economic growth" in ninth-century Puuc-Nohkakab, where "high returns on investments" ultimately "financed" central institutions and urban "services." Such terminologies inevitably reanimate the old formalist-substantivist controversy about whether or not neoclassical economics provides us with a template for understanding decision making in all conceivable cultural contexts. Were such categories and considerations somehow refractively experienced by the ancient Maya, or can their application be justified only as parts of the toolkit of the modern analyst? As Isendahl and Heckbert note, the extent to which nonmodern people think in terms of costs and tradeoffs is "a key anthropological issue." As suggested by Tainter's (1988) persuasive model of declining energy returns on complexity, the logic of tradeoffs sometimes seems to be possible to abstract from the specifics of various socioecological processes regardless of the worldviews and categories through which those processes were generated. In fact, a similar conclusion should be fundamental to the many efforts to apply world-system analysis and the zero-sum logic of capital accumulation to a number of social formations through several millennia of human history (Chase-Dunn and Hall 1991; Denemark et al. 2000; Kardulias 1999). The main difference between the two approaches appears to be whether social systems are perceived as collectivities with common objectives or as constellations of contending interests. To further illuminate such efforts to formalize the repetitively cyclical trajectories of human civilizations, anthropology urgently needs to explore the convoluted relation between mainstream concepts of money and energy (Hornborg 2016).

Tradeoffs of Growth and Decline

Like Isendahl and Heckbert, Hegmon in Chapter 7 identifies "economic growth" in premodern societies. Like them, also, she is concerned with the problem of water security as crucial to sustainability in premodern societies as well as in our contemporary world facing climate change. Among the tradeoffs of modern, high-tech irrigation, for instance in an increasingly arid California, are depleted aquifers and vulnerability to higher energy prices. In many areas of the world water is a scarce resource that traditional cultures have managed in sustainable and equitable ways (Trawick and Hornborg 2015). Reliance on fossil fuel energy to irrigate agricultural lands, however, cannot be considered sustainable. Nor is it equitable, considering the globally unequal economic access to such energy and the uneven environmental impacts of extraction, combustion, and greenhouse gas emissions. As Hegmon observes, economic growth for one social category may imply increasing disadvantages for another, and over time even for all. The economic and technological displacement of work and environmental burdens that is somewhat cynically referred to as a "tradeoff" across social groups may ultimately prove to be a disastrous temporal tradeoff even for the original beneficiaries of growth. Hegmon's suggestion that dramatic economic collapse, such as suffered by the Hohokam, Mimbres, and other societies in the American Southwest in the twelfth century, may itself have implied positive tradeoffs for some people is merely to reciprocate the cynicism. In premodern contexts, such positive tradeoffs of collapse, particularly for those at the bottom of the hierarchy, might include lower demands on labor and tribute, less inequality, less repression, more personal liberty, less pressure on the environment, and access to more arable land (i.e., better food security) per capita. As Gunn (1994:96) suggested, some individuals may have "viewed the disappearance of civilization as tax relief rather than the loss of the glory that was Rome or Calakmul."

The concept of "tradeoff" may thus be misleading when applied to a displacement of disadvantages from more to less powerful social groups. In Chapter 9, Grier and Angelbeck seem to suggest that formal ownership of resources among the Coast Salish was an adaptive strategy adopted in precontact times to promote sustainability, which had the long-term and apparently epiphenomenal consequence of increasing inequality. An alternative and less functionalist approach would be to consider the sociopolitical system of ownership as having two kinds of fundamentally unintentional consequences: promoting sustainability, on the one hand, and inequality, on the other. The implicit affinities between the discourse on tradeoffs and a generally functionalist approach appear to be confirmed when Grier and Angelbeck (Chapter 9) list the putatively beneficial social and ecological functions of potlatching. In Chapter 10, Brewington similarly suggests that the inequalities associated with community-level control of medieval Faroese resource management endorsed by the so-called Sheep Letter were a means to promote sustainability. Although he acknowledges that conservation may only have been "epiphenomenal" to the objective of local elite control, which suggests a rejection of cultural ecology in favor of a political economy approach, he concludes that "inequality of social capabilities was a tradeoff for food security," and although he concedes that this tradeoff was, "by today's standards, unacceptable," he emphasizes that sustainable resource use "inevitably *requires* tradeoffs" (emphasis added). This ambiguity regarding the benefits of an uneven distribution of resources and risks does suggest closer affinities to cultural ecology than to political ecology.

Conclusions: Reconsidering the Tradeoffs of Economic Growth in the Modern World

The chapters in this book demonstrate both the risks and the usefulness – the costs and the benefits – of framing sustainability issues in terms of tradeoffs. While it is highly useful to demonstrate how particular cultural specializations and idiosyncrasies may constitute path dependencies constraining future flexibility and resilience, it may be misleading to phrase the trajectories of socioecological transformations in terms of cost-benefit tradeoffs, as this gives the impression that social change is a matter of conscious, managerial decision making by a single agent. More often than not, the long-term consequences of a given option are unknown and the choice of that option generated by the sometimes contradictory strategies of multiple actors. Whenever the "tradeoff" for sustainability involves social inequality, as when workloads and environmental burdens are displaced to disempowered segments of society, the use of this concept seems cynical and questionable. Such displacements appear ubiquitously to be intrinsic to processes of economic and technological growth.

Central to the discourse on tradeoffs is the notion of "costs." To illustrate my point about the conceptual confusion underlying references to non-monetary "costs," I will conclude by considering a widely disseminated article in *The Guardian* (Carrington 2015), which summarized a Working Paper from the International Monetary Fund (Coady et al. 2015). Like the IMF report to which it refers, the article, titled "Fossil fuels subsidized by $10m a minute, says IMF," represents a significant intervention in the ongoing global deliberations on climate change. The article concludes that the "true cost of fossil fuels" in 2015 was around $5.3 trillion, a sum "greater than the total health spending of all the world's governments." These "true costs," however, were calculated not from actual monetary expenditures on fossil fuel subsidies, which accounted for only 6 percent of the total sum, but from estimates of damages from climate change and outdoor air pollution. In other words, non-monetary disadvantages were calculated in terms of monetary costs, as is customary in neoclassical environmental economics. Although well-intentioned, this is a conceptually misleading procedure, because it seems to assume that economic processes ideally should have no negative tradeoffs in biophysical reality. It thus completely disregards the fundamental human predicament revealed by Georgescu-Roegen (1971), who established that processes yielding increases in economic value simultaneously increase biophysical entropy. The damages from climate change and air pollution are inevitable entropic tradeoffs of modern economic growth, and money cannot compensate for entropy. Contrary to the tenets of neoclassical economics, so-called externalities simply cannot be internalized in commodity prices. The "true costs" of a commodity will remain an impossible fantasy. Moreover, the negative consequences of growth, such as environmental degradation and unhealthy working conditions, are systematically displaced to poorer segments of world society. What may appear to be global tradeoffs of economic growth are thus in reality primarily issues of unequal distribution. While most media coverage of the climate change summit in Paris in December 2015 featured cheering delegates, the climate justice movement had every reason to be dismayed. It seems very naïve to believe that what the world's leaders did in Paris was to abandon what for over two centuries has been their main source of economic growth.

References

Carrington, Damian 2015 Fossil fuels subsidized by $10m a minute, says IMF. *The Guardian*, 18 May, 2015.

Chase-Dunn, Christopher, and Tom Hall 1991 *Core/Periphery Relations in Precapitalist Worlds*. Westview Press, Boulder.

Coady, David, Ian Parry, Louis Sears, and Baoping Shang 2015 How large are global energy subsidies? *IMF Working Papers* 15/105. International Monetary Fund.

Culbert, T. Patrick, editor 1973 *The Classic Maya Collapse*. University of New Mexico Press, Albuquerque.

Denemark, Robert A., Jonathan Friedman, Barry K. Gills, and George Modelski, editors 2000 *World System History: The Social Science of Long-Term Change*. Routledge, London.

Diamond, Jared 2005 *Collapse: How Societies Choose to Fail or Succeed*. Viking, New York.

Georgescu-Roegen, Nicholas 1971 *The Entropy Law and the Economic Process*. Harvard University Press, Cambridge, MA.

Gunn, Joel D. 1994 Global Climate and Regional Biocultural Diversity. In *Historical Ecology: Cultural Knowledge and Changing Landscapes*, edited by Carole L. Crumley, pp. 67–97. School of American Research Press, Santa Fe.

Hornborg, Alf 2009 Zero-Sum World: Challenges in Conceptualizing Environmental Load Displacement and Ecologically Unequal Exchange in the World
System. *International Journal of Comparative Sociology* 50(3–4):237–262.
2016 *Global Magic: Technologies of Appropriation from Ancient Rome to Wall
Street.* Palgrave Macmillan, Houndmills.

Hornborg, Alf, and Carole L. Crumley, editors 2007 *The World System and the
Earth System: Global Socio-environmental Change and Sustainability since the
Neolithic.* Left Coast Press, Walnut Creek.

Hornborg, Alf, John R. McNeill, and Joan Martinez-Alier, editors 2007 *Rethinking
Environmental History: World-System History and Global Environmental
Change.* AltaMira Press, Lanham.

Kardulias, P. Nick, editor 1999 *World-Systems Theory in Practice: Leadership,
Production, and Exchange.* Rowman and Littlefield, Lanham.

Malm, Andreas 2016 *Fossil Capital: The Rise of Steam Power and the Roots of
Global Warming.* Verso, London.

Malm, Andreas, and Alf Hornborg 2014 The Geology of Mankind? A Critique of the
Anthropocene Narrative. *The Anthropocene Review* 1:62–69.

McAnany, Patricia A., and Norman Yoffee, editors 2010 *Questioning Collapse:
Human Resilience, Ecological Vulnerability, and the Aftermath of Empire.*
Cambridge University Press, Cambridge.

Pomeranz, Kenneth 2000 *The Great Divergence: China, Europe, and the Making of
the Modern World Economy.* Princeton University Press, Princeton.

Rappaport, Roy A. 1968 *Pigs for the Ancestors: Ritual in the Ecology of a New
Guinea People.* Yale University Press, New Haven.

Redman, Charles L. 1999 *Human Impact on Ancient Environments.* University of
Arizona Press, Tucson.

Smith, M. Estellie 2000 *Trade and Trade-offs: Using Resources, Making Choices,
and Taking Risks.* Waveland Press, Prospect Heights.

Tainter, Joseph A. 1988 *The Collapse of Complex Societies.* Cambridge University
Press, Cambridge.

Trawick, Paul, and Alf Hornborg 2015 Revisiting the Image of Limited Good: On
Sustainability, Thermodynamics, and the Illusion of Creating Wealth. *Current
Anthropology* 56(1):1–27.

Wallerstein, Immanuel 1974 *The Modern World-System: Capitalist Agriculture and
the Origins of the European World-Economy in the Sixteenth Century.*
Academic Press, San Diego.

Watts, Michael J. 2015 Now and Then: The Origins of Political Ecology and the
Rebirth of Adaptation as a Form of Thought. In *The Routledge Handbook of
Political Ecology*, edited by Tom Perreault, Gavin Bridge, and James
McCarthy, pp. 19–50. Routledge, London.

Yoffee, Norman and George L. Cowgill, editors 1988 *The Collapse of Ancient States
and Civilizations.* University of Arizona Press, Tucson.

Index

Adams, W. C., 7
Africa
  famines in, historically, 119
  food security and storage in, 20,
    254–257
  high-yield crops in, 112–113
  hunger and malnourishment in,
    255
  maize farming in, 114–121
  pearl millet crop abandonment in,
    120
agave farming, 29–34. *See also*
  agroecology model
agricultural technologies, 109–111, 114,
  121–122, 248–250
agriculture, 5–6, 224–226, 252. *See*
  also agave farming; farmers;
  high-yield crops; livestock
  farming; maize farming
  in agroecology model, 32–34
  archaeology on strategies of,
    110–111, 113–114
  biodiversity conservation in, 111–112
  energy net gain for, in Maya
    civilizations, 138–139
  environmental harm with, 172
  market demand impact on, 110,
    121–122
  marketable compared to marketed
    surplus in, 249–250, 263–265

  in Mesoamerican northern
    frontier, 29–32, 46–48
  in Mimbres region, 155–157, 160
  path dependence in, 12
  reservoir water supply for, 132–133, 141
  short-term and long-term tradeoff
    analysis in, 17, 20, 113–114, 121–122
  soil fertility and, 111–112, 117
  yield and risk considerations in,
    29–30, 114–115
agroecological niches, 113–114
agroecology model, 29–30, 35–36
  agricultural and social components
    in, 32–34
  experiment overview for, 36, 42
  generalist and specialist farmer
    integration in, 30
  reciprocity experiments in, 37–43
  specialization and exchange in,
    32–35, 47
Alaskan communities, 52, 61, 77–78.
    See also RASEM
  climate change tradeoffs in, 54–55,
    59–60
  employment scenarios for, 58–59,
    70, 73–74
  mixed economies in, 53–54, 56–57,
    71–74
  native community tradeoffs in,
    14–15, 16, 19–20